CHEROKEE GRANTED ENROLLMENT CARDS & DAWES PACKETS 1900 - 1907 VOLUME II

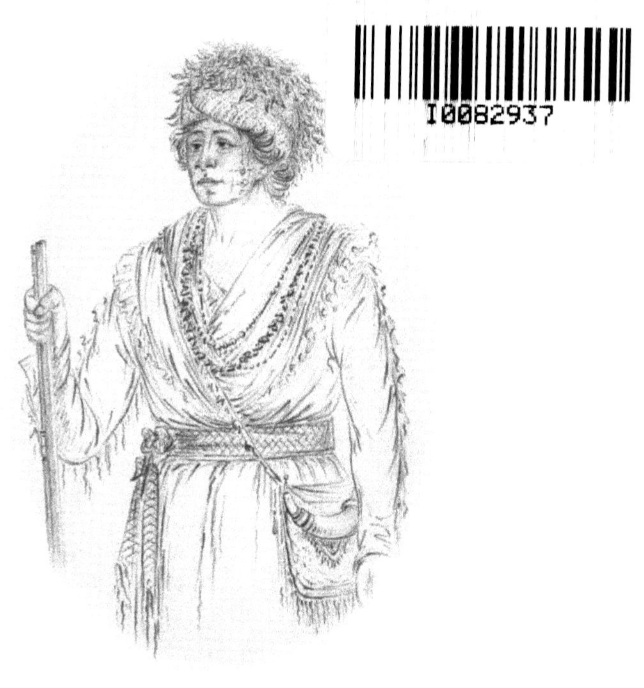

TRANSCRIBED BY

JEFF BOWEN

NATIVE STUDY
Gallipolis, Ohio
USA

Native Study LLC
Gallipolis, OH
www.nativestudy.com

Library of Congress Control Number: 2024922411

ISBN: 978-1-64968-173-7

Bookcover and Title Page: Tuch-ee or "Dutch"
By George Catlin (1796-1872) Date 1852/1860
Drawing No. 212. Portrait of a chief of a band of the Cherokee Indians, also a warrior. He wears a tunic with fringe, a large belt and carries his gun powder horn. He also wears a feathered turban, face paint and holds a rifle.
The Newberry Library (NL004918_o2.jpg)

Made in the United States of America.

Other Books and Series by Jeff Bowen

Compilation of History of the Cherokee Indians and Early History of the Cherokees by Emmet Starr with Combined Full Name Index **(Hardbound & Softbound)**

1901-1907 Native American Census Seneca, Eastern Shawnee, Miami, Modoc, Ottawa, Peoria, Quapaw, and Wyandotte Indians (Under Seneca School, Indian Territory)

1932 Census of The Standing Rock Sioux Reservation with Births and Deaths 1924-1932

Kiowa, Comanche, Apache, Fort Sill Apache, Wichita, Caddo and Delaware Indians Birth and Death Rolls 1924-1932

Census of The Blackfeet, Montana, 1897- 1901 Expanded Edition

Eastern Cherokee by Blood, 1906-1910, Volumes I **thru** *XIII*

Choctaw of Mississippi Indian Census 1929-1932 with Births and Deaths 1924-1931 Volume I
Choctaw of Mississippi Indian Census 1933, 1934 & 1937, Supplemental Rolls to 1934 & 1935 with Births and Deaths 1932-1938, and Marriages 1936-1938 Volume II

Eastern Cherokee Census Cherokee, North Carolina 1930-1939 Census 1930-1931 with Births And Deaths 1924-1931 Taken By Agent L. W. Page Volume I
Eastern Cherokee Census Cherokee, North Carolina 1930-1939 Census 1932-1933 with Births And Deaths 1930-1932 Taken By Agent R. L. Spalsbury Volume II
Eastern Cherokee Census Cherokee, North Carolina 1930-1939 Census 1934-1937 with Births and Deaths 1925-1938 and Marriages 1936 & 1938 Taken by Agents R. L. Spalsbury And Harold W. Foght Volume III

Seminole of Florida Indian Census, 1930-1940 with Birth and Death Records, 1930-1938

Texas Cherokees 1820-1839 A Document For Litigation 1921

Starr Roll 1894 (Cherokee Payment Rolls) Districts: Canadian, Cooweescoowee, and Delaware Volume One
Starr Roll 1894 (Cherokee Payment Rolls) Districts: Flint, Going Snake, and Illinois Volume Two
Starr Roll 1894 (Cherokee Payment Rolls) Districts: Saline, Sequoyah, and Tahlequah; Including Orphan Roll Volume Three

Cherokee Intruder Cases Dockets of Hearings 1901-1909 Volumes I & II

Indian Wills, 1911-1921 Records of the Bureau of Indian Affairs
Books One **thru** *Seven*
Native American Wills & Probate Records 1911-1921

Other Books and Series by Jeff Bowen

Turtle Mountain Reservation Chippewa Indians 1932 Census with Births & Deaths, 1924-1932

Chickasaw By Blood Enrollment Cards 1898-1914 Volume I thru *V*

Cherokee Descendants East An Index to the Guion Miller Applications Volume I
Cherokee Descendants West An Index to the Guion Miller Applications Volume II (A-M)
Cherokee Descendants West An Index to the Guion Miller Applications Volume III (N-Z)

Applications for Enrollment of Seminole Newborn Freedmen, Act of 1905

Eastern Cherokee Census, Cherokee, North Carolina, 1915-1922, Taken by Agent James E. Henderson
Volume I (1915-1916)
Volume II (1917-1918)
Volume III (1919-1920)
Volume IV (1921-1922)

Eastern Cherokee Census, Cherokee, North Carolina, 1923-1929, Taken by Agent James E. Henderson
Volume I (1923-1924)
Volume II (1925-1926)
Volume III (1927-1929)

Complete Delaware Roll of 1898

Applications for Enrollment of Seminole Newborn Act of 1905 Volumes I & II

North Carolina Eastern Cherokee Indian Census 1898-1899, 1904, 1906, 1909-1912, 1914 Revised and Expanded Edition

1932 Hopi and Navajo Native American Census with Birth & Death Rolls (1925-1931) Volume 1 - Hopi
1932 Hopi and Navajo Native American Census with Birth & Death Rolls (1930-1932) Volume 2 - Navajo

Western Navajo Reservation Navajo, Hopi and Paiute 1933 Census with Birth & Death Rolls 1925-1933

Cherokee Citizenship Commission Dockets 1880-1884 and 1887-1889
Volumes I thru *V*

Applications for Enrollment of Chickasaw Newborn Act of 1905
Volumes I thru *VII*
Cherokee Intermarried White 1906 Volume I thru *X*

Applications for Enrollment of Creek Newborn Act of 1905
Volumes I thru *XIV*

Other Books and Series by Jeff Bowen

Applications for Enrollment of Choctaw Newborn Act of 1905 Volumes I thru *XX*

Choctaw By Blood Enrollment Cards 1898-1914 Volumes I thru *XX*

Oglala Sioux Indians Pine Ridge Reservation 1932 Census Book I
Oglala Sioux Indians Pine Ridge Reservation Birth and Death Rolls 1924-1932 Book II

Census of the Sioux and Cheyenne Indians of Pine Ridge Agency 1896 - 1897 Book I
Census of the Sioux and Cheyenne Indians of Pine Ridge Agency 1898 - 1899 Book II

Northern Cheyenne Tongue River, Montana 1904 - 1932 Census 1904-1916 Volume I
Northern Cheyenne Tongue River, Montana 1904 - 1932 Census 1917-1926 Volume II
Northern Cheyenne Tongue River, Montana 1904 - 1932 Census 1927-1932 Volume III

Sac & Fox - Shawnee Estates 1885-1910 (Under Sac & Fox Agency) Volumes I-VIII
Sac & Fox - Shawnee Estates 1920-1924 (Under The Sac & Fox Agency, Oklahoma) & Wills 1889-1924 Volume IX
Sac & Fox - Shawnee Deaths, Cemetery, Births, & Marriage Cards (Under The Sac & Fox Agency, Oklahoma) 1853-1933 Volume X
Sac & Fox - Shawnee Marriages, Divorces, Estates Log Books Volumes 1 & 2, Log Book Births & Deaths (Under Sac & Fox Agency, Oklahoma)1846-1924 Volume XI
Sac & Fox - Shawnee Guardianships Part 1 (Under Sac & Fox Agency, Oklahoma) 1892-1909 Volume XII
Sac & Fox - Shawnee Guardianships, Part 2 (Under The Sac & Fox Agency, Oklahoma) 1902-1910 Volume XIII
Sac & Fox - Shawnee Guardianships, Part 3 (Under The Sac & Fox Agency, Oklahoma) 1906-1914 Volume XIV

Census of the Pima, Tohono O'odham (Papago), and Maricopa Indians of the Gila River, Ak Chin & Gila Bend Reservations 1932 with Birth and Death Rolls 1924-1932

Identified Mississippi Choctaw Enrollment Cards 1902-1909 Volumes I, II, III
Identified Mississippi Choctaw Enrollment Cards' Dawes Packets 1902-1909 Volumes IV, V, VI & VII

Census of the Northern Navajo, Navajo Reservation, New Mexico, 1930 Volume I
Census of the Northern Navajo, Navajo Reservation, New Mexico, 1931 Volume II

Other Books and Series by Jeff Bowen

Crow Agency Montana 1898-1905 Census Volume I 1898-1901 with Illustrations

Memoirs of a White Crow Indian (Thomas H. Leforge) As told by Thomas B. Marquis with Full Index and Illustrations

Cherokee Granted Enrollment Cards & Dawes Packets 1900 - 1907 Volume I

COMPLIMENT THIS SERIES WITH THE GREATEST CHEROKEE HISTORY AND GENEALOGICAL BOOK PUBLISHED!

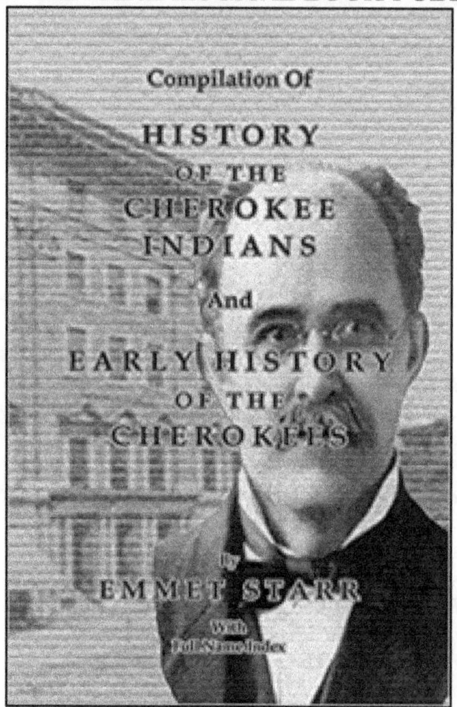

Compilation Of
HISTORY
OF THE
CHEROKEE
INDIANS
And
EARLY HISTORY
OF THE
CHEROKEES
By
EMMET STARR

- **Softback ISBN: 978-1-64968-119-5**
- **Hardback ISBN: 978-1-64968-127-0**

Visit our website at **www.nativestudy.com** to learn more about these other books and series by Jeff Bowen

"It is dangerous to be right in matters on which the established authorities are wrong."

Voltaire

Table of Contents

DEPARTMENT OF THE INTERIOR,

Commission to the Five Civilized Tribes.

CENSUS NOTICE.

The Commission to the Five Civilized Tribes will hear at MUSKOGEE, Indian Territory, from THURSDAY, JANUARY 10, 1901, to THURSDAY, FEBRUARY 28, 1901, inclusive, applicants for enrollment as citizens of the Cherokee Nation. During that time all Cherokee citizens who have not heretofore appeared before the Commission should present themselves for enrollment.

This work is done preparatory to making final rolls of Cherokee citizens under provisions of the Act of Congress, approved June 28th, 1898, viz:

That in making rolls of citizenship of the several tribes, as required by law, the Commission to the Five Civilized Tribes is authorized and directed to take the roll of Cherokee citizens of eighteen hundred and eighty (not including freedmen) as the only roll intended to be confirmed by this and preceding Acts of Congress, and to enroll all persons now living whose names are found on said roll, and all descendants born since the date of said roll to persons whose names are found thereon; and all persons who have been enrolled by the tribal authorities who have heretofore made permanent settlement in the Cherokee Nation whose parents, by reason of their Cherokee blood, have been lawfully admitted to citizenship by the tribal authorities, and who were minors when their parents were so admitted; and they shall investigate the right of all other persons whose names are found on any other rolls and omit all such that may have been placed thereon by fraud or without authority of law, enrolling only such as may have lawful right thereto, and their descendants born since such rolls were made, with such intermarried white persons as may be entitled to citizenship under Cherokee laws.

* * * * * Said commission shall make such rolls descriptive of the persons thereon, so that they may be thereby identified, and it is authorized to take a census of each of said tribes, or to adopt any other means by them deemed necessary to enable them to make such rolls. They shall have access to all rolls and records of the several tribes, and the United States court in Indian Territory shall have jurisdiction to compel the officers of the tribal governments and custodians of such rolls and records to deliver same to said commission, and on their refusal or failure to do so to punish them as for contempt; as also to require all citizens of said tribes, and persons who should be so enrolled, to appear before said commission for enrollment, at such times and places as may be fixed by said commission, and to enforce obedience of all others concerned, so far as the same be necessary, to enable said commission to make rolls as herein required, and to punish any one who may in any manner or by any means obstruct said work.

* * * * * * * * * * * *

No person shall be enrolled who has not heretofore removed to and in good faith settled in the nation in which he claims citizenship.

* * * * * * * * * * * *

The rolls so made, when approved by the Secretary of the Interior, shall be final, and the persons whose names are found thereon, with their descendants thereafter born to them, with such persons as may intermarry according to tribal laws, shall alone constitute the several tribes which they represent.

The members of said commission shall, in performing all duties required of them by law, have authority to administer oaths, examine witnesses, and send for persons and papers; and any person who shall willfully and knowingly make any false affidavit or oath to any material fact or matter before any member of said commission, or before any other officer authorized to administer oaths, to any affidavit or other paper to be filed or oath taken before said commission, shall be deemed guilty of perjury, and on conviction thereof shall be punished as for such offense.

No applicants for enrollment as Cherokee Freedmen will be heard at this appointment.

TAMS BIXBY,
T. B. NEEDLES,
C. R. BRECKINRIDGE,
COMMISSIONERS.

Muskogee, Indian Territory, December 12, 1900.

CHEROKEE ENROLLMENT NOTICE.

THE COMMISSION TO THE FIVE CIVILIZED TRIBES

WILL BE IN SESSION AT

TAHLEQUAH, INDIAN TERRITORY,

From Monday, NOVEMBER 4, Until Wednesday, DECEMBER 4, 1901, Inclusive,

For the purpose of hearing applications for enrollment of Cherokee citizens who have not heretofore applied; and also, for the purpose of hearing rebuttal and supplemental testimony with respect to applications made for enrollment as Cherokee citizens.

TAMS BIXBY,
T. B. NEEDLES,
C. R. BRECKINRIDGE,
Commissioners.

DEPARTMENT OF THE INTERIOR,

Commission to the Five Civilized Tribes.

Closing of Citizenship Rolls

OF THE MUSKOGEE OR CREEK NATION.

WHEREAS, on June 13, 1904, the Secretary of the Interior, under the authority in him vested by the provisions of the act of Congress approved March 3, 1901, (31 Stat., 1058) ordered that September 1, 1904, be and the same is hereby fixed as the time when the rolls of the Muskogee or Creek Nation shall be closed:

Notice is hereby given that the Commission to the Five Civilized Tribes will, at its office in Muskogee, Indian Territory, up to and inclusive of September 1, 1904, receive applications for the enrollment of citizens and freedmen of the Muskogee or Creek Nation, and that after that date the application of no person whomsoever for enrollment as a citizen or freedman of said nation will be received by the Commission.

Commission to the Five Civilized Tribes,

TAMS BIXBY, Chairman,
T. B. NEEDLES,
C. R. BRECKINRIDGE,
Commissioners.

Muskogee, Indian Territory,
June 25, 1904.

Citizenship Rolls Governed by this Provision of an Act of Congress

In making rolls of citizenship of the Cherokee Nation this Commission is governed by the following provision of the Act of Congress approved June 28, 1898 (30 Stats., 495);

> "That in making rolls of citizenship of the several tribes, as required by law, the Commission to the Five Civilized Tribes is authorized and directed to take the roll of Cherokee citizens of eighteen hundred and eighty (not including freedmen) as the only roll intended to be confirmed by this and preceding Acts of Congress, and to enroll all persons now living whose names are found on said roll, and all descendants born since the date of said roll to persons whose names are found thereon; and all persons who have been enrolled by the tribal authorities who have heretofore made permanent settlement in the Cherokee Nation whose parents, by reason of their Cherokee blood, have been lawfully admitted to citizenship by the tribal authorities, and who were minors when their parents were so admitted; and they shall investigate the right of all other persons whose names are found on any other rolls and omit all such as may have been placed thereon by fraud or without authority of law, enrolling only such as may have lawful right thereto, and their descendants born since such rolls were made, with such intermarried white persons as may be entitled to citizenship under Cherokee laws."

[The above quote has been transcribed from Case Cherokee D30-Nancy E. Forbes, Dawes Roll Number 21529. It will be found in similar format throughout this series.]

[Copy of the Original Treaty]

Treaty Between
The United States of America
And The
Cherokee Nation of Indians

Concluded July 19, 1866

Proclaimed August 11, 1866

[NOTICE: Within the handwritten treaty you will find Articles 12 and 13 combined, and 14 through 16 combined following up to Article 17 and continuing.]

Andrew Johnson,

President of the United States of America,

To all and singular to whom these presents shall come, greeting:

Whereas a Treaty was made and concluded at the city of Washington, in the District of Columbia, on the nineteenth day of July, in the year of our Lord one thousand eight hundred and sixty-six, by and between Dennis N. Cooley and Elijah Sells, Commissioners, on the part of the United States, and Smith Christie, White Catcher, James McDaniel, S. H. Benge, Daniel H. Ross, and J. B. Jones, Delegates of the Cherokee nation appointed by resolution of the National Council, on the part of said Cherokee nation, which Treaty is in the words and figures following, to wit:

Articles, of, agreement and Convention at the city of Washington on the nineteenth day of July in the year of our Lord One thousand Eight hundred and Sixty six between the United States. represented by Dennis N. Cooley. Commissioner of Indian affairs. Elijah Sells. Superintendent of Indian affairs for the southern Superintendency. ~~and~~ ~~[illegible]~~ and the Cherokee Nation of Indians, represented by its delegates, James McDaniel. Smith Christie. White Catcher. S.H. Benge. J.B. Jones and Daniel H. Ross—John Ross, Principal Chief of the Cherokees, being too unwell to join in these negotiations—

Preamble.

Whereas existing treaties between the United States and the Cherokee Nation are deemed to be insufficient. The said Contracting parties agree as follows viz

Article 1

The pretended treaty made with the so-called Confederate states, by the Cherokee Nation on the Seventh day of October 1861, and repudiated by the National Council of the Cherokee Nation on the 18th day of February 1863 is hereby declared to be void.

Article 2

Amnesty is hereby declared by the United States and the Cherokee Nation for all Crimes and misdemeanors committed by one Cherokee on the person or property of another Cherokee or of a citizen of the United States, prior to the 4th day of July 1866. and no right of action arising out of wrongs. committed in aid or in suppression of the rebellion. shall be prosecuted or maintained in the Courts of the United States or in the courts of the Cherokee Nation. But the cherokee nation stipulate &c

Article 3.

The confiscation laws of the cherokee Nation shall be repealed, & the same, and all sales of farms, and improvements on real estate, made or pretended to be made in pursuance thereof are hereby agreed, and declared to be null and void, and the former owners of such property so sold, their,

Article 4 7

All the Cherokees and freed persons who were formerly slaves to any Cherokee, and all free negroes not having been such slaves, who resided in the Cherokee Nation prior to June 1st 1861. who may within two years elect not to reside North East of the Arkansas River and South East of Grand River shall have the right to settle in and occupy the Canadian District South west of the Arkansas River and also all that tract of Country lying North=west of Grand River and bounded on the South East by Grand River and west by the Creek reservation to the North East Corner thereof from thence west on the North line of the Creek reservation to the Ninety sixth degree of west longitude and thence North on said line of Longitude so far that a line due East to Grand River will include a quantity of land equal to 160 acres for each person who may so elect to reside in the Territory above described in this article. Provided that that part of said District North of the Arkansas River shall not be set apart until it shall be found that the Canadian District is not sufficiently large to allow One hundred & Sixty acres to each person desiring to obtain settlement under the provisions of this Article.

Article 5

The inhabitants electing to reside in the District described in the preceding article shall have the right to elect all their local officers and Judges, and the number of delegates to which by their numbers they may be entitled in any general Council to be established in the Indian Territory under the provisions of this treaty as stated in Article 12 - and to Control all their local affairs, and to establish all necessary police regulations. and rules for the administration of justice in said District, not inconsistent with the Constitution of the Cherokee Nation, or the laws of the United States. Provided the Cherokees residing in said District shall enjoy all the rights and privileges of other Cherokees who may elect to settle in said District as hereinbefore provided, and shall hold the same rights and privileges, and be subject to the same liabilities as those who elect to settle in said District under the provisions of this treaty

Provided also that if any such police regulations or rules be adopted which in the opinion of

10

the President bear oppressively on any citizen of the Nation. he may suspend the same. And all rules or regulations in said District or in any other District of the Nation, discriminating against the Citizens of other District, are prohibited, & shall be void.

Article 6

The inhabitants of the said District herein before described shall be entitled to representation according to numbers in the National council. and all laws of the Cherokee Nation shall be uniform throughout said Nation. And should any such law either in its provisions or in the manner of its enforcement.

in the opinion of the President of the United States operate unjustly or injuriously in said District, he is hereby authorized and empowered to correct such evil, and to adopt the means necessary to secure the impartial administration of justice as well as a fair and equitable application and expenditure of the National funds as between the people of this and of every other District in said Nation —

Article 7

The United States Court to be created in the Indian Territory, and until such court is created therein the United States District Court the nearest to the Cherokee Nation shall have exclusive original jurisdiction of all causes, civil and criminal.

wherein an inhabitant of the District hereinbefore described shall be a party and where an inhabitant outside of said District in the Cherokee Nation shall be the other party as plaintiff or defendant in a civil Cause, or shall be defendant or prosecutor in a Criminal Case, and all process issued in said District by any officer of the Cherokee Nation to be executed on an inhabitant residing outside of said District. and all process issued by any officer of the Cherokee Nation Outside of said District to be executed on an inhabitant residing in said District. shall be to all intents and purposes Null & void unless endorsed by the District Judge for the District where such process is to be served. and

13

said person so arrested shall be held in custody by the Officer so arresting him, until he shall be delivered over to the United States Marshall or consent to be tried by the Cherokee Courts.

Provided, that any or all the provisions of this treaty which make any distinction in ~~the~~ rights and remedies between the citizens of any District, and the citizens of the rest of the Nation, shall be abrogated whenever the President shall have ascertained by an election duly ordered by him, that a majority of the voters of such District desire them to be abrogated, and he shall have declared such abrogation. And pro-

vided further, that No law or regulation to be hereafter enacted within said Cherokee Nation or any District thereof prescribing a penalty for its violation shall take effect or be enforced until after 90 days from the date of its promulgation either by publication in one or more Newspapers of general circulation in said Cherokee Nation or by posting up copies thereof in the Cherokee and English languages in each District where the same is to take effect, at the usual place of holding District Courts.

Art 8.

Eleventh.

No license to trade in goods wares or merchandise

Merchandize shall be granted by the United States to trade in the Cherokee Nation unless approved by the Cherokee National Council. except in the Canadian District. & such other District North of Arkansas River & West of Grand River occupied by the so called southern Cherokees. as provided in Article 4 of this treaty -

Article 9

The Cherokee Nation, having voluntarily in February 1863 by an act of their National Council forever abolished Slavery hereby Covenant and agree. that. never hereafter. shall. either. slavery or involuntary servitude exist in their Nation otherwise than in the punishment of Crime whereof the party shall have been duly Convicted. in accordance with laws applicable to all the members of said tribe alike. They further agree that all freedmen who have been liberated, by voluntary act of their former owners or by law as well as all free -

colored persons who were in the Country at the commencement of the rebellion, and are now residents therein, or who may return within six months, and their decendents, shall have all the rights of native Cherokees. Provided that owners of slaves so emancipated in the Cherokee Nation shall never receive any compensation or pay for the slaves so emancipated.

Article 10

Every Cherokee & freed person resident in the Cherokee Nation shall have the right to sell any products of his farm including his or her live stock or any Merchandize or Manufactured products and to ship & drive the same to market without restraint, paying any tax thereon which is now or may be levied by the United States on the quantity sold outside of the Indian Territory

Article 11

The Cherokee Nation hereby grant a right of way not exceeding

16—

two hundred feet wide, except at stations, switches, water stations, or crossing of rivers when more may be indispensable to the full enjoyment of the franchise herein granted, and then, only two hundred additional feet shall be taken, and only for such length as may be absolutely necessary, through all their lands, to any Company or corporation, which shall be duly authorized by Congress to construct, a rail road from any point North to any point South, and from any point East to any point West of, and which may pass through the Cherokee Nation—said Company or corporation and their employes and laborers while constructing and repairing the same and in operating said road or roads, including all necessary agents on the line, at stations, switches, water tanks and all others, necessary to the successful operation of a rail road, shall be protected, in the discharge of their duties, and at all times subject to the Indian intercourse laws, now or which may hereafter be enacted and be in force in the Cherokee Nation.

Article 12.

The Cherokees agree that a general Council consisting of delegates elected by each nation or tribe lawfully residing within the Indian Territory, may be annually convened in said Territory, which Council shall be organized in such manner and possess such powers as hereinafter prescribed.

First,- After the ratification of this treaty, and as soon as may be deemed practicable by the

18

Secretary of the Interior, and prior to the first session of said Council a Census or enumeration of each tribe lawfully resident in said Territory shall be taken under the direction of the Commissioner of Indian Affairs, who for that purpose is hereby authorized to designate and appoint Competent persons, whose Compensation shall be fixed by the Secretary of the Interior, and paid by the United States.

Second,– The first general Council shall Consist of one member from each tribe and an additional member for each one thousand Indians, or each fraction of a thousand greater than five hundred, being members of any tribe lawfully resident in said Territory, and shall be selected by said tribes respectively, who may assent to the establishment of said general Council, and if none should be thus formally selected by any Nation or tribe so assenting, the said Nation or tribe shall be represented in said general Council, by the Chief, or Chiefs & headmen of said tribes, to be taken in order of their rank as recognized in tribal usage, in the same number, and proportion as above indicated.

After the said Census shall have been taken and completed, the Superintendent of Indian Affairs shall publish and declare to each tribe assenting to the establishment of such Council the number of members of such Council, to which they shall be entitled under the provisions of this article, and the persons entitled to represent said tribes shall meet at such time and place as he shall approve: but thereafter the time, and place of the sessions of said Council shall be determined by its action Provided that no Session in any one Year shall exceed the term of thirty days. And provided, that special sessions of said Council may be called by the Secretary of the Interior, whenever in his judgment the interest of said tribes shall require such special session

Third – Said General Council shall have power to legislate upon matters pertaining to the inter-course and relations of the Indian tribes, and Nations, and Colonies of Freedmen resident in said Territory, the arrest and extradition of Criminals and offenders escaping from one tribe to another, or into any Community of Freedmen, the admin-istration of Justice between members of

21–

different tribes of said Territory and persons other than Indians and members of said tribes or nations, and the Common defense and safety of the Nations of said Territory.

All laws enacted by said Council shall take effect at such time as may therein be provided, unless suspended by direction of the President of the United States – No law shall be enacted inconsistent with the Constitution of the United States or laws of Congress or existing treaty stipulations with the United States – nor shall said Council legislate upon matters other than those above indicated – Provided however, that the legislative power of such General Council may be enlarged, by the Consent of the National Council of each nation or tribe assenting to its establishment with the approval of the President of the United States

Fourth. Said Council shall be presided over by such person as may be designated by the Secretary of the Interior

Fifth – The Council shall elect a Secretary whose duty it shall be to keep an accurate record of all the proceedings of said Council and who shall transmit a true copy of all such proceedings duly certified by the presiding officer of such Council, to the Secretary of the Interior. and to each tribe or nation represented in said Council, immediately after the sessions of said Council shall terminate. He shall be paid out of the Treasury of the United States an

20

annual salary of five hundred dollars.

21 Sixth. The members of said Council shall be paid by the United States the sum of four dollars *per diem* during the term actually in attendance on the sessions of said Council, and at the rate of four dollars for every twenty miles necessarily travelled by them in going from and returning to their homes respectively from said Council, to be certified by the Secretary and President of the said Council.

Article 13th. The Cherokees also agree that a Court or Courts may be established by the United States in said Territory, with such jurisdiction and organized in such manner

Twenty First.

24

as may be prescribed by law. provided that the Judicial tribunals of the Nation Shall be allowed to retain exclusive jurisdiction in all civil and Criminal Cases arising within their Country in which members of the Nation by nativity or adoption Shall be the only parties, or where the Cause of action Shall arise in the Cherokee Nation. except as otherwise provided in this treaty.

Article 14

The right to the Use and Occupancy of a quantity of Land not exceeding one hundred and Sixty acres To be Selected according to legal Subdivisions in one body. and To include their improvements and not including the improvements of any member of the Cherokee Nation, is hereby granted to every society or denomination which has erected, or which with the consent of the National council may hereafter erect buildings within the Cherokee country for missionary or educational purposes. But no land thus granted, nor buildings which have been or may be erected thereon shall ever be sold or otherwise disposed of, except with the consent and approval of the Cherokee National council and of the Secretary of the Interior. And whenever any such lands or build-

26

dings shall be sold or disposed of. the
44 proceeds thereof shall be applied by said
Society or societies for like purposes within
said nation subject to the approval of
the Secretary of the Interior

Article 15th The United States may settle any civilized Indians friendly with the Cherokees and adjacent tribes within the Cherokee country on unoccupied lands east of 96°, on such terms as may be agreed upon by any such tribe and the Cherokees, subject to the approval of the President of the United State which shall be consistent with the following provisions viz: should any

Twenty Fourth

such tribe or band of Indians settling in said country, abandon their tribal organization, there being first paid into the Cherokee national fund a sum of money which shall sustain the same proportion to the then existing National fund that the number of Indians sustain to the whole number of Cherokees then residing in the Cherokee Country they shall be incorporated into and ever after remain a part of the Cherokee Nation, on equal terms in every respect with native citizens.

And should any such tribe thus settling in said Country decide to

28

preserve their tribal organizations and to maintain their tribal laws, customs and usages, not inconsistent with the Constitution and laws of the Cherokee Nation, they shall have a district of country set off for their use by metes and bounds equal to 160 acres if they should so decide for each man, woman and child of said tribe and shall pay for the same into the National fund such price as may be agreed on by them and the Cherokee Nation subject to the approval of the President of the United States and in cases of disagreement the price to be fixed by the President

And the said tribe thus settled shall also pay into the National fund a sum of money to be agreed on by the respective parties not greater in proportion to the whole existing National fund and the probable proceeds of the lands herein ceded or authorized to be ceded or sold. than their numbers. bear to the whole number of Cherokees then residing in said country, and thence afterwards they shall enjoy all the rights of native Cherokees, But no Indians who have no tribal organizations.

or who shall determine to abandon their tribal organization shall be permitted to settle east of the 96° of longitude without the consent of the Cherokee National Council or of a Delegation duly appointed by it, being first obtained. And no Indians who have and determine to preserve their tribal organizations shall be permitted to settle as herein provided east of the 96° of Longitude without such consent being first obtained, unless the President of the United States after a full hearing of the objections offered by said Council or Delegation to such settle-

31—

29 ment shall determine that the objections are insufficient, in which case he may authorize the settlement of such tribe east of the 96° of longitude

Berry

Article 16 The United States may settle friendly Indians on any part of the Cherokee country west of 96° to be taken in a compact form in quantity not exceeding 160 acres for each member of each of said tribes thus to be settled: the boundaries of each of said Districts to be distinctly marked and the land conveyed in fee simple to each of said tribes to be held in common or by their members

Twenty Ninth.

32

in severalty as the United States may decide.

Said lands thus disposed of to be paid for to the Cherokee Nation at such price as may be agreed on between the said parties in interest, subject to the approval of the President and if they should not agree, then the price to be fixed by the President.

The Cherokee Nation to retain the right of possession of and jurisdiction over all of said country west of 96° of Longitude until thus sold and occupied, after which their jurisdiction and right of possession to terminate forever as to each of said districts thus sold and occupied.

Article 17

The Cherokee nation hereby cedes in trust to the United States, the tract of land in the State of Kansas, which was sold to the Cherokees by the United States under the provisions of the 2nd article of the treaty of 1835: and also that strip of the land ceded to the Nation by the 4th article of said treaty which is included in the State of Kansas, and the Cherokees consent that said lands may be included in the limits and jurisdiction of the said State.

The lands herein ceded shall be surveyed as the Public Lands of the United States are

#34—

Surveyed, under the direction of the Commissioner of the General Land Office, and shall be appraised by two disinterested persons, one to be designated by the Cherokee National Council and one by the Secretary of the Interior, and in case of disagreement by a third person to be mutually selected by the aforesaid appraisers. The appraisement to be not less than an average of One dollar and a quarter per acre exclusive of improvements.

And the Secretary of the Interior shall from time to time as such surveys and appraisements are approved by him, after due advertisement for sealed bids, sell such lands to the highest bidders for cash in parcels not exceeding one hundred and sixty acres, and at not less than the appraised value Provided that whenever there are improvements of the value of $50 made on the lands, not being mineral, and owned and personally occupied by any person for agricultural purposes at the date of the signing hereof, such person so owning and in person residing on such improvements, shall after due proof

made under such regulations as the
Secretary of the Interior may prescribe,)
be entitled to buy at the appraised value
the smallest quantity of land
in legal subdivisions which will
include his improvements not exceeding in the aggregate one hundred
and sixty acres. The expenses of
survey and appraisement to be paid
by the Secretary out of the
proceeds of sale of said land,
Provided that nothing in this article
shall prevent the Secretary of the
Interior from selling the whole of
said ~~ceded lands~~ neutral lands in a body to any

51

responsible party for Cash for a sum not less than Eight hundred Thousand dollars -] Provided &c

Article 18

That any lands owned by the Cherokees in the State of Arkansas and in States East of the Mississippi. May be sold by the Cherokee Nation in such manner as their National Council May prescribe, all such sales being first approved by the Secretary of the Interior.

Article 19

All Cherokees being heads of families residing at the date of the ratification of this treaty on any of the lands herein Ceded. or authorized to be sold and desiring to remove

38–

to the reserved country, shall be paid by the purchasers of said lands the value of such improvements to be ascertained and appraised by the Commissioners who appraise the lands, subject to the approval of the Secretary of the Interior. And if he shall elect to remain on the land, now occupied by him shall be entitled to receive a patent from the United States in fee simple for 320 acres of land to include his improvements. and thereupon he and his family shall cease to be members of the Nation

Article 20

Whenever the Cherokee National Council shall request it. the Secretary of the Interior shall cause the country reserved for the Cherokees to be surveyed and allotted among them at the expense of the United States.

Article 21

It being difficult to learn the precise boundary line between the Cherokee Country and the States of Arkansas. Missouri and Kansas it is agreed that the United States shall at its own expense cause the same to be run as far west as the

Arkansas, and marked by permanent and conspicuous monuments, by two Commissioners, one
of whom shall be designated by
the Cherokee National Council.

Article 22 The Cherokee National Council
or any duly appointed Delegation
thereof shall have the privilege
to appoint an Agent to examine
the accounts of the Nation with
the Government of the United States,
at such time as they may see
proper, and to continue or discharge such Agent and to appoint
another, as may be thought best

Thirty Eighth.

by such Council or Delegation, and such Agent shall have free access to all accounts and books in the Executive Departments relating to the business of said Cherokee Nation and an opportunity to examine the same in the presence of the Officer having such books and papers in charge.

Article 23 43-

All funds now due the Nation or that may hereafter accrue from the Sale of their lands by the United States as herein before provided for shall be invested in United States registered Stocks at their current value, and the interest on all Said funds, shall be paid semi annually on the order of the Cherokee Nation and shall be applied to the following purposes, towit. Thirtyfive percent shall be applied for the support of the common schools of the Nation, and educational pur-poses, fifteen percent for the Orphan fund and fifty per cent for general purposes, including reasonable salaries of District Officers. And the Secretary of the Interior with the approval of the President of the United States may pay out of the funds

43

due the Nation on the order of the National Council or a delegation duly authorized by it, such amount as he may deem necessary to meet. outstanding obligations of the Cherokee Nation caused by the suspension of the payment of their annuities, not to exceed the sum of one hundred & fifty thousand dollars—

Article 24

As a slight testimony for the useful and arduous services of the Rev Evan Jones for forty years a Missionary in the Cherokee Nation, now a cripple, old, and poor, it is agreed that the sum of three thousand dollars be paid to him under the direction of the Secretary of the Interior out of any Cherokee fund in or to come into his hands not otherwise appropriated.

Article 25

74

A large number of the Cherokees who served in the Army of the United States, having died, leaving no heirs entitled to receive bounties and arrears of pay on account of such service - It is agreed that all bounties and arrears for service in the Regiments of Indian United States Volunteers, which shall remain unclaimed by any person legally entitled to receive the same, for two years from the ratification of this treaty, shall be paid as the National Council may direct to be applied to the foundation and support of an asylum for the education of Orphan children, which Asylum shall be under the control of the National Council or of such benevolent Society as said Council may designate, subject

45

to the approval of the Secretary of the Interior.

Article 26   27   46—

The United States guarantee to the people of the Cherokee nation the quiet and peaceable possession of their country and protection against domestic feuds and insurrections and against hostilities of other tribes. They shall also be protected against interruptions or intrusion from all unauthorized citizens of the United States who may attempt to settle on their lands or reside in their territory. In case of hostilities among the Indian tribes, the United States agree that, the party or parties commencing the same shall so far as practicable make reparation for the damages done.

Article. 27.

The United States shall have the right to establish one or more military posts or stations in the Cherokee nation as may be deemed necessary for the proper protection of the Citizens of the United States lawfully residing therein and the Cherokees and other citizens of the Indian Country. But no sutler or other person connected therewith either

in or out of the military organization
shall be permitted to introduce any
spiritous, vinous or malt liquors into
the Cherokee nation, except the medical department, proper, and by them
only for strictly medical purposes.-
And all persons not in the military
service of the United States, not citizens of the Cherokee nation, are to
be prohibited from coming into the
Cherokee nation or remaining in the
same, except as herein otherwise
provided, and it is the duty of the
United State Indian Agent for the
Cherokees to have such persons not
lawfully residing or sojourning there
in

49

in removed from the nation as they now are, or hereafter may be required by the Indian intercourse laws of the United States.

Article 27. 28

The United States hereby agree to pay for provisions and clothing furnished the army under Appotholehala in the winter of 1861 and 1862, not to exceed the sum of ten thousand dollars, the accounts to be ascertained and settled by the Secretary of the Interior.

Article No 29 56–

The sum of ten thousand, or so much thereof as may be necessary, to pay the expenses of the delegates and representatives of the Cherokees, invited by the Government to visit Washington for the purposes of making this treaty, shall be paid by the United States on the ratification of this treaty. and the Secretary

Why allow a half.

Article ~~29~~. 30.

51

The United States agree to pay to the proper claimants all losses of property by Missionaries or Missionary Societies resulting from their being ordered or driven from the Country by United States Agents. and from their property being taken and occupied or destroyed by by United States troops, not exceeding in the aggregate. twenty thousand dollars. to be ascertained by the Secretary of the Interior

Article ~~30~~ 31.

All provisions of treaties, heretofore ratified and in force, and not inconsistent with the provisions of this treaty are hereby re-affirmed and declared to be in full force: and nothing herein shall be construed as an acknowledgement by the United States, or as a relinquishment by the Cherokee

Nation of any Claims or demands under the guaranties of former treaties except as herein expressly provided.

Bowe

In testimony whereof the said Commissioners on the part of the United States, and the said delegation on the part of the Cherokee Nation, have hereunto set their hands and seals, at the City of Washington this ninth day of July, A. D. one thousand eight hundred and sixty-six.

In presence of

W H Watson
J W Wright

D. N. Cooley,
Com. Ind. Affairs

Elijah Sells
Supt. Ind. Affs.

Smith Christie
White Catcher
James McDaniel
S. H. Benge
Danl H. Ross
J. B. Jones

Delegates of the Cherokee Nation, Appointed by Resolution of the National Council.

Signatures witnessed by the following named persons, the following interlineations being made before signing:— On page 6th the word "the" interlined, on page 11 the word "the" struck out and to said page 11 a sheet attached, requiring publication of laws, and on page 34th the word "ceded" struck out and the words "Neutral lands" inserted. Page 47th added relating to expenses of treaty.

Thomas Ewing Jr.
Wm. A. Phillips
J W Wright

Forty-Ninth

And whereas, the said Treaty having been submitted to the Senate of the United States for its constitutional action thereon, the Senate did, on the twenty-seventh day of July, one thousand eight hundred and sixty-six, advise and consent to the ratification of the same, with amendments, by a resolution in the words and figures following, to wit:

In Executive Session,
Senate of the United States,
July 27, 1866

Resolved, (two thirds of the Senators present concurring) That the Senate advise and consent to the ratification of the Articles of Agreement and convention made at the City of Washington on the nineteenth day of July, in the year of our Lord one thousand eight hundred and sixty-six, between the United States, and the Cherokee nation of Indians, with the following

Amendments.

1st Insert at the end of Article 2 the following:- But the Cherokee nation stipulate and agree to deliver up to the United States or their duly authorized agent any or all public property, particularly ordnance, ordnance stores, arms of all kinds and quartermasters stores, in their possession or control, which belonged to the United States or the so-called Confederate States, without any reservation.

over

2nd Strike out the last proviso in Article 17, and insert in lieu thereof the following:— Provided, That nothing in this Article shall prevent the Secretary of the Interior from selling the whole of said lands not occupied by actual Settlers at the date of the ratification of this Treaty, not exceeding 160 acres to each person entitled to preemption under the preemption laws of the United States; in a body to any responsible party, for Cash, for a sum not less than one Dollar per acre.

3d Insert at the end of Article 29 the following:— — And the Secretary of the Interior shall also be authorized to pay the reasonable costs and expenses of the Delegates of the Southern Cherokees.

The moneys to be paid under this Article shall be paid out of the proceeds of the sales of the National lands in Kansas.

Attest: [signature]

Secretary.

And whereas, the foregoing amendments having been fully explained and interpreted to the aforenamed Delegates of the Cherokee nation, they did, on the thirty-first day of July, one thousand eight hundred and sixty-six, give, on behalf of said nation, their free and voluntary assent to said amendments, in the words and figures following, to wit:

Whereas the Senate of the United States did on the 27th day of July 1866 advise and consent to the ratification of the Articles of Agreement and Convention made at the City of Washington on the nineteenth day of July, in the year of our Lord, one thousand eight hundred and sixty six, between the United States, and the Cherokee nation of Indians with the following,

Amendments, to wit:

1st Insert at the end of Article 2 the following:- But the Cherokee nation stipulate and agree to deliver up to the United States or their duly authorized agent any or all public property particularly ordnance, ordnance stores, arms of all kinds and quartermasters stores, in their possession or control, which belonged to the United States or the so-called Confederate States, without any reservation.

2nd Strike out the last proviso in Article 17. and insert in lieu thereof the following:- Provided, That nothing in this Article shall prevent the Secretary of the Interior from selling the whole of said lands not occupied by actual settlers at the date of the ratification of this Treaty, not exceeding

160 acres to each person entitled to preemption under the preëmption laws of the United States; in a body to any responsible party, for cash, for a sum not less than one Dollar per acre.

3rd Insert at the end of Article 29. the following:
And the Secretary of the Interior shall also be authorized to pay the reasonable costs and expenses of the Delegates of the Southern Cherokees

The moneys to be paid under this article shall be paid out of the proceeds of the sales of the National lands in Kansas.

Now therefore, we, the delegates on the part of the said Cherokee Nation, do hereby assent and agree to the said amendments above written, the same having been explained to us and being fully understood by us.

Witness our hands and seals this 31st day of July A.D. 1866 at Washington D.C.

Smith Christie
White Catcher
James McDaniel
S. H. Benge
Dan. H. Ross
J. B. Jones

In presence of
D. N. Cooley
Comr. Ind. Affairs
J. Harlan U.S. Indian Agent
Charles E. Mix
[illegible]
W. R. Irwin

Now, therefore, be it known that I, Andrew Johnson, President of the United States of America, do, in pursuance of the advice and consent of the Senate, as expressed in its resolution of the twenty-seventh of July, one thousand eight hundred and sixty-six, accept, ratify, and confirm the said Treaty with the amendments as aforesaid.

In testimony whereof I have signed my name hereto, and have caused the seal of the United States to be affixed.

Done at the city of Washington
this eleventh day
of August, in the year of
our Lord one thousand eight
hundred and sixty-six,
and of the Independence
of the United States of America
the ninety-first.

Andrew Johnson

By the President:
Henry Stanbery
Acting Secretary of State.

[Transcribed Miscellaneous Letters with Treaty]

Treaty Between
The United States of America
And The
Cherokee Nation of Indians

Concluded July 19, 1866

Proclaimed August 11, 1866

Miscellaneous Letters - July, Part II, 1866.

DEPARTMENT of the INTERIOR,
WASHINGTON D. C. July 31 1866

Sir

I have the honor to transmit for promulgation, the treaty negotiated on the 19th inst., with the Cherokee Indians together with certain amendments thereto, made by the Senate, which amendments having been submitted to said Indians, have been assented to by them as will appear from the accompanying paper signed by their duly authorized delegates.

I am sir very respect'y
Your obt servt
Jas Harlan
Secretary

Hon. Wm H Seward
Secretary of (sic) War.

#358.

Domestic Letters, Volume 73, page 551.

Department of State,
Washington August 4, 1866

Hon. O. H. Browning,
Secretary of the Interior.

Sir:

I have the honor to enclose for your consideration, letters from Mr. W. A. Phillips and Reverend John B. Jones in relation to the translation and publication of the Cherokees Treaty. It appears to me that the Government ought not to promulgate the Treaty in the language of the Cherokees, under its official sanction, without the assent of those who sign the treaty in behalf of the Cherokees to the correctness of the translation. In reply to a suggestion of that kind to Mr Phillips, he was understood to say that a translation had been made by Mr Jones, which the representatives of the Cherokees had seen and used while here in Washington. If that translation is in the possession of your Department, as was, perhaps erroneously supposed, you may have sufficient assurance of its correctness to warrant the distribution of printed copies for the information of Cherokees, incapable of reading English, under a statement of the facts which shall preclude the inference that the United States are committed to, or bound by any thing except the original English of the Treaty.

I have the honor to be Sir
Your obedient servant,
Henry Stanbery
Acting Secretary.

#358.

Miscellaneous Letters - August, Part I, 1866.

Rec^d 4th Aug:

DEPARTMENT of the INTERIOR,
WASHINGTON D. C. Aug 4 1866

Sir

I have the honor to state in reply to the letter of your Department of this date, that this Department will pay the reasonable expenses occasioned by the translation and publication in the Cherokee language and character, of the recent treaty between the United States and Cherokees, on the presentation of proper vouchers approved by the Department of State.

Very respectfully
Your ob't servt
Jas Harlan
Secretary

Hon W^m. H. Seward
Secretary of State.

#358.

Domestic Letters, Volume 73, page 583.

Department of State,
Washington August 9. 1866.

William J. McDonald
Chief Clerk Office Secretary of Senate

Sir:

With a view of facilitating the promulgation of the following named treaties with Indians, I have to request that you will cause six of the printed copies of each of them to be transmitted to this Department, viz: Treaty with the Chippewas of Saginaw Swan Creek, and Black River in Michigan, of October 18, 1864.#335

Treaty with the Seminoles, of March, 21, 1866.#352
do do do Creeks, of June, 14, 1866.#356
do do do Delawares of July 4, 1866.#357
do do do Cherokees of July 19. 1866.#358

I am, Sir, your obedient servant,
R. S. Chew.
Acting Chief Clerk.

#358.

Miscellaneous Letters - August, Part I, 1866.

RECEIVED,

Dept. of State

Aug 10 1866

Office of Secretary of U. S. Senate,

Washington, August 10 1866.

R. S. Chew Esq

Acting Chief Clerk,

State Department,

Sir,

In compliance with the request contained in your communication of the 9th instant, I herewith enclose six of the printed copies of each of the Indian Treaties therein named.

Yours Respectfully,

W: J: McDonald

Chief Clerk

#358.

Domestic Letters - Volume 74, pages 66 and 67.

Department of State,
Washington August 24, 1866.

Hon James Harlan,
Secretary of the Interior.

Sir:

Agreeably to a request contained in your letter of the 22d instant, received today, I have the honor to transmit to you herewith, 250 copies of each of the following named Treaties with Indians, viz.

Treaty with the Delawares concluded July 4, 1866. #357
do do do Creeks do June 14, do #356
do do do Cherokees do July (19) 9, do #358

Be pleased to acknowledge their receipt. A copy of these Treaties has been sent respectively to the editors of the newspapers designated by you for their promulgation.

I am, sir, your obedient servant,
William H. Seward.

#358.

[Transcription of the Original Treaty]

Treaty Between
The United States of America
And The
Cherokee Nation of Indians

Concluded July 19, 1866

Proclaimed August 11, 1866

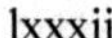

TREATY

BETWEEN

THE UNITED STATES OF AMERICA

AND THE

CHEROKEE NATION OF INDIANS.

CONCLUDED JULY 19, 1866.
RATIFICATION ADVISED, WITH AMENDMENTS, JULY 27, 1866.
AMENDMENTS ACCEPTED JULY 31, 1866.
PROCLAIMED AUGUST 11, 1866.

ANDREW JOHNSON,

PRESIDENT OF THE UNITED STATES OF AMERICA,

TO ALL AND SINGULAR TO WHOM THESE PRESENTS SHALL COME, GREETING:

Whereas a Treaty was made and concluded at the city of Washington, in the District of Columbia, on the nineteenth day of July, in the year of our Lord one thousand eight hundred and sixty-six, by and between Dennis N. Cooley and Elijah Sells, Commissioners, on the part of the United States, and Smith Christie, White Catcher, James McDaniel, S. H. Benge, Daniel H. Ross, and J. B. Jones, delegates of the Cherokee nation, appointed by resolution of the national council, on the part of said Cherokee nation, which treaty is in the words and figures following, to wit:

Articles of agreement and convention at the city of Washington on the nineteenth day of July, in the year of our Lord one thousand eight hundred and sixty-six, between the United States, represented by Dennis N. Cooley, Commissioner of Indian Affairs, [and] Elijah Sells, superintendent of Indian affairs for the southern superintendency, and the Cherokee nation of Indians, represented by its delegates, James McDaniel, Smith Christie, White Catcher, S. H. Benge, J. B. Jones, and Daniel H. Ross—John Ross, principal chief of the Cherokees, being too unwell to join in these negotiations.

Preamble.

Whereas existing treaties between the United States and the Cherokee nation are deemed to be insufficient, the said contracting parties agree as follows, viz:

Article 1.

The pretended treaty made with the so-called Confederate States by the Cherokee nation on the seventh day of October, 1861, and repudiated by the national council of the Cherokee nation on the 18th day of February, 1863, is hereby declared to be void.

Article 2.

Amnesty is hereby declared by the United States and the Cherokee nation for all crimes and misdemeanors committed by one Cherokee on the person or property of another Cherokee, or of a citizen of the United States, prior to the 4th day of July, 1866; and no right of action arising out of wrongs committed in aid or in the suppression of the rebellion shall be prosecuted or maintained in the courts of the United States or in the courts of the Cherokee nation.

ARTICLE 3.

The confiscation laws of the Cherokee nation shall be repealed, and the same, and all sales of farms, and improvements on real estate, made or pretended to be made in pursuance thereof, are hereby agreed and declared to be null and void, and the former owners of such property so sold, their heirs or assigns, shall have the right peaceably to reoccupy their homes, and the purchaser under the confiscation laws, or his heirs or assigns, shall be repaid by the treasurer of the Cherokee nation from the national funds, the money paid for said property, and the cost of permanent improvements on such real estate, made thereon since the confiscation sale; the cost of such improvements to be fixed by a commission, to be composed of one person designated by the Secretary of the Interior and one by the principal chief of the nation, which two may appoint a third in cases of disagreement, which cost so fixed shall be refunded to the national treasurer by the returning Cherokees within three years from the ratification hereof.

ARTICLE 4.

All the Cherokees and freed persons who were formerly slaves to any Cherokee, and all free negroes not having been such slaves, who resided in the Cherokee nation prior to June 1st, 1861, who may within two years elect not to reside northeast of the Arkansas river and southeast of Grand river, shall have the right to settle in and occupy the Canadian district southwest of the Arkansas river, and also all that tract of country lying northwest of Grand river, and bounded on the southeast by Grand river and west by the Creek reservation to the northeast corner thereof; from thence west on the north line of the Creek reservation to the ninety-sixth degree of west longitude; and thence north on said line of longitude so far that a line due east to Grand river will include a quantity of land equal to 160 acres for each person who may so elect to reside in the territory above described in this article: *Provided*, That that part of said district north of the Arkansas river shall not be set apart until it shall be found that the Canadian district is not sufficiently large to allow one hundred and sixty acres to each person desiring to obtain settlement under the provisions of this article.

ARTICLE 5.

The inhabitants electing to reside in the district described in the preceding article shall have the right to elect all their local officers and judges, and the number of delegates to which by their numbers they may be entitled in any general council to be established in the Indian territory under the provisions of this treaty, as stated in article 12; and to control all their local affairs, and to establish all necessary police regulations and rules for the administration of justice in said district, not inconsistent with the constitution of the Cherokee nation or the laws of the United States: *Provided*, The Cherokees residing in said district shall enjoy all the rights and privileges of other Cherokees who may elect to settle in said district as hereinbefore provided, and shall hold the same rights and privileges and be subject to the same liabilities as those who elect to settle in said district under the provisions of this treaty: *Provided also*, That if any such police regulations or rules be adopted which, in the opinion of the President, bear oppressively on any citizen of the nation, he may suspend the same. And all rules or regulations in said district, or in any other district of the nation, discriminating against the citizens of other districts, are prohibited, and shall be void.

ARTICLE 6.

The inhabitants of the said district hereinbefore described shall be entitled to representation according to numbers in the national council, and all laws of the Cherokee nation shall be uniform throughout said nation. And should any such law, either in its provisions or in the manner of its enforcement, in the opinion of the President of the United States, operate unjustly or injuriously in said district, he is hereby authorized and empowered to correct such evil, and to adopt the means necessary to secure the impartial administration of justice, as well as a fair and equitable application and expenditure of the national funds as between the people of this and of every other district in said nation.

ARTICLE 7.

The United States court to be created in the Indian territory; and until such court is created therein, the United States district court, the nearest to the Cherokee nation, shall have exclusive original jurisdiction of all causes, civil and criminal, wherein an inhabitant of the district hereinbefore described shall be a party, and where an inhabitant outside of said district, in the Cherokee nation, shall be the other party, as plaintiff or defendant in a civil cause, or shall be defendant or prosecutor in a criminal case, and all process issued in said district by any officer of the Cherokee nation, to be executed on an inhabitant residing outside of said district, and all process issued by any officer of the Cherokee nation outside of said district, to be executed on an inhabitant residing in said district, shall be to all intents and purposes null and void, unless endorsed by the district judge for the district where such process is to be served, and said person, so arrested, shall be held in custody by the officer so arresting him, until he shall be delivered over to the United States marshal, or consent to be tried by the Cherokee court: *Provided*, That any or all the provisions of this treaty, which make any distinction in rights and remedies between the citizens of any district and the citizens of the rest of the nation, shall be abrogated whenever the President shall have ascertained, by an election duly ordered by him, that a majority of the voters of such district desire them to be abrogated, and he shall have declared such abrogation: *And provided further*, That no law or regulation, to be hereafter enacted within said Cherokee nation or any district thereof, prescribing a penalty for its violation, shall take effect or be enforced until after 90 days from the date of its promulgation, either by publication in one or more newspapers of general circulation in said Cherokee nation, or by posting up copies thereof in the Cherokee and English languages in each district where the same is to take effect, at the usual place of holding district courts.

ARTICLE 8.

No license to trade in goods, wares, or merchandise *merchandise* shall be granted by the United States to trade in the Cherokee nation, unless approved by the Cherokee national council, except in the Canadian district, and such other district north of Arkansas river and west of Grand river occupied by the so-called Southern Cherokees, as provided in article 4 of this treaty.

ARTICLE 9.

The Cherokee nation having, voluntarily, in February, 1863, by an act of their national council, forever abolished slavery, hereby covenant and agree that never hereafter shall either slavery or involuntary servitude exist in their nation othererwise than in the punishment of crime, whereof the party shall have been duly convicted, in accordance with laws applicable to all the members of said tribe alike. They further agree that all freedmen who have been liberated by voluntary act of their former owners or by law, as well as all free colored persons who were in the country at the commencement of the rebellion, and are now residents therein, or who may return within six months, and their descendants, shall have all the rights of native Cherokees: *Provided*, That owners of slaves so emancipated in the Cherokee nation shall never receive any compensation or pay for the slaves so emancipated.

ARTICLE 10.

Every Cherokee and freed person resident in the Cherokee nation shall have the right to sell any products of his farm, including his or her live stock, or any merchandise or manufactured products, and to ship and drive the same to market without restraint, paying any tax thereon which is now or may be levied by the United States on the quantity sold outside of the Indian territory.

ARTICLE 11.

The Cherokee nation hereby grant a right of way not exceeding two hundred feet wide, except at stations, switches, water stations, or crossing of rivers, where more may be indispensable to the full enjoyment of the franchise herein granted, and then only two hundred additional feet shall be taken, and only for such length as may be absolutely necessary, through all their lands, to any company or corporation which shall be duly authorized by Congress to construct a railroad from any point north to any point south, and from any point east to any point west of, and which may pass through, the Cherokee nation. Said company or corporation, and their employés and laborers, while constructing and repairing the same, and in operating said road or roads, including all necessary agents on the line, at stations, switches, water tanks, and all others necessary to the successful operation of a railroad, shall be protected in the discharge of their duties, and at all times subject to the Indian intercourse laws, now or which may hereafter be enacted and be in force in the Cherokee nation.

ARTICLE 12.

The Cherokees agree that a general council, consisting of delegates elected by each nation or tribe lawfully residing within the Indian territory, may be annually convened in said territory, which council shall be organized in such manner and possess such powers as hereinafter prescribed.

First. After the ratification of this treaty, and as soon as may be deemed practicable by the Secretary of the Interior, and prior to the first session of said council, a census or enumeration of each tribe lawfully resident in said territory shall be taken under the direction of the Commissioner of Indian Affairs, who for that purpose is hereby authorized to designate and appoint competent persons, whose compensation shall be fixed by the Secretary of the Interior, and paid by the United States.

Second. The first general council shall consist of one member from each tribe, and an additional member for each one thousand Indians, or each fraction of a thousand greater than five hundred, being members of any tribe lawfully resident in said territory, and shall be selected by said tribes respectively, who may assent to the establishment of said general council; and if none should be thus formally selected by any nation or tribe so assenting, the said nation or tribe shall be represented in said general council by the chief or chiefs and headmen of said tribes, to be taken in the order of their rank as recognized in tribal usage, in the same number and proportion as above indicated. After the said census shall have been taken and completed, the superintendent of Indian affairs shall publish and declare to each tribe assenting to the establishment of such council the number of members of such council to which they shall be entitled under the provisions of this article, and the persons entitled to represent said tribes shall meet at such time and place as he shall approve; but thereafter the time and place of the sessions of said council shall be determined by its action: *Provided*, That no session in any one year shall exceed the term of thirty days: *And provided*, That special sessions of said council may be called by the Secretary of the Interior whenever in his judgment the interest of said tribes shall require such special session.

Third. Said general council shall have power to legislate upon matters pertaining to the intercourse and relations of the Indian tribes and nations and colonies of freedmen resident in said territory; the arrest and extradition of criminals and offenders escaping from one tribe to another, or into any community of freedmen; the administration of justice between members of different tribes of said territory and persons other than Indians and members of said tribes or nations; and the common defence and safety of the nations of said territory.

All laws enacted by said council shall take effect at such time as may therein be provided, unless suspended by direction of the President of the United States. No law shall be enacted inconsistent with the Constitution of the United States, or laws of Congress, or existing treaty stipulations with the United States. Nor shall said council legislate upon matters other than those above indicated: *Provided, however*, That the legislative power of such general council may be enlarged by the consent of the national council of each nation or tribe assenting to its establishment, with the approval of the President of the United States.

Fourth. Said council shall be presided over by such person as may be designated by the Secretary of the Interior.

Fifth. The council shall elect a secretary, whose duty it shall be to keep an accurate record of all the proceedings of said council, and who shall transmit a true copy of all such proceedings, duly certified by the presiding officer of such council, to the Secretary of the Interior, and to each tribe or nation represented in said council, immediately after the sessions of said council shall terminate. He shall be paid out of the treasury of the United States an annual salary of five hundred dollars.

Sixth. The members of said council shall be paid by the United States the sum of four dollars per diem during the term actually in attendance on the sessions of said council, and at the rate of four dollars for every twenty miles necessarily travelled by them in going from and returning to their homes, respectively, from said council, to be certified by the secretary and president of the said council.

Article 13.

The Cherokees also agree that a court or courts may be established by the United States in said territory, with such jurisdiction and organized in such manner as may be prescribed by law: *Provided*, That the judicial tribunals of the nation shall be allowed to retain exclusive jurisdiction in all civil and criminal cases arising within their country in which members of the nation, by nativity or adoption, shall be the only parties, or where the cause of action shall arise in the Cherokee nation, except as otherwise provided in this treaty.

ARTICLE 14.

The right to the use and occupancy of a quantity of land not exceeding one hundred and sixty acres, to be selected according to legal subdivisions in one body, and to include their improvements, and not including the improvements of any member of the Cherokee nation, is hereby granted to every society or denomination which has erected, or which with the consent of the national council may hereafter erect, buildings within the Cherokee country for missionary or educational purposes. But no land thus granted, nor buildings which have been or may be erected thereon, shall ever be sold or [o]therwise disposed of except with the consent and approval of the Cherokee national council and of the Secretary of the Interior. And whenever any such lands or buildings shall be sold or disposed of, the proceeds thereof shall be applied by said society or societies for like purposes within said nation, subject to the approval of the Secretary of the Interior.

ARTICLE 15.

The United States may settle any civilized Indians, friendly with the Cherokees and adjacent tribes, within the Cherokee country, on unoccupied lands east of 96°, on such terms as may be agreed upon by any such tribe and the Cherokees, subject to the approval of the President of the United States, which shall be consistent with the following provisions, viz· Should any such tribe or band of Indians settling in said country abandon their tribal organization, there being first paid into the Cherokee national fund a sum of money which shall sustain the same proportion to the then existing national fund that the number of Indians sustain to the whole number of Cherokees then residing in the Cherokee country, they shall be incorporated into and ever after remain a part of the Cherokee nation, on equal terms in every respect with native citizens. And should any such tribe, thus settling in said country, decide to preserve their tribal organizations, and to maintain their tribal laws, customs, and usages, not inconsistent with the constitution and laws of the Cherokee nation, they shall have a district of country set off for their use by metes and bounds equal to 160 acres, if they should so decide, for each man, woman, and child of said tribe, and shall pay for the same into the national fund such price as may be agreed on by them and the Cherokee nation, subject to the approval of the President of the United States, and in cases of disagreement the price to be fixed by the President.

And the said tribe thus settled shall also pay into the national fund a sum of money, to be agreed on by the respective parties, not greater in proportion to the whole existing national fund and the probable proceeds of the lands herein ceded or authorized to be ceded or sold than their numbers bear to the whole number of Cherokees then residing in said country, and thence afterwards they shall enjoy all the rights of native Cherokees. But no Indians who have no tribal organizations, or who shall determine to abandon their tribal organizations, shall be permitted to settle east of the 96° of longitude without the consent of the Cherokee national council, or of a delegation duly appointed by it, being first obtained. And no Indians who have and determine to preserve their tribal organizations shall be permitted to settle, as herein provided, east of the 96° of longitude without such consent being first obtained, unless the President of the United States, after a full hearing of the objections offered by said council or delegation to such settlement, shall determine that the objections are insufficient, in which case he may authorize the settlement of such tribe east of the 96° of longitude.

ARTICLE 16.

The United States may settle friendly Indians in any part of the Cherokee country west of 96°, to be taken in a compact form in quantity not exceeding 160 acres for each member of each of said tribes thus to be settled; the boundaries of each of said districts to be distinctly marked, and the land conveyed in fee simple to each of said tribes to be held in common or by their members in severalty as the United States may decide.

Said lands thus disposed of to be paid for to the Cherokee nation at such price as may be agreed on between the said parties in interest, subject to the approval of the President; and if they should not agree, then the price to be fixed by the President.

The Cherokee nation to retain the right of possession of and jurisdiction over all of said country west of 96° of longitude until thus sold and occupied, after which their jurisdiction and right of possession to terminate forever as to each of said districts thus sold and occupied.

ARTICLE 17.

The Cherokee nation hereby cedes, in trust to the United States, the tract of land in the State of Kansas which was sold to the Cherokees by the United States, under the provisions of the 2nd article of the treaty of 1835; and also that strip of the land ceded to the nation by the 4th article of said treaty which is included in the State of Kansas, and the Cherokees consent that said lands may be included in the limits and jurisdiction of the said State.

The lands herein ceded shall be surveyed as the public lands of the United States are surveyed, under the direction of the Commissioner of the General Land Office, and shall be appraised by two disinterested persons, one to be designated by the Cherokee national council and one by the Secretary of the Interior, and, in case of disagreement, by a third person, to be mutually selected by the aforesaid appraisers. The appraisement to be not less than an average of one dollar and a quarter per acre, exclusive of improvements.

And the Secretary of the Interior shall from time to time, as such surveys and appraisements are approved by him, after due advertisement for sealed bids, sell such lands to the highest bidders for cash in parcels not exceeding one hundred and sixty acres, and at not less than the appraised value: *Provided*, That whenever there are improvements of the value of $50 made on the lands not being mineral, and owned and personally occupied by any person for agricultural purposes at the date of the signing hereof, such person so owning, and in person residing on such improvements, shall, after due proof, made under such regulations as the Secretary of the Interior may prescribe, be entitled to buy, at the appraised value, the smallest quantity of land in legal subdivisions which will include his improvements, not exceeding in the aggregate one hundred and sixty acres; the expenses of survey and appraisement to be paid by the Secretary out of the proceeds of sale of said land: *Provided*, That nothing in this article shall prevent the Secretary of the Interior from selling the whole of said neutral lands in a body to any responsible party, for cash, for a sum not less than eight hundred thousand dollars.

ARTICLE 18.

That any lands owned by the Cherokees in the State of Arkansas and in States east of the Mississippi may be sold by the Cherokee nation in such manner as their national council may prescribe, all such sales being first approved by the Secretary of the Interior.

ARTICLE 19.

All Cherokees being heads of families residing at the date of the ratification of this treaty on any of the lands herein ceded, or authorized to be sold, and desiring to remove to the reserved country, shall be paid by the purchasers of said lands the value of such improvements, to be ascertained and appraised by the commissioners who appraise the lands, subject to the approval of the Secretary of the Interior; and if he shall elect to remain on the land now occupied by him, shall be entitled to receive a patent from the United States in fee simple for 320 acres of land to include his improvements, and thereupon he and his family shall cease to be members of the nation.

ARTICLE 20.

Whenever the Cherokee national council shall request it, the Secretary of the Interior shall cause the country reserved for the Cherokees to be surveyed and allotted among them, at the expense of the United States.

ARTICLE 21.

It being difficult to learn the precise boundary line between the Cherokee country and the States of Arkansas, Missouri, and Kansas, it is agreed that the United States shall, at its own expense, cause the same to be run as far west as the Arkansas, and marked by permanent and conspicuous monuments, by two commissioners, one of whom shall be designated by the Cherokee national council.

ARTICLE 22.

The Cherokee national council, or any duly appointed delegation thereof, shall have the privilege to appoint an agent to examine the accounts of the nation with the government of the United States at such time as they may see proper, and to continue or discharge such agent, and to appoint another, as may be thought best by such council or delegation; and such agent shall have free access to all accounts and books in the executive departments relating to the business of said Cherokee nation, and an opportunity to examine the same in the presence of the officer having such books and papers in charge.

ARTICLE 23.

All funds now due the nation, or that may hereafter accrue from the sale of their lands by the United States as hereinbefore provided for, shall be invested in United States registered stocks at their current value, and the interest on all said funds shall be paid semi-annually on the order of the Cherokee nation, and shall be applied to the following purposes, to wit: Thirty-five per cent. shall be applied for the support of the common schools of the nation and educational purposes; fifteen per cent. for the orphan fund, and fifty per cent. for general purposes, including reasonable salaries of district officers; and the Secretary of the Interior, with the approval of the President of the United States, may pay out of the funds due the nation, on the order of the national council or a delegation duly authorized by it, such amount as he may deem necessary to meet outstanding obligations of the Cherokee nation, caused by the suspension of the payment of their annuities, not to exceed the sum of one hundred and fifty thousand dollars.

ARTICLE 24.

As a slight testimony for the useful and arduous services of the Rev. Evan Jones, for forty years a missionary in the Cherokee nation, now a cripple, old and poor, it is agreed that the sum of three thousand dollars be paid to him, under the direction of the Secretary of the Interior, out of any Cherokee fund in or to come into his hands not otherwise appropriated.

ARTICLE 25.

A large number of the Cherokees who served in the army of the United States having died, leaving no heirs entitled to receive bounties and arrears of pay on account of such service, it is agreed that all bounties and arrears for service in the regiments of Indian United States volunteers which shall remain unclaimed by any person legally entitled to receive the same for two years from the ratification of this treaty, shall be paid as the national council may direct, to be applied to the foundation and support of an asylum for the education of orphan children, which asylum shall be under the control of the national council, or of such benevolent society as said council may designate, subject to the approval of the Secretary of the Interior.

ARTICLE 26.

The United States guarantee to the people of the Cherokee nation the quiet and peaceable possession of their country and protection against domestic feuds and insurrections and against hostilities of other tribes. They shall also be protected against inter[r]uptions or intrusion from all unauthorized citizens of the United States who may attempt to settle on their lands or reside in their territory. In case of hostilities among the Indian tribes, the United States agree that the party or parties commencing the same shall, so far as practicable, make reparation for the damages done.

ARTICLE 27.

The United States shall have the right to establish one or more military posts or stations in the Cherokee nation, as may be deemed necessary for the proper protection of the citizens of the United States lawfully residing therein and the Cherokees and other citizens of the Indian country. But no sutler or other person connected therewith, either in or out of the military organization, shall be permitted to introduce any spirit[u]ous, vinous, or malt liquors into the Cherokee nation, except the medical department proper, and by them only for strictly medical purposes. And all persons not in the military service of the United States, not citizens of the Cherokee nation, are to be prohibited from coming into the Cherokee nation, or remaining in the same, except as herein otherwise provided; and it is the duty of the United States Indian agent for the Cherokees to have such persons, not lawfully residing or sojourning therein, removed from the nation, as they now are, or hereafter may be, required by the Indian intercourse laws of the United States.

ARTICLE 28.

The United States hereby agree to pay for provisions and clothing furnished the army under Appotholehala in the winter of 1861 and 1862, not to exceed the sum of ten thousand dollars, the accounts to be ascertained and settled by the Secretary of the Interior.

ARTICLE 29.

The sum of ten thousand [dollars,] or so much thereof as may be necessary to pay the expenses of the delegates and representatives of the Cherokees invited by the government to visit Washington for the purposes of making this treaty, shall be paid by the United States on the ratification of this treaty.

ARTICLE 30.

The United States agree to pay to the proper claimants all losses of property by missionaries or missionary societies, resulting from their being ordered or driven from the country by United States agents, and from their property being taken and occupied or destroyed by *by* United States troops, not exceeding in the aggregate twenty thousand dollars, to be ascertained by the Secretary of the Interior.

ARTICLE 31.

All provisions of treaties, heretofore ratified and in force, and not inconsistent with the provisions of this treaty, are hereby reaffirmed and declared to be in full force ; and nothing herein shall be construed as an acknowledgment by the United States, or as a relinquishment by the Cherokee nation of any claims or demands under the guaranties of former treaties, except as herein expressly provided.

In testimony whereof, the said commissioners on the part of the United States, and the said delegation on the part of the Cherokee nation, have hereunto set their hands and seals, at the city of Washington, this *ninth* [nineteenth] day of July, A. D. one thousand eight hundred and sixty-six.

D. N. COOLEY,
Com'r Ind. Affairs.
ELIJAH SELLS,
Sup't Ind. Affs.
SMITH CHRISTIE,
WHITE CATCHER,
JAMES McDANIEL,
S. H. BENGE,
DANL. H. ROSS,
J. B. JONES,
Delegates of the Cherokee Nation, appointed by Resolution of the National Council.

In presence of—
W. H. WATSON.
J. W. WRIGHT.

Signatures witnessed by the following named persons, the following interlineations being made before signing: On page 1st the word "the" interlined, on page 11 the word "the" struck out, and to said page 11 a sheet attached requiring publication of laws; and on page 34th the word "ceded" struck out and the words "neutral lands" inserted. Page 47½ added relating to expenses of treaty.

THOMAS EWING, JR.
WM. A. PHILLIPS.
J. W. WRIGHT.

And whereas, the said treaty having been submitted to the Senate of the United States for its constitutional action thereon, the Senate did, on the twenty-seventh day of July, one thousand eight hundred and sixty-six, advise and consent to the ratification of the same, with amendments, by a resolution in the words and figures following, to wit:

IN EXECUTIVE SESSION, SENATE OF THE UNITED STATES,
July 27, 1866.

Resolved, (two-thirds of the Senators present concurring,) That the Senate advise and consent to the ratification of the articles of agreement and convention made at the city of Washington, on the nineteenth day of July, in the year of our Lord one thousand eight hundred and sixty-six, between the United States and the Cherokee nation of Indians, with the following

AMENDMENTS:

1st. Insert at the end of article 2 the following:

But the Cherokee nation stipulate and agree to deliver up to the United States, or their duly authorized agent, any or all public property, particularly ordnance, ordnance stores, arms of all kinds, and quartermasters' stores, in their possession or control, which belonged to the United States or the so-called Confederate States, without any reservation.

2nd. Strike out the last proviso in article 17, and insert in lieu thereof the following:

Provided, That nothing in this article shall prevent the Secretary of the Interior from selling the whole of said lands not occupied by actual settlers at the date of the ratification of this treaty, not exceeding 160 acres to each person entitled to pre-emption under the pre-emption laws of the United States, in a body, to any responsible party, for cash, for a sum not less than one dollar per acre.

3d. Insert at the end of article 29 the following:

And the Secretary of the Interior shall also be authorized to pay the reasonable costs and expenses of the delegates of the southern Cherokees.

The moneys to be paid under this article shall be paid out of the proceeds of the sales of the national lands in Kansas.

Attest:

J. W. FORNEY,
Secretary.

And whereas the foregoing amendments having been fully explained and interpreted to the aforenamed delegates of the Cherokee nation, they did, on the thirty-first day of July, one thousand eight hundred and sixty-six, give, on behalf of said nation, their free and voluntary assent to said amendments, in the words and figures following, to wit:

Whereas the Senate of the United States did, on the 27th day of July, 1866, advise and consent to the ratification of the articles of agreement and convention, made at the city of Washington, on the nineteenth day of July, in the year of our Lord one thousand eight hundred and sixty-six, between the United States and the Cherokee nation of Indians, with the following

AMENDMENTS, to wit:

1st. Insert at the end of article 2 the following:

But the Cherokee nation stipulate and agree to deliver up to the United States, or their duly authorized agent, any or all public property, particularly ordnance, ordnance stores, arms of all kinds, and quartermasters' stores, in their possession or control, which belonged to the United States or the so-called Confederate States, without any reservation.

2nd. Strike out the last proviso in article 17, and insert in lieu thereof the following:

Provided, That nothing in this article shall prevent the Secretary of the Interior from selling the whole of said lands not occupied by actual settlers at the date of the ratification of this treaty, not exceeding 160 acres to each person entitled to pre-emption under the pre-emption laws of the United States, in a body, to any responsible party, for cash, for a sum not less than one dollar per acre.

3d. Insert at the end of article 29 the following:

And the Secretary of the Interior shall also be authorized to pay the reasonable costs and expenses of the delegates of the Southern Cherokees.

The moneys to be paid under this article shall be paid out of the proceeds of the sales of the national lands in Kansas.

Now, therefore, we, the delegates on the part of the said Cherokee nation, do hereby assent and agree to the said amendments above written, the same having been explained to us and being fully understood by us.

Witness our hands and seals, this 31st day of July, A. D. 1866, at Washington, D. C.

SMITH CHRISTIE. [SEAL.]
WHITE CATCHER. [SEAL.]
JAMES McDANIEL. [SEAL.]
S. H. BENGE. [SEAL.]
DANL. H. ROSS. [SEAL.]
J. B. JONES. [SEAL.]

In presence of—
D. N. COOLEY,
Com'r Ind. Affairs.
J. HARLAN,
U. S. Ind. Agent.
CHARLES E. MIX.
J. W. WRIGHT.
W. R. IRWIN.

Now, therefore, be it known that I, ANDREW JOHNSON, President of the United States of America, do, in pursuance of the advice and consent of the Senate, as expressed in its resolution of the twenty-seventh of July, one thousand eight hundred and sixty-six, accept, ratify, and confirm the said treaty with the amendments as aforesaid.

In testimony whereof I have signed my name hereto, and have caused the seal of the United States to be affixed.

Done at the city of Washington, this eleventh day of August, in the year of [SEAL.] our Lord one thousand eight hundred and sixty-six, and of the Independence of the United States of America the ninety-first.

ANDREW JOHNSON.

By the President:
HENRY STANBERY,
Acting Secretary of State.

INTRODUCTION

It was found that the material within these pages had to contain three separate stipulations in order to be transcribed. Every page to be typed or packet to be considered for each individual involved had to be "Granted." They had to have, #1: a "D" card (Doubtful to be reconsidered); #2: had to have a follow up of a Cherokee by Blood Enrollment Card and #3; had to be entered upon the final Dawes Roll (with a Dawes Number) for the Cherokee.

Not all packets will be transcribed for this series; out of the 3,207 packets only those applying for citizenship under the Doubtful listings and fully accepted while meeting the three stipulations will fall within these pages.

Individuals fully rejected cover a lot of ground and contain no ability for searching out factual receipts in changing a decision from so long ago. "Rejected" cases being added to the "Granted" materials could only over burden these volumes being transcribed while undermining the purpose of searching the accepted bloodlines of true Cherokee descendants.

The rejections cover so much time and testimony even though maybe sometimes treated unfairly or unjustly through the Commission or Government representatives a party's circumstance at this moment can't be overturned and need not be involved with the records transcribed.

These cases are fascinating, it can easily be seen that the authorities in charge of researching the Cherokee people scrutinized these people almost with every intention of disallowing their claims whether blood or no blood. To put it bluntly it would make your blood boil.

There is no doubt that the Cherokee were being overrun by a horde of various groups all with one motive in mind; wanting a share of the take which belonged to only those that truly carried Cherokee blood in their veins.

The circumstances thrown towards the Cherokee as well as the Commission had to have been overwhelming. While at the same time making it easier to incur favor from those in power; those with ample resources sometimes likely slipped through the cracks only to create more wealth for themselves while leaving some in the cold when rightfully citizens.

The theme throughout these cases came to one final conclusion, a stamp; applied on every card in most cases, "Granted."

Time and again you will notice many stamps, Refused; Denied; Citizenship Certificate Issued; Action Approved By Secretary of Interior; Notice of Departmental Action Forwarded Attorney for The Cherokee Nation; Copy of Decision Forwarded Applicant; Record Forwarded Department; Decision Rendered; Granted Decision Rendered; Applicate Granted and Applicants Ordered Enrolled.

The confusion can be seen while many of these stamps were repeatedly applied on a single decision page time and again. So a rule of acceptance or stipulations ("Granted" as applied to the series title) for transcription had to be followed as explained in the first paragraph. In most cases the decisions are made for citizenship concerning individuals from the Western Cherokee.

The whole thing was mass hysteria. The Cherokee were being flooded with every sort of governmental intrusion imaginable. They wanted their own government run by their own laws, their own courts. It's necessary that a brief history be provided below to understand how these historically valuable papers came to be.

They just wanted the U.S. government to keep up their end of the bargain by Treaty; which was to keep the intruders out while the Cherokees took care of building their own lives. But the Government representatives told the Cherokees you either take care of the problem or we take care of the whole thing and take charge of your government thus denying Cherokee sovereignty. When the Cherokee Nation formed its own decision making policies and authorizations the Department of Interior openly overrode many of their decisions with delay tactics as well as overturning legitimate decisions in favor of following in many ways cronyism, bribery or selfish power.

To reiterate, the Cherokee relied upon their leaders to guide them but they ended up hanging in the balance after the Civil War, with their loyalties split worse than ever and their country ravished. Fathers and brothers were off fighting a war that didn't even concern them. By the time the war was over the Cherokee people had lost any form of stability. The men fighting the war came back to the same old political hatreds and in-fighting. The Nation was being overrun with many that claimed they were Cherokee, hoping to benefit from false claims of citizenship. These people, known as intruders, did nothing but make it more difficult for the Cherokees because of the pressures from the Government to control their boundaries. The blood Cherokees that were seeking their homeland were again in question as to who they were. They found nothing but scrutiny and distrust, the war had made them choose a side, and the U.S. Government didn't care for the choice of the majority.

Intruder after intruder was encroaching on Cherokee land and what was to seem like a never ending battle. Many Cherokee citizens lost their rights while intruders that didn't belong stayed using up what little resources there were. The government was telling the Cherokee leaders to settle their own intruder problems or else they would have to intercede. In an effort to clarify who were true Cherokee citizens and who were not, or who had been wrongfully taken off of the rolls, was a problem.

There were part-bloods, full-bloods, and no bloods along with mass confusion, prejudice, vendettas, and deceptions. The intruders wanted a free ride and were willing to use the confusion as a camouflage to achieve their purpose and greed.

This was a situation where the government was threatening to come in and turn the Cherokee Nation into a Federal Territory because it appeared to them that the Tribal Council would not be able to organize an effort to control the problem. But this wasn't the issue at hand as far as the Cherokee were concerned. They felt as if, according to their treaty stipulations, the United States was responsible for intruder removal. They felt as if the United States had let things get out of hand and that the government had not lived up to its contractual agreement. According to treaty stipulations this was true, but, they were told to either come up with a solution or lose their rights as a sovereign nation. Realizing the same things have been stated over and over again it needs to be repeated. The Government moved the natives to Indian Territory, they suffered and many died and now the Government intended on stealing the rest of not only their human rights but their homes forever more.

From William G. McLoughlin's book, *After the Trail of Tears, The Cherokees Struggle for Sovereignty 1839-1880,* it references on page 354, "Still, the Nation remained very uneasy about the fundamental question of its right to define who were its own citizens and its right to expect the United States to remove those who the Nation judged were not. Ever since 1872, federal agents had refused to expel from the Nation those former slaves whom the Nation considered 'aliens' and since 1874, federal agents had been under instructions from the Bureau of Indian Affairs to compile their own list of black or white persons who, in their opinion, had some claim to citizenship despite previous rulings of the Cherokee Courts on their claims."

On page 355-356, "On the basis of the affidavits and reports submitted, the Secretary of the Interior, Zachariah Chandler, sent E.C. Watkins to the Nation in 1875, to investigate the citizenship problem and gather information that Chandler could use to ask Congress to take action on behalf of these 'men without a country.' Watkins reported in February, 1876, that many of those on Ingall's list were 'clearly entitled' to Cherokee citizenship. Oochalata denied it. He counter charged that Ingalls was meddling in Cherokee affairs and wrote to the Bureau of Indian Affairs to complain. Receiving no satisfactory response, he wrote directly to President Grant on November 13, 1876, enclosing a petition from the Cherokees in Cooweescoowee District, complaining that the agent had not removed thousands of intruders in their area though ordered to do so by the Council. Some of these intruders were former slaves from the Deep South, but most were white U.S. citizens from Kansas, Missouri, and Arkansas.

Grant referred this letter to Commissioner J.Q. Smith. Annoyed that Oochalata had gone over the head of the Interior Department to the President, on December 8, Smith wrote Oochalata a long, assertive, and highly provocative letter outlining for the first time the department's position on this question. Smith said that from the evidence he had received, both from various federal agents and from the investigations of E.C. Watkins, the Cherokee Nation had failed to deal consistently and impartially with the problems of former slaves and others who claimed Cherokee citizenship. Therefore, the Bureau of Indian Affairs would continue to compile its own list of those who had "prima facie" evidence for citizenship (whether the Cherokee courts had acted negatively on their claims or not), and it would take no action to remove them until the Cherokees carried out four stipulations to resolve the issue. First, the Council must establish a clear, legal procedure providing due process for adjudicating all prima facie claims. Second, the rules by which such cases were decided must be approved by the Secretary of the Interior to ensure their impartiality.

Third, he suggested that the Cherokee Circuit Courts be designated as the appropriate bodies for such hearings. Finally, claimants' appeals of the decisions of the Cherokee Circuit Courts must be forwarded to the Secretary of the Interior, and no claimant for citizenship should be removed from the Nation until the Secretary had made his own ruling. In effect, Smith asserted the right of the Bureau of Indian Affairs to decide who was and was not a Cherokee citizen. A crucial decision concerning the issue of the sovereignty of Indian nations was about to be reached.

Oochalata was stunned and wrote a 139-page letter to Smith explaining why this procedure was totally unacceptable and contrary to law, treaties, precedent, and the U.S. Constitution."

On page 357, "Acting on instructions from Oochalata, the Cherokee Delegation sent another letter to President Grant on January 9, 1877, insisting that treaty rights, the Trade and Intercourse Act, and precedent gave the Nation the right 'to determine the question as to who are and who are not intruders.' The president referred their letter to Secretary of the Interior, Carl Schurz, who, on April 21, 1877, told the delegation that he supported Smith's four stipulations for settling the matter. Oochalata ignored this response and in August, 1877, sent to the new Commissioner of Indian Affairs, Ezra A. Hayt, a list of all the intruders whom the Cherokees wished to be immediately removed. On Nov. 7, Hayt replied flatly that the Bureau of Indian Affairs would not do so: 'while the department reserves to itself the right to finally determine who are and are not intruders under the law, **it expects the Cherokee Nation Council to enact some general and uniform law by which the Cherokee courts shall hear and determine the rights of claimants to citizenship,** subject only to the review of the Secretary of Interior after a final adjudication has been reached.'"

On page 358-9, "The department's claim that it had the right to judge intruders was, in Oochalata's opinion, 'a new doctrine for construing treaty or contracts in writing, to add to it verbally, a new clause, after the expiration of 92 years from date of that compact or treaty and without the consent of [one] party. . . . It is a dangerous doctrine to which I can never agree.'

While he urged the Council to send a protest through its delegation, Oochalata also asked it to enact a law that would establish a court to decide citizenship claims in a legal and uniform manner. The Council complied on Dec. 5, 1877, but the compromise was fatally weakened by the Council's failure to address two aspects of the law governing the Citizenship Court's actions.

First, the law provided no guidelines for deciding cases that would meet the demands of the Bureau of Indian Affairs, and consequently, in cases involving former slaves, the Citizenship Court relied, as the Cherokee Supreme Court had in 1870-71, simply on the wording in the Treaty of 1866. Second, the Council explicitly refused to allow the right of the Secretary of the Interior to review the decisions of the Court, stating that the Cherokee Citizenship Court was 'a tribunal of last resort.' The three persons appointed to the court, were John Chambers, O.P.H. Brewer, and George Downing. Also referred to as the Chamber's Commission, the Court began to hold hearings early in 1878. All persons claiming to have grounds for citizenship were required to present them or to be declared intruders."

On pages 359-360, McLoughlin continues, "By the end of 1878, Oochalata was struggling to find some new approach to the problem. On Dec. 3, he went over the head of the Bureau of Indian Affairs again, and wrote to Pres. Rutherford B. Hayes, forwarding a complete account of all of the cases adjudicated by the Citizenship Court and asking him to order the expulsion of those rejected and all other intruders. He told Hayes that the Cherokee Nation had an 'inherent national right' to define its own citizens, while the United States had a well-established obligation to expel non-citizens. Suspecting that Hayes would reject this request, Oochalata approached Commissioner Ezra A. Hayt and tried to work out a compromise. He said that the Cherokees would stop confiscating the property of those former slaves judged to be intruders pending the appointment of a joint commission of Cherokees and members of the Bureau to review the rejected claims. Hayt agreed only on the condition that decisions of this commission must be unanimous or the Bureau would retain the right to make its own decision in each case. Oochalata and the delegation could not accept such a condition, and the negotiations broke down. Finally, as a last resort, the council decided to submit a series of questions to the Secretary of the Interior, Carl Schurz, about their right to determine citizenship and the obligation of the United States to accept their determinations. They asked Schurz to present these questions to Attorney General Charles Devens for his opinion. They sent the letter on March 3, 1879, and after Hayt informed Devens of his views on the matter, Devens held hearings at which both sides presented their views. Realizing the importance of the decision, the Cherokees spent the money necessary to hire the best lawyers they could find to assist them. Hayt said that the status of at least one-thousand persons was at issue; the Council argued that there were over twice that many intruders whom the Department was refusing to remove. Throughout the dispute, the Bureau of Indian Affairs declined to act against intruding squatters from Kansas who made no pretense to citizenship.

"The three questions that the Council asked Devens to answer were: Did the Cherokee Nation have the right to determine its own citizenship? Did the former slaves who were citizens have any claim to share in the use of Cherokee land or in the money derived from the sale of the Cherokee land? Was it, or was it not, the duty of the Federal government to remove intruders under treaty stipulations and The Trade and Intercourse Act? By the time Devens sent his reply to Shurz in December, 1879, the citizenship court had heard 416 claims for citizenship and rejected 338."

Devens' opinion was clearly in the negative as far as the Cherokee Nation's sovereignty and decision processes were concerned. On page 364, McLoughlin observes, "Clearly, as since the days of Andrew Jackson, Federal refusal to honor the requirement of removing intruders was to be the means of forcing the Indian nations to do what they did not want to do." Oochalata would not run again as the election of August 1879 neared and Dennis W. Bushyhead became the new chief on August 4, 1879 but in the end it didn't matter who was chief the fight to keep Cherokee sovereignty along with self-government was all but lost by 1880.

On pages 365-366, McLoughlin wrote, "The turning point was reached in 1887 when Congress passed the Dawes Severalty Act. The act expressed what was now the national consensus among white voters (including Indian reformers, railroad magnates, and entrepreneurs)--that the solution to 'the Indian question' was to denationalize the tribes in the Indian Territory, survey and allot their land in severalty, and establish a white-dominated territorial government over 'Oklahoma' the Choctaw word for 'red man.'"

The sovereignty of the Western Cherokee tribe was taken, and to this day they still don't have a true land base as a nation. Even though others were able to take away the land that was promised to remain theirs forever; nobody was able to take away their right and ability to choose who was a true citizen and who was not. The packets transcribed within this series are exactly as they appeared on the microfilm copies from the original court records.

These cases are fascinating because of the generational bloodlines that can be verified by documentation rather than just word of mouth. From Kent Carter's book, *The Dawes Commission,* "The tribe also, continued to oppose the enrollment of whites who had married into the Cherokee tribe. That controversy dragged through the U.S. Court of Claims and then the Supreme Court, which finally ruled in favor of the tribe on November 05, 1906. The court upheld the Cherokee citizenship laws that denied rights to any white who had married into the tribe after November 1, 1877. It also upheld an 1839 law which stated that anyone who moved out of the nation lost their citizenship unless they were readmitted. The applications of 3,341 persons were rejected as a result of this ruling, and the allotment clerks were forced to undo a great deal of their work. With the issue finally settled by the courts, the commission was able to send the first schedule of Cherokees by intermarriage, containing fifty-five names, to the secretary of interior on June 10, 1907. Eventually only 286 people were enrolled as intermarried whites----far fewer than the number put on the rolls of the Choctaw and Chickasaw tribes, which had much more liberal laws on rights based on marriage."[1]

In Cohen's *Handbook of Federal Indian Law* he states, "In the *Cherokee Intermarriage Cases,* the Supreme Court considered the claims of certain white persons, intermarried with Cherokee Indians, who wanted to participate in the common property of the Cherokee Nation. Such persons were permitted by tribal law to be tribal citizens with limited rights in tribal property. The tribe had also provided for the revocation of citizenship rights of a white person who intermarried with a Cherokee if the Cherokee spouse were abandoned or if a widower or widow married a non-Cherokee. The Court found that the Cherokee Nation had authority to qualify the rights of citizenship which it offered to its 'naturalized' citizens. Such tribal action defeated the claims of the plaintiffs:

The laws and usages of the Cherokees, their earliest history, the fundamental principles of their national policy, their constitution and statutes, all show that citizenship rested on blood or marriage; that the man who would assert citizenship

---

[1] The Dawes Commission and the Allotment of the Five Civilized Tribes, 1893-1914 by Kent Carter, pg. 121, para. 2.

must establish marriage; that when marriage ceased (with a special reservation in favor of widows or widowers) citizenship ceased; that when an intermarried white married a person having no rights of Cherokee citizenship by blood it was conclusive evidence that the tie which bound him to the Cherokee people was severed and the very basis of his citizenship obliterated."[2]

An important footnote that Cohen published within his pages for the above paragraph also needs to be studied. He noted, "Under Cherokee law white persons intermarrying with Cherokees before 1875 were tribal citizens for most purposes, including allotment of tribal land, but had no interest in tribal funds except those funds derived from tribal lands. A Cherokee law that became effective in 1875 provided that whites marrying Cherokees had no rights to tribal property but could obtain full citizenship by the payment of $500 to the tribe. In 1877 the tribe provided that no intermarried citizen could obtain any rights to tribal land or funds."[3]

You will also find many of the Doubtful "D" cards as well as "Straight" Cherokee By Blood Roll cards within these pages, establishing each parties "Granted" status.

During many years of study this author has found cases that should have been accepted, especially with the particular documentation presented. It's obvious that reading a little Cherokee history you'd find the problems between the Cherokee and the Government started and continued on for decades from pre-Civil War excelling after and into the early 1900's the troubles continued to brew.

All in all the outcome of the many decisions made should have rendered a different result, not counting the misery of those that wouldn't live to see justice through. Also there have been many cases that would numb the minds of so many. How spent and frail they'd become wondering over and over how their lives could have gotten to this point with such a lack of conversation when they just wanted what was theirs. The years of struggle had given many the hopes that their ancestors were one of those that had a decent claim and an honest consideration. Like any time in history there are political struggles and the human factor that points out man is not perfect. These pages were transcribed with the wish that another person somewhere along the line will find their relation from the past and give them the answers long hoped for. These Cherokee packets or testimonies fill the genealogical curiosity to the brim in helping a descendant to understand part of what their ancestor had to endure at the hands of a bureaucrat following the will of the mindless government and the mindless questioner likely in many cases maybe not all, but with prejudice towards the Native People.

Under a select catalog of National Archive microfilm publication, covering, under a film explanation on page 73, paragraph 2, for M-1186, "The commission enrolled individuals as 'citizens' of a tribe under the following categories: Citizens by Blood, Citizens by Marriage, New Born Citizens by Blood (enrolled under an act of Congress approved March 3, 1905, 33 Stat.1071), Minor Citizens by Blood (enrolled

---

[2] Felix S. Cohen's Handbook of FEDERAL INDIAN LAW 1982 ED. pgs 20-21.

[3] Felix S. Cohen's Handbook of FEDERAL INDIAN LAW 1982 ED. pg 21 footnote16.

under an act of Congress approved April 28, 1906, 34 Stat. 137), Freedmen (former black slaves of Indians, later freed and admitted to tribal citizenship), New Born Freedmen, and Minor Freedmen. Delaware Indians adopted by the Cherokee tribe were enrolled as a separate group within the Cherokee. Within each enrollment category the commission generally maintained three types of cards: 'Straight' cards for persons whose applications were approved, 'D' cards for persons whose applications were considered doubtful and subject to question, and 'R' cards for persons whose applications were rejected. Persons listed on 'D' cards were subsequently transferred to either 'Straight' or 'R' cards depending on the commission's decisions."

Two more points can be made from paragraph 4 on page 73 also. "An applicant's census card number can be determined only by using the final rolls and the accompanying indexes reproduced on roll 1."[4]

"No indexes have been located for the majority of the "D" and "R" cards."[5]

The actual packets transcribed in this series come from National Archive film M-1301, rolls 27-31.

Jeff Bowen
Gallipolis, Ohio
NativeStudy.com

[4] American Indians; pg. 73, Para. 4

[5] American Indians; pg. 73, Para. 5

Cherokee D47 - Charles W. Devine

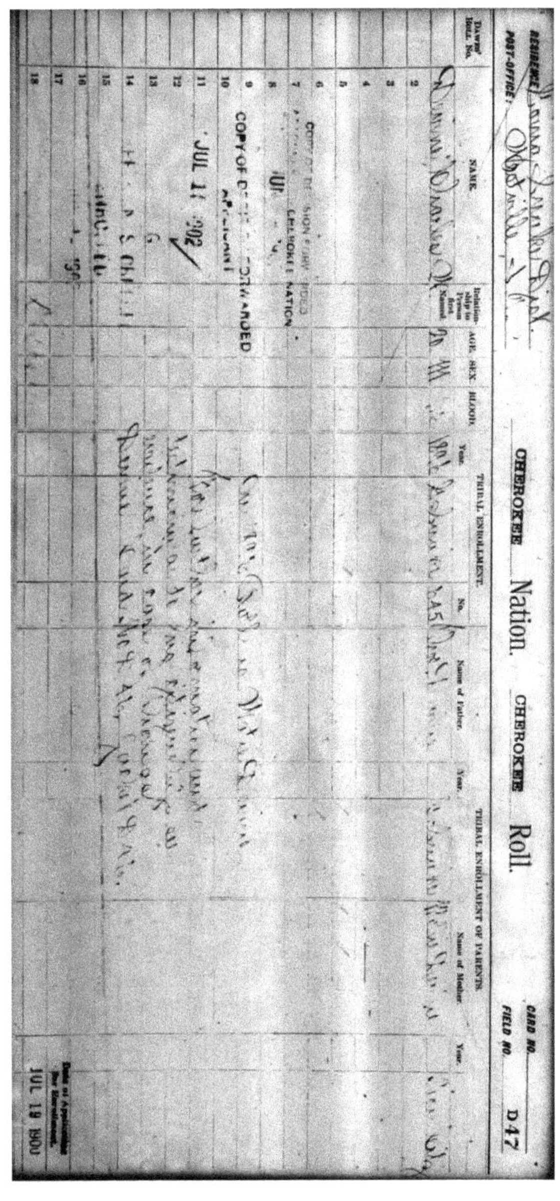

CHEROKEE Nation. CHEROKEE Roll.

CARD NO.
FIELD NO. D47

COPY OF DECISION FORWARDED

JUL 11 1902

Date of Application for Enrollment.
JUL 19 1900

DEPARTMENT OF THE INTERIOR,
COMMISSION TO THE FIVE CIVILIZED TRIBES,
WESTVILLE, I.T. JULY 19, 1900.

In the matter of the application of Charles W. Devine, foe[sic] enrollment as Cherokees[sic], said Devine being sworn by Commissioner Needles, testified as follows:

Q What is your name? A Charles W. Devine.
Q How old are you? A 20 years.
Q Your postoffice? A Westville.
Q Where do you live? A In Goingsnake.
Q How long have you lived there? A All my life. Never lived anywhere else. Was born in Kansas.
Q Hold[sic] were you when you came from Kansas? A Three months.
Q Are you a Cherokee by blood? A Yes.
Q What is your father's name? A Thomas Devine.
Q Is he living? A Yes.
Q Is his name upon the rolls of the Cherokee Nation? A Yes.
Q What is the name of your mother? A Mollie.
Q Is her name upon the Cherokee rolls? A Yes.
Q Is your name upon the '80 roll of the Cherokee Nation? A No, I don't think it is.
Rolls of '80 being examined his name is not found thereon.
Q Is your name upon the rolls of '96? A Yes.
On '96 roll, page 741, number 645 as Watie;
On '94 roll, page 642, number 716 as Chas. W.
Q Did you ever apply to the Cherokee Tribal authorities for citizenship?
A My father did.
Q Did you ever apply to the Dawes Commission? A No sir.
Q Are you married? A Yes.
Q Have you any children? A No sir.
Q What is the date of your marriage? A March 19, '00.
Q Don't apply for your wife? A No sir, don't think it's necessary.

The name of Charles W. Devine being found upon the Census rolls of '96 and also upon the pay-roll of '94, he claiming citizenship by blood, upon examination of the roll of '80 his name is not found. For further information in regard to his citizenship see testimony of Thomas Devine, it not being clear to the Commission that Charles W. Devine is a Cherokee by blood, his name is placed upon a doubtful card for further consideration, as was that of his father.

Brown McDonald, being sworn by Commissioner Needles, says as Stenographer to the Commission to the Five Civilized Tribes, he reported in full the testimony of the above named witness, and that the foregoing is a full, true and correct transcript of his notes.

Brown McDonald

Sworn to and subscribed before me this 20th day of July, 1900, at Westville, Indian Territory.

TB Needles
Commissioner.

"R"

Cherokee D-47.

Department of the Interior,
Commission to the Five Civilized Tribes,
Muskogee, I. T., February 14, 1902.

SUPPLEMENTAL TESTIMONY ON BEHALF OF APPLICANT, in the matter of the application of Charles W. Divine[sic] for enrollment as a Cherokee citizen.

Appearances:
Thomas Divine, father of applicant;
W.W. Hastings, attorney for the Cherokee Nation.

BY COMMISSION: The applicant was notified by registered mail on the 30th day of January, 1902, that his case would be taken up for final consideration by the Commission on the 15th day of February 1902, and that he would be permitted to appear before the Commission and to on said date introduce any additional testimony affecting his case. His father, Thomas Divine, this day appears in his behalf, and requests that the case be taken up on the 14th instead of the 15th inst.

THOMAS DIVINE, being sworn and examined, testified as follows:

BY COMMISSION:
Q What is your name? A Thomas Divine.
Q What is your post-office? A Westville, Indian Territory.
Q Are you the father of Charles W. Divine? A Yes sir.
Q Was he living when you were admitted to citizenship in the Cherokee Nation by the Cherokee commission on citizenship? A Yes sir.

BY COMMISSION: It appears from the records of the Cherokee Nation in the docket of the Cherokee Commission n Citizenship, page 100, No. 94, that the applicant's father was admitted to citizenship by the Cherokee Commission on the 23rd day of September, 1881. Roach Young, President of the Commission; William Harnage and G.W. Mayes, Assistant Commissioners; J.B. Mayes, Clerk.

Q Is your son willing to have this case submitted to the Commission now for final consideration? A I suppose so.
Q Did he authorize you to appear before the Commission and introduce this testimony in his application? A Yes sir.

BY MR. HASTINGS: Cherokee Nation submits this case.

M.D. Green, being first duly sworn, states that as stenographer to the Commission to the Five Civilized Tribes he correctly recorded the testimony and proceedings in this case and that the foregoing is a true and complete transcript of his stenographic notes thereof.

MD Green

Subscribed and sworn to before me this February 15, 1902.

T B Needles
Commissioner.

CHEROKEE D 47

DEPARTMENT OF THE INTERIOR,

COMMISSION TO THE FIVE CIVILIZED TRIBES.

In the matter of the application of Charles W. Devine for enrollment as a Cherokee citizen.

On the nineteenth day of July, 1900, Charles W. Devine appeared before the Commission to the Five Civilized Tribes and made application for his enrollment as a citizen by blood of the Cherokee Nation.

At the conclusion of the evidence offered at that time the name of Charles W. Devine was placed upon a "Doubtful" card pending further consideration as to his rights of citizenship.

Further evidence has been presented to the Commission and the case submitted for final consideration.

The following decision is now rendered.

DECISION.

--oOo--

From all the evidence of record in this case it appears that Charles W. Devine is a Cherokee Indian by blood, and was 20 years old at the date of this application. His father, Thomas Devine, was re-admitted to citizenship in the Cherokee Nation on the 23rd day of September, 1881 by a decree of a Cherokee Commission on Citizenship. Applicant has resided in the Cherokee Nation ever since the date of his father's re-admission, and he is identified on the Strip payment roll of 1894 and the Cherokee Census roll of 1896.

In making rolls of citizenship of the Cherokee Nation this Commission is governed by the following provisions of the Act of Congress approved June 28, 1898 (30 Stats., 495);

> "That in making rolls of citizenship of the several tribes, as required by law, the Commission to the Five Civilized Tribes is authorized and directed to take the roll of Cherokee citizens of eighteen hundred and eighty (not including freedmen) as the only roll intended to be confirmed by this and preceding Acts of Congress, and to enroll all persons now living whose names are found on said roll, and all descendants born since the date of said roll to persons whose names are found thereon; and all persons who have been enrolled by the tribal authorities who have heretofore made permanent settlement in the Cherokee Nation whose parents, by reason of their Cherokee blood, have been lawfully admitted to citizenship by the tribal authorities, and who were minors when their parents were so admitted; and they shall investigate the right of all other persons whose names are found on any other rolls and omit all such as may have been placed thereon by fraud or without authority of law, enrolling only such as may have lawful right thereto, and their descendants born since such rolls were made, with such intermarried white persons as may be entitled to citizenship under Cherokee laws."

In view of the facts and the law in this case it is considered that Charles W. Devine is entitled to be enrolled as a citizen by blood of the Cherokee Nation, and it is so ordered.

Tams Bixby

T B Needles

C. R. Breckinridge

Commissioners.

Dated at Muskogee, Indian Territory,

JUN 9 - 1902

COMMISSIONERS:

HENRY L. DAWES,
TAMS BIXBY,
THOMAS B. NEEDLES,
C. R. BRECKINRIDGE.

ALLISON L. AYLESWORTH,
SECRETARY.

ADDRESS ONLY THE
COMMISSION TO THE FIVE CIVILIZED TRIBES.

DEPARTMENT OF THE INTERIOR,
COMMISSION TO THE FIVE CIVILIZED TRIBES.

REFER IN REPLY TO THE FOLLOWING

Cher. D-47.

Muskogee, Indian Territory, June 9, 1902.

W. W. Hastings, Esq.,

Attorney for the Cherokee Nation,

Muskogee, Indian Territory.

Sir:

Enclosed herewith please find copy of the decision of the Commission rendered June 9, 1902, in the matter of the application of Charles W. Devine for enrollment as a citizen of the Cherokee Nation.

You are hereby advised that you will be allowed fifteen days from date hereof in which to file with the Commission such protest as you desire to make against the enrollment of the person above named as a citizen of the Cherokee Nation. If you fail to file the protest within the time allowed this applicant will be regularly listed for enrollment.

Yours truly,

Tams Bixby

Acting Chairman.

Encl. D-47.

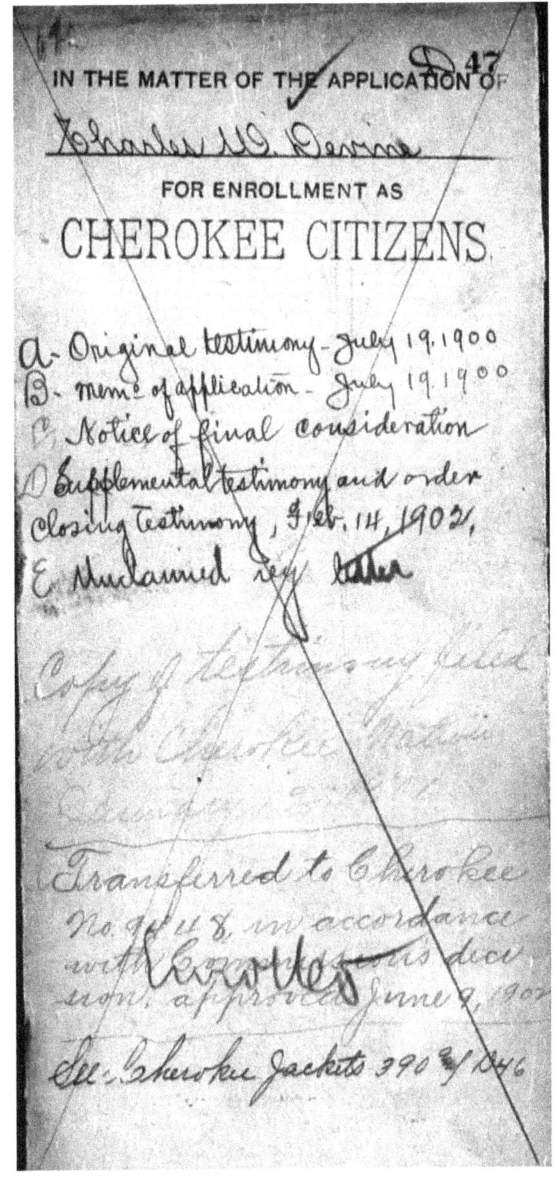

D 47

IN THE MATTER OF THE APPLICATION OF

Charles W. Devine

FOR ENROLLMENT AS

CHEROKEE CITIZENS.

A- Original testimony- July 19.1900
B- memo of application- July 19.1900
C. Notice of final consideration
D Supplemental testimony and order
Closing Testimony, Feb. 14, 1902,
E. Unclaimed reg letter

Copy of testimony filed with Cherokee Native

Transferred to Cherokee No. 9448 in accordance with Commissions decision, approved June 9, 1902

See Cherokee Jackets 390 & 1046

RESIDENCE: Goingsnake DISTRICT.
POST OFFICE: Westville I.T.

Cherokee Nation. Cherokee Roll.
(Not including Delawares, Shawnees, or Freedmen.)

CARD NO. ______
FIELD NO. 9418

Dawes' Roll No.		NAME.	Relationship to Person first Named.	AGE.	SEX.	BLOOD.	Tribal Enrollment: Year.	Tribal Enrollment: District.	Tribal Enrollment: No.	Parents: Name of Father.	Parents: Year.	Parents: District.	Parents: Name of Mother.	Parents: Year.	Parents: District.
21485	1	Devine, Charles W		20	M.	1/16	1896	Goingsnake	645	Thos Devine		G.snake	Mollie Devine		Non citz
21486	2	" James T	Son	4 mo	M	1/32		See note		No 1			May Devine		"
	3	CITIZENSHIP CERTIFICATE ISSUED FOR NO. ... AUG 13 1903													
	4														
	5														
	6														
	7	GRANTED						No 1 on 1896 roll as Watie Devine							
	8	JUN 9 1902						No 2, Birth affidavit approved August 23, 1902.							
	9														
	10														
	11														
	12														
	13														
	14														
	15												On Cherokee Card No		
	16											Date of Application for Enrollment.	D-47 July 19, 1900;		
	17	See Cherokee											On this card, August		
	18	Card No D46											22, 1902		

See N B # 1978.

Cherokee D48 - Lizzie Dry [Lizzie is white with 5-1/2 blood children. Each child has a Dawes Roll Number.]

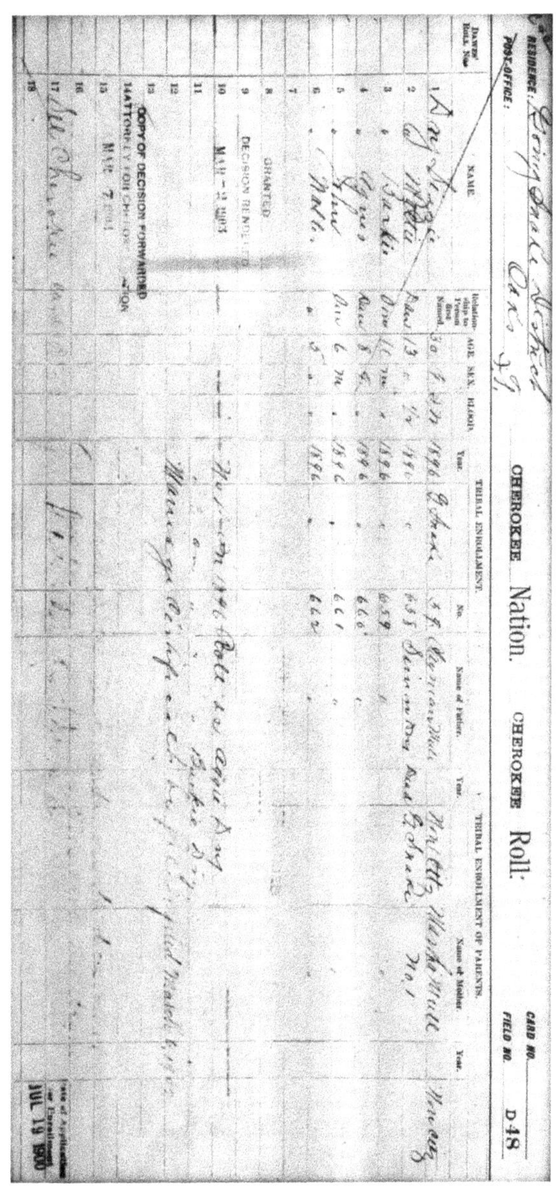
RESIDENCE:
POST-OFFICE:
CHEROKEE Nation. CHEROKEE Roll.
CARD NO.
FIELD NO. D48

Dawes' Roll No.	NAME	Relationship to Person first Named.	AGE	SEX	BLOOD	TRIBAL ENROLLMENT Year	District	No.	Name of Father	Year	District	Name of Mother	Year	District
	1		30			1896								
	2		13					655						
	3					1896		659						
	4					1896		660						
	5		6			1896		661						
	6		5			1896		662						

GRANTED
DECISION RENDERED
MAR 2 1903
COPY OF DECISION FORWARDED
ATTORNEY FOR CHEROKEE NATION
MAR 7 1903
Date of Application for Enrollment
JUL 19 1900

Department of the Interior,
Commission to the Five Civilized Tribes,
Westville, I.T., July 19, 1900.

In the matter of the application of Lizzie Dry for the enrollment of herself as a Cherokee by intermarriage, and her children as Cherokees by blood; being duly sworn and examined by Commissioner Needles, she testified as follows:

Q What is your name? A Lizzie Dry.
Q How old are you? A Going on 30.
Q What is your post office? A Oaks.
Q In what district do you live? A Going Snake.
Q How long have you lived there? A About 15 years.
Q Are you a Cherokee by blood? A No, sir.
Q What is the name of your father? A Clement Mull.
Q Was he a white man? A Yes, sir.
Q What is the name of your mother? A Martha.
Q Is she a white woman? A Yes, sir.
Q Is your name upon the roll of 1880? Are you marred? A No, sir.
Q Have you been married? A Yes, sir.
Q What was your husband's name? A Simon Dry.
Q When were you married? A 17 years ago.
Q Is Simon Dry living? A No, sir.
Q How old was your husband when you married him, about how old.
A He was a young man when I married him.
Q Was your husband a Cherokee? A Yes, sir, a full blood.
Q How long has he been dead? A About 2 years and 4 months.
Q Have you got any certificate of marriage? What proof have you got of your marriage? A Yes, sir, Comin Snell, Dave Mann, and all of them, I was lawfully married.

(On 1894 roll, page 644, No. 758, Simon Dry, Going Snake district. On 1896 toll, page 741, No. 657, Simon Dry, Going Snake.)

Comin Snell, being duly sworn, testified, through Simon R. Walkingstick, a duly sworn interpreter, as follows:

Q What is your name? A Coming Snell.
Q Are you a full blood indian[sic]? A Yes, sir.
Q Did you know Simon Dry? A Yes, sir.
Q How long did you know him? A From a csa ll[sic] child up to the time he died.
Q Was he a Cherokee by blood? A Yes, sir, he was a full blood Cherokee.
Q And lived in the Cherokee Nation? A Yes, sir.
Q Do you know whether he married this woman, Lizzie, or not? A I wasn't present at the marriage ceremony, I think that she was his wife, the lived together as man and wife until he died.
Q What was Simon's father's name? A Peter Dry.
Q What was his mother's name? A Nancy Dry.

Q They were both indians[sic] by blood? A Yes, sir, they were both Cherokees.

Lizzie Dry, recalled, testified:

Q You say you have got no marriage certificate at all? A No, sir.
Q Do you know who married you? A Yes, sir, Larnback, a preacher.
Q He didn't give you any certificate? A No, sir.
Q Couldn't you get a certificate from him? A He lives at Siloam.
Q That isn't far from you, is it? A It is called 22 miles I think.
Q Is there anybody here that saw you married? A That fellow that was here a while ago, I forgot whether he was there or not.
Q Any of these women here know where you were married or not?
A Yes, sir, all three of them there knows it.
Q Have you got any children? A Yes, sir, I have five at home.
Q What is the name of the oldest one at home? A Mattie, she is 13.
(On 1896 roll, page 741, No. 658, Mattie Dry, Going Snake dist.)
Q What is the name of the next one? A Barkie, 11 years old.
(On 1896 roll, page 741, No. 659, Barkie Dry, Going Snake dist.)
Q What is the name of the next one? A Agnes, Going on 8.
(On 1896 roll, page 741, No. 660, Aggie Dry, Going Snake district.)
Q What is the name of the next one? A John Dry, he was 6 years old last December.
(On 1896 roll, page 741, No. 661, John Dry, Going Snake dist.)
Q What is the name of the next one? A Walter, he will be 5 next December.
(On 1896 roll, page 741, Nol. 662, Walter Dry, Going Snake dist.)
Q Is that all? A Yes, sir.
Q Whose is that baby? A It is mine.
Q What is its name? A Jennie.
Q How old is Jennie? A 2 months and three weeks old.
Q What is its last name? A Jennie Stovall.
Q It isn't a child of Simon Dry? A No, sir.
Q You are not married again? A No, sir.
Q Are these children all living with you? A Yes, sir.
Q Are they all Simon Drys[sic] children? A Yes, sir.
Q Were they all born before Simon died? A Yes, sir.
(On 1895 roll, oage[sic] 820, No. 59, Lizzie Dry, Going Snake district.)

The name of Lizzie Dry is found upon the roll of 1896. She claims to have been married to Simon Dry 17 years ago. Simon Dry, the testimony shows, was a full blood indian[sic], and his name appears upon the Census Roll of 1896 and the pay-roll of 1894. A search being made, his name is not found upon the authenticated roll of 1880. From the testimony there is no doubt but what he was a full blood Cherokee citizen. She also proves that she lived with Simon Dry as man and wife until his death, but presents no certificate of marriage. The following children, she claims were born to her during her marriage with Simon Dry; Mattie, Walter, Barkie, Agnes, and John, and their names are found upon the Census Roll of 1898. The name of Lizzie Dry is ordered enrolled upon a doubtful card as an intermarried citizen, and the names of the said five children will also be enrolled upon a doubtful card as citizens by blood.

The name of Jennie Stovall, two months old, she having been born after the death of her husband, and she acknowledging it is not the child of Simon Dry, the application for its enrollment is rejected.

It will be necessary for you to get a certificate of your marriage from this minister and file it with this Commission, and that will make your case complete.

------o------

Bruce C. Jones, Being duly sworn, says that as stenographer to the Commission to the Five Civilized Tribes he reported the testimony of the above named witnesses, and that the foregoing is a full, true and correct translation of his stenographic notes.

Bruce E. Jones

Sworn to and subscribed before me this the 20th day of July, 1900.

Tams Bixby
Commissioner.

Supl. C.D.#48.

Department of the Interior,
Commission to the Five Civilized Tribes,
Muskogee, I. T., February 15, 1902.

SUPPLEMENTAL TESTIMONY in the matter of the enrollment of Lizzie Dry, et al., as citizens of the Cherokee Nation.

Mr. W. W. Hasting; Cherokee representative, present.

LIZZIE DRY, the applicant, being duly sworn, testified as follows:

By the Commission:

Q What is your name? A Lizzie Dry.
Q Where do you live? A Oaks.
Q Have you any statement that you desire to make to this Commission relative to your enrollment as a Cherokee citizen? A Here is a letter what was sent out to me.
Q Have you any evidence of your marriage to Simon Dry, your marriage license and certificate? A No, sir; when I got married, I married under Cherokee law and didn't have to have any license at that time, and I went to Westville enrolling and they said I would have to sent[sic] it and get my certificate; I have been married and every one said it was all right, and I didn't sent[sic] for the certificate.

Q Why not; they told you to send for it? A They told me that would be only helping myself; my children was[sic] all right.
Q Where is this marriage certificate; have you got a marriage certificate? A No, sir, I never sent for it.
Q Is the preacher living? A Yes, sir, at Siloam, and when I got this letter out of the office there at Oaks I was going to send for that certificate and they told me it would be too late, I had better come on, and I could get it any time I could get it.
Q Now it will be necessary for you to file that certificate with the Commission immediately.
Q Is there any other statement you desire to make relative to your enrollment?
A Yes, sir, I just want to know if I can't get that and send it on.
Q Yes, you get that and sent it to us as soon as possible.
Q Is that all? A Yes, sir.
Q You submit this case now to the Commission for final consideration do you?
A Yes, sir.

---oooOOOooo---

J. O. Rosson, being first duly sworn, states that as stenographer to the Commission to the Five Civilized Tribes he correctly recorded the testimony and proceedings in this case, and that the foregoing is a true and complete transcript of his stenographic notes thereof.

JO Rosson

SUBscribed[sic] and sworn to before me this February 19, 1902.

T B Needles

Commissioner.

Cherokee D 48

DEPARTMENT OF THE INTERIOR,

COMMISSION TO THE FIVE CIVILIZED TRIBES.

Muskogee, Indian Ter. March 8, 1902.

In the matter of the application of Lizzie Dry. et al. for enrollment as citizens of the Cherokee Nation.

Supplemental Statement.

---oOo---

An examination of the authenticated tribal rolls in the possession of this Commission shows the name of Peter Dry and Nancy Dry thereon as native Cherokees.

It is directed that copies of this statement be filed with the testimony in the above case.

T B Needles
Commissioner.

Cher
Supp'l to D 48

Department of the Interior,
Commission to the Five Civilized Tribes,
Muskogee, I.T., October 31, 1902.

In the matter of the application of LIZZIE DRY, for the enrollment of herself as a citizen by intermarriage, and her children, MATTIE, BARKIE, AGNES, JOHN and WALTER DRY, as citizens by blood, of the Cherokee Nation.

LIZZIE DRY, being duly sworn and examined by the Commission, testified as follows:

Q What is your name ? A Lizzie Dry.
Q What is your age ? A Thirty.
Q What is your post office address ? A Oaks.
Q You an applicant for enrollment as an intermarried citizen of the Cherokee Nation, are you ? A Yes sir.
Q What was the name of your husband Dry ? A Simon Dry.
Q When were you married to him ? A Pretty near 20 years.
Q Then you must be older than thirty now ? A I married when I was sixteen.
Q You must be thirty five years old then, aren't you? Do you know your age exactly? A No sir, I don't know just exactly my age, but that's the best I can guess.
Q Did you and your husband Simon Dry live together all the time from your marriage up till he died ? A Yes sir.
Q When did he die? How long has it been ? A He's been dead pretty near five years.
Q You and he never separated during his lifetime ? A No sir.
Q Have you lived in the Cherokee Nation al,[sic] the time since you and Dry were married ? A Yes sir.
Q Are the children, Mattie, Barkie, Agnes, John and Walter, all your children by Mr. Dry ? A Yes sir.
Q Are they all living now ? A Yes sir.
Q Have they lived all their lives in the Cherokee Nation ? A Yes sir.

Q Have you married since Mr. Dry's death ? A No sir.
Q You are still a widow ? A Yes sir.
Q Where do you live Mrs. Dry ? A I live a mile from Oaks, east.
Q Whose place do you live on ? A I live on my girl's place.
Q You say you have not married again since Mr. Dry's death ? A No sir.
Q You have never lived with any other man as your husband since his death?
A No sir.

E. C. Bagwell, on oath states that, as stenographer to the Commission to the Five Civilized Tribes, he correctly recorded the testimony and proceedings had in the above entitled cause, and that the foregoing is an accurate transcript of his stenographic notes thereof.

E.C. Bagwell

Subscribed and sworn to before me this December 11, 1902.

BC Jones
Notary Public.

DEPARTMENT OF THE INTERIOR,

COMMISSION TO THE FIVE CIVILIZED TRIBES.

In the matter of the application of Lizzie Dry for the enrollment of herself as a citizen by intermarriage of the Cherokee Nation, and for the enrollment of her minor children, Mattie, Barkie, Agnes, John and Walter Dry, and for Jennie Stovall as citizens by blood of the Cherokee Nation, consolidating:

Lizzie Dry, et al.,	Cherokee D 48
Jennie Stovall,	Cherokee R 28

D E C I S I O N.

The record in these cases shows that on July 19, 1900, Lizzie Dry appeared before the Commission at Westville, Indian Territory, and made application for her enrollment as a citizen by intermarriage of the Cherokee Nation, and for the enrollment of her minor children, Mattie, Barkie, Agnes, John and Walter Dry, and Jennie Stovall as citizens by blood of the Cherokee Nation. Further proceedings were had in the matter of said application at Muskogee, Indian Territory, on February 15, 1902, at Kansas, Indian Territory, on May 29, 1902, and again at Muskogee, Indian Territory, on October 31, 1902.

The evidence shows that Lizzie Dry was lawfully married in 1886, to one, Simon Dry, who died in 1898. The said Simon Dry is not identified on the authenticated tribal roll of 1880, but on examination of the tribal rolls in the possession of this Commission, it appears that he is identified on the strip payment roll of 1894 and the Cherokee census roll of 1896 as a native Cherokee, and that his parents, Peter and Nancy Dry, are identified on the authenticated tribal roll of 1880 as native Cherokees. Lizzie Dry and her minor children, Mattie, Barkie, Agnes, John and Walter Dry, are identified on the Cherokee census roll of 1896.

The evidence further shows that after the death of Simon Dry, in 1898, his said wife, Lizzie, lived with one Lewis Stovall, a Cherokee by blood. It further appears that there was born to the said Lizzie Dry and Lewis Stovall, Jennie Stovall, a female child. It appears that there was no valid marriage between said Lewis Stovall and Lizzie Dry, but that is considered immaterial, owing to the fact that said Lewis Stovall (Stover), is a Cherokee by blood and identified on the Cherokee authenticated tribal roll of 1880. The said Jennie Stovall is identified by a birth affidavit made a part of the record herein.

The evidence further shows that the said Lizzie Dry resided in the Cherokee Nation with her husband, Simon Dry, up to the time of his death; that she has continued to reside in said Nation since that time and that she has not remarried since the death of her said husband. Her children have resided in said Nation all their lives.

It is, therefore, the opinion of this Commission that Lizzie Dry should be enrolled as a citizen by intermarriage of the Cherokee Nation, and that Mattie Dry, Barkie Dry, Agnes Dry, John Dry and Walter Dry should be enrolled as citizens by blood of the Cherokee Nation, and that Jennie Stovall, being the child of a recognized citizen, should be enrolled as a citizen of the Cherokee Nation, in accordance with the provisions of section twenty-one of the Act of Congress approved June 29, 1898 (30 Stats., 495), and it is so ordered.

COMMISSION TO THE FIVE CIVILIZED TRIBES.

Tams Bixby
~~Acting~~ Chairman.

T.B. Needles
Commissioner.

C. R. Breckinridge
Commissioner.

Muskogee, Indian Territory,
this MAR -2 1903

ATTORNEYS:
W. W. HASTINGS,..........Tahlequah, I. T.
J. L. BAUGH,..........Chouteau, I. T.

STENOGRAPHER:
J. C. STARR,..........Vinita, I. T.

MARSHALS:
JOHN PARKS,..........Vinita, I. T.
W. B. WYLY,..........Tahlequah, I. T.

OFFICE OF

Attorneys for the Cherokee Nation

BEFORE THE DAWES COMMISSION, CHEROKEE ENROLLMENT.

Please return this letter with your reply or mention this Number: D. 40

Fort Gibson, I. T., 9-6-1901.

Mr. David Mann,
Oaks, I. T.

Dear Sir:

Please give us the following information, "Does Lizzie Dry live in your neighborhood?" If so do you know whether she has remarried since the death of her husband, Simon Dry.

In her application for inrollment she had a child which was Two Month and Three Weeks old her husband having died some two years previous to her application.

Yours truly,

W. W. Hastings

J. L. Baugh

Attys. for the Cherokee Nation.

[Copy of Original Handwritten Letter]

Oaks I.T.
Oct 3

Mr W. W. Hasting
Sir you wrote me a while back in regards to Lizzie Dry. she still lives in this neighborhood. in regards to her ~~husband~~ marriage since the death of her husband Simon Dry. she has not law-fully been married to her child that was (2) month 3 wk. old when at Westville it is still living. in regard to her husband Simon Dry death he has been dead about 4 years. in regards to her marriage with Simon Dry I saw the minister that married them and he said that he would give her the marriage certificate

Truly Yours
D S [illegible]

[Transcription of Handwritten Letter on opposite page]

Oaks I. T.
Oct 3

Mr W. W. Hasting

Sir you wrote me a while back in regards to Lizzie Dry; she still lives in this neighborhood, in regards to her ~~husband~~ marriage since the death of her husband Simon Dry, she has not law-fully been married

in regard to her child that was (2 month 3)wk old when at Westville it is still liveing.

in regard. to her husband Simon Dry death he has been dead about 4 years in regard to her marriage with Simon Dry I saw the minister that married them and he said that he would give her the marrage certificate

Truly Yours
D S Mann

COMMISSIONERS:
TAMS BIXBY,
THOMAS B. NEEDLES,
C. R. BRECKINRIDGE,
W. E. STANLEY.

ALLISON L. AYLESWORTH,
SECRETARY.

DEPARTMENT OF THE INTERIOR,
COMMISSION TO THE FIVE CIVILIZED TRIBES.

REFER IN REPLY TO THE FOLLOWING
Cherokee D-48
& R-28

ADDRESS ONLY THE
COMMISSION TO THE FIVE CIVILIZED TRIBES.

Muskogee, Indian Territory, March 7, 1903.

W. W. Hastings,
Attorney for the Cherokee Nation,
Vinita, Indian Territory.

Dear Sir:

There is herewith enclosed a copy of the decision of the Commission to the Five Civilized Tribes, dated March 2, 1903, granting the application of Lizzie Dry for the enrollment of herself as a citizen by intermarriage, and for the enrollment of her minor children, Mattie, Barkie, Agnes, John and Walter Dry, and Jennie Stovall, as citizens by blood, of the Cherokee Nation.

You are hereby advised that you will be allowed fifteen days from date hereof, in which to file such protest as you desire to make against the action of the Commission in this case, a copy of which protest you will be required to serve upon the applicant. If you fail to file protest within the time allowed, this decision will be considered final.

Respectfully,

Tams Bixby
Chairman.

Enc. M-7197

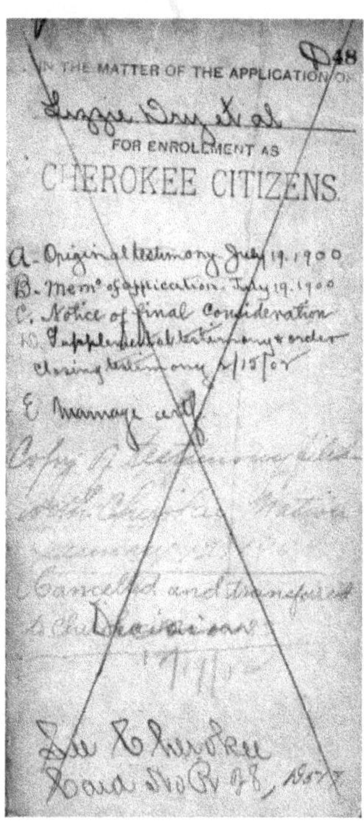

D48

IN THE MATTER OF THE APPLICATION OF

Lizzie Dry et al

FOR ENROLLMENT AS

CHEROKEE CITIZENS.

A- Original testimony July 19, 1900

B- Mem° of application. July 19, 1900

C. Notice of final Consideration

D. Supplemental testimony & order closing testimony 5/15/07

E Marriage cert

Cancelled and transferred

Residence: Going Snake District.
Post Office: Oaks, I.T.

Cherokee Nation. Cherokee Roll.
(Not Including Delawares, Shawnees, or Freedmen.)

Card No.
Field No. 10182

Dawes' Roll No.		Name	Relationship to Person first Named	Age	Sex	Blood	Tribal Enrollment Year	District	No.	Name of Father	Year	District	Name of Mother	Year	District
	1	Dry, Lizzie ×		30	F	I.W.	1896	Going Snake	59	Clayman Mull		Non citz	Martha Mull		Non citz
27865	2	" Mattie	Dau	13	F	1/2	1896	" "	658	Simon Dry	Dead	G. Snake	No1		
27866	3	" Parker	Son	11	M	1/2	1896	" "	659	" "		"	No1		
27867	4	" Agnes	Dau	8	F	1/2	1896	" "	660	" "		"	No1		
27868	5	" John	Son	6	M	1/2	1896	" "	661	" "		"	No1		
27869	6	" Walter	Son	5	M	1/2	1896	" "	662	" "		"	No1		
27870	7	Stover, Jennie	Dau	3 mo	F	1/4				Lewis Stovall			No1		
	8														

GRANTED
MAR 2 1903

Testimony of June 16, 1904 shows marriage of No1 on August 7 1903 to Lewis Stover on Cherokee Card No. 4165; Also shows correct surname of No 7 to be Stover

No 3 on 1896 Roll as Parker Dry. Aug 8 1904 in accordance with Dept.
No 4 " 1896 " " Aggie Dry. letter of July 28 1904 surname of
No 7 changed on final roll to Stover
copy of [illegible]

Nos 1 to 6 incl on Cherokee Card No D 48 July 19, 1900;
No 7 on Cherokee Card No R-28, July 19, 1900.
On this card, March 25, 1903.

Citizenship Certificate Issued for No. 3
APR 1 1905

Date of Application for Enrollment.

Testimony of August 18, 1904 shows marriage of No 2 on April 2, 1904 to Thomas [illegible] on Cher Card 6169.

Cherokee D49 - Franklin R. Mitchell

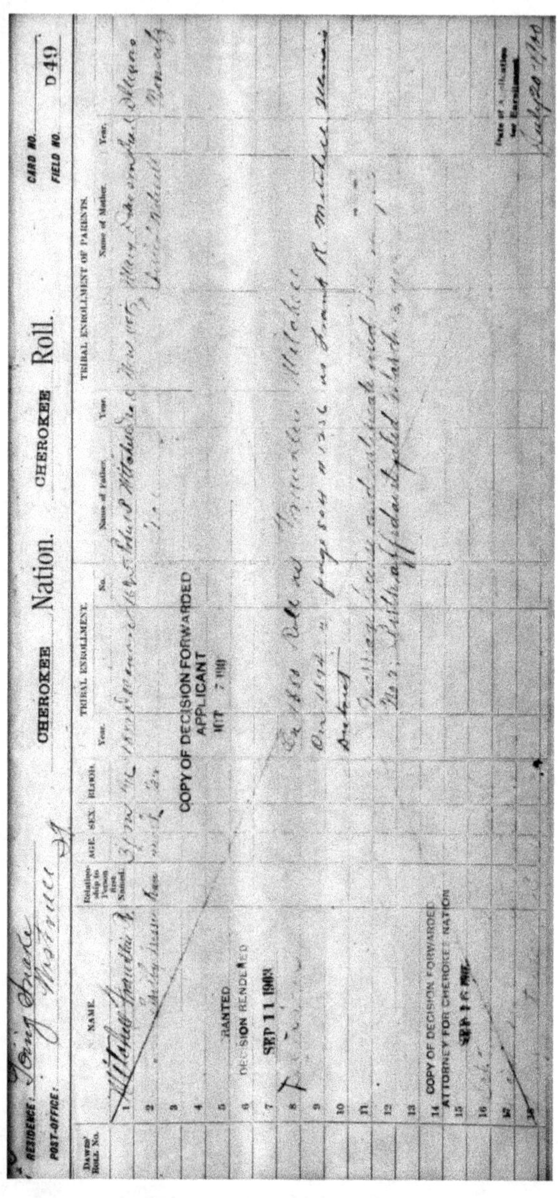

RESIDENCE: Going Snake
POST-OFFICE: Westville I.T.

CHEROKEE Nation. CHEROKEE Roll.

CARD NO.
FIELD NO. D49

Dawes' Roll No.		NAME	Relationship to Person first Named	AGE	SEX	BLOOD	Tribal Enrollment Year	District	No.	Name of Father	Year	District	Name of Mother	Year	District
	1	Mitchell, Franklin R.		37	M	1/2	1896			Edward Mitchell			Mary Mitchell		
	2														

COPY OF DECISION FORWARDED
APPLICANT
OCT 7 1903

GRANTED
DECISION RENDERED
SEP 11 1903

COPY OF DECISION FORWARDED
ATTORNEY FOR CHEROKEE NATION
SEP 16 1903

Date of Application for Enrollment.

DEPARTMENT OF THE INTERIOR,
COMMISSION TO THE FIVE CIVILIZED TRIBES,
WESTVILLE, I.T. JULY 20, 1900.

In the matter of the application of Franklin R. Mitchell ~~et als.~~, for enrollment as Cherokee citizens by blood, said Mitchell being sworn by Commissioner Breckinridge, testified as follows:

Q What is your name? A Franklin R. Mitchell.
Q Your age? A 31.
Q Your postoffice? A Westville.
Q Your district? A Goingsnake.
Q Whom do you apply for? A For myself and brother.
Q Is your brother under age? A No sir, he is 21, but he is a convict in the penitentiary.
Q Do you apply as a Cherokee by blood? A Yes.
Q What is your father's name? A Robert B. Mitchell.
Q How long have you lived in this district? A I was raised in the Nation, but have only lived here about six months.
Q Where were you before that 6 months? A My home has been principally in Illinois district, but I was enrolled in Delaware.
Q So when you speak of six months you mean you have only lived in this district six months, but you have lived in the Nation all your life? A Well, I have been out of the Nation three or four different times for six months at a time, but never gave up my residence here, and always voted here and claimed my home here.
On '80 roll, page 283, number 1683.
On '94 roll, page 804, number 1256.
Q Where have you lived for the last 5 or 6 years? A I lived in the Cherokee Nation. I was in Texas from last January a year ago until early in the fall sometime, when I came back to Illinois district, and I was there until in May again and I went to Texas and was back here again in this last January. This is the only time I have been out of the Nation in my life.
Q Have you any property in the Nation here? A No sir.
Q Any home? A Yes, I am living with my brother-in-law.
Q What has he got? A A farm.
Q What do you do there? A Work.
Q Make your home there? A Yes.
Q Got any interest in the crop? A Yes.
Q Is that where you have lived? A No sir, only lived there for six months- was raised by a cousin of mine in Illinois district.
Q Now this brother you speak of, is he over 21 years of age or not?
A He is just 21.

By Mr. Hastings, Cherokee Attorney:

Q What is your mother's name? A Mary Mitchell.
Q Is she married now? A No sir, she is dead.

Q Have you a sister? A Yes, one by the name of Mary and one by the name of Margarett[sic].
Q Have you a young brother? A Yes, by the name of Joe.
Q When did you leave Delaware? A In '82.
Q Where did you go from there? A Illinois.
Q With whom did you live over there? A Lewis Thornton.
Q You lived with him until you went to Texas two years ago? A I worked around in the neighborhood.
Q Did you work outside of the Cherokee Nation during that time? A No sir.
Q All you have lived outside of the Cherokee Nation is what you have told the Commission when you went to Texas two years ago? A Yes.
Q Were you ever married? A Yes, about three years ago; my wife is dead.
Q You married while you were in Texas? A Yes.
Q How long had you been down there prior to your marriage? A I married at Fort Gibson and we moved down to Texas and my wife died and I came back. She was a non-citizen and her folks lived in Texas. She had a brother there.
Q Did she have any property in Texas? A No sir.
Q As soon as your wife died you returned? A When we married we first came here to this district, and then when we left here we went to Texas, and then I came back here, and then I made another trip there and she died and I came back here to stay..
Q Who married you? A Tom Thornton.
Q What was her maiden name? A Goodwin.
Q Did you ever own any farm in the Cherokee Nation? A I owned places-- claims.
Q Well, why didn't you draw your strip money in '94-- where were you?
[sic] I was in Fort Gibson.
Q Why didn't you draw it then? A I could not get in at the time I needed the money-- I wanted to invest my money in buying a team and I could not get in in time to buy to buy[sic] the team and I sold my claim to Clew Gullagher and got the money.
Q Up to that time had you ever lived out of the Cherokee Nation? A No sir.
Q Were you living in the Cherokee Nation at that time? A Yes.
Q What explanation are you going to make why you are not on the '96 roll? A Me and Jim Coleman was making hay on Brock Station Prairie when the census takers came around and Louis ---- gave my name in so he told me, and I never did try to enroll or see anything more about it.

By the Commission:
Q When were you married? A In '95.
Q When did your wife die? A It will be two years in January.
By Mr. Hastings:
Q Where do you live now? A With Jim Shell, three miles southeast of here.
Q How long have you lived there? A I came there in January.
Q Came from Texas there? A Yes.
Q How long had you been in Texas that last time? A I went there the first of January, 1899.
By the Commission?[sic]
Q What did you want particularly with that team you bought with you[sic] '94 strip payment money? A I wanted it to do some hauling on the pay- grounds.

Q You did not move to Texas with that team? A No sir.
Mr. Mitchell, your name appears to be duly identified on the roll of '80 and on the roll of '94, but is not found on the roll of '96, and your different movements raise some doubt as to your continued residence and purpose of residence in the Nation, so your name will be placed upon a doubtful card for the further consideration of the Commission. If there is any further evidence you want to submit you can forward it to the Commission at its office in Muskogee-- any affidavits or any written evidence, and whatever decision the Commission may arrive at will be communicated to you in writing at your present postoffice address, and the decision will finally be forwarded with the testimony whether it be favorable or unfavorable, to the Secretary of the Interior for his approval or disapproval.

Brown McDonald, being sworn by Commissioner Breckinridge, says as Stenographer to the Commission to the Five Civilized Tribes, he reported in full the testimony of the above names witness, and the foregoing is a full, true and correct transcript of his notes.

Brown McDonald

Sworn to and subscribed before me this 23rd day of July, 1900, at Stilwell, I.T.

Clifton R. Breckinridge
Commissioner.

"R"

Cherokee D 49.

Department of the Interior,
Commission to the Five Civilized Tribes,
Muskogee, I. T., February 14, 1902.

SUPPLEMENTAL TESTIMONY ON BEHALF OF APPLICANT in the matter of the application of Franklin R. Mitchell for enrollment as a Cherokee citizen.

Appearances:
Applicant, in person;
W.W. Hastings, attorney for the Cherokee Nation.

FRANKLIN R. MITCHELL, being first duly sworn, and being examined testified as follows:

BY COMMISSION:

Q What is your name? A Franklin R. Mitchell.
Q How old are you? A I am 32 years old.
Q What is your post-office address? A Westville.

Q Are you an applicant before this Commission for enrollment as a Cherokee citizen? A Yes sir.
Q Have you any statement that you desire to make relative to your enrollment as a citizen? A Well, I don't really know why I have been objected, unless it is because I am supposed to have forfeited my rights by being out of the Nation over the limited length of time.
Q Where were you born? A I was born in the Cherokee Nation I suppose, I don't know.
Q Where were you when you can first remember? A I was in the Cherokee Nation.
Q How long did you continue to live there? A I lived there in the Cherokee Nation all my life with the exception of three short periods.
Q When did you leave the Nation the first time? A When did I?
Q Yes. A In 1896.
Q Was that the first time you have ever left the Cherokee Nation? A That is the first time I ever been out of the Nation to stay any length of time.
Q Well now, that isn't the question; when was the first time you ever left the Nation?
A First time I left the Nation was when I was summonsed to Fort Smith as a witness one time.
Q How long did you remain out? A I stayed there two or three days.
Q When was the next time you went away? A Next time was in '96.
Q Where did you go to in 1896? A I went to Texas.
Q How long did you remain there? A I remained from September 1896 until August '97.
Q Then where did you go? A I came to the Cherokee Nation, in Canadian district.
Q In '97? A Yes sir.
Q How long did you stay here before you went out again then? A I stayed then, I was in Canadian awhile; went from there to Goingsnake and stayed until August, came back to Illinois District and stayed until January.
Q In the Cherokee Nation you stayed until January 1898? A Yes sir.
Q Then where did you go? A Went to Texas.
Q Then how long did you stay in Texas that time? A I stayed until sometime in the month of April of the same year.
Q 1898? A Yes sir.
Q Well where did you go to when you left Texas in 1898? A I come back to Fort Gibson in Illinois District.
Q How long did you remain? A I remained there somewhere near two or three weeks; maybe a month; I don't know which.
Q Where did you go then? A I went back to Texas.
Q Now do you remember about what month it was you went back to Texas, about May was it? A Yes sir, about the last of April or the first of May.
Q '98? A Yes sir.
Q You went to Texas? A Yes sir.
Q How long did you stay there? A I remained until January 1899.
Q Then where did you go? A I come back to the Cherokee Nation and I have been there ever since.
Q Is there any other statement you desire to make relative to your enrollment? A I have some affidavits from parties who knew-

Q The Commission cannot file affidavits. A Well one reason I wanted to present them was because the parties was scattered so over the Nation and I am not able to bring them.

Q The Commission has been all over the Cherokee Nation since 1900.

A Yes sur[sic] I wasn't objected until you were at Westville, and you have never been any closer then[sic] here only while you were at Tahlequah[sic]

Q You were placed on a doubtful card 18 months ago almost at Westville, and since that time the Commission has been all over the country again. A You aint been no nearer than Tahlequah; and one of these witnesses is in Canadian and one in Sequoyah.

Q Do you submit this case to the Commission now for final consideration? A Well I just want to make this statement. If this is sufficient, if the Commission thinks this is sufficient for clearing up the doubts in regard to my citizenship, I will submit it as a final declaration; if not, I would like to have some kind of showing to get these witnesses before the Commission if that be agreeable.

Q You have had 18 months to get these witnesses before the Commission. A Well if you want to reject me on that, all right.

Q It is not for the Commission to say at this time whether the testimony is sufficient; that is for you to determine. A If I was to submit, would I have the privilege of producing them afterwards if I was rejected?

Q No, not after the case was once closed you would not.

Q Well you see there it is. I don't know what to do about it.

Q Have you any witnesses here that you desire to introduce in this case? A No, none here whatever; not that I know of, in town.

BY COMMISSION: On the 30th of January 1902, the applicant was notified by registered mail that his case would be taken up by the Commission for final consideration on the 15th day of February, 1902. He was also notified that he would be given the privilege of appearing before the Commission in person or by attorney, and that an opportunity would be given him at that time to introduce any additional testimony affecting his case. In view of this fact the case will be closed. Attention is also invited to the fact that this testimony is taken on the 14th, although the applicant is notified that it will be taken up on the 15th of February, but this was done at his special request. he having appeared before the Commission on this day.

M.D. Green, being first duly sworn, states that as stenographer to the Commission to the Five Civilized Tribes he correctly recorded the testimony and proceedings in this case and that the foregoing is a true and complete transcript of his stenographic notes thereof.

MD Green

Subscribed and sworn to before me this February 15, 1902.

T B Needles

Commissioner.

File with Cherokee D-49.

DEPARTMENT OF THE INTERIOR.
Commission to the Five Civilized Tribes.
Muskogee, Indian Territory, July 22nd, 1902.

In the matter of the application of Franklin R. Mitchell for the enrollment of himself as a citizen by blood of the Cherokee nation[sic].

Upon an examination of the testimony had in the matter of the application of the said Franklin R. Mitchell, it appears that when he made application at Westville, Indian Territory, July 20th, 190, he also applied for the enrollment of his brother, age 21 years, and who is confined in the penitentiary. The record in this case, however, fails to disclose that any disposition was made as to his application for the enrollment of his brother.

It further appears that subsequent to the time that he made application for the enrollment of himself he again appeared before the Commission at Westville, Indian Territory, and made a new application for his brother, Joseph A. Mitchell, and that the said Joseph A. Mitchell has been duly listed for enrollment as a citizen by blood of the Cherokee nation[sic] on Cherokee roll card, field number 441.

Copies of the foregoing statement will be filed with and made a part of the record in the matter of the application of Franklin R. Mitchell for the enrollment of himself as a citizen by blood of the Cherokee nation.

T B Needles
Commissioner.

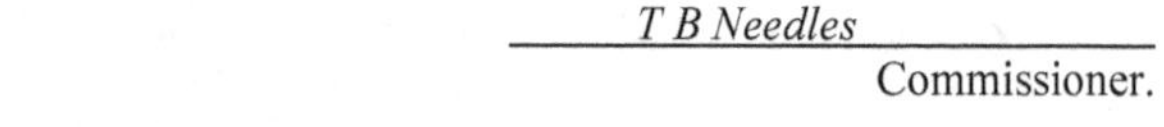

Cherokee D 49.

DEPARTMENT OF THE INTERIOR,

COMMISSION TO THE FIVE CIVILIZED TRIBES.

In the matter of the application of Franklin R. Mitchell for enrollment of himself and his daughter, Trilby Trissie Mitchell, as citizens by blood of the Cherokee Nation.

D E C I S I O N.

The record in this case shows that on July 20, 1900 Franklin R. [remainder of sentence on folded part of the paper, unreadable] Cherokee Nation. Further proceedings in the matter of said application were had at Muskogee, Indian Territory on February 14, 1902 and affidavits as to the birth of Trilby Trissie Mitchell were filed on March 13, 1902.

The evidence shows that the applicant, Franklin R. Mitchell, is a Cherokee by blood; that he is duly identified on the 1880 authenticated tribal roll of the Cherokee Nation and the 1894 strip payment roll; that he has been married twice and that his first wife died prior to his marriage to his present wife, Belle Mitchell, formerly Hayes; that his said daughter, Trilby Trissie Mitchell, was born of his last marriage; that she is too young to be on any roll, but is identified by birth affidavits on file with the Commission,

The evidence further shows that the applicant, Franklin R. Mitchell, has always claimed his home and residence to be in the Cherokee Nation and that he has resided therein all of his life, except at intervals when he has been in the State of Texas; that he was in said State from September 1896 until August 1897; also from January 1898 until April of the same year and from May 1898 until January 1899, since which time he has resided continuously in said Nation. His said daughter, Trilby Trissie Mitchell, has resided with her parents since her birth.

It is, therefore, the opinion of this Commission that Franklin R. Mitchell and Trilby Trissie Mitchell should be enrolled as citizens by blood of the Cherokee Nation, in accordance with the provisions of Section 21 of the Act of Congress, approved June 28, 1898 (30 Stats. 495), and it is so ordered.

COMMISSION TO THE FIVE CIVILIZED TRIBES.

(SIGNED). *Tams Bixby.*

Acting Chairman.

T.B. Needles

Commissioner.

C. R. Breckinridge

Commissioner.

(SIGNED). *W. E. Stanley.*

Muskogee, Indian Territory,

this SEP 11 1903

COMMISSIONERS:

TAMS BIXBY,
THOMAS B. NEEDLES,
C. R. BRECKINRIDGE,
W. E. STANLEY.

ALLISON L. AYLESWORTH,
SECRETARY.

DEPARTMENT OF THE INTERIOR,
COMMISSION TO THE FIVE CIVILIZED TRIBES.

REFER IN REPLY TO THE FOLLOWING

Cherokee D-49

ADDRESS ONLY THE
COMMISSION TO THE FIVE CIVILIZED TRIBES.

Muskogee, Indian Territory, September 16, 1903.

W. W. Hastings,

Attorney for the Cherokee Nation,

Tahlequah, Indian Territory.

Dear Sir:

There is herewith enclosed a copy of the decision of the Commission to the Five Civilized Tribes, dated September 11, 1903, granting the application for the enrollment of Franklin R. and Trilby Tressie[sic] Mitchell, as citizens by blood of the Cherokee Nation.

You are hereby advised that you will be allowed fifteen days from date hereof, in which to file such protest as you may desire to make against the action of the Commission in this case, a copy of which protest you will be required to furnish the applicant. If you fail to file protest within the time allowed you this decision will be considered final.

Respectfully,

Tams Bixby

End. D-36 Chairman.

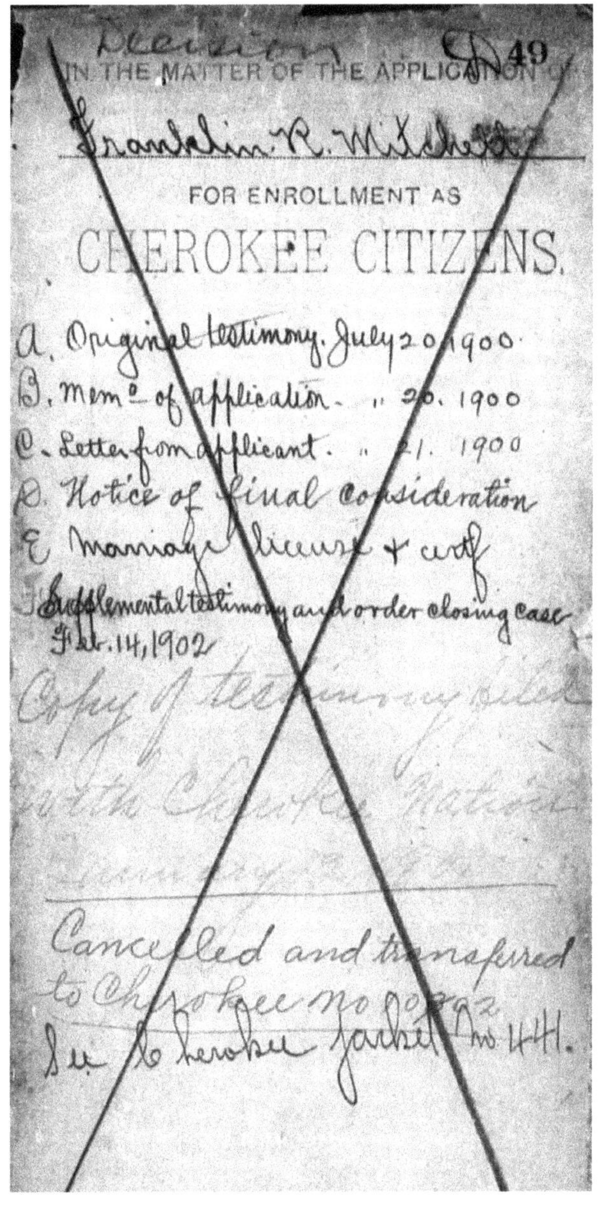

Decision 49

IN THE MATTER OF THE APPLICATION OF

Franklin R. Mitchell

FOR ENROLLMENT AS

CHEROKEE CITIZENS.

A. Original testimony. July 20 1900

B. Memo of application. " 20. 1900

C. Letter from applicant. " 21. 1900

D. Notice of final consideration

E Marriage license + cert

F Supplemental testimony and order closing case Feb. 14, 1902

Copy of testimony filed with Cherokee Nation

Cancelled and transferred to Cherokee No 90292

See Cherokee Jacket No. 441.

Cherokee Nation. Cherokee Roll.

Residence: Going Snake District. Post Office: Westville, I.T.

Field No. 103[illegible]

Dawes' Roll No.	Name	Relationship to Person first Named	Age	Sex	Blood	Tribal Enrollment Year	District	No.	Name of Father	Year	District	Name of Mother	Year	District
29424	Mitchell, Franklin P.		31	M	1/16	1880	Delaware	1625	[illegible] Mitchell	dead	Non Citz	Mary Dawson	dead	Illinois
29425	" Trilby [illegible]	Dau	[illegible]	F	1/32				No. 1			Belle L. Mitchell		Non citz

GRANTED SEP 11 190[illegible]

On 1880 Roll as Franklin Mitchell
On 1894 [illegible] page 804 #1256 as Frank P. Mitchell [illegible] District
Marriage license and certificate filed Feb 24, 1902
No. 2: Birth affidavit filed March 19, 1902

Date of Application: On Cherokee Card No. D49 July 20, 1900. On this card October 7, 1903.

See NB #2395

Cherokee D51 - Mary Crittenden by Benjamin Crittenden [Mary is not enrolled and there are 5-1/4 blood children. Each child has a Dawes Roll Number.]

Department of the Interior.
Commission to the Five Civilized Tribes
Westville, I. T., July 20, 1900.

In the matter of the application for Benjamin Crittenden for enrollment as a Cherokee citizen; further proceedings are now for wife had in this case, applicant having been previously sworn herein; Examined by Com'r Needles:

Q Your name is upon the roll of 1880 and you are a citizen by blood?
A Yes sir. (Page 422, #461.)
Q Your wife, Mary Crittenden, is a white woman? A Yes sir.
Q You have got no certificate of marriage, that was the trouble with your case?
A No sir, that was the trouble.
Q Can't you get a certificate of marriage and present here?
A No sir, Mr. Foreman never issued any.

-- -- --

Edward Foreman, being sworn and examined by Com'r Needles states:

Q What is your name? A Edward Foreman.
Q What is your age? A Sixty.
Q What is your post-office address? A Westville.
Q Are you a citizen of the Cherokee Nation? A Yes sir.
Q You know Benjamin Crittenden? A Yes sir.
Q Do you know a woman supposed to be his wife, Mary Crittenden?
A Yes sir.
Q You know whether they are married or not? A Yes sir, I married them.
Q Was[sic] you a minister then? A No sir, I was Judge of the Court, District Judge of Goingsnake District.
Q Didn't you issue him a certificate of marriage? A No sir, I just placed his marriage on the record.
Q You married him then according to the Cherokee Laww[sic]? A Yes sir and also reported the marriage to the clerk.
Q You know whether he has lived with his wife from that time until this?
A I couldn't say. He lives a good piece from me, I guess he does.
Q You have never heard anything to the contrary? A No sir.

-- -- --

Applicant, Benjamin Crittenden, re-called and examined further by Com'r Needles:
Q Have you lived with your wife continuously since you married her? A Yes sir.
Q Have you got any children under twenty-one years of age?
A All under twenty-one.
Q How many is all? A Four.
Q Give their names? A Emily, nine years old. (On 1896 roll, page 736, #512, Emily Crittenden, Goingsnake District.) David, five years old, (On 1896 roll, page 736, #514, David Crittenden, Goingsnake District) Lewis Crittenden, seven years old. (On 1896 roll, page 736, #513, Lewis Crittenden, Goingsnake District.) Lula, four years old. (On 1896 roll, page 736, #515, Lula Crittenden, Goingsnake District.)

Q Are these children, living at home with you? A Yes sir.
Examined by Cherokee Representative Baugh:
Q Wasn't your wife sister of a man they called Bullet Weaver?
A Yes sir.
Q He is on the roll as an adopted colored isn't he? A Yes sir, I think so.
Q He swore here the other day that he was part negro? A They are part Cherokee and part darkey.
Examined by Com'r Needles:
Q Do you know your wife's mother, what her name was[sic] A I don't know what her name was before; I knw[sic] her given name.
Q You don't know what her other name was? A No sir, not until she married, she married Weaver and had two children by him.
Q And is your wife one of them? A Yes sir.
Q Your wife's name was Mary Weaver before you married her? A Yes sir.
Q Do you know anything in regard to your wife's Indian blood?
A Only what her father and mother swore to.
Q What's her mother's name? A Emily.
Q Emily what? A I told you I couldn't give her surname.
Q What is her brother's name, has she got a brother named Lewis Weaver,- your wife? A Yes sir.
Q You don't know anything about the mother of Lewis and your wife, as to who she was? A No sir.

Com'r Needles: The name of Benjamin Crittenden appearing upon the authenticated roll of 1880 and also upon the roll of 1898, and he having made sufficient proof as to his residence, he is ordered enrolled as a Cherokee citizen by blood.

The name of his wife, Mary Crittenden, formerly Mary Weaver, appears upon the roll of 1896; proof of their marriage has been made to-day satisfactory to the Commission; the Commission not being satisfied as to the lineage of his wife, as to whether she was a white woman or otherwise, suspends its judgment as to her citizenship, and her name with that of her four children, Emily, Lewis, David and Lula, will be placed upon a doubtful card. Mr. Crittenden will be permitted to and is requested to present to this Commission proof necessary to establish either the Indian or white blood of his wife.

M.D. Green, being first duly sworn, states that as stenographer to the Commission to the Five Civilized Tribes he reported the foregoing case and that the above and foregoing is a full, true and complete transcript of his stenographic notes in said case.

MD Green

Subscribed and sworn to before me this 23 day of July 1900.

Clifton R. Breckinridge
Commissioner.

Department of the Interior,
Commission to the Five Civilized Tribes,
Westville, I.T., July 20, 1900.

In the matter of the application of Benjamin Crittenden for the enrollment of himself and children as Cherokees by blood, and for the enrollment of his wife as an intermarried citizen; being duly sworn and examined by Commissioner Needles, he testified as follows:

Q What is your name? A Benjamin Crittenden.
Q What is your age? A 53.
Q What is your post office? A Westville.
Q What district do you live in? A Going Snake.
Q How long have you lived there? A I was raised here.
Q Have you lived there all your wife[sic]? A Yes, sir.
Q What is the name of your father? A William Crittenden.
Q Is he living? A No, sir.
Q How long has he been dead? A He has been dead about 15 years.
Q What is the name of your mother? A Lyda.
Q Is she living? A No, sir, she is dead.
Q Have you ever been enrolled by the Cherokee authorities? A Yes, sir.
(On 1880 roll, page 422, No. 461, Going Snake dist., Been Critdenten[sic]. On 1896 roll, page 736, No. 510, Benjamin Crittenden, Going Snake.)
Q What proportion of Cherokee blood do you claim? A 1/4, I guess.
Q Are you married? A Yes, sir.
Q Your wife living? A Yes, sir.
Q What is her name? A Mary Weaver it was before I married her.
Q Is she an indian[sic]? A She claimed to be an indian and applied for her rights, but failed to get them.
Q When were you married? A In 1891.
Q Have you a certificate of marriage? A No, sir, but uncle[sic] Ned Foreman married me.
Q Is the name of Mary Weaver on the rolls of 1880? A No, sir, she is on the 1896 rolls(On 1896 roll page 736, No. 511, as Mary Crittenden, Going Snake district.)
Q Is she a white woman? A She is not a white woman, she is Cherokee and got a little drakey[sic] mixed with her so they tell me.
Q Have you got any children? A Got four.
Q By her? A Yes, sir.
Q Is Ned Foreman here? A Yes, sir, he is on the ground.
Q Can you prove your marriage by anybody else? A No, sir, only his son and him was there.

Well, we will continus[sic] your case until you can find him and have him testify sometime this afternoon.

-----o-----

Bruce C Jones, being duly sworn, says that as stenographer to the Commission to the Five Civilized Tribes he reported the testimony of the above named witness, and that the foregoing is a full, true and correct translation of his stenographic notes.

Bruce C Jones

Sworn to and subscribed before me this the 23rd day of July, 1900.

T B Needles
Commissioner.

Supl.-C.D.#51.

Department of the Interior,
Commission to the Five Civilized Tribes.
Muskogee, I. T., February 17, 1902.

SUPPLEMENTAL in the matter of the enrollment of MARY CRITTENDEN ET al., as Cherokee citizens:

Commission: Applicant was notified by registed[sic] letter January 31, 1902, that her case would be taken up for final consideration by the Commission on the 17th day of February, 1902, and that she would on said date be offered an opportunity to introduce any further testimony affecting her case.

Applicant has been called three times and fails to respond either in person or by attorney and the case is closed.

T B Needles
Commissioner.

Cherokee D 51

DEPARTMENT OF THE INTERIOR,
COMMISSION TO THE FIVE CIVILIZED TRIBES.

In the matter of the application for the enrollment of Mary Crittenden as a citizen by intermarriage of the Cherokee Nation, and for the enrollment of her minor children Emily, Lewis, David and Lula Crittenden as citizens by blood of the Cherokee Nation.

D E C I S I O N.

The record in this case shows that on July 20, 1900, Benjamin Crittenden appeared before the Commission at Westville, Indian Territory, and made personal application for the enrollment of himself and his minor children Emily, Lewis, David and Lula Crittenden as citizens by blood of the Cherokee Nation, and for the enrollment of his wife Mary Crittenden as a citizen by intermarriage of the Cherokee Nation. Benjamin Crittenden has been differently classified and is not therefore embraced in this decision.

The evidence shows that Mary Crittenden was lawfully married in 1891 to Benjamin Crittenden, a citizen by blood of the Cherokee Nation. Her children Emily, Lewis, David and Lula Crittenden are the issue of that marriage. They and their said mother are identified on the Cherokee Census roll of 1896.

The evidence further shows that the said Mary Crittenden has lived with her husband in the Cherokee Nation since 1891, and that she was a resident of said Nation at the date of the application herein.

It is, therefore, the opinion of this Commission that Mary Crittenden should be enrolled as a citizen by intermarriage of the Cherokee Nation, and that Emily Crittenden, Lewis Crittenden, David Crittenden and Lula Crittenden should be enrolled as citizens by blood of the Cherokee Nation, in accordance with the provisions of Section twenty-one of the Act of Congress approved June 28, 1898, (30 Stats., 495), and it is so ordered.

COMMISSION TO THE FIVE CIVILIZED TRIBES.

Tams Bixby
Acting Chairman.

T.B. Needles
Commissioner.

C. R. Breckinridge
Commissioner.

Muskogee, Indian Territory,
this JUN 9- 1902

DEPARTMENT OF THE INTERIOR,
Commission to the Five Civilized Tribes,
Muskogee, I. T. June 13th 1902.

In the matter of the application of Mary Crittenden for enrollment as a citizen of the Cherokee Nation, by intermarriage.

Cherokee D 51.

Protest of the Cherokee Nation.

The Cherokee Nation respectfully desires to pray an appeal from the Decision of the Commission in this case, rendered on June 9th 1902, and asks that the same be forwarded to the Honorable Secretary of the Interior for review.

The testimony in this case shows that Mary Crittenden, nee Weaver, is a colored person and that she married Benjamin Crittenden, a Cherokee by blood, in 1891.

The testimony further shows that she is a full sister of Bullette Weaver who is classified as a colored man and not as a white person or a Cherokee by blood.

The Cherokee Nation desires to call the attention of the Honorable Secretary of the Interior to Section 4593, Mansfields[sic] Digest, being the laws of Arkansas extended over and put in force in the Indian Territory by the act of Congress of date May 2nd 1890, and was therefore in force when this marriage took place in 1891, as follows:

"All marriages of white persons with negroes or mulattoes are declared to be illegal and void."

Your attention is also invited to that section of the Cherokee law which provides for the intermarriage of white persons or foreigners with Cherokees, delawares[sic] or Shawnees by blood but no provision is made whatever for the intermarriage of a colored person with an Indian and in as much as there is no provision for the same we contend that this marriage was illegal and void both under the Cherokee laws as well as the laws of the United States then in force in the Indian Territory; and if the marriage was void it conferred no citizenship whatever upon the applicant, Mary Crittenden.

We are sustained in our construction of the Cherokee Intermarriage Law by the decision of the Supreme Court of the Cherokee Nation in 1871, the Court saying in that opinion that the Chapter of the Cherokee laws entitled "Relating to Intermarriage with white men etc" "only alludes to and was intended for white men and Cherokee women." This is our contention exactly. No marriage in the Cherokee Nation was ever by any court regarded as legal between a colored person and a Cherokee citizen by blood.

Now the Commission in a great number of cases where white women have intermarried with their husbands before their readmission to citizenship in the Cherokee Nation have cited the Rogers case and held that it was binding upon the

Commission. The same court that passed upon the Rogers case is the one that rendered this decision and this construction was made thirty years ago and has never been changed by any court subsequent to that time. For the information of the Honorable Secretary of the Interior, a certified copy of this decision is attached hereto.

But we are not confined to the Cherokee Law or the Arkansas Laws put in force in the Indian Territory but this woman is not entitled to be enrolled under section twenty-one of the Curtis Bill which provides that in enumerating the persons to be enrolled by this Commission in the last line of the first paragraph of the section, the Commission shall enroll "Such intermarried white persons as may be entitled to citizenship under Cherokee laws." Now the applicant is not a white person, but the proof clearly shows that ~~she~~ *her mother* was a slave and her full brother has been enrolled as a colored citizen of the Cherokee Nation. With reference to the enrollment of Cherokee Freedmen the Commission is instructed to be governed by the decree of the court of claims rendered the third day of February 1896 and if this applicant has any rights whatever in the Cherokee Nation she must apply as a Cherokee Freedman and not as an intermarried white person.

Your attention is further invited to the fact that the decision of the Commission fails to make any note of the applicant as a colored person[sic]

For the reasons above stated, we submit that this marriage was illegal and void and if our contention be true then this woman is not entitled to be enrolled as a citizen of the Cherokee Nation by intermarriage.

Respectfully submitted,

W. W. Hastings

J. C. S. Attorney for the Cherokee Nation.

"Tuesday Morning, June 20, 1871."

"Court convened—Present same as yesterday. The making out of report continued until the court announced the following decision regarding certain colored men who have married colored women of the nation, towit:"

"The Court of Commission after mature reflection feel authorized to decide against all cases before it wherein colored or black men are claiming citizenship from marrying black female citizens under the law 'Regulating Intermarriage with White Men,' as they are convinced a correct interpretation of said law will not authorize a clerk of any of the courts to issue a license to a black man to marry a black woman as it only alludes to, and was intended for white men and Cherokee women."

"The Court believes it is further sustained in the opinion that colored citizens, are such by adoption, and as such, cannot confer rights upon others, without further legislation upon the matter; therefore decides 'The following named persons are not entitled to Cherokee citizenship as claimed, to-wit:'"

"George Washington, Cooweescoowee District.
"Henry Johnson, Tahlequah "
"Lee Cooper, " "
"Henry Bird, " "
"William Madden, " "
"Alonzo Cullen, "
"Solomon Foster, Illinois "
"William Hudson, " "
"Haywood Youngblood, Sequoyah District."

Executive Department, Cherokee Nation.

Tahlequah, I. T., June 22, 1901.

I, J. T. Parks, Executive Secretary of the Cherokee Nation, Indian Territory, do hereby certify that the above and foregoing is a true and correct copy of the decision of the Supreme Court of the Cherokee Nation sitting as a "Special Court of Commission" as found on pages 86 and 87 Record Book No. Five entitled "Minutes of Special Court of Commission," on file in this department.

Given under my hand and the Great Seal of the Cherokee Nation at Tahlequah, Indian Territory, on this the day and date above written.

J. T. Parks
Executive Secretary of Cherokee Nation.

NOTE:—"Decision regarding colored citizens of the United States intermarrying with colored women citizens of the Cherokee Nation made June 20, 1871.

Cherokee D-51.

DEPARTMENT OF THE INTERIOR,
COMMISSION TO THE FIVE CIVILIZED TRIBES.

In the matter of the application for the enrollment of Mary Crittenden as a citizen of the Cherokee Nation, and for the enrollment of her minor children, Emily, Lewis, David, Lula and Walter Crittenden, as citizens by blood of the Cherokee Nation.

D E C I S I O N.

The record herein shows that on July 20, 1900, Benjamin Crittenden appeared before the Commission at Westville, Indian Territory, and made application for the enrollment of his wife, Mary Crittenden, as a citizen of the Cherokee Nation, and for the enrollment of his minor children, Emily, Lewis, David and Lula Crittenden, as citizens by blood of the Cherokee Nation. The application also included the said Benjamin Crittenden, but he has been differently clacsified[sic] and is not embraced in this decision. On June 9, 1902, the Commission rendered a decision herein, enrolling Mary Crittenden as a citizen by intermarriage and her minor children a citizens by blood of the Cherokee Nation, and transmitted the same to the Secretary of the Interior for his approval. Such decision was not approved, and on August 5, 1902, the record was returned to this Commission for an expression of their views on the objections, raised by the Cherokee Nation, to the enrollment of Mary Crittenden as a citizen of the Cherokee Nation by intermarriage, on the ground that she was shown to be of African descent, and could not, under Cherokee laws and customs, acquire citizenship by intermarriage.

On October 31, 1902, a birth affidavit was filed for Walter Crittenden, born since the date of the original decision herein, and on December 6, 1902, at Muskogee, Indian Territory, a supplemental statement and order was made in the matter of this application, and the same is filed herewith and made a part of this record.

While the evidence tends to show that Mary Crittenden is, in part, of African descent, her mother being apparently, part negro, the record, as now made, also shows that she is of Cherokee descent; that she was born in 1865, and is the daughter of Emily Weaver and Joseph Weaver, who appear to have resided together as husband and wife for about five years. Joseph Weaver is identified on the authenticated tribal roll of 1880 as a Cherokee by blood, and the said Emily Weaver and her daughter, Mary Crittenden, are both identified on the Cherokee census roll of 1896 as a Cherokee by blood.

The minor applicants herein are the children of said Mary Crittenden by her husband, Benjamin Crittenden, a citizen by blood of the Cherokee Nation. The four older children are identified on the Cherokee census roll of 1896 with their mother, and Walter Crittenden is identified by a birth affidavit made a part of this record.

This record, as supplemented by the order of December 6, 1902, confirms the former finding of the Commission as to the three minor applicants herein, and it now appears that Mary Crittenden is a Cherokee Indian by blood.

The evidence further shows that said Mary Crittenden has resided in the Cherokee Nation all her life, and her said children are therefore considered to have been residents of the Cherokee Nation since their birth.

It is, therefore, the opinion of this Commission that Mary Crittenden, Emily Crittenden, Lewis Crittenden, David Crittenden, Lula Crittenden and Walter Crittenden should be enrolled as citizens by blood of the Cherokee Nation, in accordance with the provisions of section twenty-one of the Act of Congress approved June 28, 1898 (30 Stats., 495), and t is so ordered.

COMMISSION TO THE FIVE CIVILIZED TRIBES.

(SIGNED). *Tams Bixby.*
Chairman.

(SIGNED). *T. B. Needles.*
Commissioner.

(SIGNED). *C. R. Breckinridge.*
Commissioner.

Dated Muskogee, Indian Territory,

this ______________________

DEPARTMENT OF THE INTERIOR,

Commission to the Five Civilized Tribes,

Muskogee, I. T. December 9th 1902.

In the matter of the application of Mary Crittenden et al for enrollment as a citizens of the Cherokee Nation.

Cherokee D 51.

Protest of the Cherokee Nation.

Comes now the Cherokee Nation and protests against the decision of the Commission in this case, rendered on December 15th 1902, and respectfully asks that same be forwarded to the Honorable Secretary of the Interior for review.

The testimony in this case clearly shows that the mother of Mary Crittenden, Emily Weaver was part negro and that the grand mother of Mary Crittenden, Nellie

Cole, had no Cherokee blood but claimed as a Cherokee Freedman. The testimony of Emily Weaver, the alleged mother of Mary Crittenden is to the effect that she had never been recognized as a citizen of the Cherokee Nation and in answer to this question "Did you ever draw any money in the Cherokee Nation?" she said "No sir."

She also testified that she applied to the Commission in 1896 and that she was never admitted and the testimony further shows that all of the rolls of the Cherokee Nation in the possession of the Commission were examined and the name of Emily Weaver the alleged mother of Mary Crittenden could not be found thereon.

The testimony further shows that Mary Crittenden is a full sister to Bullette Weaver whose name appears upon the roll of 1880 as an "Adopted Colored" and on June 13th 1902 the Cherokee Nation filed an appeal setting forth the reasons why the judgment of the Commission theretofore rendered on June 9 1902 enrolling the applicant as a citizen by intermarriage should not be affirmed and reference is again made to said appeal for the purpose of showing our reasons why no marriage is legal between a Cherokee and a woman of African descent.

It will be noted that upon Benjamin Crittendens[sic] second appearance before the Commission on July 20th 1900 in answer to the question put to him by the Commissioner in charge " Your wife Mary Crittenden is a white woman?" he said "Yes sir." Hence it will be seen that he applied for her as a citizen by intermarriage and not as a Cherokee by blood. The Commission of its own Notion on December 6th 1902 caused a supplemental statement to be filed in this case averring that the father of the said Mary Crittenden is one Joseph Weaver and further on in said statement appears the statement that the tribal rolls in the possession of the Commission show that "That said Joseph Weaver is identified on the Cherokee tribal roll of 1880" giving the page and number etc. How the Commission could ascertain that a Joseph Weaver whose name appears upon the roll of 1880 is the alleged father of the applicant is not clear to us. Joseph Weaver has never sworn to it yet he was alive and accessible; this is a common name and for all we know there might be several Joseph Weavers who lived in that section of the country and in fact there is no evidence whatever that the Joseph Weaver whose name appears upon this roll is the father of the applicant; neither is there any evidence of a marriage between any Joseph Weaver and the applicants[sic] mother; on the other hand the applicants[sic] mothers[sic] testimony while it is uncertain and not to the point leaves the impression that the Joe Weaver that she refers to was her illegal husband for about five years next last past because in answer to this question: "What is the name of your present husband?" She said "Joe Weaver." Later on when asked "When were you married to him?" She answered "Never was married to him just lived with him five years." She also states that she had lived with one man by the name of Robbins and had children by him and that she was never married to any man.

Again we want to call the attention of the Department to the fact that Joseph Weaver has never been called to the stand and we desire to call the attention of the Department to the further fact that Mary Crittenden herself, although married in 1881, was never called to the stand and although there have been numerous payments in 1875, 1880, 1883, 1886, 1890 and 1894 the name of Mary Crittenden nor her mother Emily Weaver does not appear upon one of them nor is it contended that she ever drew any money as a Cherokee by blood.

Now the examination of the 1896 roll shows that the said Mary Crittenden was at that time thirty-nine years of age which would have made her have been born in the year 1867 and yet as above stated her name does not appear upon any roll except that of 1896 which was not a pay roll and never authenticated and not binding upon the Commission or the Department and the name of her mother ever appears upon the 1896 roll when she admits that she never drew one cent of money and that she was never recognized before as a citizen of the Cherokee Nation that her mother was of African descent and that she was never legally married to any man.

Now Section 692 of the Compiled laws of the Cherokee Nation 1892 provides for legitmatizing[sic] children where there was a form of marriage taken place which was prohibited on account of consanguinity or where either of the parties had a former husband or wife living and it will be noted that there must have been a form of marriage which would of itself tend to show that the children of such unlawful marriages were in fact the children of this man and his wife. The same section of the Cherokee law also legitimatizes illegitimate children where the parents afterwards intermarry and this publicly recognizes the parentage of the children but illegitimate children are not legitimatized by any law where there has never been a form of a marriage either before or after the birth of the children.

This is a most serious question and one that we hope will be well considered by the Department in this case. Suppose the Department holds other wise, the evil consequences will be apparent. Every lewd woman with an illegitimate child in the country would immediately lay the parentage of said child to some ignorant Cherokee Indian and demand its enrollment as a citizen of the Cherokee Nation. She would appear before the Commission and swear that a certain man was the father of the child, no proof of marriage would be required and we submit that the testimony of a woman of such loose morals should not commend itself to the Commission or to the Secretary of the Interior. In other words if the Cherokee Nation has not heretofore recognized an illegitimate child by enrolling it and paying it money we insist that the testimony of the mother of the child is insufficient to show its parentage.

Section 21 of the Curtis act requires the commission to enroll all Cherokee citizens whose names are found upon the Cherokee authenticated roll of 1880 <u>and all descendants born since the date of said roll,</u> to persons whose names are found thereon. Now it will be noted the descendants must mean of course all legitimate descendants. The words could have no other proper legal meaning. How could you prove who the descendants were unless they were the descendants of a legal union. Again you will note that the descendants must be born since the date of said roll hereas, Mary Crittenden was born in 1867 or 13 years before the roll of 1880 was made and there is no evidence that she was ever recognized by Joe Weaver as his child, but on the other hand there is evidence that her mother was a woman of loose morals, was never married to any man, but had numerous other children, none of whom were ever recognized as citizens of the Cherokee Nation but were always refused and never drew any money.

Now the act of Congress approved June 10th 1896 requires this Commission to respect all laws of the Cherokee Nation in making the rolls of the Cherokee Nation and if this be true, then respecting section 692 of the compiled laws of the Cherokee Nation of date 1893 and respecting section twenty-one of the Curtis Bill which requires them to enroll descendants since born to those whose names appear upon the roll of 1880, then the applicant should not be enrolled as a citizen by blood of the Cherokee Nation.

For the reasons assigned heretofore on June 13th 1902 we do not believe that Mary Crittenden should be enrolled as a citizen of the Cherokee Nation by intermarriage and for the reasons herein given we do not believe she is entitled to be enrolled as a Cherokee by blood.

Respectfully Submitted.

W W Hastings
Attorney for the Cherokee Nation.

Attest:
J C Starr
Stenographer for the Cherokee Nation.

COMMISSIONERS:

HENRY L. DAWES,
TAMS BIXBY,
THOMAS B. NEEDLES,
C. R. BRECKINRIDGE.

ALLISON L. AYLESWORTH,
SECRETARY.

ADDRESS ONLY THE
COMMISSION TO THE FIVE CIVILIZED TRIBES.

DEPARTMENT OF THE INTERIOR,
COMMISSION TO THE FIVE CIVILIZED TRIBES.

REFER IN REPLY TO THE FOLLOWING
Cher. D-51.

Muskogee, Indian Territory, June 9, 1902.

W. W. Hastings, Esq.,
Attorney for the Cherokee Nation,
Muskogee, Indian Territory.

Sir:

Enclosed herewith please find copy of the decision of the Commission rendered June 9, 1902, in the matter of the application of Mary Crittenden et al for enrollment as citizens of the Cherokee Nation.

You are hereby advised that you will be allowed fifteen days from date hereof, in which to file with the Commission such protest as you desire to make against the action of the enrollment of the persons named as citizens of the Cherokee Nation. If you fail to file protest within the time allowed these applicants will be regularly listed for enrollment.

Yours truly,

Tams Bixby
Acting Chairman.

Encl. D-51.

COMMISSIONERS:

HENRY L. DAWES,
TAMS BIXBY,
THOMAS B. NEEDLES,
C. R. BRECKINRIDGE.

ALLISON L. AYLESWORTH,
SECRETARY.

ADDRESS ONLY THE
COMMISSION TO THE FIVE CIVILIZED TRIBES.

DEPARTMENT OF THE INTERIOR,
COMMISSION TO THE FIVE CIVILIZED TRIBES.

REFER IN REPLY TO THE FOLLOWING

Cherokee D-51.

Muskogee, Indian Territory, July 9, 1902.

Mr. W. W. Hastings,
Attorney for the Cherokee Nation,
Muskogee, Indian Territory.

Sir:

You are hereby advised that the decision of the Commission to the Five Civilized Tribes, granting the application of Benjamin Crittenden for the enrollment of his wife, Mary Crittenden, as a citizen by intermarriage of the Cherokee Nation, and for the enrollment of his four minor children, Emily, Lewis, David and Lula Crittenden, as citizens by blood of the Cherokee Nation, a copy of which decision was furnished you on June 9, 1902, has this day been transmitted to the Secretary of the Interior for his review and decision.

The action of the Secretary will be made known to you as soon as the Commission is informed of same.

Respectfully,
Tams Bixby
Acting Chairman.

COMMISSIONERS:

HENRY L. DAWES,
TAMS BIXBY,
THOMAS B. NEEDLES,
C. R. BRECKINRIDGE.

ALLISON L. AYLESWORTH,
SECRETARY.

ADDRESS ONLY THE
COMMISSION TO THE FIVE CIVILIZED TRIBES.

DEPARTMENT OF THE INTERIOR,
COMMISSION TO THE FIVE CIVILIZED TRIBES.

REFER IN REPLY TO THE FOLLOWING

Cherokee D-51.

Muskogee, Indian Territory, December 15, 1902.

W. W. Hastings,
Attorney for Cherokee Nation,
Muskogee, Indian Territory.

Dear Sir:-

There is transmitted herewith decision of the Commission to the Five Civilized Tribes, dated December 15, 1902, granting the application for the enrollment of Mary Crittenden and her minor children, Emily, Lewis, David, Lula and Walter Crittenden, as citizens by blood of the Cherokee Nation.

You are advised that on June 9, 1902, the Commission rendered a decision granting the application of Mary Crittenden for the enrollment of herself as a citizen by intermarriage of the Cherokee Nation, and for the enrollment of her children as citizens by blood of the Cherokee Nation, which decision was forwarded to the Secretary of the Interior for review and approval.

Under date of August 5, 1902, the Department remanded the record of proceedings had in said application and requested an expression of the views of the Commission on the objections raised by the Nation to the enrollment of Mary Crittenden as a citizen of the Cherokee Nation by intermarriage, on the ground that she was shown to be of African descent, and could not under Cherokee laws and customs acquire citizenship by intermarriage.

The record as supplemented by the order of December 6, 1902, confirms the former finding of the Commission as to the three minor applicants, and it now appears that Mary Crittenden is a Cherokee Indian by blood.

You are advised that you will be allowed fifteen days from date hereof in which to file such protest as you desire to make against the action of the Commission in granting the enrollment of Mary Crittenden, as a citizen by blood of the Cherokee Nation, December 15, 1902. You will be required to make proof of service of a copy of such protest on the applicant.

At the expiration of fifteen days from date hereof, this case will be forwarded to the Secretary of the Interior for review and approval.

Respectfully,

Tams Bixby

Acting Chairman.

Enc. P-138.

COMMISSIONERS:

HENRY L. DAWES,
TAMS BIXBY,
THOMAS B. NEEDLES,
C. R. BRECKINRIDGE.

ALLISON L. AYLESWORTH,
SECRETARY.

ADDRESS ONLY THE
COMMISSION TO THE FIVE CIVILIZED TRIBES.

DEPARTMENT OF THE INTERIOR,
COMMISSION TO THE FIVE CIVILIZED TRIBES.

REFER IN REPLY TO THE FOLLOWING

Cherokee D 51.

Muskogee, Indian Territory, December 23, 1902.

W. W. Hastings,

Attorney for Cherokee Nation,

Muskogee, Indian Territory.

Dear Sir:

You are hereby advised that the Commission's decision, dated December 15, 1902, granting the application of Mary Crittenden for the enrollment of herself and her five minor children, Emily, Lewis, David, Lula and Walter Crittenden, as citizens by blood of the Cherokee Nation, a copy of which decision was furnished you on December 15, 1902, has this day been transmitted to the Secretary of the Interior for is review and decision.

The action of the Secretary will be made known to you as soon as the Commission is informed of same.

Respectfully,

Tams Bixby Acting Chairman.

COMMISSIONERS:

TAMS BIXBY,
THOMAS B. NEEDLES,
C. R. BRECKINRIDGE,
W. E. STANLEY.

ALLISON L. AYLESWORTH,
SECRETARY.

ADDRESS ONLY THE
COMMISSION TO THE FIVE CIVILIZED TRIBES.

DEPARTMENT OF THE INTERIOR,
COMMISSION TO THE FIVE CIVILIZED TRIBES.

REFER IN REPLY TO THE FOLLOWING

Cherokee D 51

Muskogee, Indian Territory, January 20, 1904.

W. W. Hastings,

Attorney for the Cherokee Nation,

Tahlequah, Indian Territory.

Dear Sir:

In regard to the Commission's decision of December 23, 1902, in the matter of the application of Benjamin Crittenden for the enrollment of his wife, Mary Crittenden, as a citizen by intermarriage of the Cherokee Nation and for the enrollment of his five minor children, Emily, Lewis, David, Lula and Walter Crittenden, as citizens by blood of the Cherokee Nation, which said decision was protested by the Cherokee Nation as to the said Mary Crittenden, you are advised that the Commission is in receipt of Departmental letter, dated November 20, 1903, directing that Mary Crittenden be enrolled as a Cherokee Freedman.

Respectfully,

T B Needles

Commissioner in Charge.

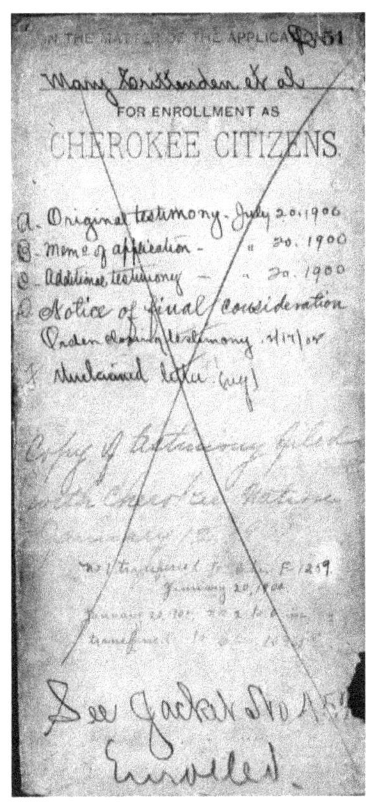

IN THE MATTER OF THE APPLICATION

Mary Crittenden et al

FOR ENROLLMENT AS

CHEROKEE CITIZENS.

A. Original testimony. July 20, 1900

B. Memo of application " 20. 1900

C. Additional testimony " 20. 1900

D. Notice of final consideration

Order closing testimony. 3/17/04

Copy of testimony filed with Cherokee Nation

See Jacket No.

Enrolled.

[Copy of the children's enrollment card showing Dawes Roll numbers.]

RESIDENCE: Going Snake DISTRICT.
POST OFFICE: Westville I.T.

Cherokee Nation. Cherokee Roll.
(Not including Delawares, Shawnees, or Freedmen.)

CARD NO.
FIELD NO. 10365

Dawes' Roll No.		NAME.	Relationship to Person first Named.	AGE.	SEX.	BLOOD.	Tribal Enrollment: Year.	Tribal Enrollment: District.	Tribal Enrollment: No.	Parents: Name of Father.	Parents: Year.	Parents: District.	Parents: Name of Mother.	Parents: Year.	Parents: District.
30819	1	Crittenden, Emily		9	F	1/4	1896	G. Snake	512	Benjamin Crittenden		G. Snake	Mary Crittenden		Going Snake
30820	2	" Lewis	Bro.	7	M	1/4	1896	" "	513	" "		"	" "		"
30821	3	" David	"	5	"	"	1896	" "	514	" "		"	" "		
30822	4	" Lula	Sister	4	F	"	1896	" "	515	" "			" "		
30823	5	" Walter	Bro.	2½	M	"		See note		" "					
	6	GRANTED								#1356					
	7		CITIZENSHIP CERTIFICATE ISSUED FOR NO. MAR 10 1905												
	8	ACTION APPROVED BY SECRETARY OF INTERIOR.													
	9	NOV 2 1903													

No 5: Birth affidavit approved October 31, 1902.

See Cherokee Card No. 1259

On Cherokee Card D. Date of Application for enrollment: July 20 1900.
Transfer On this card, January 20, 1904.

[Mary Crittenden's Freedmen Card -- Front]

RESIDENCE: Going Snake DISTRICT.
POST OFFICE: Westville I.T.

Cherokee Nation. Freedmen Roll.

CARD NO. ______
FIELD NO. 123[illegible]

Dawes' Roll No.		NAME.	Relationship to Person first Named.	AGE.	SEX.	Tribal Enrollment Year	Tribal Enrollment District	Tribal Enrollment No.	SLAVE OF—	REMARKS.
349[illegible]	1	Crittenden; Mary		35	F	1896	Going Snake	511		
4061	2	Woodall, Rachel	Sister	27	F	1880	Tahlequah	2566		

No 2 on 1896 roll page 810 #2495 Going Snake Dist.

MAY 12 1905

CITIZENSHIP CERTIFICATE ISSUED

See Cherokee card No 10365.

No 1 on Cherokee card No. D. 51 July 20, 1900. On this card January 20, 1904. No 2 on Cherokee card No. D. 2443, July 1, 1902. On this card May 13, 1905.

ADDITIONAL INFORMATION ON REVERSE SIDE.

[Mary Crittenden's Freedmen Card -- Back]

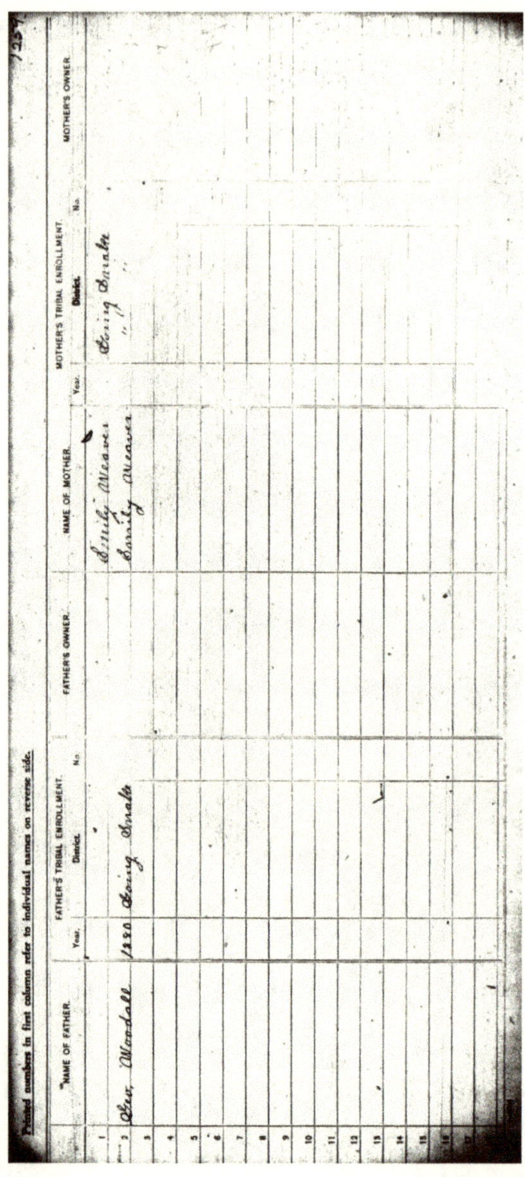

1257

Printed numbers in first column refer to individual names on reverse side.

	NAME OF FATHER.	FATHER'S TRIBAL ENROLLMENT. Year.	District.	No.	FATHER'S OWNER.	NAME OF MOTHER.	MOTHER'S TRIBAL ENROLLMENT. Year.	District.	No.	MOTHER'S OWNER.
1						Emily Weaver		Going Snake		
2	Geo. Woodall	1880	Going Snake			Emily Weaver		"		
3										
4										
5										
6										
7										
8										
9										
10										
11										
12										
13										
14										
15										
16										
17										

Cherokee D52 - Jim Harlin

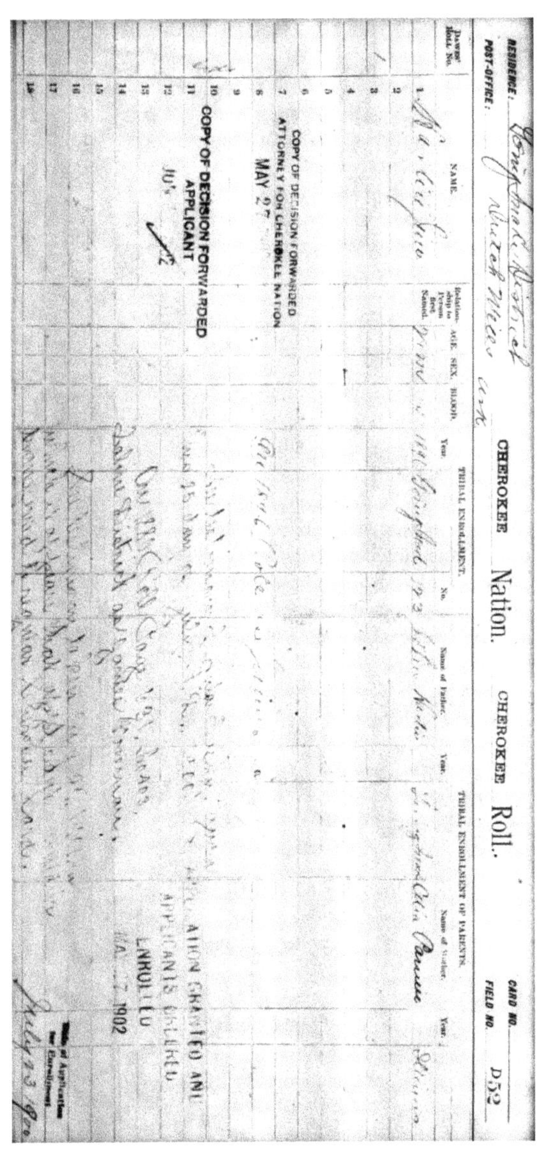

CHEROKEE Nation. CHEROKEE Roll.

RESIDENCE:

POST-OFFICE:

CARD NO.

FIELD NO. D52

COPY OF DECISION FORWARDED ATTORNEY FOR CHEROKEE NATION MAY 27

COPY OF DECISION FORWARDED APPLICANT

APPLICATION GRANTED AND APPLICANTS ENROLLED

ENROLLED

1902

DEPARTMENT OF THE INTERIOR.
COMMISSION TO THE FIVE CIVILIZED TRIBES.
STILWELL, I. T., JULY 23rd, 1900.

IN THE MATTER OF THE APPLICATION OF Jim Harlin, for enrollment as a citizen of the Cherokee Nation, and he being sworn by Commissioner, C. R. Breckinridge, testified as follows:

Q What is your name? A Jim Harlin.
Q What is your age? A Will be twenty one tomorrow.
Q What is your Postoffice? A Dutch Mills.
Q Your District? A Going Snake.
Q How long have you lived in this District? A All my life.
Q What is your father's name? A Harlin.
Q Full name? A John Harlin.
(Identified on the roll of 1894, Page 647, #804, James Harlin, Going Snake District)
Q Did you draw your strip money in 1894? A Yes sir.
Q You were living in 1894 in the family of Andrew and Mary Easky; your name appears on the roll of 1894 as enrolled in that family.
(Identified on the roll of 1896, Page 744, #723, James Easky.[sic]
Q It seems you were put down in 1896 James Easky; were you some times called James Easky, and some times James Harlin? A Yes sir.
Q You say you were some times known as James Easky and some times as James Harlin? A Yes sir.
Q Any one around here who has known you all your life? [No answer given]

George W. Christie, being called and sworn, testified as follows:

Q What is your full name? A George W. Christie
Q Your age? A Forty.
Q Your Postoffice? A Westville.
Q Your District? A Going Snake.
Q How long have lived in this District and Nation?
A In Going Snake About thirty years.
Q Do you know this young man here, James Easky or James Harlin?, who is applying for enrollment? A Yes sir.
Q Do you know he is living and has lived with his kin folks, the Easkys? A Yes sir.
Q You have just known of him as James Easky? A Yes sir.

Andrew J. Alberty, being called and sworn, testified as follows:

Q What is your name? A Andrew J. Alberty.
Q What is your age? A Fifty six.
Q What is your Postoffice address? A Stilwell.
Q How long have you lived in this District? A I was born and raised here.

Q Do you know this applicant, here, James Harlin? A I do not know him by that name; know him by Jim Easky.
Q Do you know his mother? A Yes sir.
Q Do you know that he is not in fact an Easky, but is a Harlin; that he was just raised by the name of Easky? A He was raised by the name of Easky; I can not say whether he is a Harlin.
Q You say you know his mother? A Yes sir.
Q What is her name? A Sealy Easky.
Q How far does she live from you? A When she lived here; about three miles.
Q How long since she lived up here? A About fifteen years.
Q Did you know this boy along back about that time? A I have known him since he was a nursing child.
Q Was her name Easky then? A Yes sir.
Q Was her name Easky when this boy was born? A Yes sir.
Q But she gave him the name of Harlin; Do you know she claimed this boy as her child? A Yes sir.
Q Do you know she is living at this time? A No sir.
Q Do you understand she is? A The last time I ever heard of her, she was living; I never heard of her death.
Q You would be likely to have heard of it, if she had died? A I guess I would.

By Mr. W. W. Hastings, Cherokee Representative:
Q Was she a Cherokee by blood? A Yes sir.

By the Commission?[sic] A[sic] She was recognized as a Cherokee by blood?
A Yes sir.
Q And her name was Easky when this child was born? A Yes sir.
Q What did you say her name was? A Sealy Easky.

By Mr. W. W. Hastings, Cherokee Represenative[sic]:
Q Do you know what family she lived with then? A Her father and mother.
Q His name was Andrew Easky or Dick? A Yes sir.
Q She always, so far as you knew, lived in Going Snake District, at that time, I mean? A Yes sir.
Q How far did she live from Flint Line; Dutch Mills? A Two miles, I reckon.

By the Commission:
James Harlin, you are identified on the rolls of 1894 and 1896, but you are old enough to have been on the roll of 1880, and your name is not found there; neither is your mother's name identified on the roll of 1880, and there is some doubt of course about her child being entitled to enrollment or not, as she is not on the roll of 1800, or her child; therefore, your name will be placed on a doubtful card, and it will be well for you to see your mother and have her take steps to identify herself as a Cherokee by blood, or to show where she was enrolled in 1880; and when you do that, then you should call the attention of this Commission to your mother established that way, and write to the Commission, giving it the information about your mother being on the roll

of 1880, or you under some name of that roll, as additional evidence that can be looked up.
When the Commission decides in your case, it will let you know at your postoffice what the decision is, and whatever evidence you furnish will be considered with your case.

R. R. Cravens, being sworn, states that as stenographer to the Commission to the Five Civilized Tribes, he reported the foregoing case, and that the above and foregoing is a true, full and correct transcript of his stenographic notes in said case.

R R Cravens

Sworn to and subscribed before
me this 24th day of July, 1900.

T B Needles
COMMISSIONER.

Department of the Interior,
Commission to the Five Civilized Tribes,
Stillwell[sic], I.T., July 25, 1900.

D. 52.

In the matter of the application for the enrollment of Jim Harlin.

Additional testimony.

Lula Easky, being duly sworn and examined by Commissioner Breckinridge, testified as follows:
Q What is your name? A Lula Easky.
Q What is your post office? A Dutch Mills.
Q How old are you? A 29.
Q What is your district? A Going Snake.
Q How long have you lived in this district? A All my life.
Q You appear now with reference, I understand you to say, to the application of Jim Harlin? A Yes, sir.
Q I understand that you are able to indicate where he is enrolled in 1880 and in 1894? A Yes, sir, in 1894 and 1896 he is enrolled with us.
Q First you ought to show where he is enrolled in 1880. Under what name is he enrolled in 1880? A Jim Freeman,
Q What is his age now? A I don't know exactly, he was a baby then.
Q Do you consider him at least 20 years of age? A Yes, sir.
Q Under what name was he enrolled in 1880? A Jim Freeman.
Q How did he happen to be called Jim Freeman at that time? A His mother done that, she had two through a Freeman and one through a Harlin.
Mr. Baugh, representing the Cherokee Nation: What[sic] is the mother of this boy?
A His mother is Celia Parnell.

Q Where does she live at? A Cookston[sic], Illinois district.
Q In 1880 did she have this boy enrolled? A Yes, sir, in Saline district.
Q Under what name? A Jim Freeman.
Q Do you know that James Freeman enrolled on the 1880 roll in Saline is the same as James Easky, enrolled in 1896 as in Going Snake? A Yes, sir.
Q How do you know he is the same identical person? A We have raised him ever since he was about 2 years old.
Q Did his mother have any other children besides him? A Yes, sir, she had one before him and she has got three since, there are five in all.
Q Did she have any other in 1880? A No, sir, she didn't have any other; yes, sir she had one older than this one, she had two children in 1880.
Commissioner Breckinridge: Where is this boy's mother living? A In Illinois district.
Q Does he live with his mother? A No, sir, he lives with us.
Q You see that this is a very confused record, the boy's name has been chanced[sic] around so much it is almost impossible to identify him, and yet we want to do what is just by the boy. You tell the boy to appear before the Commission in his own case, and if he can to bring his mother that she can testify as to her having him enrolled back when he was a child. That seems to be the only way that we can get the straight of this case. Was the father of this Jim Harlin living in 1880? A Yes, sir, he is living yet.
Q What is his name? A Jim Harlin.
Q And what name did his mother beat in 1880? A Celia Parnell.
Q And you say that this child of hers was enrolled in 1880 as Freeman? A Yes, sir.
Q How do you know that Jim Freeman on the roll of 1880 is the same person as this Jim Harlin we are talking about now? A We have raised him.
Q When did you get possession of him? A I don't know what time, he was about 2 years old.
Q What name did he have at the time that you got possession of him, was he known then as Jim Freeman? A We always did call him Jim Easky, but she enrolled him as Jim Freeman, I don't know what made her do it.
Q When did she get the name of Freeman? A She had one child name Freeman and she enrolled this one as Freeman.
Q Is the mother a Cherokee by blood? A Yes, sir.
Mr. Baugh: Q What was his brother's name? A George.
Q Did you raise George? A Yes, sir, I raised him until he was about 14 years old.
Commissioner Breckenridge[sic]: George what? A George Freeman.
Q Was this Jim Harlin married? A No, sir.

------o------

Bruce C. Jones, being duly sworn, says that as stenographer to the Commission to the Five Civilized Tribes he reported the testimony of the above named witness, and that the foregoing is a full, true and correct translation of his stenographic notes.

---- *Bruce C Jones*

Sworn to and subscribed before me this the 30th day of July, 1900.

T B Needles
Commissioner.

Department of the Interior,
Commission to the Five Civilized Tribes,
Stilwell, I.T., July 27, 1900.

D. 52.

In the matter of the application of James Harlin.
Additional testimony.

James Harlin, being duly sworn and examined by Commissioner Breckenridge[sic], testified as follows:
Q What is your name? A James Harlin.
Q What is your age? A 22.
Q What is your post office? A Dutch Mills, Ark.
Q In what district do you live? A Going Snake.
Q How long have you lived in Going Snake? A All my life.
Q Are you enrolled in 1880? A Yes, sir.
Q Under what name do you appear on the roll of 1880? A James Harlin.
Q Do you claim as a Cherokee by blood? A Yes, sir.
Q How much Cherokee blood do you claim? A About a half breed.
(Not identified on roll of 1880 as James Harlin.)

Celia Parnell, being sworn and examined by Commission Breckenridge, testified as follows:
Q What is your name? A Celia Parnell.
Q What is your age? A 51.
Q What is your post office? A Cookston[sic], I. T.
Q What is your district? A Illinois.
Q How long have you lived in this section of country, in the Cherokee Nation?
A I have lived all my life; I was born and raised here.
Q Do you know this young man here that calls himself James Harlin?
A Yes, sir.
Q What kin are you to him? A He is my son.
Q He is under the impression that he was enrolled in 1880 as James Harlin, do you know anything about his enrollment in 1880?
A He is enrolled in 1880 as James Freeman.
(On 1880 roll, page 631, No. 403, James Freeman, Saline district, 2 years old.)

Q You say the James Freeman of 1880 is one and the same person as this James Harlin here now? A Yes, sir.
Q How did he happen to be enrolled as James Freeman? A His step-father enrolled him, my oldest child was Freeman and this was a Harlin, and he gave them both the same name. Mr and Mrs. Parnell married January 11, 1880.
Q And this was the child born before that marriage? A Yes, sir, he was enrolled with some Freemans?[sic] A I had two named Freeman, and this was a younger one named Harlin, and my husband, Parnell, enrolled them and he gave them all the name of Freeman.
Q Did Parnell have him enrolled? A Yes, sir.
Q He put them both in as Freeman? A Yes, sir.
Mr. W.W. Hastings, representative of the Cherokee Nation: What was the other child's first name? A George Freeman.
Q About how much older was George than James? A George was born in 1872 and James was born in 1878.
Commissioner Breckenridge[sic]: Was this boy enrolled in 1894? A I can't tell you that, because he didn't live with me, my father drawed it for him.
Q Who was he living with in 1894? A My father.
Q What was your father's name? A Andy Dick Easkey[sic].
Q You think he might have been down with his family in 1894? A Yes, sir.
(On 1894 roll, page 647, No. 804, James Harlin, Going Snake dist. In the family of Andrew Easkey and Mary Easkey.)
Q Now Mrs. Parnell, under what name were you enrolled in 1880? A As a Parnell.
(On 1880 roll, page 853, No. 817, S. A. E. Parnell, Saline dist. Duly identified by enrollment with other members of family.)
Q Is there some old citizen here that knows this is your boy, and all his changes of name? A Yes, sir, John Paden.

John Paden, being duly sworn and examined by Commissioner Breckenridge, testified as follows:
Q What is your name? A John Paden.
Q What is your age? A 38.
Q What is your post office? A Tulu, Ark.
Q Do you know this woman sitting her[sic], Celia Parnell? A Yes, sir.
Q How long have you known her? A All my life, nearly.
Q Do you know this man here, James Harlin, as he calls himself? A Yes, sir.
Q How long have you known him? A I have known him ever since he was three or four years old.
Q Have you always known him as the child of this woman? A Yes, sir.
Q He claiming her as his mother and she claiming him as her child? A Yes, sir.
Q Have you ever known him under any other name than James Harlin?
A He went by the name of James Easkey, his grandfather raised him, old man Andrew Easkey.
Q Did he ever have anything to do with a family named Freeman?
A I don't know, sir, she had one by the name of Freeman.
Q Did this boy have a half brother named Freeman? A Yes, sir.

Commissioner Breckenridge[sic]: James, you are duly identified on the roll of 1880, and also on the roll of 1894 and 1896, and you will be enrolled as a Cherokee by blood.

-------0-------

Bruce C. Jones, being duly sworn, says that as stenographer to the Commission to the Five Civilized Tribes he reported the testimony of the above named witnesses, and that the foregoing is a full, true and correct translation of his stenographic notes.

Bruce C Jones

Sworn to and subscribed before me this the 2nd day of August, 1900.

Clifton R. Breckinridge
Commissioner.

CHEROKEE D 52

DEPARTMENT OF THE INTERIOR,

COMMISSION TO THE FIVE CIVILIZED TRIBES.

In the matter of the application of Jim Harlin, for enrollment as a Cherokee citizen.

On the 23rd day of July, 1900, Jim Harlin, appeared before the Commission to the Five Civilized Tribes, and made application for his enrollment as a citizen by blood of the Cherokee Nation.

At the conclusion of the evidence offered at that time his name was placed upon a "Doubtful" card as he could not be identified upon the authenticated tribal roll of 1880.

Further evidence in the matter of this application has been submitted to the Commission and the following decision is rendered.

DECISION.

--oOo--

From all the evidence of record in this case it appears that Jim Harlin is the son of Celia Parnell, who is identified on the tribal roll of 1880. It appears that Celia

Parnell had another son whose name was Freeman. It further appears that the husband of Celia Parnell when enrolling the family in 1880 enrolled the two boys under the name of Freeman. This applicant is identified on the 1880 roll as James Freeman and on the 1896 roll as James Easky, and on the 1894 roll as James Harlin. He has resided in the Cherokee Nation all his life.

In making rolls of citizenship of the Cherokee Nation this Commission is governed by the following provisions of the Act of Congress approved June 28, 1898, (30 Stats., 495);

> "That in making rolls of citizenship of the several tribes, as required by law, the Commission to the Five Civilized Tribes is authorized and directed to take the roll of Cherokee citizens of eighteen hundred and eighty (not including freedmen) as the only roll intended to be confirmed by this and preceding Acts of Congress, and to enroll all persons now living whose names are found on said roll, and all descendants born since the date of said roll to persons whose names are found thereon; and all persons who have been enrolled by the tribal authorities who have heretofore made permanent settlement in the Cherokee Nation whose parents, by reason of their Cherokee blood, have been lawfully admitted to citizenship by the tribal authorities, and who were minors when their parents were so admitted; and they shall investigate the right of all other persons whose names are found on any other rolls and omit all such as may have been placed thereon by fraud or without authority of law, enrolling only such as may have lawful right thereto, and their descendants born since such rolls were made, with such intermarried white persons as may be entitled to citizenship under Cherokee laws."

In view of the facts and the law in this case it is considered that Jim Harlin is entitled to enrollment as a citizen by blood of the Cherokee Nation, and it is therefore so ordered.

Tams Bixby

T B Needles

C. R. Breckinridge

Commissioners.

Dated at Muskogee, Indian Territory,

MAY 27 1902

COMMISSIONERS:

HENRY L. DAWES,
TAMS BIXBY,
THOMAS B. NEEDLES,
C. R. BRECKINRIDGE.

—

ALLISON L. AYLESWORTH,
SECRETARY.

ADDRESS ONLY THE
COMMISSION TO THE FIVE CIVILIZED TRIBES.

DEPARTMENT OF THE INTERIOR,
COMMISSION TO THE FIVE CIVILIZED TRIBES.

Muskogee, Indian Territory, May 27, 1902.

W. W. Hastings, Esq.,

Attorney for the Cherokee Nation,

Muskogee, Indian Territory.

Sir:

There is herewith transmitted a copy of the decision of the Commission to the Five Civilized Tribes rendered May 27th, in the matter of the application of Jim Harlin for enrollment as a citizen by blood of the Cherokee Nation.

You are hereby advised that you will be allowed fifteen days from the date hereof in which to file with the Commission such protest as you desire to make against the enrollment of said person as a citizen of the Cherokee Nation. If you fail to file the protest within the time allowed this applicant will be regularly listed for enrollment.

Very respectfully,

Tams Bixby
Acting Chairman.

Encl. D-52.

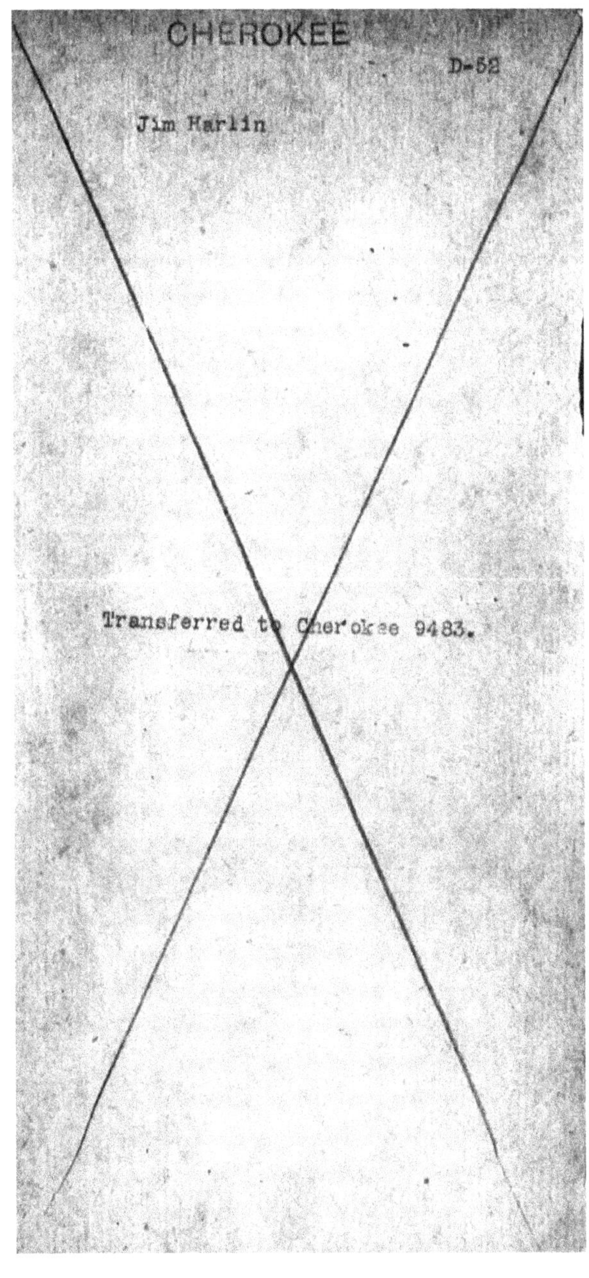

CHEROKEE

D-52

Jim Harlin

Transferred to Cherokee 9483.

RESIDENCE: Going Snake DISTRICT.
POST OFFICE: Dutch Mills, Ark.

Cherokee Nation. Cherokee Roll.

CARD NO.
FIELD NO. 9483

Dawes' Roll No.		NAME	Relationship to Person first Named	AGE	SEX	BLOOD	Tribal Enrollment Year	Tribal Enrollment District	Tribal Enrollment No.	Name of Father	Year	District	Name of Mother	Year	District
21540	1	Harlin, Jim	X	21	M	1/4	1896	Going Snake	723	John Harlin		Going Snake	Celia Russell		Illinois

GRANTED
MAY 27 1902

On 1896 Roll as James Early
On 1880 Roll, page 631, No 403, Saline District,
as James Freeman

Date of Application for Enrollment.

Cherokee D54 - Slater Cowart

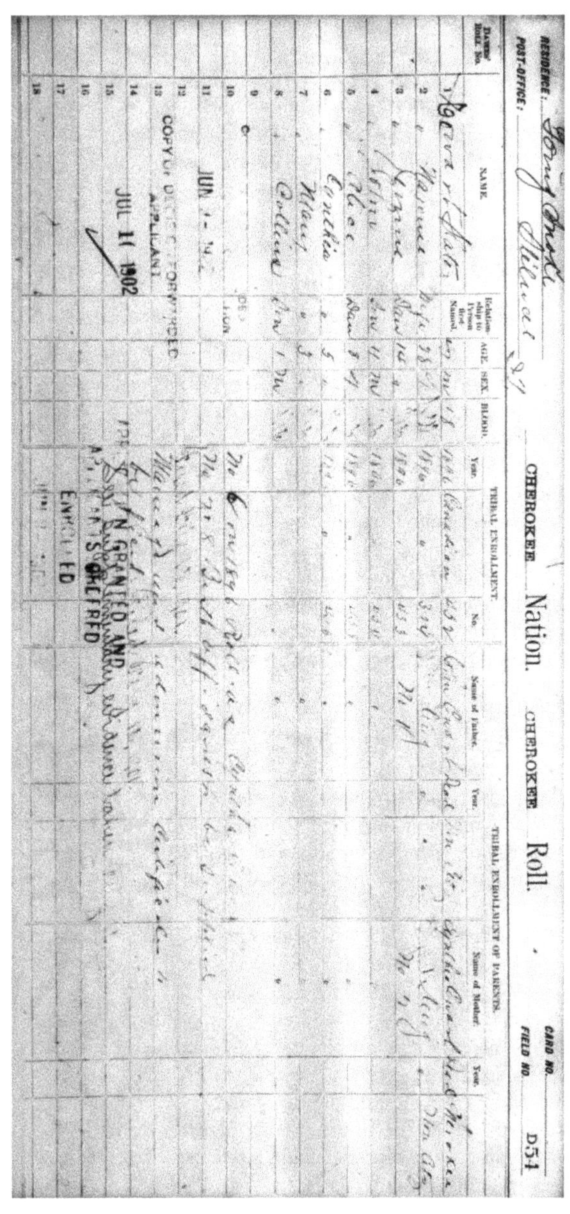

RESIDENCE:
POST-OFFICE:

CHEROKEE Nation. CHEROKEE Roll.

CARD NO.
FIELD NO. D54

JUN 1 - 1902

COPY OF DECISION FORWARDED APPLICANT

JUL 11 1902

Department of the Interior,
Commission to the Five Civilized Tribes,
Stillwell[sic], I.T., July 24, 1900.

In the matter of the application of Slater Cowart for the enrollment of himself and children as Cherokees by blood, and for the enrollment of his wife as an intermarried Cherokee; being duly sworn and examined by Commissioner Breckenridge[sic], he testified as follows:

Q What is your name? A Slater Cowart.
Q How old are you? A 47.
Q What is your post office? A Stillwell.
Q What is your district? A Going Snake.
Q How long have you lived in that district? A About a year.
Q Where did you live before that? A Canadian district.
Q How long did you live there? A 25 or 26 years.
Q Do you mean to say your residence is now in the Indian Territory and has been for the last 25 or 26 years and in the Cherokee Nation? A Yes, sir.
Q Who do you apply for enrollment for now? A Myself, wife and children.
Q Do you apply as a Cherokee by blood? A Yes, sir, for myself.
Q Were you enrolled in 1880? A I must have been, I was in Illinois district at that time.
Q Do you remember whether you were on the roll of 1880 or not?
A No, sir, it must have been I was off on a trip at that time in Tennessee.
Q Were you admitted to citizenship by the action of the Council?
A Yes, sir.
Q Have you got your certificate? A No, sir.
Q When were you first admitted A First in 1874, and in about 1883 or 84 or 85 or somewhere along there.
Q What has become of your certificate? A I never had one.
Q How do you know you were admitted? A I applied to the Council.
Q What district were you living in in 1894? A Canadian.
Q Did you draw money in 1894? A Yes, sir.
Q Is James S. your name? A No, sir.
(On 1896 roll, page 16, No. 452, Slater Cowart, Canadian district.)
Q[sic] I think I gave an order to James S. Harris for the money in 1894 and then he drew it, and that is the way that James S. comes in.
(On 1894 roll, page 20, No. 451, Slater Coward, Canadian dist.)
Q Is your wife a Cherokee by blood? A Yes, sir, by adoption.
Q She is a white woman? A Yes, sir.
Q When were you married? A In 1885.
Q Have you got any certificate of marriage? A No, sir.
Q Have you got any personal testimony here of your marriage?
A No, sir, I can't get any.
Q Anybody around here knows anything about it? A No, sir, I have only been around here about 12 months, I can get plenty of testimony there.

Q You have got plenty of testimony where? A In Canadian.
Q You have got some children you want to apply for? A Yes, sir.
Q Give their names please? A Jennie, age 14.
(On 1896 roll, page 16, No. 453, Jennie Coward, Canadian dist.)
Q Your next child now? A John, age 11.
(On 1896 roll, page 16, No. 454, John Cowart, Canadian dist.)
Q Now your next child? A Alice, age 8.
(On 1896 roll, page 16, No. 455, Alice Cowart, Canadian dist.)
Q Your next child? A Cynthia, 5 years old.
(On 1896 roll, page 16, No. 456, Cynthia Coward, Canadian dist.)
Q Any more children? A Mary.
Q How old is Mary? A Three.
Q Have you got a certificate of birth for Mary? A Yes, sir.
Q What is the next one? A Collins, 1 year old.
Q What is your wife's name? A Nannie Cowart.
Q What is her age? A 28.
(On 1896 roll, page 95, No. 324, Nannie Cowart, Canadian district.)
Q How old was she when you married her? A About 14.
Q Mr. Cowart, are you and your wife living together at this time? A Yes, sir.
Q Are these children all living? A Yes, sir.
Q Why haven't you got a certificate of your re-admission in 1884
A I don't know why, they never have given me any certificate, they just put it on record.

Q The rights of yourself and your family depent[sic] largely on evidence of your re-admission in 1884. You then need to supply the Commission with a satisfactory certificate of your marriage, or if you cannot present a copy of your certificate of marriage, you need to supply the Commission with affidavits from people who know of your marriage, if possible, some who were present when you were married, and who can testify that you and your wife have lived together as man and wife according to the testimony that you have given here, confirming that testimony by neighbors.

Now you are identified on the roll of 1896, and also on the pay-roll of 1894, but it is not sufficient under the circumstances at present. Your wife is identified on the roll of 1896, but both of these things simply give us jurisdiction, they do not determine the matter in your favor. Your children are all identified on the roll of 1896, except the two youngest children. In the case of the two youngest children are are[sic] desired to have properly filled out the certificates of their birth and supply that to the Commission. So you understand now there are three things you are to do, first to get a copy of your certificate of admission by the Council, presumably in 1884, and the other is to more clearly establish the fact of your marriage, and the other is to properly fill out and certificy[sic] these certificates of birth of your children. If you will attend to these things, no reason is seen at this time why you should not be duly enrolled, and all of your family, but for the present, for the lack of such evidence, your application will be put upon a doubtful card, to await such action upon your part as has been indicated.

--------o--------

Bruce C. Jones, being duly sworn, says that as stenographer to the Commission to the Five Civilized Tribes he reported the testimony of the above named witness, and that the foregoing is a full, true and correct translation of his stenographic notes.

Bruce C Jones

Sworn to and subscribed before me this the 30th day of July, 1900.

T B Needles
Commissioner.

SUPPLEMENTAL TESTIMONY.

D #54.

DEPARTMENT OF THE INTERIOR,
COMMISSION TO THE FIVE CIVILIZED TRIBES,
MUSKOGEE, I.T., FEBRUARY 16th, 1901.

SUPPLEMENTAL TESTIMONY in the matter of the enrollment of Slater Cowart for Cherokee citizenship; said Cowart being sworn and examined by Commissioner Breckinridge, testified as follows:

Q Give me your full name? A Slater Cowart.
Q How old are you? A 48.
Q You applied for enrollment at Stillwell[sic] back in July? A Yes, sir.

Com'r Breckinridge:--The applicant now presents a certificate of marriage showing that he and his wife, Nannie King, were united in marriage October 4, 1885, by R. G. Parks, who is known as a Minister of the gospel and whose credentials are of record Book A. page 55 as indicated in the certificate. This is filed herewith.

Q Now your wife's maiden name was King was it, Nannie King? A Yes, sir.
Q Were you ever married except to this wife? A No, sir.
Q Was she ever married except to you? A No, sir.

Com'r Breckinridge:--The applicant also presents an official copy of an Act of the Cherokee Council approved November 19th, 1880 admitting him to citizenship as a Cherokee by blood. This is filed herewith.

Q Have you certificates of the birth of your two younger children?
A That's them there if they are fixed up right.

Com'r Breckinridge:--This testimony with the documents referred to will be filed with case D. #56 and attention will be called to it on the card.

---oooOOOooo---

J. O. Rosson, being first duly sworn, states that as stenographer to the Commission to the Five Civilized Tribes, states[sic] that as suck he correctly recorded the testimony and proceedings in this case and that the foregoing is a true and complete transcript of his stenographic notes thereof.

J O Rosson

Subscribed and sworn to before me this 18th day of February, 1901.

T B Needles

Commissioner.

CHEROKEE D 54

DEPARTMENT OF THE INTERIOR,

COMMISSION TO THE FIVE CIVILIZED TRIBES.

In the matter of the application of Slater Cowart, et.al. for enrollment as Cherokee citizens,

On the 24th day of July, 1900, Slater Cowart appeared before the Commission to the Five Civilized Tribes, and made application for the enrollment of himself and minor children, Jennie, John, Alice, Cynthia, Mary and Collins Cowart as citizens by blood of the Cherokee Nation, and for his wife Nannie Cowart as a citizen by intermarriage of the Cherokee Nation.

At the conclusion of the evidence offered at that time the names of all the parties herein were placed upon a "Doubtful" card awaiting proof of the re-admission of Slater Cowart to citizenship in the Cherokee Nation as alleged, also proof of marriage between himself and wife, and proof of birth of his two youngest children.

Further evidence in these matter has been submitted to the Commission and the following decision is rendered.

DECISION

--oOo--

From all the evidence of record in this case it appears that Slater Cowart was re-admitted to citizenship in the Cherokee Nation by an Act of the Cherokee National

Council on the 19th day of November, 1880. He testified that he had lived in the Cherokee Nation for twenty five or twenty-sic years prior to the date of his application for enrollment. He is identified on the Cherokee Census roll of 1896, and on the strip payment roll of 1894. His wife, Nannie Cowart is a white woman, and was duly married to him on the fourth day of October, 1885, The children of this marriage, Jennie, John, Alice and Cynthia are identified on the Cherokee Census roll of 1896. The two children Mary and Collins Cowart are of course too young to be upon any roll of the Cherokee Nation, but it appears that Mary was born March fourth, 1897 and that Collins was born May second, 1899, and that they were both living on the 23rd day of July, 1900, the date at which the evidence of their birth was furnished to this Commission. It further appears that Slater Cowart and his wife were living together at the time of this application.

This Commission in making rolls of citizenship of the Cherokee Nation is governed by the following provisions of the Act of Congress approved June 28, 1898 (30 Stats. 495);

> "That in making rolls of citizenship of the several tribes, as required by law, the Commission to the Five Civilized Tribes is authorized and directed to take the roll of Cherokee citizens of eighteen hundred and eighty (not including freedmen) as the only roll intended to be confirmed by this and preceding Acts of Congress, and to enroll all persons now living whose names are found on said roll, and all descendants born since the date of said roll to persons whose names are found thereon; and all persons who have been enrolled by the tribal authorities who have heretofore made permanent settlement in the Cherokee Nation whose parents, by reason of their Cherokee blood, have been lawfully admitted to citizenship by the tribal authorities, and who were minors when their parents were so admitted; and they shall investigate the right of all other persons whose names are found on any other rolls and omit all such as may have been placed thereon by fraud or without authority of law, enrolling only such as may have lawful right thereto, and their descendants born since such rolls were made, with such intermarried white persons as may be entitled to citizenship under Cherokee laws."

Under the law and the facts in this case it is considered that Slater Cowart and his six minor children, Jennie, John, Alice, Cynthia, Mary and Collins Cowart are entitled to be enrolled as citizens by blood of the Cherokee Nation, and that Nannie Cowart is entitled to be enrolled as a citizen by intermarriage of the Cherokee Nation.

It is therefore so ordered.

Tams Bixby

T B Needles

C. R. Breckinridge

Commissioners.

Dated at Muskogee, Indian Territory,

JUN 9 - 1902

COMMISSIONERS:

HENRY L. DAWES,
TAMS BIXBY,
THOMAS B. NEEDLES,
C. R. BRECKINRIDGE.

ALLISON L. AYLESWORTH,
SECRETARY.

ADDRESS ONLY THE
COMMISSION TO THE FIVE CIVILIZED TRIBES.

DEPARTMENT OF THE INTERIOR,
COMMISSION TO THE FIVE CIVILIZED TRIBES.

REFER IN REPLY TO THE FOLLOWING

Cher. D-54.

Muskogee, Indian Territory, June 9, 1902.

W. W. Hastings, Esq.,

Attorney for the Cherokee Nation,

Muskogee, Indian Territory.

Sir:

Enclosed herewith please find copy of the decision of the Commission rendered June 9, 1902, in the matter of the application of Slater Cowart et al for enrollment as citizens of the Cherokee Nation.

You are hereby advised that you will be allowed fifteen days from the date hereof in which to file with the Commission such protest as you desire to make against the enrollment of the persons above named as citizens of the Cherokee Nation. If you fail to file protest within the time allowed these applicants will be regularly listed for enrollment.

Yours truly,

Tams Bixby
Acting Chairman.

Encl. D-54.

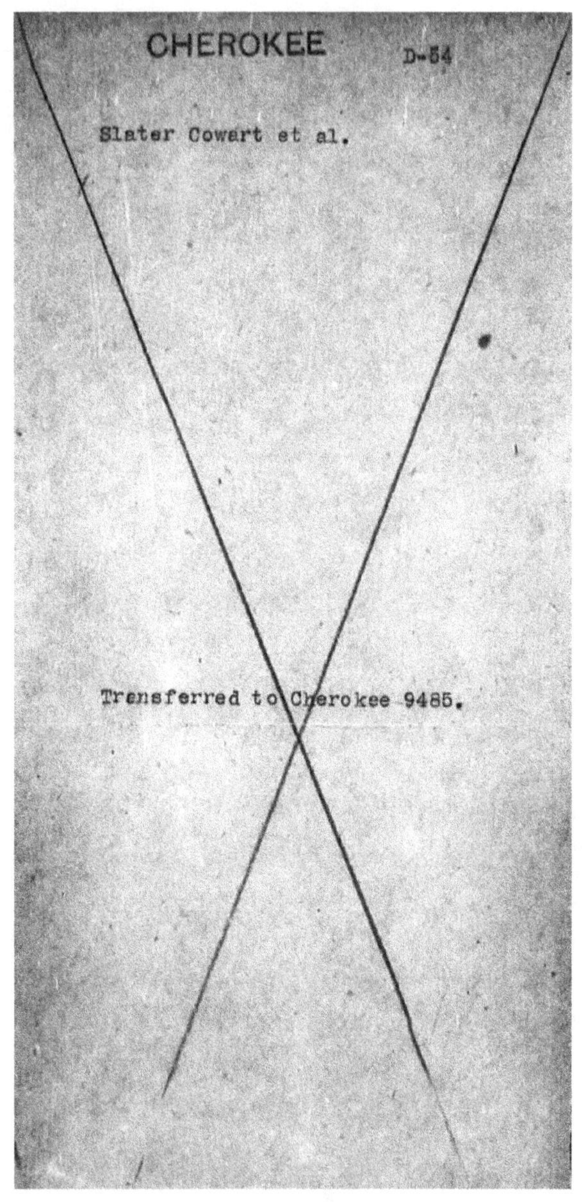

CHEROKEE D-54

Slater Cowart et al.

Transferred to Cherokee 9485.

RESIDENCE: Going Snake DISTRICT.
POST OFFICE: Stilwell I.T.

Cherokee Nation. Cherokee Roll.

CARD No.
FIELD No. [illegible]

Dawes' Roll No.		NAME.	Relationship to Person first Named.	AGE.	SEX.	BLOOD.	Tribal Enrollment Year.	District.	No.	Name of Father.	Year.	District.	Name of Mother.	Year.	District.
21541	1	Cowart Slater		47	M	1/8	1896	Canadian	452	John Cowart	Dead	Non citz	Cynthia Cowart	Dead	Cherokee
	2	" Nannie	Wife	28	F	I.W.	1896	"	2726	Wm King	"	"	Elizabeth King	"	Non citz
21542	3	" Jennie	Dau	14	"	1/16	1896	"	453	No 1			No 2		
21543	4	" John	Son	11	M	1/16	1896	"	454	"			"		
21544	5	" Alice	Dau	8	F	1/16	1896	"	455	"			"		
21545	6	" Cynthia	"	5	"	1/16	1896	"	456	"			"		
21546	7	" Mary	"	3	"	1/16							"		
21547	8	" Collins	Son	1	M	1/16									
21548	9	" Nittie	Dau	1	F	1/16									

GRANTED
JUN - 9 1902

No 6 on 1896 Roll as Cynthia Cowart
No 9, Birth affidavit approved October [illegible]
No 3 died December 20 1902: Evidence of death filed April 11, 1908

CITIZENSHIP CERTIFICATE
ISSUED FOR NO. [illegible]
FEB 10 1906

RESERVATION CERTIFICATE
ISSUED FOR No.
FEB 1909

Cherokee D55 - John W. Collins by Green B. Callahan

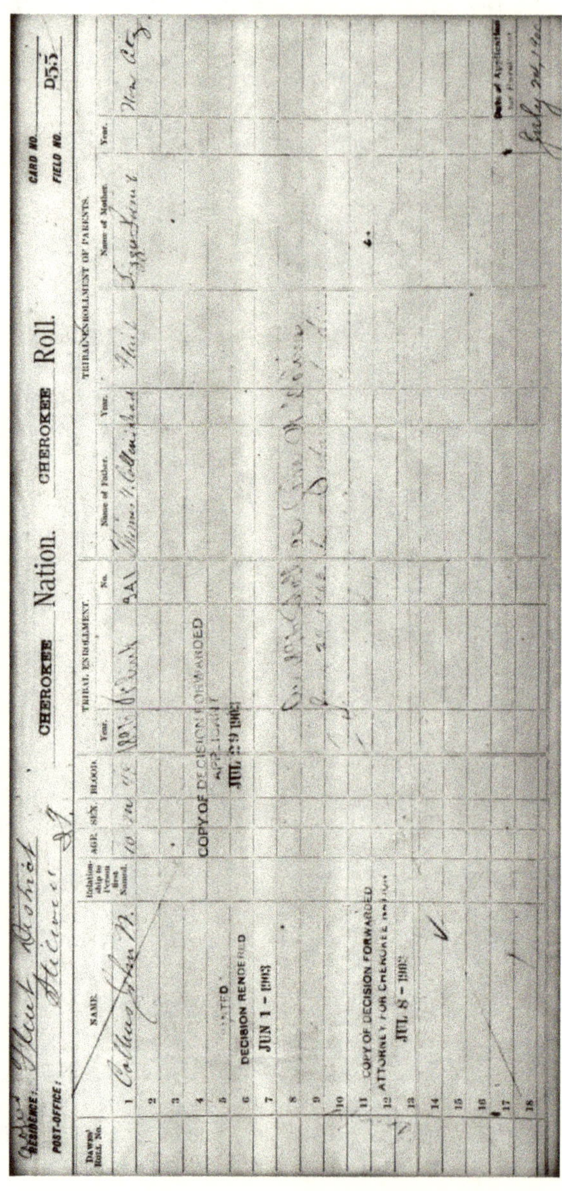
CHEROKEE Nation. CHEROKEE Roll.

CARD NO.
FIELD NO. D55

RESIDENCE:
POST-OFFICE:

Dawes' Roll No. | NAME | Relationship to Person first Named | AGE | SEX | BLOOD | TRIBAL ENROLLMENT | TRIBAL ENROLLMENT OF PARENTS

COPY OF DECISION FORWARDED APPLICANT JUL 29 1903

DECISION RENDERED JUN 1 - 1903

COPY OF DECISION FORWARDED ATTORNEY FOR CHEROKEE NATION JUL 8 - 1903

Date of Application for Enrollment.

Department of the Interior,
Commission to the Five Civilized Tribes,
Stillwell[sic], I.T., July 30, 1900.

In the matter of the application for the enrollment of John W. Collins, made by Green B. Callahan, guardian: Green B. Callahan, being duly sworn and examined by Commissioner Breckenridge[sic], testified as follows:

(See No.____, for application of Green B. Callahan for himself and family.)

Q What is your name? A Green B. Callahan.
Q What is your age? A 71.
Q What is your post office? A Stillwell.
Q What is your district? A Flint.
Q How long have you lived in this district? A 13 years.
Q Where did you live before that? A In Georgia.
Q Mr. Callahan, I understand there is an additional member of your family you want to apply for, a minor for whom you are guardian? A Yes, sir.
Q You hand me here letters of guardianship, by which you are appointed the guardian of John W. Collins, and duly signed by Benjamin F. Paden, Judge of the District Court, Flint district, December 27, 1893. Now the mother of this child is said to be Lizzie Land? A Yes, sir.
Q How old is this child? A About 10 years old.
Q The father of this child is said to be Tim Collins? A Yes, sir.
Q Now what was its mother named? A Callahan, my daughter.
Q How old is the mother of this child? A She is 33.
Q How does this mother get her right to citizenship? A By marrying Tim Collins.
Q She isn't admitted as a citizen at the time the others were?
A No, sir, she isn't any Cherokee.
Q Is Collins dead? A Yes, sir.
Q What evidence have you that she married Tim Collins? A I have not got any, John McPherson married her.
Q When did Collins die? A About a year ago, I think, I don't recollect.
Q Was Tim Collins and his wife Lizzie separated? A Yes, sir, they were not living together.
Q Well, that goes into the question of who was to blame; did he leave his wife, or did she leave him? A I don't know which it was.
Q Was a divorce granted? A No, sir, no divorce was ever granted.
Q Is this woman still living? A Yes, sir, the mother of that child is living.
Q You will have to explain this relationship that she had with Tim Collins to legitimatize the child. A I know they were married.
Q I have no evidence of that, and I don't know who did the abandoning, one of them abandoned the other and no divorce was granted; you have no decree to show to whom a divorce was granted? A No, sir, they just quit, and I don't know which one of them was to blame.

Q Well, Mr. Callahan, this application will be placed for the present on a doubtful card. The Commission does not see any material ground on which this claim can be advanced at this time, and it is disposed to reject the applicant, but the child's mother is living and for the present it will put it on a doubtful card in order that she may appear if she wishes in order to strengthen the case, or supply any additional testimony, written or otherwise, you or she may be able to produce, showing that this child was born in lawful wedlock. That will be the status for the present.

(On 1898 roll, page 651, No. 341, as John W. Colins[sic], Flint dist.)

----------o----------

Bruce C. Jones, being duly sworn, says that as stenographer t\o the Commission to the Five Civilized Tribes he reported the testimony of the above named witness, and that the foregoing is a full, true and correct translation of his stenographic notes.

Bruce C Jones

Sworn to and subscribed before me this the 30th day of July, 1900.

T B Needles
Commissioner.

D-55.

Department of the Interior.
Commission to the Five Civilized Tribes.
Tahlequah, I. T., December 8, 1900.

In the matter of the application of Green B. Callahan for the enrollment of John W. Collins.

Supplementary testimony.

Green B. Callahan, being sworn by Commissioner T. B. Needles, testified as follows:

Q What is your name? A Green B. Callahan.
Q What is your age? A 71.
Q What is your postoffice address? A Stilwell.
Q Are you a recognized citizen of the Cherokee Nation? A Yes sir, by adoption.
Q Who do you want to apply for enrollment, John W. Collins? A Yes sir.
Q What was his mother's name? A Lizzie Collins.
Q What was his father's name? A Thomas Tim Collins.
Q Was Thomas T. Collins a Cherokee by blood? A Yes sir.
Q Was his wife? A No sir.
Q Are they both dead? A No sir, he[sic] child's mother's alive.
Q How old is John Collins? A 10 years old.

1880 roll: page 360, #402, Tim T. Collins, Flint district
Q You know when he was married to his wife, Lizzie? A I think it was in '88. I won't be certain.
Q When did Tim Collins die? A I don't recollect. Its[sic] been two or three years.
Q What district would he be in in 1896? A In Flint.
1894 roll: page 526, #424, John W. Collins, Flint district
1894 roll: page 526, #423, Thomas T. Collins, Flint district.
Q You know whether Thomas T. Collins was married to Lizzie Collins or not; you got any proof? A Yes sir, John McPherson here.

Witness, John McPherson, being sworn, testified as follows:
Q What is your name? A John V. McPherson.
Q What is your age? A 56.
Q What is your postoffice? A Sallisaw.
Q Do you know Thomas T. Collins? A Yes sir, as Tim Collins.
Q You know when he died? A About three years ago.
Q You know his wife, Lizzie? A Yes sir.
Q Was she a citizen? A No sir.
Q You know whether they were married or not? A Yes sir.
Q How do you know that? A I married them myself.
Q Was Tim Collins a Cherokee by blood? A Yes sir, always recognized as that.
Q You know whther[sic] he lived with her until his death? A No sir, they were parted.
Q You know anything about their having a child, named John? A They had one child, but don't recollect its name.
Q Before they parted? A Yes sir.
Q Tim Collins you say is dead? A Yes sir.
Q Is his wife living? A Yes sir.
Q Is she married again? A Yes sir.
Q Is she married to an Indian or white man? A White man.

Applicant recalled-
Q Where is this child? A Up with her now.
Q Won't she apply for its enrollment? A Yes, she would have, but as I thought as I was guardian that I was enough.
Q Has she been here and had him enrolled? A No sir.
Q This child is already enrolled? A I didn't know it had been enrolled.
Q Are you the father of Lizzie, the wife of Tim Collins? A Yes sir.
Q Do you know of your own knowledge that this child was born while they were living together as man and wife? A Yes sir.

Witness, John McPherson, recalled-
Q When were these parties married? A In '88.

Applicant recalled-
Q When did they separate? A I dn't[sic] exactly recollect.

Q How long did they live together before they separated? A No sir, I don't know exactly how long. I ain't certain whether they lived together until the child was born or not. I won't be certain about it.
Q You don't know how long after that separation this child was born? A No sir, I don't. The parted before it was born. There is a midwife that was there when it was born.
Q Why didn't you bring the mother of this child here? A I could have done so. I didn't know; I thought McPherson would be evidence enough.
Q Where does she live? A At Flint.
Q How far from here? A Thirty miles.

Witness, Minerva T. Thomas, being sworn, testified as follows:
Q What is your name? A Minerva T. Thomas.
Q How old are you? A 57 years old.
Q What is your postoffice? A Stilwell.
Q Did you know Tim Collins during his life? A Yes sir.
Q Did you know his wife, Lizzie? A Yes sir.
Q Do you know their child, John W. Collins? A Yes sir.
Q Were you there when it was born? A Yes sir, I was the midwife.
Q Do you recollect whether Tim Collins and his wife were living together or not?
A No sir, they weren't.
Q How long had they lived tgether[sic]? A I don't recollect how long. It wasn't more than two or three months.
Q They never lived together after that? A No sir.
Q Did Tim Collins acknowledge this child as his child? A Yes sir, I think he did.

Commissioner Needles-

The testimony taken today shows that Tim Collins was legally married to Lizzie Lamb, mother of John W. Collins, and the said John W. Collins is found upon the Census roll of 1896 as well as the pay roll of 1894. While the testimony[sic] says that the child was born a very short time after the separation of the father and the mother of said child, but there is no question from the testimony, but what the child, John W., was conceived in wedlock. The fact that his name is on the Census roll of 1896 and also the pay roll of 1894, the further evidence as to the legitimacy of the child, John W. Collins; and the opinion of the Commission at this time is that the said John W. Collins should be listed for enrollment as a Cherokee citizen by blood, and its name taken from D-Card 55, and placed upon a straight card.

E.G. Rothenberger, being duly sworn, states that as stenographer to the Commission to the Five Civilized Tribes, he reported in full the supplementary testimony in the above case, and that the foregoing is a full, true and correct transcript of his stenographic notes in said case.

E. G. Rothenberger

Subscribed and sworn to before me this 8th day of December, 1900.

T B Needles

Commissioner.

Cherokee D 55

DEPARTMENT OF THE INTERIOR,

COMMISSION TO THE FIVE CIVILIZED TRIBES.

In the matter of the application of John W. Collins, for enrollment as a citizen of the Cherokee Nation.

On the 24th day of July, 1900, Green B. Callahan appeared before the Commission to the Five Civilized Tribes and made application as guardian of John W. Collins for the enrollment of his ward, the said John W. Collins, as a citizen by blood of the Cherokee Nation.

At the conclusion of the evidence offered at that time the name of John W. Collins was placed upon a "Doubtful" card as the examiner was not satisfied with the proof as to the child's right to enrollment. Further evidence has been submitted to this Committee and the following decision is rendered.

D E C I S I O N.

--oOo--

From the evidence in this case it appears that John W. Collins is the ten year old son of Lizzie and Thomas T. Collins, known as Tim Collins. The said Thomas T. Collins is identified on the authenticated tribal roll of 1880 as Tim T. Collins and on the Strip payment roll of 1894 as Thomas T. Collins.

Thomas T. Collins was married to his wife Lizzie in 1888 and separated soon after marriage. The child John W. Collins was born soon after the separation of his parents. His name appears upon the Cherokee Census roll of 1896, and he lives with his guardian, who has been a resident of the Nation for fifteen years.

In making roll of citizenship of the Cherokee Nation this Commission is governed by the following provisions of the Act of Congress approved June 28, 1898 (30 Stats., 495);

> "That in making rolls of citizenship of the several tribes, as required by law, the Commission to the Five Civilized Tribes is authorized and directed to take the roll of Cherokee citizens of eighteen hundred and eighty (not including freedmen) as the only roll intended to be confirmed by this and

preceding Acts of Congress, and to enroll all persons now living whose names are found on said roll, and all descendants born since the date of said roll to persons whose names are found thereon; and all persons who have been enrolled by the tribal authorities who have heretofore made permanent settlement in the Cherokee Nation whose parents, by reason of their Cherokee blood, have been lawfully admitted to citizenship by the tribal authorities, and who were minors when their parents were so admitted; and they shall investigate the right of all other persons whose names are found on any other rolls and omit all such as may have been placed thereon by fraud or without authority of law, enrolling only such as may have lawful right thereto, and their descendants born since such rolls were made, with such intermarried white persons as may be entitled to citizenship under Cherokee laws."

In view of the facts and the law in this case it is considered that John W. Collins being the lineal descendant of a person whose name appears upon the 1880 roll is entitled to be enrolled as a citizen of the Cherokee Nation, and it is therefore so ordered.

(SIGNED). *Tams Bixby.*

T B Needles

C. R. Breckinridge

Commissioners.

(SIGNED). *W. E. Stanley.*

Dated at Muskogee, Indian Territory,

JUN 1 - 1903

COMMISSIONERS:
TAMS BIXBY,
THOMAS B. NEEDLES,
C. R. BRECKINRIDGE,
W. E. STANLEY.

ALLISON L. AYLESWORTH,
SECRETARY.

DEPARTMENT OF THE INTERIOR,
COMMISSION TO THE FIVE CIVILIZED TRIBES.

REFER IN REPLY TO THE FOLLOWING
Cherokee D-55.

ADDRESS ONLY THE
COMMISSION TO THE FIVE CIVILIZED TRIBES.

Muskogee, Indian Territory, July 9, 1903.

W. W. Hastings,

Attorney for Cherokee Nation,

Tahlequah, Indian Territory.

Dear Sir:

There is herewith inclosed a copy of the decision of the Commission to the Five Civilized Tribes, dated June 1, 1903, granting the application of Green B. Callahan for the enrollment of his ward, John W. Collins, as a citizen by blood of the Cherokee Nation.

You are hereby advised that you will be allowed fifteen days from date hereof in which to file such protest as you may desire to make against the action of the Commission in this case, a copy of which protest you will be required to serve upon the applicant. If you fail to file protest within the time allowed this decision will be considered final.

Respectfully,

T B Needles
Commissioner in Charge.

Enc. H-33.

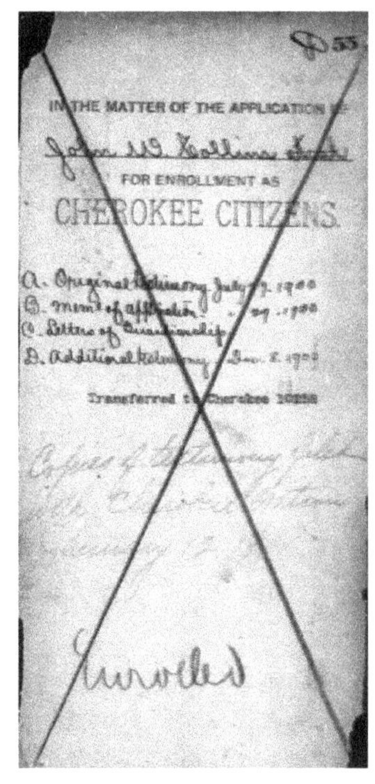

IN THE MATTER OF THE APPLICATION OF

John W. Collins

FOR ENROLLMENT AS

CHEROKEE CITIZENS.

Enrolled

RESIDENCE: Flint DISTRICT.
POST OFFICE: Stilwell, I.T.

Cherokee Nation. Cherokee Roll.
(Not including Delawares, Shawnees, or Freedmen.)

CARD NO. ______
FIELD NO. 10258

Dawes' Roll No.	NAME.	Relationship to Person first Named.	AGE.	SEX.	BLOOD.	Tribal Enrollment Year.	Tribal Enrollment District.	Tribal Enrollment No.	Name of Father.	Year.	District.	Name of Mother.	Year.	District.
29301	Collins, John W		10	M	1/8	1896	Flint	341	Thomas T. Collins	Dead	Flint	Lizzie Lamb		Non citz

CITIZENSHIP CERTIFICATE
ISSUED FOR NO. ______

GRANTED
JUN 1 1903

No1 on 1896 Roll as John W Colins

Date of Application for Enrollment: On Cherokee Card No D-55, July 24, 1900; On this card, July 29, 1903

Cherokee D56 - French Scott

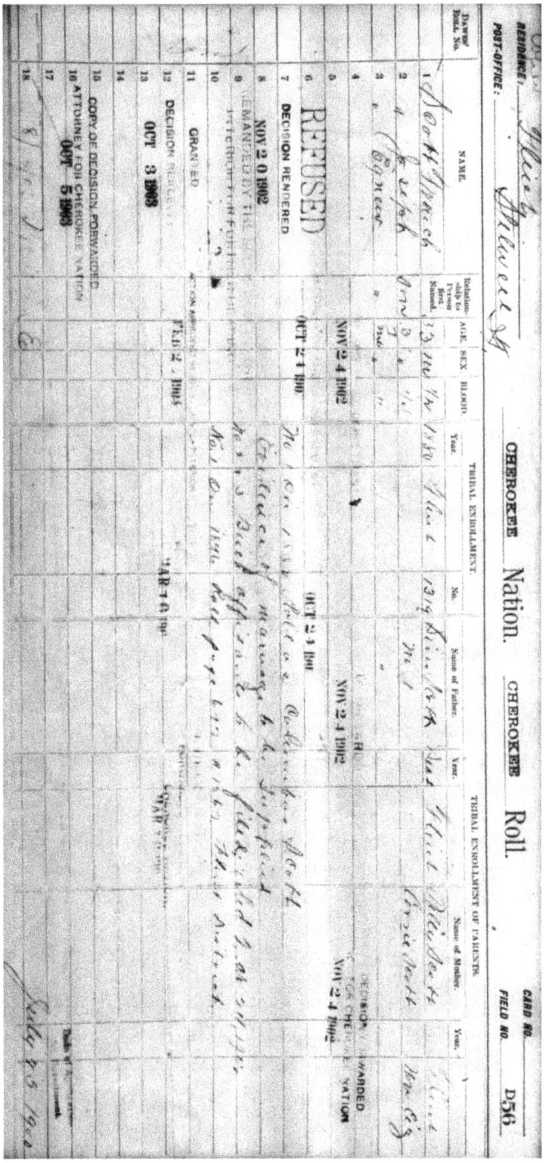

RESIDENCE: Illinois
POST-OFFICE: Stilwell I.T.

CHEROKEE Nation. CHEROKEE Roll.

CARD NO.
FIELD NO. D56

REFUSED

DECISION RENDERED NOV 20 1902

DECISION FORWARDED FOR CHEROKEE NATION NOV 24 1902

GRANTED FEB 2 1904

DECISION RENDERED OCT 3 1903

COPY OF DECISION FORWARDED ATTORNEY FOR CHEROKEE NATION OCT 5 1903

Cherokee D-56

Department of the Interior,
Commission to the Five Civilized Tribes,
Cherokee Land Office
Tahlequah, I.T., July 24, 1903.

In the matter of the application of French Scott for the enrollment of himself and his children, Joseph and Egnew Scott, as citizens by blood of the Cherokee Nation.

SUPPLEMENTAL TESTIMONY.

FRENCH SCOTT, being duly sworn and examined by the Commission, testified as follows:

Q What is your name? A French Scott.
Q How old are you? A 36.
Q What is your postoffice address? A Stilwell.
Q Have you a son named Joseph? A Yes sir.
Q And one named Egnew? A Yes sir.
Q Are they both living now? A Yes sir.
Q Are they all the children you have? A That's all.
Q Have you heretofore applied to this Commission for the enrollment of yourself and children as citizens of the Cherokee Nation? A Yes sir.
Q You claim to be citizens by blood, do you? A Yes sir.
Q Where do you live? A Live a mile north of Stilwell; born and raised right there.
Q Have you lived there all your life? A In about 1889 I think it was, I got into a little difficulty and had to leave the country, but I was in and out all the time, but I didn't let myself be known.
Q What year was it you left the Cherokee Nation? A '89.
Q Had you ever been out of the nation any length of time prior to 1889?
A Only just three or four months at a time.
Q Were you married in 1889? A Married in '96.
Q You were a single man at that time? A Yes sir.
Q Where did you go? A Part of the time I was in the Choctaw Nation and part of the time in Fort Smith, Arkansas, and part of the time in North Carolina.
Q Where did you go first? A When I first went, I went to North Carolina.
Q How long did you stay? A One month, then I come back to the Cherokee Nation.
Q What were you doing in North Carolina? A Wasn't doing anything.
Q Were you working there? A Yes sir.
Q Did you stay in any one place? A Yes sir. I boarded with a family named J. H. Shark; postoffice is Robbinsville.
Q Did you acquire any property in North Carolina? A No sir.
Q Did you vote in any election they had there? A No sir. Didn't pay no taxes nor nothing.

Q Then where did you go? A Came back to the Cherokee Nation.
Q How long did you stay here then? A Staid about thirteen months.
Q Then where did you go? A Choctaw Nation.
Q Where did you go from there? A Came back here again.
Q How long did you stay here then? A About eight weeks I think.
Q Then where did you go? A Spring of '95 I went back to North Carolina.
Q How long did you stay in the Choctaw Nation? A About four years.
Q You didn't claim to be a citizen of that nation did you? A No sir; I had an uncle as citizen there.
Q How long did you stay in North Carolina when you went back in '95? A I made two trips between '95 and 1900 but I don't remember just what years. Made two trips back to the Cherokee Nation.
Q They were just visits, were they? A Yes sir.
Q You were living in North Carolina continuously from 1895 to 1900, were you?
A Wasn't living there; just boarding there.
Q You were in North Carolina these five years? A With the exception of the two visits between the time.
Q Were you working there? A A little.
Q Did you acquire any property there? A No.
Q Did you ever vote there? A No.
Q You came back to the Cherokee Nation in 1900 and have lived here ever since?
A Yes sir.
Q Where were you married? A Married in North Carolina.
Q In what year? A '96.
Q Where was Joseph born? A Born there.
Q Egnew born there? A Yes sir.
Q Your wife's home was in North Carolina? A Yes.
Q Did you keep house with her there? A No.
Q Did you board there the four years after you were married? A Yes.
Q Did you board with your wife's people? A Yes.
Q You made your home then where your wife's home had been before you were married? A I didn't consider that my home at all; I considered my home here.
Q Irrespective of where you lived that is where you staid? A That's where I staid; didn't consider it my home.
Q That is where your two children were born, is it not? A Yes sir.
Q Has your wife been back to North Carolina to visit since she came here?
A No sir.
Q I believe you said you never acquired any property there? A No, didn't own any property there.
Q And never voted? A No.
Q When you left the Cherokee Nation the first time, in 1889, what property did you have here? A Had some cattle, had a mule, three head of horses - - - -
Q Did you have a farm? A Yes sir.
Q What did you do with that stock? A Left it here.
Q Where is it now? A Some of it is here. I have got some of the cattle yet, but the older stock died out; but then I have got some of the same stock from that stock.

Q You have the increase from that stock? A Yes sir. I sold some of it when I come back the last time.
Q That was the property you had here in 1889, was it? A Yes sir.
Q And when you left here in 1895, what property did you have then? A Had the same property.
Q And you still have that property now? A The increase, yes sir.
Q You still own the farm? A Own the same place.
Q When you were out of the nation, did you get the rents for your farm? A Yes sir.
Q Got the rents every year, did you? A Yes sir.
Q You were not here when they made the 1896 census roll, were you? A Yes, I came home; and I was put on the '96 roll by the Cherokee Senators and Council here at Tahlequah.
Q You and your wife are living together now, are you? A Yes sir.
Q These two children are living with you? A Yes sir.
Q The first time these two children ever came to the Cherokee Nation was in 1900?
A Yes that's the first time.
Q Have you voted in all the elections of the Cherokee Nation when you were present in the nation? A I didn't vote in one election when I was absent, but ever since I been back; I have helped in the elections as a clerk or as supervisor for 12 years.
Q You never voted anywhere else except in the Cherokee Nation? A That's all.

++++++++++++++++++++

Mabel F. Maxwell, being duly sworn, states that, as stenographer to the Commission to the Five Civilized Tribes, she correctly recorded the supplemental testimony in this case, and that the above and foregoing is a true and complete transcript of her stenographic notes thereof.

Mabel F. Maxwell

Subscribed and sworn to before me
this 25th day of July, 1903.

Samuel Foreman
Notary Public.

MFM

Cherokee D 56.

DEPARTMENT OF THE INTERIOR,

COMMISSION TO THE FIVE CIVILIZED TRIBES.

In the matter of the application of French Scott for the enrollment of himself and his minor children, Joseph and Egnew Scott, as citizens by blood of the Cherokee Nation.

D E C I S I O N.

The record in this case shows that on July 25, 1900, French Scott appeared before the Commission at Stilwell, Indian Territory, and made application for the enrollment of himself and his minor children, Joseph and Egnew Scott, as citizens by blood of the Cherokee Nation. The record further shows that on November 20, 1902, the Commission rendered its decision in the matter of said application and forwarded the same to the Department for approval; that the Department did not approve said decision, but on May 19, 1903, remanded the case to the Commission for further proceedings and readjudication; and that on July 24, 1903, further proceedings in the matter of said application were had at Tahlequah, Indian Territory.

The evidence shows that the said French Scott is a Cherokee by blood; that he is identified on the 1880 authenticated Cherokee roll, on the 1894 Cherokee strip payment roll and on the 1896 Cherokee census roll; that the said Joseph and Egnew Scott are his children, born since 1896, and are duly identified by birth affidavits made a part of the record herein.

The evidence further shows that the said French Scott resided in the Cherokee Nation all his life up to 1889, at which time he was sent to the penitentiary; that since 1889, he has at various times resided temporarily beyond the limits of the Cherokee Nation, but his home has always been in said Nation. During his absence he has always maintained ownership of live stock in the Cherokee Nation and has also maintained possession and control of a farm in said Nation. The residence of the said minor children is considered to have been in the Cherokee Nation since their birth.

It is, therefore, the opinion of this Commission, following the decision of the Department in the case of Joseph D. Yeargain, et al. (I.T.D. 2900-1903), that French Scott, Joseph Scott and Egnew Scott should be enrolled as citizens by blood of the Cherokee Nation, in accordance with the provisions of section twenty-one of the Act of Congress, approved June 28, 1898 (30 Stats., 495), and it is so ordered.

COMMISSION TO THE FIVE CIVILIZED TRIBES.

(SIGNED). *Tams Bixby.*
Chairman.

(SIGNED). *T. B. Needles.*
Commissioner.

(SIGNED). *C. R. Breckinridge.*
Commissioner.

Commissioner.

Muskogee, Indian Territory,
this OCT 3 1903

COMMISSIONERS:

HENRY L. DAWES,
TAMS BIXBY,
THOMAS B. NEEDLES,
C. R. BRECKINRIDGE.

—

ALLISON L. AYLESWORTH,
SECRETARY.

ADDRESS ONLY THE
COMMISSION TO THE FIVE CIVILIZED TRIBES.

DEPARTMENT OF THE INTERIOR,
COMMISSION TO THE FIVE CIVILIZED TRIBES.

Cherokee D-56.

Muskogee, Indian Territory, November 24, 1902.

Mr. W. W. Hastings,

Attorney for Cherokee Nation,

Muskogee, Indian Territory.

Dear Sir:

There is herewith inclosed a copy of the decision of the Commission to the Five Civilized Tribes, dated November 20, 1902, rejecting the application of French Scott for the enrollment of himself and his two minor children, Joseph and Egnew Scott, as citizens by blood of the Cherokee Nation.

The decision, with the record of proceedings had in the case, has this day been transmitted to the Secretary of the Interior for his review and decision.

The action of the Secretary will be made known to you as soon as the Commission is informed of same.

Respectfully,

Tams Bixby Acting Chairman.

Enc. H-108.

COMMISSIONERS:
TAMS BIXBY,
THOMAS B. NEEDLES,
C. R. BRECKINRIDGE,
W. E. STANLEY.

ALLISON L. AYLESWORTH,
SECRETARY.

DEPARTMENT OF THE INTERIOR,
COMMISSION TO THE FIVE CIVILIZED TRIBES.

REFER IN REPLY TO THE FOLLOWING
Cherokee D-56

ADDRESS ONLY THE
COMMISSION TO THE FIVE CIVILIZED TRIBES.

Muskogee, Indian Territory, July 6, 1903.

W. W. Hastings,
Attorney for the Cherokee Nation,
Tahlequah, Indian Territory.

Dear Sir:

You are hereby notified that on May 19, 1903, the Secretary of the Interior remanded, for the taking of additional testimony, the application of French Scott for the enrollment of himself and children as citizens by blood of the Cherokee Nation, Cherokee D-56. Additional testimony is particularly required as to the residence of the applicants.

The principal applicant has this day been notified that any further testimony he may have to present in this case can be introduced before the Cherokee Land Office at Tahlequah, on or before August 4, 1903, and on that day you can, if you desire, appear and introduce additional testimony on behalf of the Cherokee Nation.

Respectfully,

T B Needles

Commissioner in Charge.

MFM

COMMISSIONERS:

TAMS BIXBY,
THOMAS B. NEEDLES,
C. R. BRECKINRIDGE,
W. E. STANLEY.

ALLISON L. AYLESWORTH,
SECRETARY.

DEPARTMENT OF THE INTERIOR,
COMMISSION TO THE FIVE CIVILIZED TRIBES.

REFER IN REPLY TO THE FOLLOWING

Cherokee D-56

ADDRESS ONLY THE
COMMISSION TO THE FIVE CIVILIZED TRIBES.

Muskogee, Indian Territory, October 5, 1903.

W. W. Hastings,

Attorney for Cherokee Nation,

Tahlequah, Indian Territory.

Dear Sir:

There is herewith enclosed a copy of the decision of the Commission to the Five Civilized Tribes, dated October 3, 1903, granting the application of French Scott for the enrollment of himself and his two minor children, Joseph and Egnew Scott, as citizens by blood of the Cherokee Nation.

You are hereby advised that you will be allowed fifteen days from date hereof in which to file such protest as you may desire to make against the action of the Commission in this case, a copy of which protest you will be required to furnish the applicant. If you fail to file protest within the time allowed this decision will be considered final.

Respectfully.

Tams Bixby

Chairman.

Enc. D-21[sic].

COMMISSIONERS:

TAMS BIXBY,
THOMAS B. NEEDLES,
C. R. BRECKINRIDGE,
W. E. STANLEY.

ALLISON L. AYLESWORTH,
SECRETARY.

DEPARTMENT OF THE INTERIOR,
COMMISSION TO THE FIVE CIVILIZED TRIBES.

REFER IN REPLY TO THE FOLLOWING

Cherokee D 56

ADDRESS ONLY THE
COMMISSION TO THE FIVE CIVILIZED TRIBES.

Muskogee, Indian Territory, March 10, 1904.

W. W. Hastings,

Attorney for the Cherokee Nation,

Tahlequah, Indian Territory.

Dear Sir:

You are hereby advised that the Commission's decision dated October 3, 1903, granting the application of French Scott for the enrollment of himself and his two minor children, Joseph and Egnew Scott, as citizens by blood of the Cherokee Nation, was affirmed by the Secretary of the Interior on February 29, 1904.

Respectfully.

TB Needles

Commissioner in Charge.

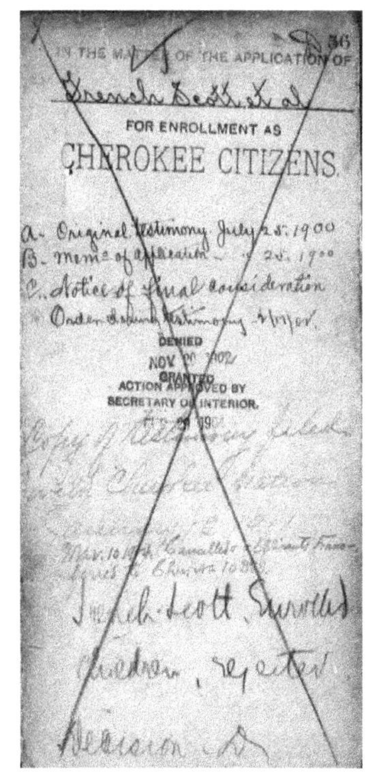

IN THE MATTER OF THE APPLICATION OF

French Scott et al

FOR ENROLLMENT AS

CHEROKEE CITIZENS.

A- Original testimony July 25, 1900

B- Mem of application 25, 1900

C. Notice of final consideration

DENIED

NOV 1902

GRANTED

ACTION APPROVED BY

SECRETARY OF INTERIOR.

Joseph Scott, Enrolled

RESIDENCE: Flint DISTRICT.
POST OFFICE: Stilwell I.T.

Cherokee Nation. Cherokee Roll.
(Not including Delawares, Shawnees, or Freedmen.)

CARD NO.
FIELD NO. 10388

Dawes' Roll No.		NAME.	Relationship to Person first Named.	AGE.	SEX.	BLOOD.	Tribal Enrollment Year.	District.	No.	Tribal Enrollment of Parents: Name of Father.	Year.	District.	Name of Mother.	Year.	District.
30892	1	Scott, French		33	M	1/2	1880	Flint	1319	Liver Scott	dead	Flint	Polly Scott		Flint
30893	2	" Joseph	son	3	"	1/4				No1			Carrie Scott		Non citz
30894	3	" Eghew	"	7/12	"	"				"			"		"

GRANTED
ACTION APPROVED BY
SECRETARY OF INTERIOR
FEB 29 19

NOV 1 19

CITIZENSHIP CERTIFICATE
ISSUED FOR NO.

No1 on 1880 roll as Columbus Scott
No1 on 1896 roll page 697 #1567, Flint District
Nos 2 and 3 birth affidavits filed Mar. 24, 1903
No1 died December 26, 1906 affidavit filed June 25, 1907

See NB #647

Date of Application for Enrollment: On Cher. Card No 10 56 July 25, 1900: On this Card March 10, 1904

Cherokee D59 - Isabell U. Moore

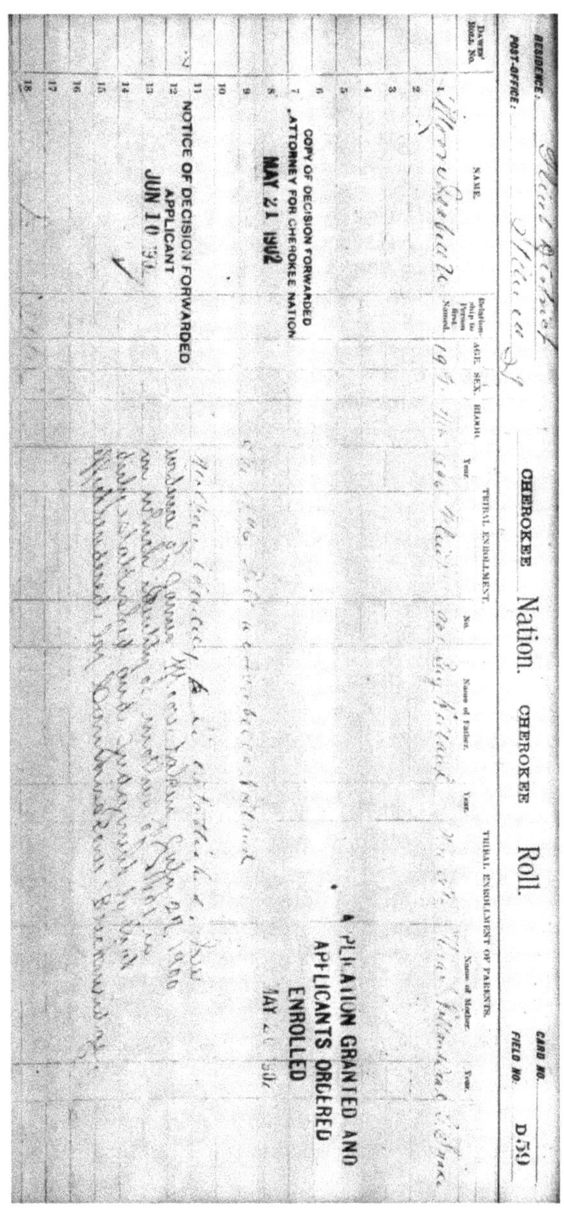

RESIDENCE:
POST-OFFICE:

CHEROKEE Nation. CHEROKEE Roll.

CARD NO.
FIELD NO. D59

Dawes' Roll No.	NAME.	Relationship to Person first Named.	AGE.	SEX.	BLOOD.	TRIBAL ENROLLMENT. Year.	TRIBAL ENROLLMENT. No.	Name of Father.	Year.	TRIBAL ENROLLMENT OF PARENTS. Name of Mother.	Year.

COPY OF DECISION FORWARDED
ATTORNEY FOR CHEROKEE NATION
MAY 21 1902

NOTICE OF DECISION FORWARDED
APPLICANT
JUN 10 '02

APPLICATION GRANTED AND
APPLICANTS ORDERED
ENROLLED
MAY 20 1902

Department of the Interior,
Commission to the Five Civilized Tribes,
Stilwell, I.T., July 27, 1900.

D. 59.

In the matter of the application for the enrollment of Isabell U. Moore.

James Moore, being duly sworn and examined by Commissioner Breckenridge[sic], testified as follows:

Q What is your name? A James Moore.

Q Mr. Moore, you appear now to supplement the evidence in the application you made for the enrollment of your wife, Isabell Moore. As I understand it, the trouble was that your wife's mother couldn't be identified on the roll of 1880?

A Yes, sir.

Q What did you give as your wife's name before you married her?

A Isabell Holland.

Q How do you spell that last name? A H-o-l-l-a-n-d.

Q I believe you gave this morning the name of her mother as Flora S. Holland?

A Yes, sir.

Q You present now a duly authenticated marriage license signed by W. C. Ghormley, Clerk of Going Snake district, dated January 22, 1881, and given under the seal of his office, authorizing the marriage between B. G. Holland, a citizen of the United States, and Mrs. F. S. Crittendin[sic], a Cherokee citizen by blood. The certificate of marriage shows that the marriage was duly consummated on the 24th of January, 1881, and the documents are properly recorded. This indicates that your wife's mother only acquired the name of Holland in 1881, and that her right name in 1880 was Crittenden? A Yes, sir.

(On 1880 roll, page 421, No. 431, Susan Critdenten[sic], Going Snake district, 20 years old.)

Benjamin G. Holland, being sworn and examined by Commissioner Breckenridge, testified as follows:

Q What is your name? A Benjamin G. Holland.

Q What is your age? A 60.

Q What is your post office? A Stilwel.

Q How long have you lived in this section of the country? A I came here in 1877.

Q Did you know one F. S. or Susan Crittendin? A Yes, sir, she was my first wife.

Q Do you know this applicant here, James Moore, who applies for his wife, Isabell? A Yes, sir.

Q What kin is his wife to you? A She is my daughter.

Q Is she your daughter by this Susan Crittendin? A Yes, sir.

Q Do you identify the enrollment that you have heard here of her in 1880 as Susan Crittendin? A Yes, sir.

Q Her family connections and all as being her enrollment at the time? A Yes, sir.

Mr. Hastings, rpresentative[sic] of the Cherokee Nation: What was your wife's father's name? A James Crittenden.

Q And her mother's name? A Isabell Crittenden.

Commissioner Breckenridge[sic]: Your daughter and this gentleman are living together now as man and wife? A Yes, sir.

Mr. Moore, your wife being duly identified as indicated in the testimony, and identified as the daughter of F S. or Susan Crittenden, who is duly identified on the roll of 1880, she will herself be enrolled at this time as a Cherokee by blood.

-------o-------

Bruce C. Jones, being duly sworn, says that as stenographer to the Commission to the Five Civilized Tribes he reported the testimony of the above names witnesses, and that the foregoing is a full, true and correct transcript of his stenographic notes.

Bruce C Jones

Sworn to and subscribed before me this the 2nd day of August, 1900.

Clifton R. Breckinridge
Commissioner.

Department of the Interior,
Commission to the Five Civilized Tribes,
Stilwell, I.T., July 27, 1900.

In the matter of the application for the enrollment of Isabell U. Moore as a Cherokee citizen. James Robert Moore, being duly sworn and examined by Commissioner Breckenridge, testified as follows:

Q What is your name? A James Robert Moore.
Q What is your age? A 26.
Q What is your post office? A Stilwell.
Q And your district? A Flint.
Q How long have you lived in Flint district? A About 2 years, and 10 or 11 months.
Q Where did you live before that? A In Georgia.
Q For whom do you make application now for enrollment? A I want to make application for myself and wife, but I see it is not necessary to make application for myself, it is only for my wife.
Q Is your wife a Cherokee by blood? A Yes, sir.
Q What is your wife's name? A Isabell Unitia Moore.
Q How old is your wife? A 19 years old.
Q What was your wife's name before your married her? A Holland.
Q What was your wife's mother's name? A Flora S. Holland.

Q Is she living? A No, sir, she died in 1883.

Q When were you married? A In 1898.

Q What district was your wife's mother in in 1880? A The district above here, Going Snake.

(On 1894 roll, page 549, No. 886, Isabella W. Holland, Flint dist. On 1896 roll, page 674, No. 961, Isabelle Holland, Flint district.)

Q Mr. Moore, you present here a duly certified marriage license and certificate of marriage showing that marriage between yourself and Isabella Holland was authorized the 2nd of November, 1898, signed by James A. Winston, Clerk of the United States Court, said license being under the seal of the United States Court. The certificate of marriage is duly authenticated by J. G. Brendel, a minister of the Gospel, showing that your marriage took place in accordance with the license on the 7th of November, 1898. This identifies your wife as the Isabell Holland indicated in the enrollment. What proportion of Cherokee blood do you claim for your wife?

A 1/16 is my understanding.

Q Does she claim exclusively through her mother? A Yes, sir.

Mr. Moore, your wife is not to be found on the roll of 1880. As stated, she is identified on the rolls of 1894 and 1896, and duly identified through the certificate of marriage and marriage license cited, but her being on the rolls of 1894 and 1896 does not conclusively establish her right to enrollment. It simply gives this Commission jurisdiction over her case as an absolute matter of fact. It is found impossible at present to identify her mother upon the roll of 1880, her mothers[sic] name you have given in the testimony. Now at present your application for your wife will be placed upon a doubtful card, and you are desired to find out what was the real name of your wife's mother in 1880, and under what name she was enrolled, so that this Commission can identify her on the 1880 enrollment, provided that she was there, and also can identify your wife as the child of that woman enrolled in 1880, whatever her name may be; you get that information and supply it to this Commission either personally or by writing, and it will be taken into further consideration of your wife's application through you.

-------o-------

Bruce C. Jones, being duly sworn, says that as stenographer to the Commission to the Five Civilized Tribes he reported the testimony of the above named witness, and that the foregoing is a full, true and correct translation of his stenographic notes.

Bruce C Jones

Sworn to and subscribed before me this the 2nd day of August, 1900.

Clifton R. Breckinridge
Commissioner.

Cherokee D 59

DEPARTMENT OF THE INTERIOR,

COMMISSION TO THE FIVE CIVILIZED TRIBES.

In the matter of the application for the enrollment of Isabell U. Moore as a citizen by blood of the Cherokee Nation.

D E C I S I O N.

--oOo--

The record in this case shows that on July 27, 1900, James Robert Moore appeared before the Commission at Stillwell[sic],Indian Territory, and then and there made personal application for the enrollment of his wife Isabell U. Moore as a citizen by blood of the Cherokee Nation. It appears from the evidence that one Susan Crittenden is identified on the authenticated tribal roll of 1880, and that the said Isabell U. Moore is the descendants[sic] of said Susan Crittenden, born to her since the preparation of such roll. Isabell U. Moore is identified on the Strip payment roll of 1894 and the Cherokee Census roll of 1896. She was married to James Robert Moore on November 2, 1898. Her husband is not an applicant for enrollment.

The authority of the Commission herein is defined in Paragraph 1, Sec. 21 of the Act of Congress june[sic] 28, 1898 (30 Stats., 495).

It is therefore the opinion of this Commission that Isabell U. Moore is lawfully entitled to be enrolled as a member by blood of the Cherokee Tribe of Indians in Indian Territory, and that the application for her enrollment as such should be granted, and it is so ordered.

COMMISSION TO THE FIVE CIVILIZED TRIBES.

Tams Bixby
Acting Chairman.

T.B. Needles
Commissioner.

C. R. Breckinridge
Commissioner.

Dated Muskogee, Indian Territory,
this MAY 20 1902

COMMISSIONERS:

HENRY L. DAWES,
TAMS BIXBY,
THOMAS B. NEEDLES,
C. R. BRECKINRIDGE.

—

ALLISON L. AYLESWORTH,
SECRETARY.

ADDRESS ONLY THE
COMMISSION TO THE FIVE CIVILIZED TRIBES.

DEPARTMENT OF THE INTERIOR,
COMMISSION TO THE FIVE CIVILIZED TRIBES.

REFER IN REPLY TO THE FOLLOWING

D. 59.

Muskogee, Indian Territory, May 21, 1902.

W. W. Hastings, Esq.,

Attorney for the Cherokee Nation,

Sir:

Enclosed herewith please find copy of a decision of the Commission rendered May 20th, in the matter of the application of Isabell U. Moore as a citizen of the Cherokee Nation.

You are hereby advised that you will be allowed fifteen days from the date hereof in which to file with the Commission such protest as you desire to make against the enrollment of the above person as a citizen of the Cherokee Nation. If you fail to file protest within the time allowed you this decision will be considered final. the protest within the time allowed this applicant will be regularly listed for enrollment.

Very respectfully,

T B Needles

Commissioner in Charge.

Encl. D-59.

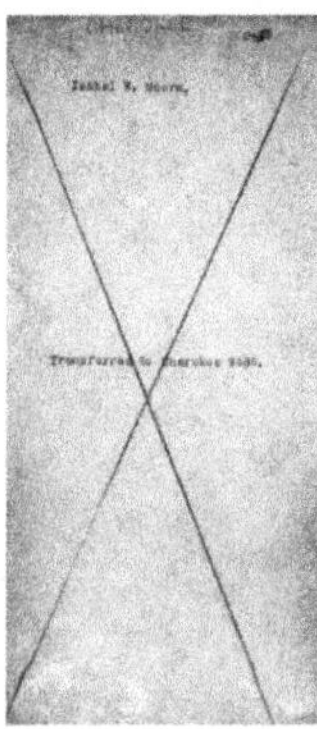

Isabel W. Moore,

Transferred to Cherokee [illegible].

RESIDENCE: Flint DISTRICT.
POST OFFICE: Stilwell I.T.

Cherokee Nation. Cherokee Roll.

CARD No.
FIELD No. 9486

Dawes' Roll No.	NAME.	Relationship to Person first Named.	AGE.	SEX.	BLOOD.	TRIBAL ENROLLMENT: Year.	District.	No.	TRIBAL ENROLLMENT OF PARENTS: Name of Father.	Year.	District.	Name of Mother.	Year.	District.
21549	Moore, Isabell U	X	19	F	1/16	1896	Flint	961	Benj. Holland		non cit	Flora S Holland	Dead	G. Snake

GRANTED
MAY 20 1902

On 1896 Roll as Isabelle Holland

CITIZENSHIP CERTIFICATE
ISSUED FOR NO.
OCT 14 1904

Date of Application for Enrollment

Cherokee D60 - Annie Aley or Alie Stayathome

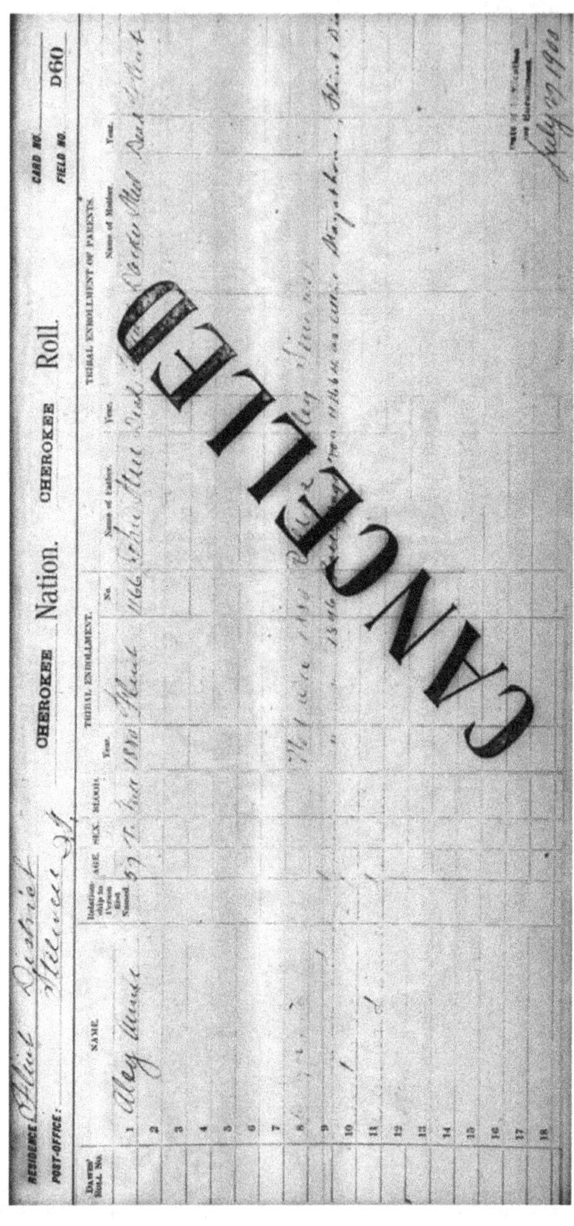

RESIDENCE: Flint District
POST-OFFICE: Stilwell I.T.

CHEROKEE Nation. CHEROKEE Roll.

CARD NO.
FIELD NO. D60

Dawes' Roll No.		NAME	Relationship to Person first Named	AGE	SEX	BLOOD	Tribal Enrollment: Year	Tribal Enrollment: District	Tribal Enrollment: No.	Name of Father	Year	District	Name of Mother	Year	District
	1	Aley Annie		57	F	Full	1880	Flint	1166	[illegible]	Dead	[illegible]	[illegible]	Dead	Flint

CANCELLED

July 27 1900

Department of the Interior,
Commission to the Five Civilized Tribes,
Stilwell, I.T., July 27, 1900.

In the matter of the application of Annie Aley for the enrollment of herself and two children as Cherokees by blood; being sworn and examined by Commissioner Breckenridge[sic], through Simon R. Walkingstick, a duly sworn interpreter, she testified as follows:

Q What is your name? A Annie Aley.
Q How old are you? A About 57.
Q What is your post office? A Stilwell.
Q What is your district? A Flint district.
Q How long have you lived in Flint district? A I have been here a long time, lived here all my life. I was raised here.
Q For whom do you apply for enrollment? A For myself and two children.
Q Do you apply as a Cherokee by blood? A Yes, sir.
Q What proportion of blood do you claim? A Full blood.
Q Are you on the roll of 1880? A Yes, sir.
Q What name did you have then? A Annie Stay-at-home.
Q Were you ever called Darkie? A No, sir, my mother was called Darkie.
Q Was your mother living in 1880? A No, sir, she died during the war.

William McLemore, being sworn and examined by Commissioner Breckenridge[sic], through Simon R. Walkingstick, interpreter, testified as follows:
Q What is your name? A William McLemore.
Q What is your age? A 51.
Q How long have you lived in this country? A I have lived here all my life.
Q What is your post office? A Stilwell.
Q How long have you know this woman here? A Since I have been a young man.
Q By what name have you always known her? A I have known her as Stay-at-home, Aley Stay-at-home.
Q Did you know any of her family? A Yes, sir.
Q What members of her family do you know, any brothers and sisters?
A I knew her brother, Johnson Simmons.
Q What was her name before she was married? A I remember this woman being called Still. [could be Steel]

William McLemore, recalled, testified:
Q What blood are you, are you a full blood? A Yes, sir.
Q Do you know this woman as a full blood Cherokee? A Yes, sir.
Q Did you know her mother? A No, sir, I didn't know her.
Q Did you know her father? A No, sir.
Q Have you known this woman all her life? A Well, from the time I was a young man I have known her.

Q Has she always been regarded by the Cherokees as a full blood Cherokee?
A Yes, sir, she is regarded as a full blood.

Annie Aley, recalled, testified:
Q Did you have a brother named Simons? A Yes, sir.
Q Did you sometimes go by the name of Simmons? A I think so.
Q Give the names of your brothers? A Johnson Simons was one, Charlie Gettingdown was another.
Q Have you got another brother named Joe Simons? A That is my son.
Q Ave? A That is my daughter.
Q John? A I have a son named John.

(On 1880 roll, page 390, No. 1166, Alley Simons, Flint district, 30 years old. Identified in connection with her children as indicated by previous questions. On 1896 roll, page 700, No. 1864, Allie Stay-at-home, Flint district. Not identified on 1894 roll.)

Q Now give the names and ages of your children? A William Stay-at-home, 15 years old.
Q What is the name of the next child? A Joe Stay-at-home, 13 years old.
Q Was he ever called Wakie? A I don't remember that they ever called him that. At the time the census takers came around I was away from home and some relatived[sic] had him enrolled.
Q Have you got a child named Ollie Stay-at-home, 16 years old?
A Yes, sir, 16 years old.
Q Who is Hooley? A I think that is my other son, he is 13.
Q Who is Colbin? A I think that Colbin is one of the boys I gave.
Q Did you ever call him Colbin? A That is pretty close to it.
Q Is your husband living? A No, sir, he is dead.

Madam, your application for the present will be placed on a doubtful card, along with the application that you made for your children, and you are desired to try and get some information about your claim, and introduce t to the Commission at a later date. The decision when finally rendered will be communicated to you by mail at your present post office address and all the papers in the case will be finally transmitted to the Honorable Secretary of the Interior for his approval or disapproval.

-------o-------

Bruce C. Jones, being duly sworn, says that as stenographer to the Commission to the Five Civilized Tribes he reported the testimony of the above named witnesses, and that the foregoing is a full, true and correct translation of his stenographic notes.

Bruce C Jones

Sworn to and subscribed before me this the 2nd day of August, 1900.

Clifton R. Breckinridge
Commissioner.

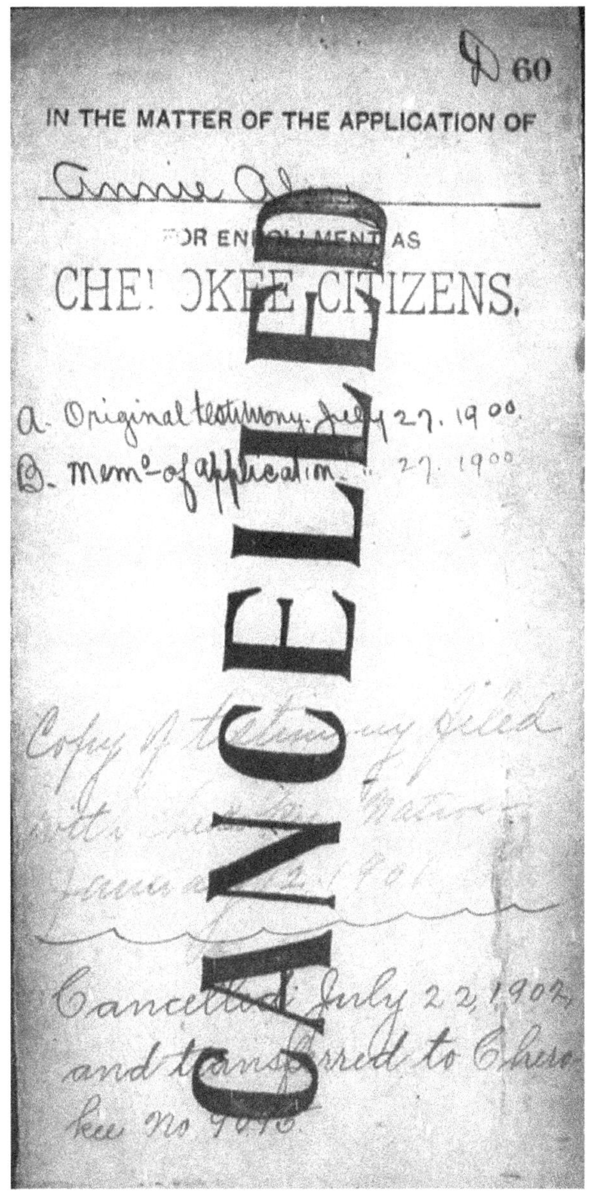
D 60

IN THE MATTER OF THE APPLICATION OF

Annie A

FOR ENROLLMENT AS

CHEROKEE CITIZENS.

CANCELLED

A. Original testimony July 27. 1900.
B. Mem^o of application " 27. 1900

Copy of testimony filed with ... ... Nation ... 1901

Cancelled July 22, 1902, and transferred to Cherokee No 9040

RESIDENCE: Flint DISTRICT.
POST OFFICE: Stilwell I.T.

Cherokee Nation. Cherokee Roll.
(Not Including Delawares, Shawnees, or Freedmen.)

CARD NO.
FIELD NO. 9095

Dawes' Roll No.		NAME	Relationship to Person first Named	AGE	SEX	BLOOD	TRIBAL ENROLLMENT Year	District	No.	TRIBAL ENROLLMENT OF PARENTS Name of Father	Year	District	Name of Mother	Year	District
20859	1	Stay at home, Elie		55	F	Full	1880	Flint	1166	John Steel	dead	Flint	Dorcus Steel	dead	Flint
20860	2	" William	Son	17	M	"	1896	"	1666	Stay at home	"	G. Snake	No 1		
20861	3	" Joe	"	14	M	"	1896	"	1667	"	"	" "	"		
	4														
	5	CITIZENSHIP CERTIFICATE ISSUED FOR NO. 1				ISSUED FOR No.									
	6	JUN 30 1905				APR 1 - 1908									
	7														
	8						No 1 On 1880 roll as Ally Simmons.								
	9						No 2 " 1896 " " Hooley Stay at home								
	10						No 3 " " " " Calbin " " "								
	11														
	12														
	13														
	14														
	15														
	16														
	17														
	18														

6/3/02 Date of Application for Enrollment.

Cherokee D63 - Luke and Benjamin Whitfield by Mathew J Whitfield

Department of the Interior.
Commission to the Five Civilized Tribes.
Bunch, I. T., July 30th, 1900.

In the matter of the application of Matthew J. Whitfield etal[sic] for enrollment as Cherokee citizens; being sworn and examined by Commissioner Breckinridge, testified as follows:

Q What is your full name? A Matthew J. Whitfield.
Q What's your age? A 45.
Q Your post-office? A Wauhillau.
Q Your district? A Tahlequah.
Q How long have you lived there? A 17 years.
Q Where did you live before that? A I came from Texas.
Q Have you lived in the Nation continuously for the last 17 years? A Yes sir.
Q For whom do you make application now to have enrolled? A Myself and two children.
Q Do you apply as a Cherokee by blood? A No sir, I don't.
Q Is your wife dead? A My first wife is dead.
Q Mother of these children, she's dead? A Yes sir.
Q You claim through that wife? A I claim through that wife, yes sir.
Q You claim for yourself through your present wife, do you? A Yes sir.

Mr. Whitfield, you present here a certified copy of the Cherokee authorities in regard to the admission of one Emma Whitfield. The certificate referred to is dated the 12th of September, 1884. It is signed by Eli Spears, President; John Lee and Andrew Young, Committee on Citizenship, and attested by John L. Adair, Clerk of the Committee. The endorsement on the back is under the hand and seal of W. H. Mayes, Ass't. Executive Secretary, dated Dec. 27th, 1893, and is to the effect that the paper just referred to is a correct copy of the decision in question as appears by the record of the Court.

Q When were you and Emma Whitfield married? A In 1875.
Q When did she die? A In 1890.
Q Have you any evidence of your marriage to Emma Whitfield? A Yes sir.
Q What evidence have you? A I have no certificate; not here. I was not married here to her.
Q Have you some personal testimony you can produce here? A Yes.

(I will proceed to that directly.)

Q You moved in here from Texas? A Yes sir.
Q What year did you come from Texas? A 1883.
Q When Emma Whitfield was admitted to citizenship as shown by the certificate you present here, she was at that time your wife, was she? A Yes sir.
Q Now did you and she live here from '83 to '90 to the time she died; all the time.[sic] A All the time, yes sir.
Q You spent that 17 years in the territory? A Yes, 17 years in the territory.
Q And these children were born during that time you lived in the territory?
A No sir; they were born before I come here.

Q Are these two children that you speak of on any of the rolls of the Cherokee Nation? A Yes sir.
Q Are they on the blood roll of 1894? A Yes sir.
Q And on the Census roll of 1896? A Yes sir.
Q Give me the names of these children and their ages? A Luke Whitfield, 19.
Q And the next child? A Benjamin, 17 years old.
Q They are both you say on the roll of '94 and '96? A Yes sir.
Q And you understand that their names are not in the certificate of citizenship that admitted their mother? A Yes sir, I understand that.
Q They are not in any other certificate of admission to citizenship? A Not that I know of.

John M. Sanders, being brought in as a witness, was sworn and examined by Commissioner Breckinridge, and testifies as follows:

Q Give your full name? A John M. Sanders.
Q What is your age? A 47.
Q What is your post-office? A Wauhillau.
Q How long have you lived in this section of the country? A All my life.
Q Do you know the applicant Mr. Matthew J. Whitfield? A Yes.
Q How long have you known him? A I have known him ever since he came into my neighborhood.
Q When did he come into your neighborhood? A I don't remember exactly what year.
Q Did you understand that it was when he first came from Texas?
A Yes sir.
Q Was that some 15 or 20 years ago? A I could not exactly tell just what it was.
Q Has it been a long or short time? A A good while ago, I can't say how long ago.
Q Do you remember his wife, Emma? A Yes sir.
Q Was she a Cherokee by blood.[sic] A She claimed to be.
Q Was she considered a full blood Cherokee? A I could not tell you about that.
Q Did she look like she was? A She was dark skinned.
Q Mr. Whitfield came here some time before his wife died? A Yes sir.
Q Do you know how long his wife has been dead? A Died somewhere about '90.
Q Did you know Mr. Whitfield some years before her death? A Yes sir. They lived in the neighborhood some time before she died, but I don't remember how long.
Q Some years was it? A I could not say how long it was.
Q A few months or a few years? A I do not remember, I could not say.
Q Do you know their children, Luke and Benjamin? A Yes sir.
Q Were they living before their mother died? A Yes sir.
Q Were they looked upon as the children of this woman, Emma? A Yes sir.
Q She and Mr. Whitfield were living together as husband and wife and claiming these children as their own? A Yes sir.

- Redirect.-

Note: 1894 roll; page 1174, #3484, Luke Whitfield, Tahlequah Dist.
1894 roll; page 1174, #3485, Benj. Whitfield, Tahlequah Dist.
1896 roll; page 1262, #3539, Whitfield, Luke, Tahlequah Dist.
1896 roll; page 1262, #3540, Whitfield, Benjaman[sic], Tahlequah Dist.

Now Mr. Whitfield, I will consider your present application as applying to these two children, but they go to a card for themselves, and the Commission will place their names on a doubtful card. They are enrolled in '94 and '96, but they are not enumerated in the certificate admitting your wife to citizenship, and they were alive at that time according to your own testimony. Therefore, the Commission will have to consider their rights in connection with the Cherokee law. Their residence, I understand from you has been in the Nation continuous ever since they came from Texas with their mother in 1883.

Mr. Whitfield you now call attention to a clause that had escaped my notice in reading the certificate of admission of your wife which is to the effect that she and her children are entitled to all the rights admitting them to citizenship in the Cherokee Nation. Now in every other certificate that has so far come before this Commission within my knowledge, the children have been enumerated by name. I request therefore that you let this certificate go with this application in order that this statement may appear in your case. The Commission will consider any question that arises in that connection and will let you know its decision through the mails[sic], at your present post-office address.

Edward G. Rothenberger, being sworn by Commission Breckinridge as Stenographer to the Commission to the Five Civilized Tribes, he reported in full the testimony of the above named witness, Matthew J. Whitfield, and that the foregoing is a full, true and correct transcript of his notes.

Edward G. Rothenberger

Sworn to and subscribed before me this 1st day of August, 1900, at Bunch, I. T.

Commissioner.

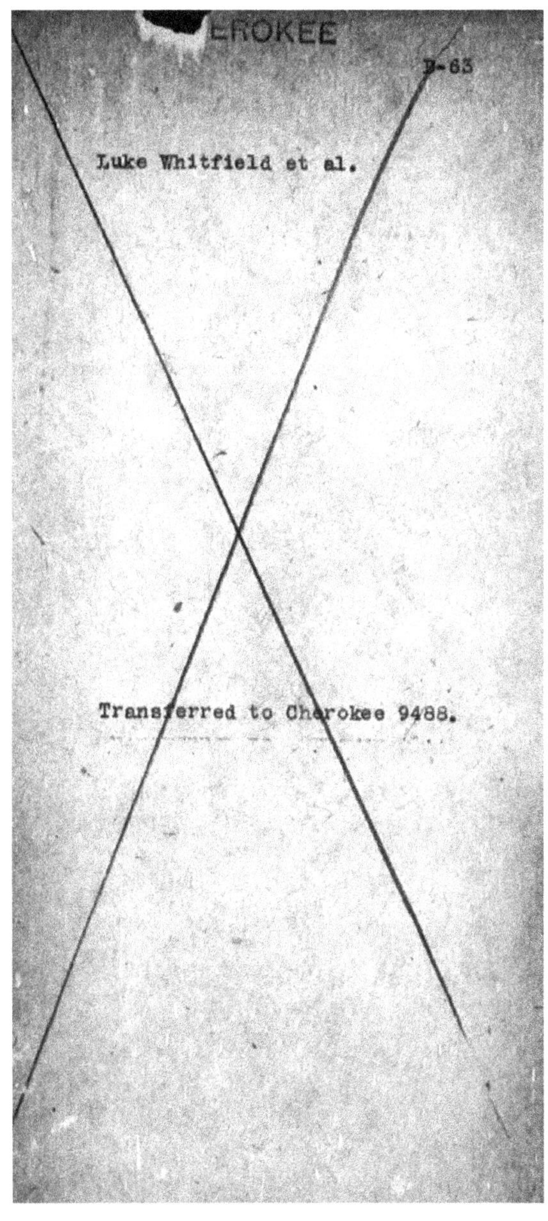

CHEROKEE

D-63

Luke Whitfield et al.

Transferred to Cherokee 9488.

RESIDENCE: Tahlequah DISTRICT.
POST OFFICE: [illegible], I.T.

Cherokee Nation. Cherokee Roll.

CARD NO.
FIELD NO. 9388

Dawes' Roll No.		NAME.	Relationship to Person first Named.	AGE.	SEX.	BLOOD.	Tribal Enrollment Year	Tribal Enrollment District	Tribal Enrollment No.	Name of Father	Year	District	Name of Mother	Year	District
21551	1	Whitfield, Luke		19	M	1/4	1896	Tahlequah	3539	Mathew J Whitfield		Non citz	Emma Whitfield	Dead	Tahlequah
21552	2	" Benjamin	Bro.	17	"	"	1896	"	3540	" "					

GRANTED
MAY 20 1902

No. 2 on 1896 Roll as Benjaman Whitfield

CITIZENSHIP CERTIFICATE
ISSUED FOR NO.
OCT 14 1904

CITIZENSHIP CERTIFICATE
ISSUED FOR NO.
OCT 14 1904

[illegible]

See NB 2847

Date of Application for Enrollment.

Cherokee D65 - Mary & Zakrona Feather by Samuel E. Adair

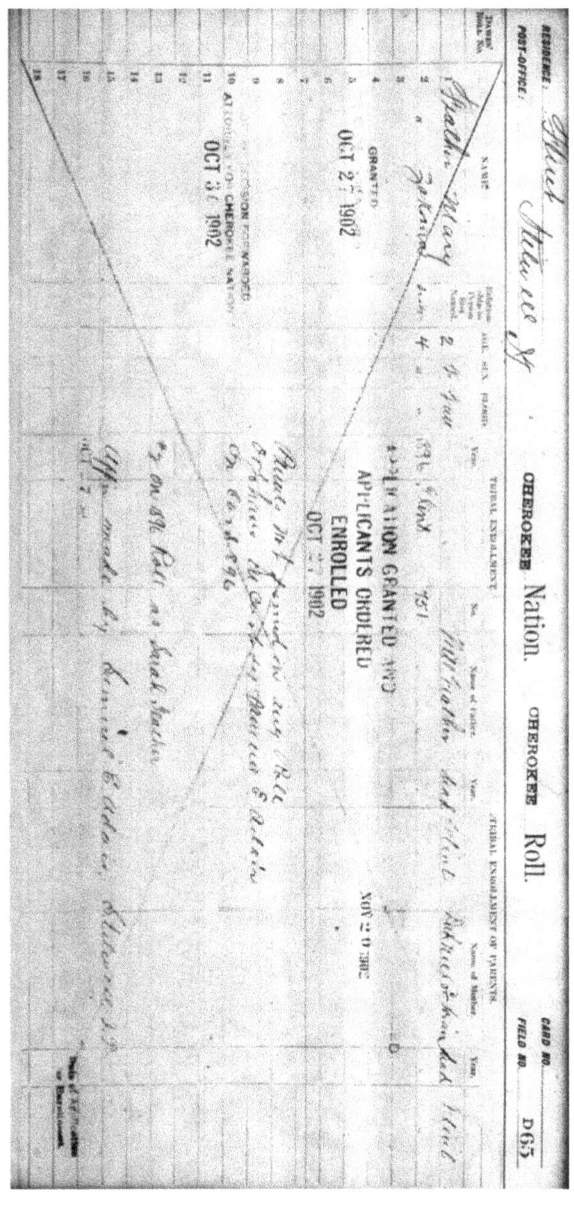

RESIDENCE: Flint
POST-OFFICE: Stilwell I.T.

CHEROKEE Nation. CHEROKEE Roll.

CARD NO.
FIELD NO. D65

GRANTED
OCT 27 1902

DECISION FORWARDED
ATTORNEYS FOR CHEROKEE NATION
OCT 31 1902

APPLICATION GRANTED AND
APPLICANTS ORDERED
ENROLLED
OCT 27 1902

NOV 20 1902

DEPARTMENT OF THE INTERIOR,
COMMISSION TO THE FIVE CIVILIZED TRIBES?[sic]
BUNCH, I.T. July 31st, 1900.

In the matter of the application of Samuel E. Adair for enrollment of his step children as Cherokee citizens, being first sworn by Commissioner Breckinridge, testified a[sic] follows:

Q Give your full name? A Samuel E. Adair.
Q What is your age? A Twenty nine.
Q What is your postoffice? A Stilwell.
Q What is your district? A Flint.
Q How long have you lived in this district? A All my life.
Q For who[sic] do you apply for enrollment? A Two step children.
Q Give their names? A Mary and Zakrona.
Q The oldest daughter? A Zakrona.
Q How old is Zakrona? A About four years old.
Q How old is Mary? A She is two years old.
Q Is Zakrona on the roll of 1896? A I dont[sic] know.
Q Was their father your wifes[sic] brother? A Yes sir.
Q Was the father a Cherokee by blood? A Yes sir.
Q Was their mother a Cherokee by blood? A Yes sir.
Q What was their fathers[sic] name.[sic] A Bill Fether[sic]
Q When did he die? A This January, two years ago.
Q How old was he? A I don't know exactly, but about twenty four or five.
Q What was their mothers[sic] name? A Dove Fether.
Q What was her name before she was a Fether? A Cochrum.
Q The mother is dead? A Yes sir.
Q How old was she when she died? A I don't know.
Q How long has she been dead? A Not quite a year.
Q Was she about as old as her husband? A I think not.
Q Is their mother found on the roll of 1880? A I don't know.
Q Under there what name would she be enrolled? A The daughter of Jim Cochrum.
80 roll, page 364, #526, Spade Feather.
96 roll, page 666, #749, William Feather.
Q Was the older child ever known as Sarrah[sic]? A No sir.

The evidence and a large amount of inquiry in and about the record indicates that these two orphan children are full blood Cherokees, but the names of their father and mother are so much obscured and varied that it is not found possible at this time to identify them in a satisfactory manner, and these applicants will be placed for the present on a doubtful card, Samuel E. Adair, who makes the application for these children is dirrected[sic] to make deliberate inquiry among the relatives of these children and to supplement the personal application if possible with information of a more accurate character.

| |

W.J. Hastain, being sworn states as stenographer to the Commission to the Five Civilized Tribes that the foregoing is a full true and complete transcript of his stenographic notes in said case.

Subscribed and sworn to before me this __________ day of August, 1900.

____
COMMISSIONER.

Supl.-C.D.#65.

Department of the Interior,
Commission to the Five Civilized Tribes,
Muskogee, I. T., February 17, 1902.

SUPPLEMENTAL TESTIMONY in the matter of the enrollment of MARY FETHER[sic], et al., as citizens of the Cherokee Nation:

Samuel E. Adair, Guardian, was notified on the 31st day of January, 1902, that on the 17th day of February, 1902, the application of Mary Feather and Zakomo[sic] Feather for enrollment as citizens of the Cherokee Nation would be taken up for final consideration by the Commission, and that he would on said date be given an opportunity to introduce any additional testimony affecting this case. Application has been called three times and fails to respond either in person or by attorney, and the case is closed.

C. R. Breckinridge
Commissioner.

WHA
Cherokee

Department of the Interior,
Commission to the Five Civilized Tribes,
Flint C. H., I. T., June 5, 1902.

In the matter of the application of Samuel E. Adair, for the enrollment of his two wards, Zackrona[sic] and Mary Feather, as citizens of the Cherokee Nation.

SAMUEL E. ADAIR, being duly sworn, and examined by the Commission, testified as follows:

Q What is your name ? A Samuel E. Adair.
Q What is your age ? A 30.
Q What is your post office address ? A Stilwell, I. T.
Q In what district do your reside ? A Flint.
Q Are you a citizen by blood of the Cherokee Nation ? A Yes sir.
Q Have you resided in the Cherokee Nation all your life ? A Yes sir.
Q For whom are you now making application ? A For my two wards.
Q What are their names and ages ? A Zakrona Feather, age about 5 years; Mary Feather, age about 3.
Q Are they both now living ? A Yes sir.
Q Do they live with you ? A Yes sir.
Q How long have they lived with you ? A About two years.
Q Are you their guardian ? A No sir, I never was appointed their guardian.
Q How did you secure the custody of these children.[sic]
A Well, their father and mother died, and they sent word for my woman to come and get them and raise them, and she went and got them.
Q What is the name of your wife ? A Martha Adair.
Q Is she related in any way to these children ? A Yes sir, she is their aunt.
Q Are these two children for whom you now make application full blood Cherokees?
A Yes sir full blood Cherokees.
Q Have they ever been recognized as citizens by the tribal authorities of the Cherokee Nation ? A Yes sir.
Q What is the name of their father ? A Bill Feather.
Q Is he living ? A No sir.
Q Was he a full blood Cherokee ? A Yes sir.
Q In what district did he reside ? A Flint.
Q What is the name of their mother ? A Tahney was her Cherokee name; her English name was Nannie Feather.
Q Is she living ? A No sir.
Q Was she a full blood Cherokee ? A Yes sir.
Q In what district did she reside ? A Flint.
Q Did Bill Feather have any Cherokee name ? A Yes sir his name is Spade.
Q Spade Feather ? A Yes sir.
Q How long have the father and mother of these two children been dead ? A I would guess about two years. The father died first. It has been a little ever two years since his death.

NANCY FOGG, called as a witness, being duly sworn, and examined by the Commission through official interpreter Thomas Sanders, testified as follows:

Q What is your name ? A Nancy Fogg.
Q What is your age ? A 33.
Q What is your post office address ? A Stilwell, I. T.
Q Are you a citizen by blood of the Cherokee Nation ? A Yes sir.

Q Have you been enrolled by the Commission as a citizen of the Cherokee Nation ?
A Yes sir.

--The records of the Commission examined, and it appears therefrom that Nancy Fogg was listed for enrollment by the Commission at Stilwell, I. T., during the month of May, 1902, as a citizen of the Cherokee Nation.

Q Do you know Samuel E. Adair who makes application for the enrollment of Zakrona and Mary Feather ? A Yes sir.
Q Do these two children now reside with him ? A Yes sir.
Q Do you lived in the neighborhood in which Samuel E. Adair lives ?
A Yes sir.
Q Did you know the father and mother of Zakrona and Mary Feather ?
A Yes sir.
Q Are they living ? A No sir.
Q What was the name of the mother of these children ? A Tahney Feather.
Q What was her maiden name ? A Tahney Cockrum.
Q Were you related go Tahney Cockrum ? A Yes sir.
Q What relation were you to her ? A She was my sister.
Q Was she your full sister ? A Yes sir.
Q Was she a full blood Cherokee Indian ? A Yes sir.
Q About how old was she when she died ? A She was about 21 years of age at the time she died.
Q How long ago did she die ? A About two years.
Q How many brothers did you have in your family ? A Only two.
Q Did you ever have a brother by the name of Tom Cockrum ? A No sir.
Q Have you a sister by the name of Bettie Cockrum ? A Yes sir.
Q Was Tahney Feather older or younger than Bettie ? A She was younger.
Q Was Tahney the next child in age to Bettie ? A Yes sir.

CINDY COCKRUM, called as a witness, being duly sworn and examined by the Commission through official interpreter Thomas Sanders, testified as follows:

Q What is your name ? A Cindy Cockrum.
Q What is your age ? A 32.
Q What is your post office address ? A Stilwell, I. T.
Q Are you a citizen by blood of the Cherokee Nation ? A Yes sir.
Q Have you been enrolled by the Commission as a citizen of the Cherokee Nation ?
A Yes sir.

--The records of the Commission examined and the name of Cindy Cockrum is found to be listed for enrollment as a citizen of the Cherokee Nation on Cherokee Indian Card #905.

Q Do you know Samuel E. Adair who makes application for the enrollment of Zakrona and Mary Feather ? A Yes sir.
Q Do these two children live with him ? A Yes sir.
Q Do you reside in his neighborhood ? A Yes sir.
Q Did you know the mother of these two children ? A Yes sir.
Q Was she a full sister of yours ? A Yes sir.
Q What was her maiden name ? A Tahney Cockrum.
Q How many brothers did you have in your family ? A Two.
Q Did you have a brother by the name of Tom Cockrum ? A No sir.
Q Have you a sister by the name of Bettie ? A Yes sir
Q Is she living ? A Yes sir.
Q Is she older or younger than Tahney ? A Bettie is older than Tahney.
Q Was Tahney next in age to Bettie ? A Yes sir.

--The 1880 Cherokee roll examined and the name of the father of Zakrona and Mary Feather is found and identified thereon as Spade Feather, at page 364, #526, Flint District;

--The 1896 Cherokee roll examined and the name of the father of Zakrona and Mary Feather is found and identified thereon as William Feather, at page 666, #749, Flint District;

--The 1880 Cherokee roll examined and the name of Tahney Feather, the mother[sic] of Zakrona and Mary Feather is found and identified thereon as Tom Cockrum, at page 359, #389, Flint District; together with the name of her sister Bettie Cockrum, at page 359, #388, Flint District;

E. C. Bagwell, on oath states that as stenographer to the Commission to the Five Civilized Tribes, he correctly recorded the testimony and proceedings had in the above entitled cause, and that the foregoing is an accurate transcript of his stenographic notes thereof.

E.C. Bagwell

Subscribed and sworn to before me this JUL 15 1902, 1902.

PJ Reuter
NOTARY PUBLIC. ~~Commissioner.~~

Sup'l. D - 65.

Department of the Interior,
Commission to the Five Civilized Tribes,
Muskogee, Indian Territory, August 5, 1902.

Supplemental proceedings in the matter of the enrollment of Mary Feather and Zacoma[sic] Feather as citizens, by blood, of the Cherokee Nation, Cherokee Doubtful Card, No. 65.

By the Commission:

Upon a further examination of the 1896 census roll of citizens of the Cherokee Nation Zakoma[sic] Feather, for whom application is made in this case, is identified upon said roll, page 666, #751, as Sarah Feather, Flint District, native Cherokee, 1 year of age.

Tams Bixby
Commissioner.

Cherokee D 65.

DEPARTMENT OF THE INTERIOR,
COMMISSION TO THE FIVE CIVILIZED TRIBES.

In the matter of the application for the enrollment of Zakrona and Mary Feather as citizens by blood of the Cherokee Nation.

D E C I S I O N.

The record in this case shows that on July 31, 1900, Samuel E. Adair appeared before the Commission at Bunch, Indian Territory, and made personal application for the enrollment of his minor nieces, Zakrona Feather and Mary Feather, as citizens by blood of the Cherokee Nation. Further proceedings in the matter of said application were had at Flint Court House, Indian Territory, June 5, 1902.

The evidence shows that the said Zakrona Feather and Mary Feather are the minor children of William Feather and his wife, Nannie Feather, who are both duly identified on the 1880 authenticated roll and the 1896 Census roll of the Cherokee Nation, as native Cherokees. The evidence further shows that the father and mother of the applicants are both dead. Sail Zakrona Feather is duly identified on the 1896 Census roll of the Cherokee Nation as a native Cherokee. Mary Feather is too young to be identified on any of the tribal rolls of said Nation, but is identified by personal testimony.

The evidence further shows that the applicants were born and have always resided in the Cherokee Nation, up to and including the date of this application.

It is, therefore, the opinion of the Commission that Zakrona Feather and Mary Feather should be enrolled as citizens by blood of the Cherokee Nation, in accordance with the provisions of Section twenty-one of the Act of Congress, approved June 28, 1898, (30 Stats., 495), and it is so ordered.

COMMISSION TO THE FIVE CIVILIZED TRIBES.

(SIGNED). *Tams Bixby.*
Acting Chairman.

T.B. Needles
Commissioner.

C. R. Breckinridge
Commissioner.

Dated Muskogee, Indian Territory,

this OCT 27 1902

COMMISSIONERS:

HENRY L. DAWES,
TAMS BIXBY,
THOMAS B. NEEDLES,
C. R. BRECKINRIDGE.

ALLISON L. AYLESWORTH,
SECRETARY.

ADDRESS ONLY THE
COMMISSION TO THE FIVE CIVILIZED TRIBES.

DEPARTMENT OF THE INTERIOR,
COMMISSION TO THE FIVE CIVILIZED TRIBES.

REFER IN REPLY TO THE FOLLOWING
Cherokee D - 65.

Muskogee, Indian Territory, October 30, 1902.

W. W. Hastings,

Attorney for the Cherokee Nation,

Muskogee, Indian Territory.

Dear Sir:

There is herewith enclosed a copy of the decision of the Commission to the Five Civilized Tribes, dated October 27, 1902, granting the application of Samuel E. Adair for the enrollment of his minor nieces, Zakrona and Mary Feather, as citizens by blood of the Cherokee Nation.

You are hereby advised that you will be allowed fifteen days from date hereof in which to file such protest as you desire to make against the action of the Commission in this case. If you fail to file protest within the time allowed this decision will be considered final.

Respectfully,

C. R. Breckinridge

Acting Chairman.

Commissioner in Charge.

Enclosure C. No. 65

Department of the Interior,
Commission to the Five Civilized Tribes,
Muskogee, Ind. Ter.
Official Business.
Penalty for private use, $300.

W. V. Hastings,
Muskogee, I. T.

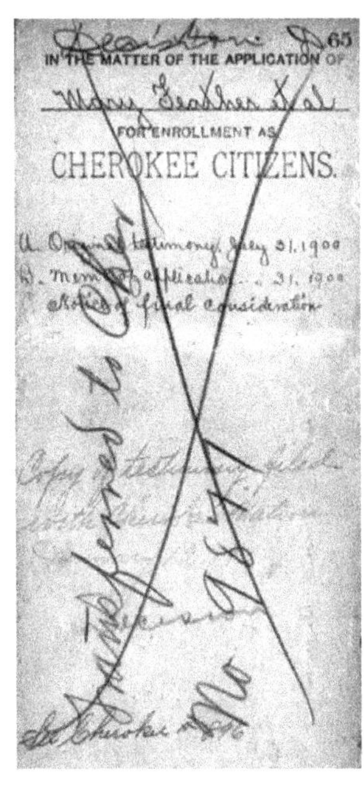

65

IN THE MATTER OF THE APPLICATION OF

Mary Feather et al

FOR ENROLLMENT AS

CHEROKEE CITIZENS.

a. Original testimony July 31, 1900
b. Mem of application " 31, 1900
Notice of final consideration

RESIDENCE: Flint DISTRICT.
POST OFFICE: Stilwell I.T.

Cherokee Nation. Cherokee Roll.

(Not including Delawares, Shawnees, or Freedmen.)

CARD NO.
FIELD NO. 9877

Dawes' Roll No.		NAME.	Relationship to Person first Named.	AGE.	SEX.	BLOOD.	Tribal Enrollment: Year.	Tribal Enrollment: District.	Tribal Enrollment: No.	Tribal Enrollment of Parents: Name of Father.	Year.	District.	Name of Mother.	Year.	District.
22144	1	Feather, Mary		7	F	Full				Will Feather		Flint	Sakie Cochran		Flint
22145	2	" Jakeonee	Sister	4	"	"	1896	Flint							
	3														
	4														
	5						Parents not found on any R								
	6						Orphans, in custody Samuel E Adair								
	7	GRANTED													
	8	OCT 2 7 1900					No. 2 on 1896 Roll as Susan								
	9														
	10						Application made by Samuel E Adair								
	11														
	12														
	13														
	14														
	15														
	16														
	17														
	18														

CITIZENSHIP CERTIFICATE
ISSUED FOR No. 1-2
APR

OCT 2 7 1902
Date of Application for Enrollment.

Cherokee D66 - Mige L. Brackett

RESIDENCE: Flint
POST-OFFICE: Dutch Mills Ark

CHEROKEE Nation. CHEROKEE Roll.

CARD NO.
FIELD NO. D66

Dawes' Roll No.	NAME	Relationship to Person first Named	AGE	SEX	BLOOD	Year	District	No.	Name of Father	Year	District	Name of Mother	Year	District
1	Brackett Mige L.		17	m		1896	Flint	1147	Wylie Brackett	dead	Cherokee	Mary Brackett	dead	Non Cit

No 1 on 1896 roll as Mige Brooker

COPY OF DECISION FORWARDED ATTORNEY FOR CHEROKEE NATION MAY 21 1902

APPLICATION GRANTED AND APPLICANTS ORDERED ENROLLED MAY 20 1902

COPY OF DECISION FORWARDED APPLICANT JUN 10 1902

Department of the Interior,
Commission to the Five Civilized Tribes,
Bunch, I. T., August 1st, 1900.

In the matter of the application of Mige L. Brackett et al for enrollment as Cherokee citizens; being sworn and examined by Commissioner Breckinridge he testifies as follows:

Q What is your name? A Mige L. Brackett.
Q What is your age[sic] A Twenty-seven.
Q In what disyrict[sic] do you live? A Flint.
Q How long have you lived in Flint? A Four or five years, I wont[sic] be certain.
Q Where did you live before that? A I lived in Tahlequah District six years ago.
Q Where did you live before that? A In Georgia.
Q For whom do you make application for enrollment at ths[sic] time?
A Myself and family.
Q Wife and children? A Yes sir.
Q Do you apply as a Cherokee by blood? A Yes sir.
Q Is your wife a Cherokee by blood? A Yes sir.
Q Do you apply for her as such? A Yes sir.
Q Are you what is known as an admitted citizen? A Yes sir.

Com'r Breckinridge: Mr. Brackett the certificate of admission to Cherokee citizenship that you hand me is dated August 16th, 1889, it is signed by Will P. Ross, Chairman of the Committee on Citizenship, and attested by D. S. Williams, Assistant Clerk of the Committee, approved and indorsed by J. B. Mayes, Principal Chief of the Nation, and under the Great Seal of the Nation; it admits, among others, one Mige Brackett, a child at that time sixteen years old; is that intended for you? A Yes sir.
Q I see the initial L is not in that name, how did that happen to be left out? A It was through carelessness of our guardian, we had a guardian at that time.
Q Was the name sometimes given a Migh and sometimes as Mige L.?
A Yes sir.
Q Mr. Bracket[sic], this certificate is a little different in some respects, it has the following citation from what is called the Act of December 5th 1888, entitled "An Act Creating a Committee on Citizenship, to-wit: That the persons to whom certificates of citizenship shall be issued by the Decree of the Commission created by this Act, shall be required as a condition precedent to the delivery of said certificates, to return to and permanently locate within the limits of the Cherokee Nation, and it shall be further the duty of all such persons to enroll their names with the names of their families (if any such) at the date of their arrival within the limits of the Nation in a book to be kept for that purpose in the office of the Principal Chief and no certificate of citizenship issued by said Commission shall entitle an applicant for admission into the Nation for (not) a longer period than one year from its date who shall fail to become a bona fide citizen within that period."
Now I observe on the back of your certificate the following indorsement[sic], "Enrolled in the Executive Department May 14th 1890" signed "C. J. Harris, Assistant Executive Secretary." This indicates, Mr. Brackett that you moved to the Cherokee Nation and were duly enrolled within the time prescribed by the Cherokee law; now

have you made your home permanently and consistently in the Cheroee[sic] Nation from May 1890 down to this time? A Yes sir.
Q Have you ever been out of the Nation? A Well, I went to mill a few times to Evansville, that's just across the line, but as for moving out, I never did.
Q Never more than going to mill? A No sir.
Q You have made you home and transacted business consistently in the Nation ever since your enrollment? A Yes sir.
Q Are you on the rolls of the Nation that have been made out since 1890? A Yes sir.
Q You say you wish to apply also for your wife? A Yes sir.
Q Does her name appear in the certificate you have just presented to me? A No sir, she is on the 1880 roll.
Q What is her name? A Susie. Her maiden name was Susie Christie.
Q How old is she? A She is twenty-two years old.
Q When were you married? A In 1893, I think it was, I wont[sic] be certain. It was either '93 or '94. I have got a certificate of marriage here, I guess it will show. (Produces certificate.)

Com'r Breckinridge: Mr. Brackett, you present here a certificate of marriage to the effect that you were lawfully joined in marriage to Susie Christie on the 23rd day of January 1893, by James A. Orr a Minister of the Gospel; it is signed by him, and he states that his credentials are recorded in the Clerk's office of the United States Court at Muskogee, in the book of Credentials page 166; now you say your wife is on the 1880 roll as Susie Christie? A Yes sir[sic]
Q And on the 1896 roll under your name? A Yes sir.
Q What district is your wife enrolled from in 1880? A In Illinois I think.
Q Now Mr. Brackett you say you want to have some children enrolled, give me their names and ages please? A Elizabeth J., five years old; Annie M., four months old.
Q Is that all, these two? A Yes sir, just two.
Q Where were you in 1894? A In Tahlequah District.

Note: 1896 roll examined for applicant; page 1018 #132 as Mige Brackett, Tahlequah District. 1894 roll, applicant's wife, page 1018 #133 as Susan Brackett, Tahlequah District. 1880 roll as applicant's wife; page 520 #510 as Susan Christie, Illinois District. 1896 roll examined for applicant; page 644 #147 as Mige Brackett, Flint District. 1896 roll, applicant's wife; page 644 #148 as Susie Brackett, Flint District. 1896 roll examined for their child; page 645 #149 as Elizabeth J. Brackett, Flint District.

Com'r Breckinridge: You present here a duly authenticated certificate of birth of your youngest child, Annie M. Brackett, on the 23rd day of March 1900. Has your wife lived with you ever since your marriage? A Yes sir.
Q And is she living with you at this time? A Yes sir.
Q Are these two children both living at this time? A Yes sir.
Q And living with you and their mother? A Yes sir.
Q Is there anything further that you want to say at this time in regard to the use of the initial L. in your name at present, and the omission of that letter when you were a boy and much younger than you are now? A Nothing only I was always known by that name, and it was just through carelessness of my guardian; you see I was raised an orphan and it was through carelessness of him in not giving it to the Commission.

Com'r Breckinridge: You are identified as stated in the testimony, and you certificate of admission dated August 16th 1889, according to the indorsement[sic] on your certificate of admission, and the testimony you have given about your residence, your residence in the Territory appears to be entirely satisfactory as regards your rights in that respect; you are further identified on the blood roll of 1894 and on the census roll of 1896; no hesitation would be felt at this time in enrolling you as a Cheroee[sic] by blood, except that the representatives of the Cherokee Nation have received a protest from one or more presumably citizens of the Cherokee Nation, saying that they wish to introduce evidence at Sallisaw contesting your right to enrollment. Now you application for yourself will for the present be placed upon what is called a doubtful or suspended card; but I wish to say, in the present light of the evidence that this is done without detriment to you, but simply to give a reasonable time within which any adverse testimony may be produced by the parties protesting, if they have it; otherwise your case appears entirely satisfactory.

Now your wife is found duly enrolled on the roll of 1880; her marriage to you is established by certificate of marriage which you have presented; she is identified on the rolls of 1894 and 1896; you claim for her as a Cherokee by blood. Your child, Elizabeth J. is identified on the roll of 1896, and your youngest child, Annie M., by a duly authenticated certificate which you have presented, and your wife and your two children just enumerated will not be enrolled as Cherokees by blood.

M.D. Green, being first duly sworn, states that as stenographer to the Commission to the Five Civilized Tribes he reported the foregoing case and that the above and foregoing is a full true and complete transcript of his stenographic notes in said case.

MD Green

Subscribed and sworn to before me this 3rd day of August 1900.

T B Needles
Commissioner.

Supl.-C.D.#66.

Department of the Interior,
Commission to the Five Civilized Tribes,
Muskogee, I. T., February 17, 1902.

SUPPLEMENTAL in the matter of the enrollment of Mige L. Brackett as a citizen of the Cherokee Nation:

Applicant was notified by registered letter January 31, 1902, that his case would be taken up for final consideration by the Commission on the 17th day of February, 1902, and that he would on said date be given an opportunity to introduce any additional testimony affecting his case. Applicant has been called three times and fails to respond either in person or by attorney and the case is closed.

C. R. Breckinridge

Commissioner.

J.O.R.

Cherokee D 66

DEPARTMENT OF THE INTERIOR,

COMMISSION TO THE FIVE CIVILIZED TRIBES.

In the matter or the application of Mige L. Brackett for enrollment as a Cherokee citizen.

On the first day of August, 1900, Mige L. Brackett appeared before the Commission to the Five Civilized Tribes and made application for the enrollment of himself, wife and children as citizens by blood of the Cherokee Nation.

At the conclusion of the evidence his wife and children were listed for enrollment on a regular card and the name of Mige L. Brackett was placed upon a "Doubtful" card at the request of the representatives of the Cherokee Nation present, they stating to the Commission that they would be able to present further evidence relative to applicant's rights to enrollment.

No further evidence has been submitted to the Commission and the following decision is rendered.

DECISION.

---oOo---

From the evidence of record in this case it appears that Mige L. Brackett is a Cherokee Indian, and that he was admitted to citizenship on the 16th day of August, 1889, by a decree of a Cherokee Commission on Citizenship. He came to the Cherokee Nation on the fourteenth day of May, 1890 and has resided there ever since. He is identified on the Strip payment roll of 1894 and the Cherokee Census roll of 1896.

In making rolls of citizenship of the Cherokee Nation this Commission is governed by the following provisions of the Act of Congress approved June 28, 1898 (30 Stats., 495);

> "That in making rolls of citizenship of the several tribes, as required by law, the Commission to the Five Civilized Tribes is authorized and directed to take the roll of Cherokee citizens of eighteen hundred and eighty (not including freedmen) as the only roll intended to be confirmed by this and preceding Acts of Congress, and to enroll all persons now living whose names are found on said roll, and all descendants born since the date of said roll to persons whose names are found thereon; and all persons who have been enrolled by the tribal authorities who have heretofore made permanent settlement in the Cherokee Nation whose parents, by reason of their Cherokee blood, have been lawfully admitted to citizenship by the tribal authorities, and who were minors when their parents were so admitted; and they shall investigate the right of all other persons whose names are found on any other rolls and omit all such as may have been placed thereon by fraud or without authority of law, enrolling only such as may have lawful right thereto, and their descendants born since such rolls were made, with such intermarried white persons as may be entitled to citizenship under Cherokee laws."

In view of the facts and the law cited it is considered that Mige L. Brackett is entitled to be enrolled as a citizen by blood of the Cherokee Nation, and it is so ordered.

Tams Bixby

T B Needles

C. R. Breckinridge

Commissioners.

Dated at Muskogee, Indian Territory,

MAY 20 1902

COMMISSIONERS:

HENRY L. DAWES,
TAMS BIXBY,
THOMAS B. NEEDLES,
C. R. BRECKINRIDGE.

—

ALLISON L. AYLESWORTH,
SECRETARY.

ADDRESS ONLY THE
COMMISSION TO THE FIVE CIVILIZED TRIBES.

DEPARTMENT OF THE INTERIOR,
COMMISSION TO THE FIVE CIVILIZED TRIBES.

REFER IN REPLY TO THE FOLLOWING

D - 66.

Muskogee, Indian Territory, May 21, 1902.

W. W. Hastings, Esq.,

Attorney for the Cherokee Nation,

Muskogee, Indian Territory.

Sir:

Enclosed herewith, please find a copy of the decision of the Commission rendered May 20, 1902, in the matter of the application of Mige L. Brackett for enrollment as a citizen of the Cherokee Nation.

You are hereby advised that you will be allowed fifteen days from date hereof in which to file with the Commission such protest as you desire to make against the enrollment of the above named person as a citizen of the Cherokee Nation. If you fail to file protest within the time allowed this applicant will be regularly listed for enrollment

Very respectfully,

T B Needles

Acting Chairman.

Enc. D-66.

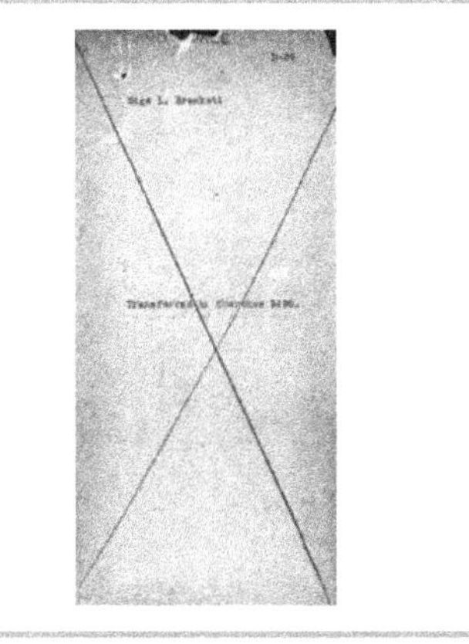

Mige L. Brackett

Transferred to Cherokee [illegible]

RESIDENCE: Flint DISTRICT.
POST OFFICE: Dutch Mills, Ark

Cherokee Nation. Cherokee Roll.

CARD NO. ______
FIELD NO. 9480

Dawes' Roll No.	NAME.	Relationship to Person first Named.	AGE.	SEX.	BLOOD.	Tribal Enrollment Year.	Tribal Enrollment District.	Tribal Enrollment No.	Name of Father.	Year.	District.	Name of Mother.	Year.	District.
21553	Brackett, Mige L.		27	M	1/[illegible]	1896	Flint	147	Baylis Smith	dead	Cherokee	Nancy Smith	dead	Non Citz

GRANTED
MAY 20 1902

No 1 on 1896 Roll as Mige Brackett

See [illegible]
[illegible] 1904

Date of Application for Enrollment.

Cherokee D68 - Mary White by William H. White

RESIDENCE:
POST-OFFICE:

CHEROKEE Nation. CHEROKEE Roll.

CARD NO.
FIELD NO. D68

COPY OF DECISION FORWARDED
ATTORNEY FOR CHEROKEE NATION
MAY 21 1907

APPLICATION GRANTED AND
APPLICANTS ORDERED
ENROLLED

Department of the Interior.
Commission to the Five Civilized Tribes.
Bunch, I. T., August 1st, 1900.

In the matter of the application of William H. White et al for enrollment as Cherokee citizens; being sworn and examined by Commissioner Breckinridge, testifies as follows:

Q What is your full name? A William H. White.
Q Your age? A 50.
Q Your post-office? A Stilwell.
Q District? Flint.
Q How long have you lived in Flint? A In Flint, about 4 years.
Q Where did you live before that? A Goingsnake and Tahlequah.
Q How long in Goingsnake? A One year.
Q How long in Tahlequah? A 2 years.
Q Where did you live before that? A Coowee-Scoowee[sic]
Q For whom do you apply for enrollment? A Wife and minor children.
Q And yourself? A No, I am not entitled to anything.
Q You're a white man? A Yes sir.
Q You never married under Cherokee law? A No sir, married in Georgia.
Q And you're not on any certificate of admission? A No sir.
Q And you're not on any of the rolls of the Cherokee Nation? A No sir.
Q You apply only then for your wife and children? A Yes sir.
Q Do you apply for your wife as a Cherokee by blood? A Yes sir.
Q What is your wife's full name? A Mary White.
Q Was she admitted under that name? A Yes sir.

You hand me here Mr. White, a certificate of admission to Cherokee citizenship. It is dated Sept. 22nd, 1888; it is signed by J. T. Adair, Chairman of the Committee on citizenship. It is attested by Connell Rogers, Clerk of the Committee, approved and endorsed by J. B. Mayes, Principal Chief of the Nation, and under the great seal of the Nation. This certificate shows that among others, one Mary White, was admitted to citizenship on the date mentioned.

Q Is that your wife? A Yes sir.
Q How old is your wife now? A 52.

Her age is given in the certificate of admission as[sic] that time 40 years of age.

Q Has your wife lived with you in the Cherokee Nation ever since her admission? A Yes sir.

You have given your residence here showing that you have lived at different times in different districts.

Q How long have you lived continuously in the Cherokee Nation?
A Since '94, when we made the first permanent settlement. We were here in '90, came from Georgia.
Q Then you moved out again? A Yes sir.
Q Where did you go? A We went back again to our native home temporarily to settle up some business and came back again in '94.

Q Your wife was admitted in '88? A Yes sir.
Q And you did not come until 1890? A No sir.
Q Something like two years after her admission? A Yes sir.
Q How long did you stay here? A I don't remember; not a very great while; sometime in '90 staid a few months, something like that.
Q Staid a few months? A Yes sir.
Q Then went back to Georgia? A Yes sir.
Q Staid there until '94? A Yes sir.
Q And then moved back here? A Yes sir.
Q You and your wife have lived continuously in the Nation ever since 1894?
A Yes sir; all the time. We bought our first property in August, '94.
Q You mean your first property in the Cherokee Nation? A Yes sir.
Q She drew strip money did she? A Yes sir.
Q Is your wife on the roll of 1894? A Yes sir.
Q She is also on the roll of 1896? A Yes sir.
Q Give me the names of your children, under age and unmarried?
A Lewis R.
Q How old is he? A He's 19.
Q Next? A Mary P.
Q How old is she? A She's 12.
Q Now what is your next child? A That's all I have under age, except one son that is 21 that is sick at home.
Q Is he a confirmed invalid? A Just recently taken sick.
Q Soon will be well and can apply for himself? A I guess so, I hope so.

It is not the practice or considered proper to let one of age be applied for unless it is quite impossible for him to apply for himself. Better for your son to meet the Commission at some of its other appointments.

Q It is only a temporary illness, you say? A Yes sir.
Q These three are the only ones you are applying for now? A Yes sir.
Q Now are these three children all on the roll of 1896? A Yes sir.
Q And all on the roll of 1894? A Yes sir.
Q Are these three children on the certificate of admission? A No sir.
Q I see Lewis R. White mentioned on the certificate of admission just quoted. Is that the child whose name you have just given? A Yes sir.

He was then 7 years of age.

Q I see Mary P. White's name on the certificate of admission; is that the same name of the child you have just mentioned? A Yes sir.

She is there given as two years of age at that time.

Now the name of the last child whom you have mentioned, Ursley P., is not on the certificate you have exhibited.

Q You give the age of Ursley P. as 12 years? A Yes sir.

And the certificate is dated about 12 years ago.

Q Why is it that her name is not on that certificate? A It was through mistake, and she was very young, just a baby, but a few months old.
Q She was living at the time the certificate was made out? A Yes sir.
Q And you claim that her name was omitted simply by mistake? A Yes sir.
Q Has that mistake ever been remedied? A Yes sir.
Q How was it? A She was placed on the roll.
Q When attention was called to it, her name was placed on the official roll?
A Yes sir.
Q Have you a certificate of that fact? A No sir, I don't believe I have. I have a copy. (Showing a paper)

This, Mr. White is simply a statement purporting to be signed by your wife and yourself from what is called the undersigned officer, but the officer does not sign his name nor state what officer he is. It is to the effect that the herein named child of yours was through mistake left off the strip payment rolls, but the name of the child is not mentioned in the statement; therefore Mr. White this paper is nothing.

Q I am not asking you about the certificate relating to the strip payment, I am asking you about the certificate of admission to citizenship corresponding to the one admitting your wife and certain members of your children; has that omission you speak of in the original certificate of admission to citizenship ever been corrected?
A Only by putting her name on the roll.
Q What roll? A Only by placing her name on the roll[sic] of '91-9496.
Q You have never gone to the Commission on citizenship and got them to correct it or by issuing a certificate? A No sir.

1894 roll; page 1182, #3669, Mary White, Tahlequah Dist.
1894 roll; page 1182, #3676, Louis R. White, Tahlequah Dist.
1894 roll; page 1182, #3678, Mary P. White, Tahlequah Dist.
1896 roll; page 814, #2618, Mary White, Goingsnake Dit[sic].
1896 roll; page 814, #2623, Lewis R. White, Goingsnake Dist.
1896 roll; page 814, #2625, Mary P. White, Goingsnake Dist.
1896 roll; page 814, #2626, Ursula[sic] P. White, Goingsnake Dist.

Mr. Baugh: Q I believe your wife was admitted in 1888 to citizenship? A Yes sir.
Q And immediately thereafter you moved to this country, ostensibly for the purpose of living there, is that not a fact? A Yes sir.
Q After remaining here a short time, you moved back to Georgia? A Yes sir.
Q You lived in Georgia six years did you not? A No sir.
Q When did you move back in this country? A '94.
Q Where was you at in '94 when the Census was taken? A I was in Georgia.
Q Who drew your money in the payment of 1894? A Gus Ivey.
Q What time after that did you move into this country? A That payment was made in September 1894, I believe.

Q What time did you move back to this country? A The first day of November I landed here.

Q Then you were out of the country four years? A No sir, not all of four years.

Q I understood you to say that you moved out in '90? A Yes sir.

Q And that you returned in November, '94? A Yes sir, I ame back in July and bought a place.

Q While you were living in Georgia, after moving back you lived there as a citizen in Georgia? A Why no sir.

Q Did not exercise any rights of citizenship at all? A No sir, just worked.

Q Did you vote while you were there? A No sir.

Q At no election at all? A No sir.

Q Well, after being gone out for four years, did you ask the National Council for re-admission again? A No sir; says it was unnecessary.

Com. Breckinridge:

Q Mr. White, when you came here with your family in 1890, did you come here for the purpose of making it your home at that time? A Yes sir.

Q Did you bring your effects here? A Yes sir, part of them.

Q You closed out your affairs in Georgia? A No sir.

Q Did you come here for the purpose of making it your home from that time on?

A Yes sir that was my intention. Our business were[sic] unsettled in Georgia and impossible to get a settlement prior to that time.

Q Prior to what time? A 1890. We understood that it was necessary to come then or soon in order to establish ourselves.

Q When you left Georgia in 1890 was your business still unsettled? A Yes sir; was in a law suit and could not settle it until the Court convened.

Q But you came here in 1890 for the purpose of making this a permanent home for yourself and family from that time on if circumstances permitted? A Yes sir.

Q Now when you got here in 1890 what did you find to be the condition of your affairs? A We found them to be alright and our family was all placed on the roll of 1890.

I am not talking about your enrollment but your business affairs. I know that some of your family were on the roll of 1890. I am talking about the affairs of your own not about your enrollment.

Q What did you find the condition of your business affairs to be when you came here in 1890 and started to make this your home? A They were in bad shape.

Q Do you mean that lot of you assests[sic] in Georgia had not been wound up?

A Yes sir we were very short here.

Q Did you make any purchase of a home or property in 1890 when you came out here? A No sir did not.

Q Did you go back to Georgia for the purpose of putting your affairs in better shape? A Yes sir.

Q Did you take back the household effects and other things that you brought here wit you? A Yes sir.

Q Do you mean to say that at no time after you went back to Georgia, that is between 1890 and 1894, you exercised the right to vote in the state of Georgia?

A No sir, I did not vote,

Q Didn't vote during that period in Georgia? A No sir. It was my intention to get here as soon as I could and did.

Q You swear that you did not vote during that period in Georgia?

A No sir, I did not vote.

Q You know that do you? A Don't know when I ever did vote in Georgia.

Q Didn't you vote in Georgia before 1890 before you came out here? A Yes sir, a few times.

Q Do you mean to say that you did not take much interest in political matters?

A No sir.

Q And didn't vote very often? A No sir, very seldom.

Q If you did not vote between 1890 and 1894, why was it because you didn't vote?

A I didn't recognize myself as a citizen there.

Q Was it because you were there with the firm purpose of coming back here as soon as you could wind up your affairs? A Yes sir.

Q Well what was the condition of your property and business in Georgia in 1894 when you came to the territory the second time? A We had pit business permanently settled I think.

Q You mean by that that your property is all sold out? A Yes sir, final settlement.

Q Different members of your family whose name you have given here you say drew strip money in '94? A Yes sir.

Q They were in Georgia at that time? A Yes sir.

Q How did you arrange for them to draw strip money when they were in Georgia?

A We arranged through our attorney.

Q Where is your attorney? A At Tahlequah.

Q Who was your attorney? A Augustus E. Ivey.

Q Is he living there now? A Yes sir.

Q Did you write him or did your family write him that they claimed to be Cherokees by blood? A Yes sir.

Q And to Cherokee citizenship? A Yes sir.

Q Was it represented to him that you were coming to the Territory as soon as you could? A Certainly so, and would have been here prior to that if it had not been for sickness.

Q At what time did you write to your attorney about this business?

A I don't remember; the first time we had considerable correspondence that it required during the year '94.

Q Do you remember about what time during the year 1894 that roll was made up?

A No sir I do not.

Q Did you write to your lawyer about it in the early part of the year or latter[sic].[sic]

A If I ain't mistaken in 1893 we had some correspondence in regard to it; kept it up all the time from the time we went away until we got back.

Q Was the money received by your family before you moved back in '94?

A Part of it.

Q Well what became of the other part? A Got it after we cam[sic] here.

Q Why didn't you get it all at once? A Because we contemplated coming.

Q What caused part of it to stay here and part of it to be sent to you in Georgia?
A My attorney supposed that my family was needing it in coming.
Q You mean to say that he only sent you a part of it to come on? A Part of it.
Q How much? A $1000.00
Q How much did you draw all together? A $2700.00 I think it was.
[First part of next question and answer cut off at bottom of page and impossible to read] exactly. We had five hundred and some dollars deposited with Ivey when we came and then we got Ursley's last payment after the Council met; $265.00 and something.
Q Youngest child was paid in '94? A Yes sir.
Q Altogether then there was $3000.00 coming. A Nearly.
Q How much did you get altogether; did you get anything over half? A Yes sir.
Q How much more than half? A I can't tell exactly.
Q Not much you think? A Yes sir.
Q You think a good deal over half, do you? A Well if I remember we got $1700.00 and some odd dollars.
Q And the balance you didn'y[sic] get? A No sir.
Q Though it was paid on the claims of your family? A Yes sir.
Q Well, what time in '94 did you come out to the Nation? A First day of November that I landed at my place that I had bought prior to, or about that day.

Mr. Baugh::
Q Did you not write to Mr. Gus Ivey that if he would have your family enrolled and then draw the money for you that you would give him half? A No sir I did not.
Q How come Mr. Ivey to have your family enrolled? A They had been enrolled always and they were on the roll of '91 and drew their pay and we were expecting to return immediately as soon as we got out[sic] business fixed, and prior to that we had a severe sickness which detained us almost a year in getting back.
Q You say that Mr. Ivey drew this money for you; the book shows he drew $2657.00; you state that he sent you $1000.00; that when you returned here you had on deposit $500.00 with Mr. Ivey? A $500. and something.
Q By what authority did Mr. Ivey hold $1157.00. A We agreed to pay him the necessary fees and expenses. We gave him the power of attorney to fix this business and he claimed that was our part after the expenses.

Com'r. Breckinridge: Mr. White the record shows that your wife, Mary White, was duly admitted to citizenship by the Cherokee authorities on the 22nd of September, 1888. It also shows that at the same time and in the same manner your wife and her children, Lewis R. and also Mary P. White, were duly admitted. The names of your wife and of these two children are identified on the roll of 1894 and also on the roll of 1896. The evidence shows that you moved to the Cherokee Nation in the year 1890 with your family for the purpose of making your permanent home here. In a very short time, not exceeding a few months you returned with your family to Georgia, taking the household effects that you had brought here. You claim that you returned owing to the embarrassment of your affairs and your desire to wind them up and get them into better shape before permantly[sic] locating in the Cherokee Nation. You claimed that you looked upon yourself and family after this time as only temporarily sojourning in Georgia, it being the purpose for all of you to return to the Nation as soon as practicable. You claim that the autumn of 1894, owing to the state of your business and sickness in your family, was the earliest date upon which you could return to the territory and that you did return here with your family and effects on or about that time, and that you and your family as enumerated in the testimony have lived here continually and consistently ever since. Now the representative present of the Cherokee Nation claims that by your return to Georgia with your family in 1890 and your stay there as indicated, they forfeited their rights of citizenship and that they should have been re-admitted by action of the Cherokee authorities in order to entitle them to enrollment at this time. The Cherokee representative will probably file his own statement with this case. In order that the Commission may more fully consider the case, your application for your wife, Mary, and for your two children, Lewis R. and Mary P., are at present placed upon a doubtful card. When the decision is finally reached yo[sic] will be informed at your present post-office address, and that decision whether favorable or unfavorable will be forwarded to the Secretary of the Interior for his final approval. Now, as you're your child, Ursley, his name appears upon the roll of 1896, but it does not appear upon the certificate of admitting her[sic] mother and other members of the family, and you testify that this child has never been admitted to Cherokee citizenship by or through any certificate of admission. You claim that the omission of this child's name from the certificate admitting other members of this family was a mistake, but that mistake has never been remedied by those who have or had the lawful authority to remedy the mistake. The child, you testify was living at the time that its mother and other members of the family were admitted to citizenship. The Commission holds that this child has never been admitted to citizenship as contemplated by the law to give it the right to enrollment at this time. I will add that the childs[sic] name is not found also on the roll of 1894, Your application therefore for your child, Ursley is rejected.

Edward G. Rothenberger, being duly sworn by Commissioner Breckinridge as Stenographer to the Commission to the Five Civilized Tribes, he reported in full the testimony of the above named witness, William H. White, and that the foregoing is a full, true and correct transcript of his note.

Edward G. Rothenberger

Sworn to and subscribed before me this 3rd day of August, 1900, at Bunch, I.T.

Commissioner.

Now comes the Cherokee Nation through its representatives and protests against the enrollment of Mary White and her children, Lewis R. White and Mary P. White, as citizens of the Cherokee Nation for the following reasons as shown in the evidence:

What the said Mary White and the above named children did move to the Cherkee[sic] Nation after their admission but subsequently removed to the State of

Georgia thereby forfeiting their rights to the acquired Citizenship, and that they failed to avail themselves of Sec. 2 of Article 1 of the Constitution of the Cherokee Nation. See Sec. 2 Art. 1, of the Cherokee Constitution.

W. W. Hastings

J. L. Baugh

Attorneys for the
Cherokee Nation.

"R"

File with Cherokee D-
68, Mary White.

Department of the Interior,
Commission to the Five Civilized Tribes,
Muskogee, I. T., February 17, 1902.

SUPPLEMENTAL TESTIMONY AND PROCEEDINGS in the matter of the application of Mary White for enrollment as a Cherokee citizen.

WILLIAM H. WHITE being sworn and examined testified as follows:

Appearances:
William H. White, for applicant;
W. W. Hastings, attorney for the Cherokee Nation.

BY COMMISSION:
Q What is your name? A William H. White.
Q How old are you? A I am 53 years old.
Q What is your post-office? A Stilwell.
BY COMMISSION: There is offered in evidence a certificate from the Cherokee Commission on citizenship, bearing date of September 22, 1888, admitting one Mary White and her children, Lewis R. White and Mary P. White to citizenship in the Cherokee Nation. The document is signed by J. T. Adair, Chairman of the Commission on citizenship, attested by Connell Rogers, Clerk of the Commission on citizenship, approved and indorsed by J. B. Mayes, Principal Chief of the Cherokee Nation, and bears the seal thereof. It is filed herewith.

It further appears that William J[sic]. White, whose name appears on doubtful card No. 69, is found in said certificate.

Q Is there any other statement you desire to make relative to the enrollment of these parties? A No sir not that I know of; I want to say something in regard to our youngest child; it was rejected; it is out youngest child; I would like to make some explanation if it is necessary. When that application was made for citizenship she was not born.

BY COMMISSION: That child will come in all right.

It further appears that the name of Thomas J. White is found in the certificate of admission admitting Mary White and others to citizenship in the Cherokee Nation on the 22nd day of September, 1888.

The name of James A. White appears in the certificate issued by the Cherokee Commission on citizenship admitting Mary White, and others to citizenship in the Cherokee Nation, on the 22nd day of September, 1888.

Q Any other statement you desire to make relative to the enrollment of your wife and children? A As to James A. White he was requested to bring a marriage certificate and it was left here with the other papers and never received it back. It was left with the Commission at the time he was placed on a doubtful list. Marriage certificate and also the certificate of the birth of his child.

BY COMMISSION: The name of George W. White appears in the certificate admitting Mary White and others to citizenship in the Cherokee Nation on the 22nd day of September 1888.

Q Do you submit this case to the Commission for final consideration? A Yes sir.

BY MR. HASTINGS: Cherokee Nation submits it.

M.D. Green, being first duly sworn, states that as stenographer to the Commission to the Five Civilized Tribes he correctly recorded the testimony and proceedings in this case and that the foregoing is a true and complete transcript of his stenographic notes thereof.

M.D. Green

Subscribed and sworn to before me this February 21, 1902.

T B Needles

Commissioner.

Cherokee D 68

DEPARTMENT OF THE INTERIOR,

COMMISSION TO THE FIVE CIVILIZED TRIBES.

In the matter of the application of Mary White, et. al. for enrollment as Cherokee citizens.

On the first day of August, 1900, William H. White appeared before the Commission to the Five Civilized Tribes and made application for the enrollment of his wife Mary and his minor children Lewis R., Mary P. and Ursley P. White as citizens by blood of the Cherokee Nation.

At the conclusion of the evidence offered at that time Ursley P. White was listed for rejection, but she has since been enrolled. The names of Mary White and Lewis R. and Mary P. White were place upon a "Doubtful" card pending further consideration of their right to be enrolled.

Further evidence has been submitted to the Commission and the case submitted for final consideration.

The following decision is now rendered.

D E C I S I O N.

---oOo---

From the evidence of record in this case it appears that Mary White and her minor children Lewis R. and Mary P. White are Cherokee Indians and were admitted to citizenship in the Cherokee Nation on the 22nd day of September, 1888 by a decree of a Cherokee Commission on Citizenship, Mary White was then married to William H. White and the evidence shows that she and her husband came to the Cherokee Nation in 1890. It further appears that a few months thereafter they returned to Georgia for the purpose of winding up their business affairs. It seems that owing to the embarrassed condition of their business matters in the State of Georgia they found it necessary to stay there until 1894. They seem however, to have regarded themselves as citizens of the Cherokee Nation and exercised none of the privileges of citizens in the State of Georgia. William H. White testified that they came back to the

Cherokee Nation as soon as they possibly could consistent with a satisfactory settlement of their affairs in Georgia.

It is the opinion of this Commission that the citizenship rights of Mary White and her children were not forfeited by virtue of the facts here recited. They are identified on the strip payment roll of 1894 and the Cherokee Census roll of 1896, and are considered to be lawfully upon said rolls.

This Commission in making rolls of citizenship of the Cherokee Nation is governed by the following provisions of the Act of Congress approved June 28, 1898 (30 Stats., 495);

> "That in making rolls of citizenship of the several tribes, as required by law, the Commission to the Five Civilized Tribes is authorized and directed to take the roll of Cherokee citizens of eighteen hundred and eighty (not including freedmen) as the only roll intended to be confirmed by this and preceding Acts of Congress, and to enroll all persons now living whose names are found on said roll, and all descendants born since the date of said roll to persons whose names are found thereon; and all persons who have been enrolled by the tribal authorities who have heretofore made permanent settlement in the Cherokee Nation whose parents, by reason of their Cherokee blood, have been lawfully admitted to citizenship by the tribal authorities, and who were minors when their parents were so admitted; and they shall investigate the right of all other persons whose names are found on any other rolls and omit all such as may have been placed thereon by fraud or without authority of law, enrolling only such as may have lawful right thereto, and their descendants born since such rolls were made, with such intermarried white persons as may be entitled to citizenship under Cherokee laws."

In view of the facts and the law cited it is considered that Mary White and her minor children Lewis R. and Mary P. White are entitled to be enrolled as citizens by blood of the Cherokee Nation, and it is so ordered.

Tams Bixby

T B Needles

C. R. Breckinridge

Commissioners.

Dated at Muskogee, Indian Territory,

MAY **20** 1902

COMMISSIONERS:

HENRY L. DAWES,
TAMS BIXBY,
THOMAS B. NEEDLES,
C. R. BRECKINRIDGE.

—

ALLISON L. AYLESWORTH,
SECRETARY.

ADDRESS ONLY THE
COMMISSION TO THE FIVE CIVILIZED TRIBES.

DEPARTMENT OF THE INTERIOR,
COMMISSION TO THE FIVE CIVILIZED TRIBES.

REFER IN REPLY TO THE FOLLOWING

D 68.

Muskogee, Indian Territory, May 21, 1902.

W. W. Hastings, Esq.,

Attorney for the Cherokee Nation,

Muskogee, Indian Territory.

Sir:

Enclosed herewith, please find a copy of the decision of the Commission rendered May 20, 1902, in the matter of the application of Mary White et al. for enrollment as citizens of the Cherokee Nation.

You are hereby advised that you will be allowed fifteen days from date hereof in which to file with the Commission such protest as you desire to make against the enrollment of the above named persons as citizens of the Cherokee Nation. If you fail to file protest within the time allowed these applicants will be regularly listed for enrollment.

Very respectfully,

T B Needles

Commissioner in Charge.

Enc. D-68.

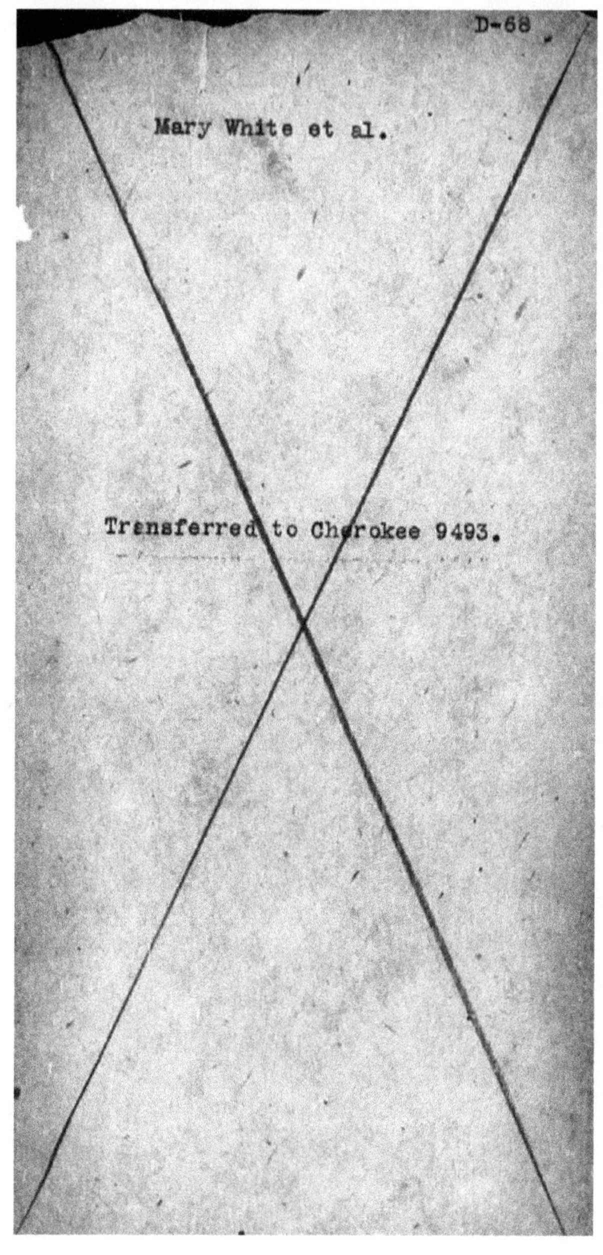

D-68

Mary White et al.

Transferred to Cherokee 9493.

RESIDENCE: Flint DISTRICT.
POST OFFICE: Stilwell I.T.

Cherokee Nation. Cherokee Roll.
(Not including Intermarried, Shawnees, or Freedmen.)

CARD NO.
FIELD NO. 9493

Dawes' Roll No.		NAME.	Relationship to Person first Named.	AGE.	SEX.	BLOOD.	Tribal Enrollment Year.	Tribal Enrollment District.	Tribal Enrollment No.	Name of Father.	Year.	District.	Name of Mother.	Year.	District.
21561	1	White, Mary E.	Named	52	F	1/8	1896	G. Snake	2618	John Tidwell		G. Snake	Lucinda Tidwell		G. Snake
21562	2	" Lewis R.	Son	19	M	1/16	1896	"	2625	Wm. H. White		non citz	No. 1		
21563	3	" Mary R.	Dau	14	F	"	1896	"	2626	"		"	"		

GRANTED
MAY 20 1902

CITIZENSHIP CERTIFICATE
ISSUED FOR NO.

See N.B. #864

See Cherokee ... 9...

Date of Application for Enrollment.

Cherokee D69 - William J. White

RESIDENCE: Flint
POST-OFFICE: Stilwell, I.T.

CHEROKEE Nation. CHEROKEE Roll.

CARD NO.
FIELD NO. D 69

Dawes' Roll No.		Name	Relationship to Person first Named	Age	Sex	Blood	Tribal Enrollment Year	District	No.	Name of Father	Year	District	Name of Mother	Year	District
	1	White William J		28	m	1/16	1896	Snake	7619	Hiram White		Non Citz	Mary White		[illegible]

See testimony in case of Mary White

COPY OF DECISION FORWARDED ATTORNEY FOR CHEROKEE NATION MAY 21 1902

APPLICATION GRANTED AND APPLICANTS ORDERED ENROLLED MAY 20 1902

COPY OF DECISION FORWARDED APPLICANT

Department of the Interior.
Commission to the Five Civilized Tribes.
Bunch, I. T., August 1st, 1900.

In the matter of the application of William J. White for enrollment as a Cherokee citizen, being sworn and examined by Commissioner Breckinridge, testifies as follows:

Q What is your full name? A William J. White.
Q What is your age? A 28 years.
Q What is your post-office? A Stilwell.
Q District? A Flint.
Q How long have you lived in Flint? A I believe about three years if I am not mistaken.
Q Where did you libe[sic] before that? A Lived in Goingsnake.
Q How long did you live in Goingsnake? A Somewhere about 6 or 8 months, I dont[sic] know exactly.
Q Where did you live before that? A In Tahlequah.
Q How long did you live in Tahlequah? A About one year, I reckon.
Q Where did you live before that? A Cooweescoowee.
Q How long did you live in Cooweescoowee? A Short time; two or three months, don't know exactly how long.
Q Where did you live before that? A Georgia.
Q How long do you claim to have lived in the Nation continuously? A 6 years I guess.
Q When did you come from Georgia? A I believe it was in '92. I came when my father did.
Q But your father has testified that he came here in '94? A Well that is right I guess, he knows.
Q Are you on any of the rolls of the Cherokee Nation or have you ever been admitted to citizenship by action of the Cherokee Authorities? A Yes sir.
Q You hand me here a certificate; do you claim that this is your certificate of admission? A Yes sir.

This certificate is dated Sept. 22nd, 1888. It is signed by J. T. Adair, Chairman of the Committee on Citizenship. It is attested by Connell Rogers, Clerk of the Committee, approved and endorsed by J. B. Mayes, Principal Chief of the Cherokee Nation, and it is under the great seal of the Nation. It states that on the date given among others, one William J. White was admitted to citizenship. At that time 15 years of age.

Q Is that your name, Mr. White? A Yes sir.
Q Do you apply for enrollment for anybody else besides yourself?
A No sir, just myself only.

Now it is observed Mr. White, that you were admitted to citizenship in 1888 at which time you were 15 years of age, and that you came to the Cherokee Nation to make it your home in 1894, some six years after you were admitted to citizenship.

Q Were you here in 1888 at the time the application was made for your enrollment?
A No sir.
Q Were you here at any time between 1888 and 1894? A Yes sir I came here with my father and mother when I came the first time.
Q Was that in 1890? A I don't remember what year it was.
Q How long did you stay here on that visit? A About three months, I believe; as near as I can recollect.
Q And then you went back to Georgia before you came out here again? A I declare I don't know.
Q All you remember is that you came here again in 1894? A Yes sir.
Q You claim to have made your home here ever since? A Yes sir.
Q Are you on the blood roll of '94? A Yes sir.
Q And roll of '96? A Yes sir.

1894 roll; page 1182, #3072, Wm. J. White, Tahlequah Dist.
1896 roll; page 814, #2619, William J. White, Goingsnake Dist.

Mr. Baugh:

Q You say you came out here with your father and mother the first time they came to this country? A Yes sir.
Q And you returned with them? A Yes sir.
Q While you were in Georgia Mr. White did you exercise any rights as a citizen in that state.[sic] A No sir; nothing only as a laborer. Wasn't old enough to vote or anything of of[sic] the kind.
Q You never voted in Georgia in your life? A Never voted in a United States election in my life. The only voting I ever did was in the Cherokee Nation.

Com'r Breckinridge:

Mr. White you admission to citizenship is duly indicated by the certificate that you exhibit, dated Sept. 22nd, 1888. You are identified on the roll of 1894 and on the roll of 1896. It appears from the testimony that you did not reside in the Cherokee Nation after your admission in 1888 until some time during the year 1894, but that you have resided here consistently since the latter time. Now the representative present of the Cherokee Nation protests against your enrollment upon the ground of virtual abandonment of citizenship as claimed in the case of other members of your family by your being brought here as it appears in 1890 and then taken back to Georgia and not returning here until 1894. For the further consideration of the merits of this protest, your application is at present placed upon a doubtful card and the final decision will not now be rendered. When the Commission finally decides upon your application, you will be informed of the result at your present post-office address, and that decision whether favorable or unfavorable will be forwarded to the Honorable Secretary of the Interior for his approval.

Edward G. Rothenberger, being duly sworn by Commissioner Breckinridge as Stenographer to the Commission to the Five Civilized Tribes, he reported in full the testimony of the above named witness, William J. White, and that the foregoing is a full, true and correct transcript of his notes.

Edward G. Rothenberger

Sworn to and subscribed before me this 3rd day of August, 1900, at Bunch, I.T.

Commissioner.

Now comes the Cherokee Nation through its representatives and protests against the enrollment of William J. White as a citizen of the Cherokee Nation for the following reasons as shown in the evidence:

That the said William J. White did move to the Cherokee Nation after his admission but subsequently removed to the State of Georgia thereny[sic] forfeiting his right to the acquired Citizenship, and that they failed to avail themselves of Sec. 2 of Article 1 of the Constitution of the Cherokee Nation. See Sec. 2, Art. 1 of the Cherokee Constitution.

W. W. Hastings

J. L. Baugh

Attorneys for the
Cherokee Nation.

"R"

File with Cherokee D-

69, William J. White.
Department of the Interior,
Commission to the Five Civilized Tribes,
Muskogee, I. T., February 17, 1902.

SUPPLEMENTAL TESTIMONY AND PROCEEDINGS in the matter of the application of Mary White for enrollment as a Cherokee citizen.

WILLIAM H. WHITE being sworn and examined testified as follows:

Appearances:
William H. White, for applicant;
W. W. Hastings, attorney for the Cherokee Nation.

BY COMMISSION:

Q What is your name? A William H. White.

Q How old are you? A I am 53 years old.

Q What is your post-office? A Stilwell.

BY COMMISSION: There is offered in evidence a certificate from the Cherokee Commission on citizenship, bearing date of September 22, 1888, admitting one Mary White and her children, Lewis R. White and Mary P. White to citizenship in the Cherokee Nation. The document is signed by J. T. Adair, Chairman of the Commission on citizenship, attested by Connell Rogers, Clerk of the Commission on citizenship, approved and indorsed by J. B. Mayes, Principal Chief of the Cherokee Nation, and bears the seal thereof. It is filed herewith.

It further appears that William J. White, whose name appears on doubtful card No. 69, is found in said certificate.

Q Is there any other statement you desire to make relative to the enrollment of these parties? A No sir not that I know of; I want to say something in regard to our youngest child; it was rejected; it is out youngest child; I would like to make some explanation if it is necessary. When that application was made for citizenship she was not born.

BY COMMISSION: That child will come in all right.

It further appears that the name of Thomas J. White is found in the certificate of admission admitting Mary White and others to citizenship in the Cherokee Nation on the 22nd day of September, 1888.

The name of James A. White appears in the certificate issued by the Cherokee Commission on citizenship admitting Mary White, and others to citizenship in the Cherokee Nation, on the 22nd day of September, 1888.

Q Any other statement you desire to make relative to the enrollment of your wife and children? A As to James A. White he was requested to bring a marriage certificate and it was left here with the other papers and never received it back. It was left with the Commission at the time he was placed on a doubtful list. Marriage certificate and also the certificate of the birth of his child.

BY COMMISSION: The name of George W. White appears in the certificate admitting Mary White and others to citizenship in the Cherokee Nation on the 22nd day of September 1888.

Q Do you submit this case to the Commission for final consideration? A Yes sir.

BY MR. HASTINGS: Cherokee Nation submits it.

M.D. Green, being first duly sworn, states that as stenographer to the Commission to the Five Civilized Tribes he correctly recorded the testimony and proceedings in this case and that the foregoing is a true and complete transcript of his stenographic notes thereof.

M.D. Green

Subscribed and sworn to before me this February 21, 1902.

T B Needles

Commissioner.

Cherokee D 69

DEPARTMENT OF THE INTERIOR,

COMMISSION TO THE FIVE CIVILIZED TRIBES.

In the matter of the application of William J. White for enrollment as a Cherokee citizen.

On the first day of August 1900, William J. White appeared before the Commission to the Five Civilized Tribes and made application for his enrollment as a citizen by blood of the Cherokee Nation.

At the conclusion of the evidence offered at that time he was placed upon a "Doubtful" card awaiting further consideration of his right to enrollment.

Further evidence has been submitted to the Commission and the case submitted for final consideration. The following decision is now rendered.

D E C I S I O N.

--oOo--

From the evidence of record in this case it appears that William J. White is a Cherokee Indian and was admitted to citizenship in the Cherokee Nation on the 22nd day of September, 1888, by a decree of the Cherokee Commission on Citizenship. It further appears that he came with his parents to the Cherokee Nation in 1890, and that a few months thereafter he returned with them to Georgia and remained there until 1894, at which time he returned to the Cherokee Nation. At the time of his return to Georgia applicant was eighteen years old.

Section 2, article 1, Constitution of the Cherokee Nation provides:

". . . . whenever any citizen shall remove with his effects out of the limits of this Nation, and becomes a citizen of any other Government all his rights and privileges as a citizen of this Nation shall cease. . . . ."

There is no evidence in this case to show that William J. White became a citizen of any other Government after his admission to citizenship in the Cherokee Nation, and as he was a minor and living with his parents at the time of his return to Georgia this Commission is of the opinion that the citizenship rights of the applicant were not forfeited by reason of the facts in this case. He is identified on the Strip payment roll of 1894, and the Cherokee Census roll of 1896, and he has lived continuously in the Cherokee Nation since 1894.

This Commission in making rolls of citizenship of the Cherokee Nation is governed by the following provisions of the Act of Congress approved June 28, 1898, (30 Stats., 495);

> "That in making rolls of citizenship of the several tribes, as required by law, the Commission to the Five Civilized Tribes is authorized and directed to take the roll of Cherokee citizens of eighteen hundred and eighty (not including freedmen) as the only roll intended to be confirmed by this and preceding Acts of Congress, and to enroll all persons now living whose names are found on said roll, and all descendants born since the date of said roll to persons whose names are found thereon; and all persons who have been enrolled by the tribal authorities who have heretofore made permanent settlement in the Cherokee Nation whose parents, by reason of their Cherokee blood, have been lawfully admitted to citizenship by the tribal authorities, and who were minors when their parents were so admitted; and they shall investigate the right of all other persons whose names are found on any other rolls and omit all such as may have been placed thereon by fraud or without authority of law, enrolling only such as may have lawful right thereto, and their descendants born since such rolls were made, with such intermarried white persons as may be entitled to citizenship under Cherokee laws."

In view of the facts and the law cited it is considered that William J. White is entitled to be enrolled as a citizen by blood of the Cherokee Nation, and it is so ordered.

Tams Bixby

T B Needles

C. R. Breckinridge

Commissioners.

Dated at Muskogee, Indian Territory,

MAY 20 1902

COMMISSIONERS:

HENRY L. DAWES,
TAMS BIXBY,
THOMAS B. NEEDLES,
C. R. BRECKINRIDGE.

—

ALLISON L. AYLESWORTH,
SECRETARY.

ADDRESS ONLY THE
COMMISSION TO THE FIVE CIVILIZED TRIBES.

DEPARTMENT OF THE INTERIOR,
COMMISSION TO THE FIVE CIVILIZED TRIBES.

REFER IN REPLY TO THE FOLLOWING

D - 69.

Muskogee, Indian Territory, May 21, 1902.

W. W. Hastings, Esq.,

Attorney for the Cherokee Nation,

Muskogee, Indian Territory.

Sir:

Enclosed herewith, please find a copy of the decision of the Commission rendered May 20, 1902, in the matter of the application of William J. White for enrollment as a citizen of the Cherokee Nation.

You are hereby advised that you will be allowed fifteen days from date hereof to file with the Commission such protest as you desire to make against the enrollment of the above named person as a citizen of the Cherokee Nation. If you fail to file the protest within the time allowed this applicant will be regularly listed for enrollment.

Very respectfully,

T B Needles

Acting Chairman.

Enc. D-69.

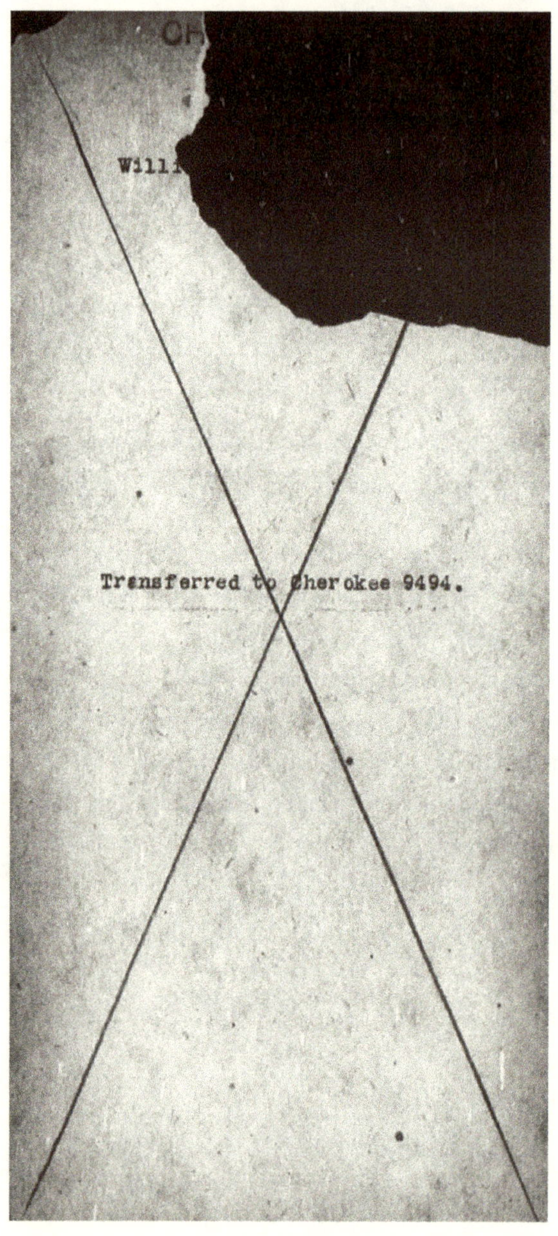
Ch

Willi

Transferred to Cherokee 9494.

RESIDENCE: Flint DISTRICT.
POST OFFICE: Stilwell I.T.

Cherokee Nation. Cherokee Roll.
(Not including Delawares, Shawnees, or Freedmen.)

CARD NO.
FIELD NO. 9494

Dawes' Roll No.	NAME.	Relationship to Person first Named.	AGE.	SEX.	BLOOD.	TRIBAL ENROLLMENT. Year.	District.	No.	TRIBAL ENROLLMENT OF PARENTS. Name of Father.	Year.	District.	Name of Mother.	Year.	District.
21564	White, William J.		28	M	1/16	1896	G Snake	2619	Harrison White		non citz	Mary White		Flint
	2													
	3 CITIZENSHIP CERTIFICATE ISSUED FOR NO. NOV 13 1901													
	4													
	5 GRANTED													
	6 MAY 20 1902													
	7													
	8													
	9													
	10													
	11													
	12													
	13													
	14													
	15													
	16													
	17 See Cherokee													
	18 Card No 9975													

Date of Application for Enrollment.

Cherokee D70 - Thomas J. White

RESIDENCE: Flint
POST-OFFICE: Stilwell I.T.

CHEROKEE Nation. CHEROKEE Roll.

CARD NO.
FIELD NO. D 70

Dawes' Roll No. | NAME | Relationship to Person first Named | AGE | SEX | BLOOD | TRIBAL ENROLLMENT: Year, District, No. | TRIBAL ENROLLMENT OF PARENTS: Name of Father, Year, District | Name of Mother, Year, District

1 White, Thomas J. | | | | 1896 | Cherokee | ... | Wm White | ... | Mary White

See testimony in case of Mary White ... card ...

COPY OF DECISION FORWARDED
ATTORNEY FOR CHEROKEE NATION
MAY 21 1902

APPLICATION GRANTED AND
APPLICATION IS ORDERED
ANNULLED
MAY 20 1902

COPY OF DECISION FORWARDED
APPLICANT
... 1902

DEPARTMENT OF THE INTERIOR,
COMMISSION TO THE FIVE CIVILIZED TRIBES,
BUNCH, I.T., AUGUST 1, 1900.

In the matter of the application of Thomas J. White for enrollment as a citizen of the Cherokee Nation, said White being sworn by Commissioner Needles, testified as follows:

Q What is your name? A Thomas J. White.
Q Your age? A 24.
Q Your postoffice address? A Stilwell.
Q Have you been recognized by the tribal authorities of the Cherokee Nation as a citizen of the Cherokee Nation? A Yes.
Q Have you ever been enrolled by the tribal authorities of the Cherokee Nation as a citizen of the Cherokee Nation? A Yes.
Q What district do you live? A Flint.
Q How long have you lived there? A For three years.
Q Where did you live before that? A In Goingsnake.
Q How long did you live in Goingsnake district? A About one year.
Q Where did you live before that? A Tahlequah.
Q How long did you live there? A Couple of years.
Q Where did you live before that? A Pryor Creek.
Q How long did you live there? A I lived there about three or four motnhs[sic].
Q Where did you live before that? A Came from Georgia.
How long have you lived continuously in the Cherokee Nation?
A I think about 6 years to the best of my knowledge since I came here last.
Q Do you recollect the year you came here last? A No sir.
Q Where did you come from when you came here last? A From Georgia.
Q What is the name of your father? A W. H. White.
Q Is he living? A Yes.
Q Is his name upon the rolls of the Cherokee Nation? A No sir, my mother's is.
Q What is the name of your mother? A Mary;
Q Is she living? A Yes.
Q Have you been outside of the Indian Territory within the past three years? A No sir.
Q Does our name appear upon the '80 roll of authenticated citizens of the Cherokee Nation? A No sir.
Q Does your name appear upon the '94 strip-payment roll? A Yes.
Q Does your name appear upon the '96 census roll? A Yes.
On '96 roll, page 814, number 2621;
On '94 roll, page 1182, number 3674, as Thos. J. *White*
Q What proportion of Cherokee blood do you claim? A 1/16.
Q Are you married? A No sir.

You present a certificate of admission to Cherokee citizenship dated at the office of the Commission on citizenship, Tahlequah, on the 22nd day of September,

1888, signed by J. T. Adair, Chairman of the Committee on Citizenship, attested by Connell Rogers, Clerk of the Citizenship Commission, approved and endorsed[sic] by J. B. Mayes, Principal Cheif[sic] of the Cherokee Nation; also signed by Henry Eiffort, Assistant Executive Secretary, under great seal of the Cherokee Nation. In the certificate there appears the name of Thomas J. White, purporting to be the son of Mary White. Are you the identical Thomas J. mentioned in this certificate of admission as Thomas J. White. A Yes.

By Mr. Baugh: Q Did you move here with your father in '90? A Yes.
Q How long did you remain in this country? A Somewhere's[sic] near three months.
Q Then you moved back to Georgia from here? A Yes.
Q While living in Georgia did you people exercise any of the rights of citizenship there? A No sir.
Q None of you--- your father did not? A No sir, not that I know of.
Q What time did you return to this country? A It was near '94 or '95 to the best of my knowledge.
Q Have you acquired a home here of your own since you returned here? A Yes.
Q Been living here ever since? A Yes.
Q Did you people apply to the National Council after your return for readmission?
A No sir.

Mr. Baugh, representative of the Cherokee Nation, protests against the enrollment of Thomas J. White. Said protest will be written out and inserted in this testimony at the proper time.

By the Commission:

Q Did you or your father ever apply to the Dawes Commission in '96 for admission?
A I could not say--- I never did myself.

The name of Thomas J. White appearing upon the census roll of '96 and pay-roll of '94 as indicated by page and number in the testimony in his case, and his name appearing in a certificate of admission to citizenship as a Cherokee citizen, described in the testimony here taken, and a protest being filed by the representatives of the Cherokee Nation against the admission of said Thomas J. White or his enrollment by this Commission at this time, the final judgment as to her enrollment at this time will be suspended, and his name will be placed upon what is known as a doubtful card. The final decision of the Commission as to the application of said applicant will be forwarded to him by mail to his postoffice address in the near future, and the testimony taken herein will be forwarded to the Secretary of the Interior, when the rolls of the Cherokee Nation are made up and completed by this Commission and forwarded to him for approval. Any further testimony that the applicant desires to produce before this Commission at any time before final judgment is rendered, he will be permitted to do so.

Brown McDonald, being duly sworn, says as Stenographer to the Commission to the Five Civilized Tribes, he reported in full the testimony of the above named witness and that the foregoing is a full, true and correct transcript of his notes.

Brown McDonald

Sworn to and subscribed before me this 13th day of August, 1900, at Muldrow, I.T.

Clifton R. Breckinridge
Commissioner.

"R"

File with Cherokee D-
70, Thomas J. White.

Department of the Interior,
Commission to the Five Civilized Tribes,
Muskogee, I. T., February 17, 1902.

SUPPLEMENTAL TESTIMONY AND PROCEEDINGS in the matter of the application of Mary White for enrollment as a Cherokee citizen.

WILLIAM H. WHITE being sworn and examined testified as follows:

Appearances:
William H. White, for applicant;
W. W. Hastings, attorney for the Cherokee Nation.

BY COMMISSION:
Q What is your name? A William H. White.
Q How old are you? A I am 53 years old.
Q What is your post-office? A Stilwell.

BY COMMISSION: There is offered in evidence a certificate from the Cherokee Commission on citizenship, bearing date of September 22, 1888, admitting one Mary White and her children, Lewis R. White and Mary P. White to citizenship in the Cherokee Nation. The document is signed by J. T. Adair, Chairman of the Commission on citizenship, attested by Connell Rogers, Clerk of the Commission on citizenship, approved and indorsed by J. B. Mayes, Principal Chief of the Cherokee Nation, and bears the seal thereof. It is filed herewith.

It further appears that William J. White, whose name appears on doubtful card No. 69, is found in said certificate.

Q Is there any other statement you desire to make relative to the enrollment of these parties? A No sir not that I know of; I want to say something in regard to our youngest child; it was rejected; it is out youngest child; I would like to make some explanation if it is necessary. When that application was made for citizenship she was not born.

BY COMMISSION: That child will come in all right.

It further appears that the name of Thomas J. White is found in the certificate of admission admitting Mary White and others to citizenship in the Cherokee Nation on the 22nd day of September, 1888.

The name of James A. White appears in the certificate issued by the Cherokee Commission on citizenship admitting Mary White, and others to citizenship in the Cherokee Nation, on the 22nd day of September, 1888.

Q Any other statement you desire to make relative to the enrollment of your wife and children? A As to James A. White he was requested to bring a marriage certificate and it was left here with the other papers and never received it back. It was left with the Commission at the time he was placed on a doubtful list. Marriage certificate and also the certificate of the birth of his child.

BY COMMISSION: The name of George W. White appears in the certificate admitting Mary White and others to citizenship in the Cherokee Nation on the 22nd day of September 1888.

Q Do you submit this case to the Commission for final consideration? A Yes sir.

BY MR. HASTINGS: Cherokee Nation submits it.

M.D. Green, being first duly sworn, states that as stenographer to the Commission to the Five Civilized Tribes he correctly recorded the testimony and proceedings in this case and that the foregoing is a true and complete transcript of his stenographic notes thereof.

M.D. Green

Subscribed and sworn to before me this February 21, 1902.

T B Needles

Commissioner.

Cherokee D. 70

DEPARTMENT OF THE INTERIOR,

COMMISSION TO THE FIVE CIVILIZED TRIBES.

In the matter of the application of Thomas J. White for enrollment as a Cherokee citizen.

On the first day of August, 1900, Thomas J. White appeared before the Commission to the Five Civilized Tribes and made application for his enrollment as a citizen by blood of the Cherokee Nation.

At the conclusion of the evidence offered at that time he was placed upon a "Doubtful" card awaiting further consideration of his right to enrollment.

Further evidence has been submitted to the Commission and the case submitted for final consideration. The following decision is now rendered.

D E C I S I O N.

---oOo---

From the evidence of record in this case it appears that Thomas J. White is a Cherokee Indian and was admitted to citizenship in the Cherokee Nation on the 22nd day of September, 1888, by a decree of the Cherokee Commission on Citizenship. It further appears that he came with his parents to the Cherokee Nation in 1890, and that a few months thereafter he returned with them to Georgia and remained there until 1894, at which time he returned to the Cherokee Nation. At the time of his return to Georgia applicant was fourteen years old.

Section 2, article 1, Constitution of the Cherokee Nation provides:

" . . . whenever any citizen shall remove with his effects out of the limits of this Nation, and becomes a citizen of any other Government all his rights and privileges as a citizen of this Nation shall cease. . . ."

There is no evidence in this case to show that Thomas J. White became a citizen of any other Government after his admission to citizenship in the Cherokee Nation, and as he was a minor and living with his parents at the time of his return to Georgia this Commission is of the opinion that the citizenship rights of the applicant were not forfeited by reason of the facts in this case. He is identified on the Strip payment roll of 1894, and the Cherokee Census roll of 1896, and he has lived continuously in the Cherokee Nation since 1894.

This Commission in making rolls of citizenship of the Cherokee Nation is governed by the following provisions of the Act of Congress approved June 28, 1898, (30 Stats., 495);

> "That in making rolls of citizenship of the several tribes, as required by law, the Commission to the Five Civilized Tribes is authorized and directed to take the roll of Cherokee citizens of eighteen hundred and eighty (not including freedmen) as the only roll intended to be confirmed by this and preceding Acts of Congress, and to enroll all persons now living whose names are found on said roll, and all descendants born since the date of said roll to persons whose names are found thereon; and all persons who have been enrolled by the tribal authorities who have heretofore made permanent settlement in the Cherokee Nation whose parents, by reason of their Cherokee blood, have been lawfully admitted to citizenship by the tribal authorities, and who were minors when their parents were so admitted; and they shall investigate the right of all other persons whose names are found on any other rolls and omit all such as may have been placed thereon by fraud or without authority of law, enrolling only such as may have lawful right thereto, and their descendants born since such rolls were made, with such intermarried white persons as may be entitled to citizenship under Cherokee laws."

In view of the facts and the law cited it is considered that Thomas J. White is entitled to be enrolled as a citizen by blood of the Cherokee Nation, and it is so ordered.

Tams Bixby

T B Needles

C. R. Breckinridge

Commissioners.

Dated at Muskogee, Indian Territory,

MAY 20 1902

COMMISSIONERS:

HENRY L. DAWES,
TAMS BIXBY,
THOMAS B. NEEDLES,
C. R. BRECKINRIDGE.

—

ALLISON L. AYLESWORTH,
SECRETARY.

ADDRESS ONLY THE
COMMISSION TO THE FIVE CIVILIZED TRIBES.

DEPARTMENT OF THE INTERIOR,
COMMISSION TO THE FIVE CIVILIZED TRIBES.

REFER IN REPLY TO THE FOLLOWING

D - 70.

Muskogee, Indian Territory, May 21, 1902.

W. W. Hastings, Esq.,

Attorney for the Cherokee Nation,

Muskogee, Indian Territory.

Sir:

Enclosed herewith, please find a copy of the decision of the Commission rendered May 20, 1902, in the matter of the application of Thomas J. White for enrollment as a citizen of the Cherokee Nation.

You are hereby advised that you will be allowed fifteen days from date hereof to file with the Commission such protest as you desire to make against the enrollment of the above named person as a citizen of the Cherokee Nation. If you fail to file the protest within the time allowed this applicant will be regularly listed for enrollment.

Very respectfully,

T B Needles

Acting Chairman.

Enc. D-70.

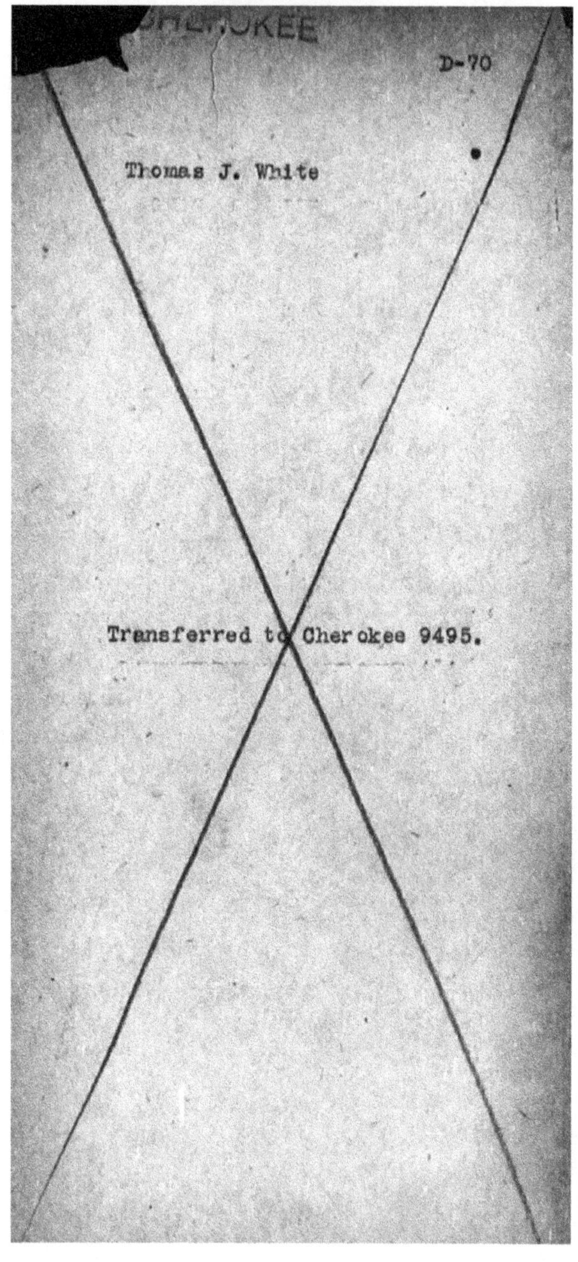

CHEROKEE

D-70

Thomas J. White

Transferred to Cherokee 9495.

RESIDENCE: Flint DISTRICT.
POST OFFICE: Stilwell I.T.

Cherokee Nation. Cherokee Roll.

(Not including Delawares, Shawnees, or Freedmen.)

CARD NO.
FIELD NO. 9495

Dawes' Roll No.	NAME	Relationship to Person first Named	AGE	SEX	BLOOD	Tribal Enrollment: Year	Tribal Enrollment: District	Tribal Enrollment: No.	Name of Father	Year	District	Name of Mother	Year	District
21565	1 White, Thomas J. x		24	M	1/16	1896	G Snake	2621	W H White		non citz	Mary White	-	Flint
	2													
	3													
	4 GRANTED													
	5 MAY 20 1902													
	6													
	7													
	8													
	9													
	10													
	11													
	12													
	13													
	14													
	15													
	16													
	17 See Cherokee													
	18 Card No 9975													

Date of Application for Enrollment.

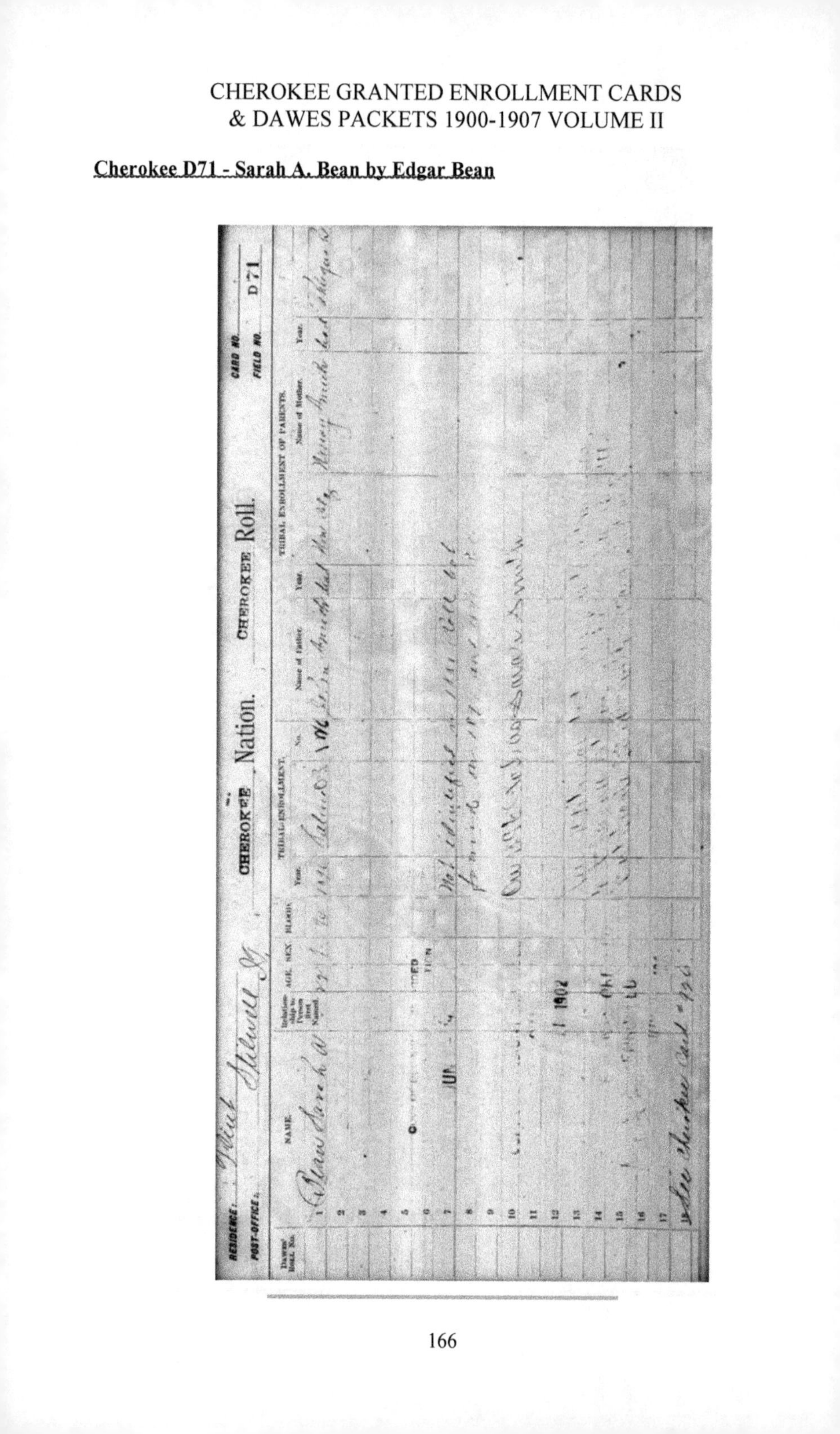

Cherokee D71 - Sarah A. Bean by Edgar Bean

Department of the Interior,
Commission to the Five Civilized Tribes,
Bunch, I.T., August 1, 1900.

In the matter of the application of Edgar Bean for the enrollment of himself, wife and child as Cherokees by blood; being duly sworn and examined by Commission Breckenridge[sic], he testified as follows:

Q What is your name? A Edgar Bean.
Q What is your age? A I am 28.
Q What is your post office? A Stilwell.
Q Your district? A Flint district.
Q How long have you lived in Flint district? A I have lived here 28 years I guess.
Q Lived in Flint district all of your life pretty much? A Yes, sir.
Q For whom do you apply now to have enrolled, yourself? A Myself and my wife and one child.
Q Do you apply as a Cherokee by blood? A Yes, sir.
Q What proportion of Cherokee blood do you claim? A About 1/4, I guess.
Q And you wife, is she a Cherokee by blood? A Yes, sir.
Q How much? A I reckon about 1/4,
Q Are you on the roll of 1880? A Yes, sir.
Q And 1896? A Yes, sir, I think so.
Q Now your wife, what is her name? A Sarah A. Bean.
Q What was her name when you married? A Sarah A. Smith.
Q Was that her maiden name? A Yes, sir.
Q How old is she? A 22.
Q When were you married? A I was married 2 years ago.
Q Is she on the roll of 1880 as Sarah Smith? A Yes sir, I guess so.
Q What is the name of your child? A Mark.
Q How old is that child? A About 10 days old.
Q That is all the children you have? A Yes, sir, that is all.
Q Were your father and mother living when you were eight or nine years old?
A Yes, sir, they are living yet.
Q What is your father's name? A Mark Bean.
Q Whose family were you enrolled with? A Mary Fulsom, my mother.
Q In what district? A Flint district.

(On 1880 roll, page 365, No. 554, Edward Fulsom, Flint district. On 1894 roll, page 12, No. 1, Edward Bean, Convict Roll. On 1896 roll, page 647, No. 232, Edward Bean, Flint district. Sarah Bean on 1896 roll, page 1040, No. 126, as Sarah Smith, Orphan Roll, Saline dist. On 1894 roll, page 5, No. 77, as Sarah Smith, Orphan Roll, Tahlequah district.)

Q You say you have been married two years? A Yes, sir.
Q Have you a certificate of marriage? A Yes, sir, here it is.
Q Mr. Bean, you present here a duly authenticated marriage license signed James A. Winston, Clerk of the United States Court, by H.W.C. Shelton, Deputy, under the

seal of the Court for the Northern District of the Indian Territory, under date of June 16, 1898. The certificate shows that you were duly married on the 19th of June, 1898, by Milton A. Clark, a minister of the Methodist Episcopal Church South, and the endorsement shows that this document has been duly recorded on the 21st of June, 1898. This satisfactorily establishes your marriage and the legitimacy of your child. You will leave this with your application. Now in regard to the birth of your child, you hand me a certificate, which is somewhat defective. You will be required to have it perfected, and the matter will be explained to you.

Now you are duly identified on the roll of 1880, and also on the roll of 1894 and the roll of 1896, and you will be enrolled as a Cherokee by blood; your marriage is satisfactorily established in 1898. You present a certificate of the birth of your child, Mark Bean, which is somewhat defective. When you have this certificate perfected and supply the Commission with it in due form, then your child Mark Bean will also be enrolled as a Cherokee by blood.

Now as to your wife, Sarah A. Bean, she is identified on the roll of 1894 and on the roll of 1896, but she cann't[sic] be identified on the roll of 1880. As the testimony discloses, there may be some question as to her being a Cherokee by blood. Upon the other hand, you state in the evidence that she was admitted and for some years continued as an inmate of the Cherokee Orphan Asylum. This is said to be a strong endorsement by responsible Cherokee officials, as no one was admitted except Cherokees by blood; but that will not be inquired into now by this Commission, it will need to be inquired into before coming to a final conclusion, as well as any other matters pertaining to the application for the enrollment of your wife. Therefore, your wife's application will be placed upon a doubtful card for the present. When a decision is finally reached in her case, you will be advised at your present post office address of that decision, and it will, whether favorable or unfavorable, be forwarded to the Honorable Secretary of the Interior for his Approval.

-------o-------

Bruce C. Jones, being duly sworn, says that as stenographer to the Commission to the Five Civilized Tribes he reported the testimony of the above named witness, and that the foregoing is a full, true and correct translation of his stenographic notes.

Bruce C Jones

Sworn to and subscribed before me this the 3rd day of August, 1900.

T B Needles
Commissioner.

D- 71.

Department of the Interior.
Commission to the Five Civilized Tribes.
Tahlequah, I. T., December 15, 1900.

Supplementary Testimony in the case of Sarah A. Bean.

Witness, Ezekiel P. Parris, being sworn and examined by Commissioner C. R. Breckinridge, testified as follows:

Q Give me your full name. A Ezekiel P. Parris.
Q How old are you? A 43 years old.
Q What is your postoffice? A Tahlequah.
Q In what district do you live? A Tahlequah
Q You want to give some information in the case of Sarah A. Bean, I believe?
A Yes sir.
Q There appears to be some trouble about her identification on the roll of 1880?
A Yes sir.
Q Can you assist us in identifying this woman on the rol[sic] of 1880? A Yes sir, she wasn't here in 1880. She was admitted in 1887 or '88 with Mrs. Martha Beck, my wife's aunt.
Q What was her name when she was admitted? A Sarah Smith.
Q That was her maiden name? A Yes sir.
Q Is there any certificate of admission that you know of? A Yes sir, I gave in the certificate with this Hampton's girl's case that came from the Choctaw Nation.
Q What is her name? A Zoa M. Hampton was her name. I can't think of her name now. She is married.
Q Did you present a certificate in that case? A Yes sir, she did.
Q Was it filed in that case? A Yes sir.
Q When did she come? A My aunt, Mrs. Martha Beck brought the five children here, and they were admitted by Council, and before she died she turned the children over to me, a d[sic] they were admitted to the Orphan Asylum by the Cherokee authorities.
Q What was Sarah A. Bean's name at the time of her admission? A Sarah Smith.
Commissioner- In case D-964, the same being the case of Zoa M. Cannon, formerly Zoa M. Hampton, there is found an official copy of the records of the Cherokee Commission on Citizenship, showing that certain people were admitted to citizenship and among them appears the name of Sarah Smith.
Q Now that is the Sarah Smith who is now known as Sarah A. Bean? A Yes sir.
Q Who is Fannie E. Hampton? A A half sister to Sarah Smith.
Q Who is Fred Beck who was admitted at that time -- was he any kin to her? A Half brother to her.
Q And what kin is Zoa M. Hampton to this Sarah Smith? A Half sister.
Q Were they half sister and brother through their mother, or through their father?
A Through their mother.

By J. L. Baugh, representative of the Cherokee Nation-
Q Who did these children live with after their admission? A With their grandmother, Mrs. Martha Beck.
Q Is she dead? A She lived with them until she died.
Q What become of them after their grandmother died? A I took them to the Orphan Home.
Q Were you ever appointed guardian for them? A Yes sir, I was taking care of their property and winding up their estate.
Q What age was this girl at the time she married Bean? A Between 16 and 18. I don't know exactly.
Q Had she lived in the Cherokee Nation all the time; has she made this her residence? A Yes sir, until she went away to the Chocraw[sic] Nation.
Q How long had she been in the Choctaw Nation? A I don't know.
Q Was she only a minor -- she was a minor before she married Bean?
A Yes sir, she was a minor when she married Bean. I think she was something like 18. Sarah Smith has never been out of the Cherokee Nation. I thought you were talking about the Hampton children.

E.G. Rothenberger, being duly sworn, states that as stenographer to the Commission to the Five Civilized Tribes, he reported in full the supplementary testimony in the above case, and that the foregoing is a full, true and correct transcript of his stenographic notes in said case.

E. G. Rothenberger

Subscribed and sworn to before me this 18th day of December, 1900.

T B Needles
Commissioner.

CHEROKEE D 71

DEPARTMENT OF THE INTERIOR,

COMMISSION TO THE FIVE CIVILIZED TRIBES.

In the matter of the application of Sarah A. Bean, for enrollment as a Cherokee citizen.

On the first day of August, 1900, Edgar Bean appeared before the Commission to the Five Civilized Tribes and made application for the enrollment of himself, his wife Sarah A. Bean, and his child Mark Bean as citizens by blood of the Cherokee Nation.

At the conclusion of the evidence offered at that time Edgar Bean and his child Mark were listed for enrollment on a regular card, and the name of his wife Sarah A.

Bean was placed upon a "Doubtful" card as she could not be identified upon the Tribal roll of 1880, being then 22 years old.

Further evidence has been submitted to the Commission and the following decision is rendered.

D E C I S I O N.

--oOo--

From all the evidence of record in this case it appears that Sarah A. Bean under her maiden name of Sarah Smith was admitted to citizenship in the Cherokee Nation by a decision of the Cherokee Commission on Citizenship in the year 1887 or 1888. She has lived in the Cherokee Nation ever since the date of her admission. It is evident of course that she could not be identified on the 1880 roll. She is identified, however, on the strip payment roll of 1894, and the Cherokee Census roll of 1896.

In making rolls of citizenship of the Cherokee Nation this Commission is governed by the following provisions of the Act of Congress approved June 28, 1898 (30 Stats., 495);

> "That in making rolls of citizenship of the several tribes, as required by law, the Commission to the Five Civilized Tribes is authorized and directed to take the roll of Cherokee citizens of eighteen hundred and eighty (not including freedmen) as the only roll intended to be confirmed by this and preceding Acts of Congress, and to enroll all persons now living whose names are found on said roll, and all descendants born since the date of said roll to persons whose names are found thereon; and all persons who have been enrolled by the tribal authorities who have heretofore made permanent settlement in the Cherokee Nation whose parents, by reason of their Cherokee blood, have been lawfully admitted to citizenship by the tribal authorities, and who were minors when their parents were so admitted; and they shall investigate the right of all other persons whose names are found on any other rolls and omit all such as may have been placed thereon by fraud or without authority of law, enrolling only such as may have lawful right thereto, and their descendants born since such rolls were made, with such intermarried white persons as may be entitled to citizenship under Cherokee laws."

Under the facts and the law in this case it is considered that Sarah A. Bean is entitled to be enrolled as a citizen by blood of the Cherokee Nation, and it is therefore so ordered.

Tams Bixby

T B Needles

C. R. Breckinridge

Commissioners.

Dated at Muskogee, Indian Territory,

JUN 9 - 1902

COMMISSIONERS:

HENRY L. DAWES,
TAMS BIXBY,
THOMAS B. NEEDLES,
C. R. BRECKINRIDGE.

—

ALLISON L. AYLESWORTH,
SECRETARY.

ADDRESS ONLY THE
COMMISSION TO THE FIVE CIVILIZED TRIBES.

DEPARTMENT OF THE INTERIOR,
COMMISSION TO THE FIVE CIVILIZED TRIBES.

REFER IN REPLY TO THE FOLLOWING

Cher. D-71.

Muskogee, Indian Territory, June 9, 1902.

W. W. Hastings, Esq.,

Attorney for Cherokee Nation,

Muskogee, Indian Territory.

Sir:

Enclosed herewith please find copy of the decision of the Commission rendered June 9, 1902, in the matter of the application of Sarah A. Bean for enrollment as a Cherokee citizen.

You are hereby advised that you will be allowed fifteen days from the date hereof in which to file with the Commission such protest as you desire to make against the enrollment of the person above named as a citizen of the Cherokee Nation. If you fail to file protest within the time allowed this applicant will be regularly listed for enrollment.

Yours truly,

Tams Bixby

Acting Chairman.

Encl. D-71.

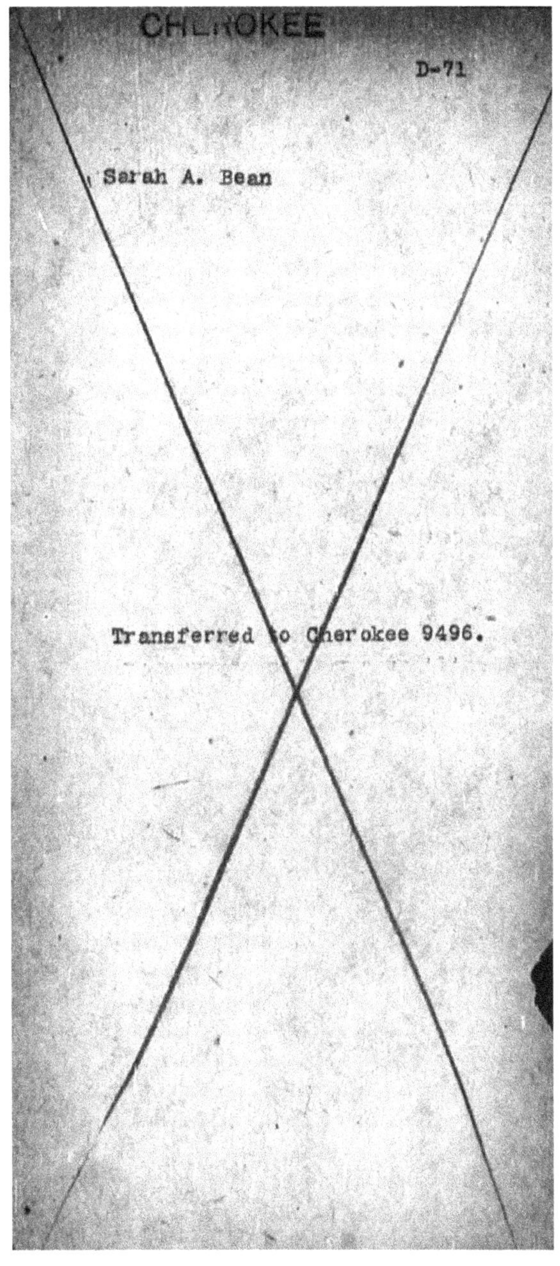

CHEROKEE

D-71

Sarah A. Bean

Transferred to Cherokee 9496.

RESIDENCE: Flint DISTRICT.
POST OFFICE: Stilwell I.T.

Cherokee Nation. Cherokee Roll.
(Not including Delawares, Shawnees, or Freedmen.)

CARD NO.
FIELD NO. 9536

Dawes' Roll No.		NAME.	Relationship to Person first Named.	AGE.	SEX.	BLOOD.	Tribal Enrollment: Year.	Tribal Enrollment: District.	Tribal Enrollment: No.	Parents: Name of Father.	Parents: Year.	Parents: District.	Parents: Name of Mother.	Parents: Year.	Parents: District.
21566	1	Bean, Sarah A		22	F	1/4	1896	Saline OR	126	John Smith	dead	Non citz	Nancy Smith	dead	Tahlequah
	2														
	3														
	4	GRANTED													
	5	JUN - 9 1902					Not identified on 1880 Roll but								
	6						found on 1894 and 1896 Rolls								
	7														
	8						On 1896 Roll as Sarah Smith								
	9														
	10														
	11														
	12														
	13														
	14														
	15														
	16														
	17														
	18														

Date of Application for Enrollment.

Cherokee D72 - Caldonia S. Sumpter by John E. Sumpter

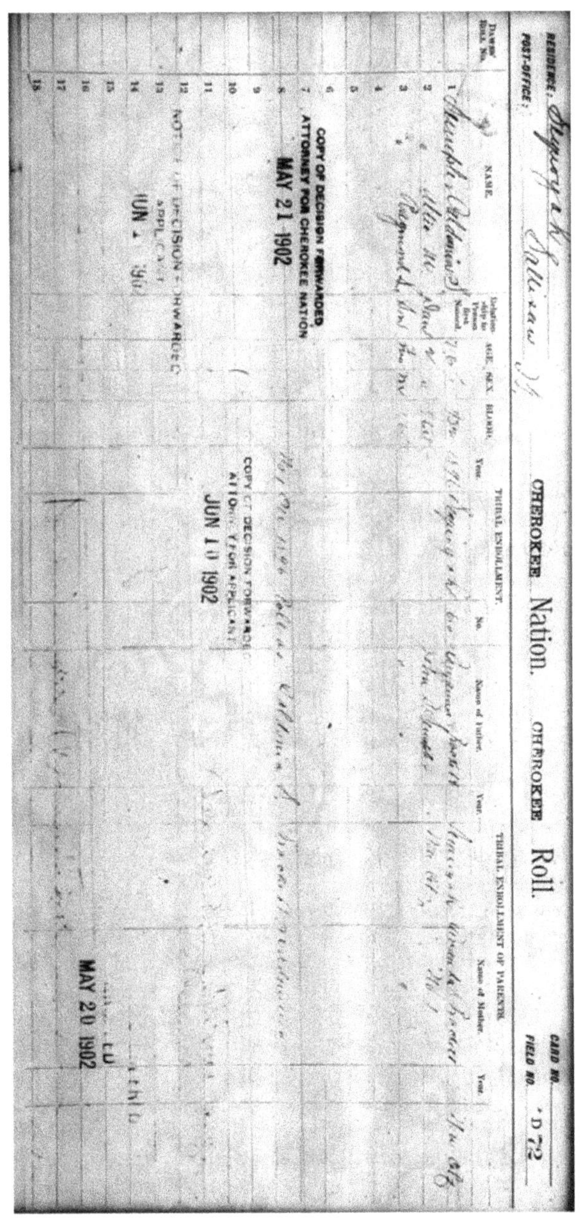

RESIDENCE:
POST-OFFICE:

CHEROKEE Nation. CHEROKEE Roll.

CARD NO.
FIELD NO. D 72

COPY OF DECISION FORWARDED
ATTORNEY FOR CHEROKEE NATION
MAY 21 1902

COPY OF DECISION FORWARDED
ATTORNEY FOR APPLICANT
JUN 10 1902

NOTICE OF DECISION FORWARDED
APPLICANT
JUN 1902

MAY 20 1902

Department of the Interior,
Commission to the Five Civilized Tribes,
Bunch, I. T., August 1st, 1900.

In the matter of the application of John E. Sumpter et al for enrollment as Cherokee citizens; being sworn and examined by Commissioner Needles he testifies as follows:

Q What is your name? A John E. Sumpter.
Q How old are you? A Twenty-seven.
Q What is your post-office address? A Sallisaw.
Q Have you been recognized by the Tribal authorities of the Cherokee Nation as a citizen? A No sir.
Q Have you ever been enrolled by the Cherokee Tribal authorities as a citizen of the Cherokee Nation? A No sir.
Q Does your name appear upon any of the Tribal rolls of the Cherokee Nation?
A No sir.
Q Were you admitted by the Commission to the Five Civilized Tribes as a citizen?
A No sir.
Q Were you admitted by the United States Court in the Indian Territory upon appeal from the decision of the Tribal authorities? Were you ever admitted by the Tribal authorities of the Cherokee Nation? A As adopted.
Q Are you an intermarried citizen? A Yes sir.
Q In what district do you live? A Sequoyah.
Q How long have you lived there? A Nine years.
Q Are you married? A Yes sir.
Q Under what law were you married? A Cherokee law.
Q Have you a marriage license and certificate with you? A Yes sir. (Produces papers.)
Q Where were you living at the time you were married? A Sequoyah.
Q You don't apply for yourself? A No sir. My wife and my children.
Q What was your wife's name before she was married? A Caldonia S. Brackett.
Q What was her father's name? A Benjamin Brackett.
Q Is he living? A Yes sir.
Q Is he a citizen by blood of the Cherokee Nation? A Yes sir.
Q His name upon the rolls of the Cherokee Nation? A Yes sir.
Q What was her mother's name? A Mandy Brackett.
Q Is she living? A Yes sir.
Q Is she a Cherokee citizen by blood? A No sir.
Q What is the age of your wife? A Twenty-six.
Q Is she on the 1880 roll? A No sir.
Her name appears upon the 1894 in Goingsnake District, and 1896 in Sequoyah.
Q By what authority does it appear upon there? A Cherokee authority.
Q Have you got a certificate to show? A Yes sir. (Produces paper.)
Q You present here a certificate of admission to Cherokee citizenship issued in the office of the Commission on Citizenship at Tahlequah, Cherokee Nation, certifying that on the 2nd day of April 1887 Caldonia S. Brackett was admitted to citizenship,

said certificate being signed 24th day of September 1889 by William P. Ross Chairman of the Committee on Citizenship, attested by D. Williams Assistant Clerk, and approved and indorsed by J. B. Mayes Principal Chief under the Great Seal of the Cherokee Nation, is the Caldonia S. Brackett mentioned in this certificate the identical Caldonia S. Brackett for whom you apply for citizenship and to whom you have been married? A Yes sir.
Q How long has Caldonia S. Brackett lived in the Cherokee Nation?
A I don't know exactly how long.
Q You don't know when she came to the Cherokee Nation? A No sir.

-- -- --

Benjamin Brackett being sworn and examined by Commissioner Needles testifies as follows:

Q What is your name? A Benjamin Brackett.
Q What is your age? A Fifty-one.
Q Where do you live? A In Sequoyah District.
Q How long have you lived there? A Six years.
Q Where did you come from to Sequoyah District? A I came from Goingsnake.
Q How long have you lived continuously in the Indian Territory and Cherokee Nation? A Thirteen years.
Q Without moving out? A Yes sir.
Q Do you know Caldonia S. Brackett? A Yes sir.
Q Is she any relation of yours? A Yes sir.
Q What? A Daughter.
Q Her husband applies for her admission here, and presents a certificate of citizenship as already described in the testimony given by him, with which you are familiar, when did Caldonia S. Brackett come to the Cherokee Nation? A The same time, about thirteen years ago.
Q Has she been living here continuously? A Yes sir.
Q Are you the identical Benjamin Brackett admitted to Cherokee citizenship on the 2nd day of April 1887 in this certificate signed by William P. Ross, Chairman and J. B. Mayes Principal Chief? A Yes sir.
Q The law under which you were re-admitted provides that as a condition precedent to the delivery of this certificate it should be the duty of all such persons admitted by it to enroll the names with the names of their family on their arrival in a book to be kept in the office of the Principal Chief, did you enroll your name? A No sir, I was already here.
Q You didn't enroll your name for the reason that you was a resident here at that time? A Yes sir.
Q You had been residing here before that time? A Yes sir.
Q You were admitted on the 2nd day of April 1887, were you living in the Cherokee Nation in 1887? A Yes sir.
Q What year did you come from the State of Georgia to the Cherokee Nation?
A I disremember.

Examined by Cherokee Representative Baugh:

Q Mr. Brackett I wanted to ask you if Mige Brackett belonged to the same family as yours did? A He was an uncle of mine.
Q Did he live here at the same time that you did when he was admitted? A There is two, there is a young Mige Brackett and an old Mige Brackett.
Q The young one is the one that was admitted? A He wasn't here when I came here.
Q He went and had his name enrolled did he not? A I couldn't tell you.

Commissioner Needles examining applicant, re-called:
Q You present a marriage license issued on the 19th day of January 1897 by the Clerk of Sequoyah District, George W. Bethel authorizing marriage between John E. Sumpter and Caldonia S. Brackett, are you the identical John E. Sumpter mentioned in this license? A Yes sir.
Q And a certificate, stating that Caldonia S. Brackett and John E. Sumpter were married on the 24th day of January 1897, this certificate of marriage is duly certified to; now have you any children? A Yes sir.
Q What are the names of your children? A Altie M. Sumpter, born the 1st day of November, 1897. Raymong[sic] L., Sumpter, seven months old.

Note: 1890 roll examined for applicant's wife; page 1051 #60 as Caldonia S. Brackett, Sequoyah District. 1894 roll, page 616 #150 as Caldonia S. Brackett, Goingsnake District.

Com'r Needles: The name of Caldonia S. Brackett being found upon the certificate of admission to Cherokee citizenship as described in the evidence herein, and being duly identified as the identical person, and her name also being found upon the census roll of 1896 and the pay roll of 1894, and being duly identified according to page and number, and the marriage license being presented in due form and marriage certificate as to her marriage with John E. Sumpter on the 24th day of January 1897, and there is also presented certificates of the birth, duly executed, proving the birth of their two children Altie M. Sumpter and Raymond L. Sumpter, all of which appears satisfactory and in due form as to the Cherokee citizenship of Caldonia Sumpter and the two children named herein; but come the Cherokee Nation, by its representative, J. L. Baugh, and files protest against the enrollment of said Caldonia Sumpter and her two children as Cherokee citizens; final judgment therefore in regard to the admission of these parties is suspended and their names will be placed upon a doubtful card.

Caldonia S. Sumpter, or her husband, will have the privilege at any time of presenting any further testimony, either oral or documentary, as to her rights and that of her children to Cherokee citizenship. The day for the hearing of any further testimony in regard to this case to be submitted by the authorities of the Cherokee Nation or the applicants herein, will be set at some future date, and the applicant and her husband will be notified in due season in order that they may appear at said hearing.

M.D. Green, being first duly sworn, states that as stenographer to the Commission to the Five Civilized Tribes he reported the foregoing case and the above and foregoing is a full true and complete transcript of his stenographic notes in said case.

MD Green

Subscribed and sworn to before me this 2nd day of August 1900.

T B Needles
Commissioner.

"R"

Cherokee D 72.

Department of the Interior,
Commission to the Five Civilized Tribes,
Muskogee, I. T., February 17, 1902.

SUPPLEMENTAL PROCEEDINGS, in the matter of the application of Caldonia S. Sumpter et al., for enrollment as Cherokee citizens.

Appearances:
James N. Huckleberry, Sr., Sallisaw, I.T., Attorney for the applicants;
Daniel Brackett, relative of applicants;
W.W. Hastings, attorney for the Cherokee Nation.

BY COMMISSION, of attorney Huckleberry:
Q Do you submit this case to the Commission for final consideration?
A Yes sir.
BY MR. HASTINGS: We do.

M.D. Green, being first duly sworn, states that as stenographer to the Commission to the Five Civilized Tribes he correctly recorded the testimony and proceedings in this case and that the foregoing is a true and complete transcript of his stenographic notes thereof.

MD Green

Subscribed and sworn to before me this February 19, 1902.

T B Needles
Commissioner.

Cherokee D 72

DEPARTMENT OF THE INTERIOR,

COMMISSION TO THE FIVE CIVILIZED TRIBES.

Muskogee, Indian Territory, March 11;02

In the matter of the application of Caldonia S. Sumpter, et.al. for enrollment as Cherokee citizens,

----

Supplemental Statement.

---oOo---

From affidavits of birth duly executed on the 31st day of July, 1900, and received by this Commission on the first day of August, 1900, it appears that Altie M. Sumpter was born to Caldonia S. and John E. Sumpter on the 12th day of November, 1897, and that Raymond L. Sumpter was born to the said parties on the second day of December, 1899, and that both of said children were living at the date of the execution of said affidavits. The same have been approved and filed with this Commission.

It is directed that copies of this statement be filed with the testimony in the above case.

T B Needles

Commissioner.

Cherokee D 72

DEPARTMENT OF THE INTERIOR,

COMMISSION TO THE FIVE CIVILIZED TRIBES.

In the matter of the application for the enrollment of Caldonia S. Sumpter, Altie M. Sumpter and Raymond L. Sumpter as citizens by blood of the Cherokee Nation.

DECISION.

--oOo--

The record in this case shows that on August 1, 1900, John E. Sumpter appeared before the Commission at Bunch, Indian Territory, and made application for the enrollment of his wife Caldonia S. Sumpter and his minor children Altie M. and Raymond L. Sumpter as citizens by blood of the Cherokee Nation.

On February 17, 1902, applicants, by their attorney, appeared before the Commission at Muskogee, Indian Territory and submitted the case for final consideration.

The evidence shows that Caldonia S. Sumpter is a Cherokee Indian and was admitted to citizenship in the Cherokee Nation under the name of Caldonia S. Brackett by a decree of the Cherokee Commission on Citizenship on April 2, 1887. She was then residing in the Cherokee Nation and has lived there continuously since the date of her admission to citizenship. She is identified on the Strip payment roll of 1894 and the Census roll of 1896. On January 24, 1897, she was married to John E. Sumpter, a non-citizen. The children Altie M. and Raymond L. are the issue of such marriage. They are too young to be upon any roll, but they are identified as having been living at the date of this application.

The authority of the Commission herein is defined in Paragraph 1, Sec. 21, of the Act of Congress, June 28, 1898 (30 Stats., 495).

It is therefore the opinion of this Commission that Caldonia S. Sumpter and her minor children Altie M. Sumpter and Raymond L. Sumpter are lawfully entitled to be enrolled as members by blood of the Cherokee tribe of Indians in Indian Territory, and that the application for their enrollment as such should be granted, and it is so ordered.

COMMISSION TO THE FIVE CIVILIZED TRIBES.

Tams Bixby
Acting Chairman.

T.B. Needles
Commissioner.

Muskogee, Indian Territory,
this MAY 20 1902

C. R. Breckinridge
Commissioner.

COMMISSIONERS:

HENRY L. DAWES,
TAMS BIXBY,
THOMAS B. NEEDLES,
C. R. BRECKINRIDGE.

ALLISON L. AYLESWORTH,
SECRETARY.

ADDRESS ONLY THE
COMMISSION TO THE FIVE CIVILIZED TRIBES.

DEPARTMENT OF THE INTERIOR.
COMMISSION TO THE FIVE CIVILIZED TRIBES.

REFER IN REPLY TO THE FOLLOWING

D. 72.

Muskogee, Indian Territory, May 21, 1902.

W. W. Hastings, Esq.,

Attorney for the Cherokee Nation,

Sir:

Enclosed herewith please find copy of a decision of the Commission rendered May 20th, in the matter of the application of Caldonia S. Sumpter, Altie M. Sumpter and Raymond L. Sumpter for enrollment as citizens of the Cherokee Nation.

You are hereby advised that you will be allowed fifteen days from the date hereof in which to file with the Commission such protest as you desire to make against the enrollment of the above persons as citizens of the Cherokee Nation. If you fail to file the protest within the time allowed these applicants will be regularly listed for enrollment.

Very respectfully,

T B Needles

Acting Chairman.

Encl. C-72.

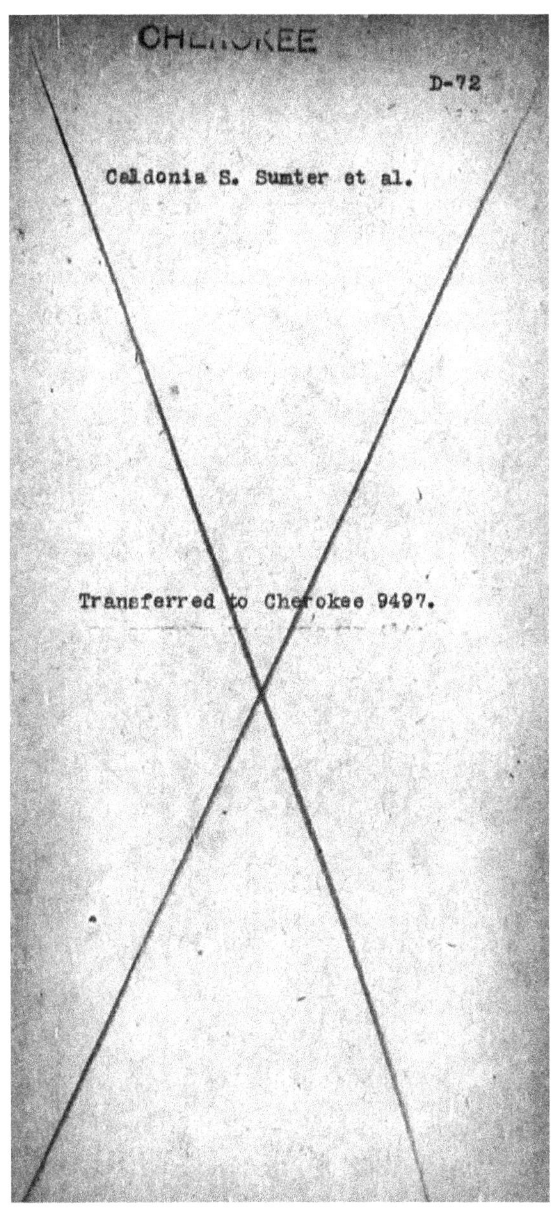
CHEROKEE

D-72

Caldonia S. Sumter et al.

Transferred to Cherokee 9497.

RESIDENCE: Sequoyah DISTRICT.
POST OFFICE: Sallisaw I T

Cherokee Nation. Cherokee Roll.
(Not including Delawares, Shawnees, or Freedmen.)

CARD No. ______
FIELD No. 9497

Dawes' Roll No.	NAME.	Relationship to Person first Named.	AGE.	SEX.	BLOOD.	Tribal Enrollment: Year.	District.	No.	Name of Father.	Year.	District.	Name of Mother.	Year.	District.
21567	Sumpter, Caldonia S.		26	F	1/32	1896	Sequoyah	60	Benjamin Brackett		Sequoyah	Amanda Brackett		non citz
21568	" Attie M.	Dau	2	"	1/64				John B Sumpter		non citz	" No 1		
21569	" Raymond L.	Son	7mo	M	1/64				" "		"	No 1		
21570	" Cecil Victor	Son	5mo	M	1/64		See note		"			No 1		

GRANTED
MAY 20 1902

No. 1 on 1896 Roll as Caldonia S Brackett, readmitted
No 4: Birth affidavit approved September 4, 1902
Represented by J H Huckleberry, Sallisaw I T
No 1 died February 14, 1902; affidavit filed [illegible]
No 4 " July 7 1902; " " [illegible]

CITIZENSHIP CERTIFICATE
ISSUED FOR NO.
NOV 17 1904

CITIZENSHIP CERTIFICATE
ISSUED FOR NO.
NOV 17 1904

CITIZENSHIP CERTIFICATE
ISSUED FOR NO.
NOV 17 1904

Date of Application for Enrollment.

Cherokee D74 - James A. White

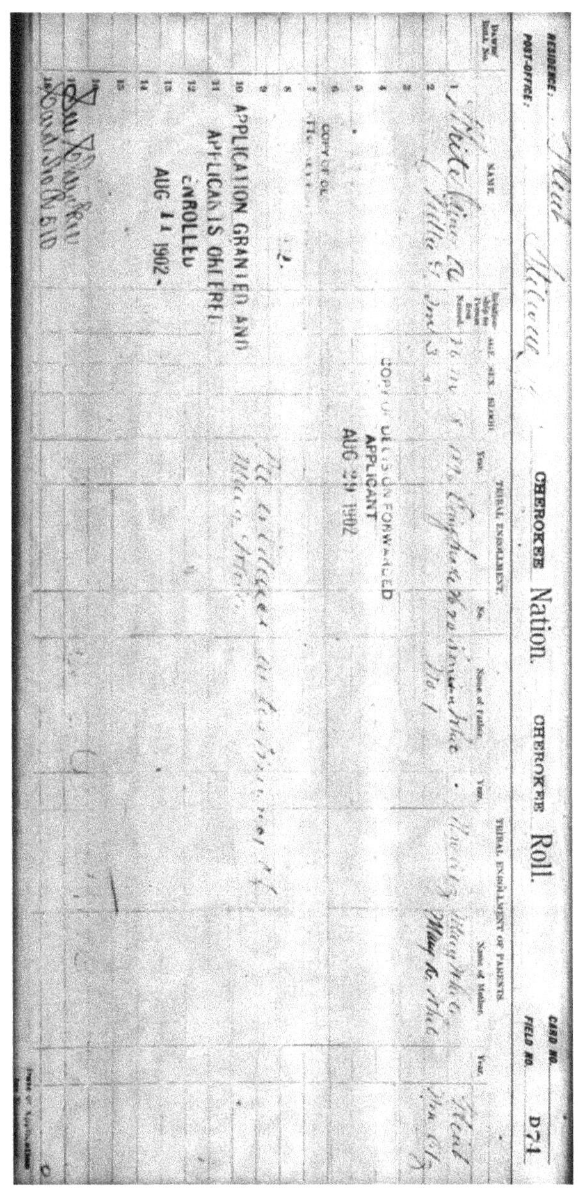

CHEROKEE Nation. CHEROKEE Roll.

CARD NO.

FIELD NO. D74

RESIDENCE: Flint

POST-OFFICE: Stilwell

COPY OF DECISION FORWARDED
APPLICANT
AUG 29 1902

APPLICATION GRANTED AND
APPLICANTS ORDERED
ENROLLED
AUG 11 1902

Department of the Interior.
Commission to the Five Civilized Tribes.
Bunch, I. T., August 2nd, 1900.

In the matter of the application of James A White et al for enrollment as Cherokee citizens; being sworn and examined by Commissioner Breckinridge, testifies as follows:

Q What is your full name? A James A. White.
Q What's your age? A 26.
Q What's your post-office? A Stilwell.
Q What's your district? A Flint.
Q How long have you lived in Flint? A About 4 years.
Q Where did you live before that? A I lived in Goingsnake before that.
Q How long did you live in Goingsnake? A Hardly a year.
Q Where did you live before that? A Tahlequah.
Q How long did you live in Tahlequah? A About one and a half year[sic].
Q Where did you live before that? A I lived in Georgia.
Q For whom do you apply for enrollment? A For myself, wife and baby.
Q One child? A Yes sir.
Q Were you admitted by the action of the Cherokee authorities? A Yes sir.

You hand me here Mr. White, a duly authenticated certificated[sic] of admission to Cherokee citizenship. It is signed by J. T. Adair, Chairman of the Committee on Citizenship, it is attested by Connell Rogers, Clerk of the Committee, approved and endorsed by J. B. Mayes, Principal Chief of the Cherokee Nation and it is under the great seal of the Nation. It is dated, Sept. 22nd, 1888. In this certificate, I find the name of James A. White along with some other people.
Q Is that your name? A Yes sir.
Q You present this as your certificate to admission? A Yes sir.

It is in due form and you are duly identified in this certificate. It is returned to you.
Q Are you on the roll of 1894? A Yes sir, I guess so.
Q Roll of 1896? A I guess so.
Q Give the name of your wife? A Mary Kindness White.
Q What was her name when you married her? A Culver.

You hand here a marriage license, Mr. White, which is in due form. It is issued by James A. Winston, Clerk of the United States Court, H. W. C. Shelton, Deputy, on the 12th of February, 1897, dated at Tahlequah and under the seal of the Court and authorizing your marriage to Miss Kindness Culver. The certificate of marriage shows that you were duly married according to the license on the 21st of February, 1897. The document shows that it has been duly recorded, having been filed for record April 14th, 1897.
Q Mr. White, you claim for your wife as an intermarried Cherokee? A Yes sir.
Q Do you know the Cherokee law of 1895 preventing the acquirements of right to citizenship by intermarriage after that date; are you aware of that law? A Well, I have heard of it, yes sir; I don't claim to know much about law.

Q But you make your application for your wife? A Yes sir.
Q She's living at this time and living with you? A Yes sir.
Q Now Mr. White, you seem to want to apply for a child? A Yes sir.
Q What is the name of your child? A Willie Guy.
Q How old is that child? A Three years old, the 8th of November.
Q Is that child upon any roll of the Cherokee Nation? A No sir.
Q Its name is Willie Guy White? A Yes sir.
Q That is the child of your present marriage? A Yes sir.

You present here a sworn certificate of the birth of this child from its mother, Mary K. White, and from J. C. Boger, M.D., duly attested by a Notary Public. You file this with your application.

1896 roll; page 814, #862, James A. White, Goingsnake Dist.
1894 roll; page 1182, #3673, Jas. A. White, Tahlequah Dist.

Now, Mr. White, it is observed that you were admitted to citizenship in 1888 and that you only appear to have been in the Cherokee Nation about 6 1/2 years; in other words, according to the statement you have submitted, you did not come to the Cherokee Nation until something like six years had expired after your admission. I will stop at this point and let you be interrogated by the representative present of the Cherokee Nation.

Mr. Baugh: A Mr. White, is your mother Mary White? A Yes sir.
Q Was she admitted to citizenship in 1888? A Yes sir.
Q When did she first come to this country after admission? A In '91, I believe; I will not be positive.
Q You come with her? A Yes sir.
Q How long did you live in the Cherokee Nation after you first came here?
A It wasn't a great while.
Q About how long? A Three or four months.
Q What was your object of the move to this country? A The object was to make our home here.
Q When you returned or went back to Georgia, did you take all your effects with you? A Folks did, yes sir.
Q How long did you remain in Georgia before you returned to this country?
A Something over three years.
Q What was you doing while you were in Georgia this last time? A Just farming.
Q Living on your own place? A No sir.
Q What was the object in going back to Georgia? A I had to follow my father then as I was under age then. I don't know the reason.
Q What time did you return here then? A In November, 1894, I, believe.
Q Did you draw strip money? A Yes sir.
Q Where was[sic] you at when the Census Roll was made for the purpose of paying out this money? A In Georgia, I guess.
Q How come your name to be placed upon that roll? A I don't know anything about that.
Q You didn't give the names in yourself, you nor your folks? A No sir.
Q Were you of age when you returned to this country the last time? A No sir.
Q Did you or your folks make application to the National Council for readmission?

A I don't know.
Q Do you know whether your father while he was in the state of Georgia exercised any of the rights as a citizen of that State? A No sir, I don't know.
Q Do you know whether he voted at any election either municipal or otherwise?
A No, I don't.

I wish in the name of the Cherokee Nation to file a protest against the enrollment of this applicant and his child, Willie Guy, on the ground that they have forfeited their rights by removing from the Cherokee Nation back to Georgia with all their effects; and that when they came back, they failed to avail themselves of the privilege granted under section 2nd, article one, of the Cherokee Constitution, which provides for the readmission of persons so removing out of the limit of the Cherokee Nation.

Com'r. Breckinridge: Mr. White, you present a duly authenticated certificate of your admission to citizenship on the 22nd of September, 1888, and you are founf[sic] on the roll of 1894 and also on the roll of 1896; but it appears from your testimony that after your admission in 1888, you came with your family to the Cherokee Nation and then returned for several years to Georgia as shown in the testimony, returning again to the Nation some six years ago. The question of your having forfeited your citizenship and having failed to take necessary steps for readmission presents itself in this case for consideration and is also raised by the representative present of the Cherokee Nation. Your residence in the Nation for the last six years or nearly six years at least, appears to be very well established, but in view of the question of forfeiture involved, your application will be placed upon a doubtful card for further consideration. When the decision of the Commission is finally reached, you will be advised of it at your present post-office and that decision whether favorable or unfavorable, will be forwarded with all the papers in your case to the Honorable Secretary of the Interior for his final approval.

Now, you have made application for your wife, Kindness White. Your marriage is duly established, but it took place in 1897 after the Cherokee law prohibited the acquirement of rights of citizenship by intermarriage, and therefore the enrollment of your wife at this time is refused; but that does not effect[sic] the rights of your child, Willie Guy; he is duly identified by a certificate of birth, which you have presented and which is shown to be born in lawful wedlock, but the child can only derive its rights through you under lawful marriage and therefore your application for the child will be placed with yours upon a doubtful card, and the final decision respecting the child will be communicated to you as with your own application.

Edward G. Rothenberger, being duly sworn by Commissioner Breckinridge as Stenographer to the Commission to the Five Civilized Tribes, he reported in full the testimony of the above named witness, James A. White, and that the foregoing is a full, true and correct transcript of his notes.

Edward G. Rothenberger

Sworn to and subscribed before me this 6th day of August, 1900.

Commissioner.

"R"

File with Cherokee D-
74, James A. White.

Department of the Interior,
Commission to the Five Civilized Tribes,
Muskogee, I. T., February 17, 1902.

SUPPLEMENTAL TESTIMONY AND PROCEEDINGS in the matter of the application of Mary White for enrollment as a Cherokee citizen.

WILLIAM H. WHITE being sworn and examined testified as follows:

Appearances:
William H. White, for applicant;
W. W. Hastings, attorney for the Cherokee Nation.

BY COMMISSION:
Q What is your name? A William H. White.
Q How old are you? A I am 53 years old.
Q What is your post-office? A Stilwell.

BY COMMISSION: There is offered in evidence a certificate from the Cherokee Commission on citizenship, bearing date of September 22, 1888, admitting one Mary White and her children, Lewis R. White and Mary P. White to citizenship in the Cherokee Nation. The document is signed by J. T. Adair, Chairman of the Commission on citizenship, attested by Connell Rogers, Clerk of the Commission on citizenship, approved and indorsed by J. B. Mayes, Principal Chief of the Cherokee Nation, and bears the seal thereof. It is filed herewith.

It further appears that William J. White, whose name appears on doubtful card No. 69, is found in said certificate.

Q Is there any other statement you desire to make relative to the enrollment of these parties? A No sir not that I know of; I want to say something in regard to our youngest child; it was rejected; it is out youngest child; I would like to make some explanation if it is necessary. When that application was made for citizenship she was not born.

BY COMMISSION: That child will come in all right.

It further appears that the name of Thomas J. White is found in the certificate of admission admitting Mary White and others to citizenship in the Cherokee Nation on the 22nd day of September, 1888.

The name of James A. White appears in the certificate issued by the Cherokee Commission on citizenship admitting Mary White, and others to citizenship in the Cherokee Nation, on the 22nd day of September, 1888.

Q Any other statement you desire to make relative to the enrollment of your wife and children? A As to James A. White he was requested to bring a marriage certificate and it was left here with the other papers and never received it back. It was left with the Commission at the time he was placed on a doubtful list. Marriage certificate and also the certificate of the birth of his child.

BY COMMISSION: The name of George W. White appears in the certificate admitting Mary White and others to citizenship in the Cherokee Nation on the 22nd day of September 1888.

Q Do you submit this case to the Commission for final consideration? A Yes sir.

BY MR. HASTINGS: Cherokee Nation submits it.

M.D. Green, being first duly sworn, states that as stenographer to the Commission to the Five Civilized Tribes he correctly recorded the testimony and proceedings in this case and that the foregoing is a true and complete transcript of his stenographic notes thereof.

M.D. Green

Subscribed and sworn to before me this February 21, 1902.

T B Needles

Commissioner.

CherokeeD74

DEPARTMENT OF THE INTERIOR,

COMMISSION TO THE FIVE CIVILIZED TRIBES.

Muskogee, Indian Territory, March 10, 1902.

In the matter of the application of James A. White for enrollment as a Cherokee citizen.

Supplemental Statement.

----oOoo------

On the second day of August, 1900, there was received by this Commission an affidavit of birth duly executed on the said second day of August, 1900, from which it appears that Willie G. White was born to Mary Kindness and James A. White on the eighth day of November, 1897, and was living at the date of the execution of said affidavit. The same has been approved and filed with this Commission.

It is directed that copies of this statement be filed with the testimony in the above case.

T B Needles
Commissioner.

DEPARTMENT OF THE INTERIOR,
COMMISSION TO THE FIVE CIVILIZED TRIBES.

In the matter of the application of James A. White for the enrollment of himself and his child Willie G. White as citizens by blood of the Cherokee Nation.

D E C I S I O N.

The record in this case shows that on August 2, 1900, James A. White appeared before the Commission at Bunch, Indian Territory, and made application for the enrollment of himself and his child, Willie G. White, as citizens by blood of the Cherokee Nation, and for the enrollment of his wife Mary Kindness White as a citizen by intermarriage of the Cherokee Nation. Mary Kindness White has been differently classified and is not embraced in this decision. A copy of the testimony taken at Muskogee, Indian Territory on February 17, 1902, in the matter of the application of Mary White has been filed herewith and made a part of the record herein.

The evidence, and an examination of the records of the Cherokee Nation, in the possession of this Commission, show that James A. White was admitted to citizenship in the Cherokee Nation by the duly constituted authorities of said Nation on September 22, 1888. The evidence further shows that the applicant came with his parents to the Cherokee Nation in 1890, and that a few months thereafter he returned with them to Georgia and remained there until 1894, at which time he returned to the Cherokee Nation, being then 20 years old. He is identified on the Cherokee Strip payment roll of 1894, and the Cherokee Census roll of 1896. The child Willie G. is the issue of a marriage between applicant and one Kindness Culver, on February 21, 1897. He is identified by a birth affidavit on file with this Commission.

The evidence further shows that the said James A. White has resided continuously in the Cherokee Nation since 1894, and that he and his said child were residents of said Nation at the date of the application herein.

It is, therefore, the opinion of this Commission that James A. White and Willie G. White should be enrolled as citizens by blood of the Cherokee Nation in accordance with the provisions of Section twenty-one of the Act of Congress approved June 28, 1898 (30 Stats., 495), and it is so ordered.

COMMISSION TO THE FIVE CIVILIZED TRIBES.

Tams Bixby
Acting Chairman.

T.B. Needles
Commissioner.

C. R. Breckinridge
Commissioner.

Dated Muskogee, I. T.
this AUG 11 1902

COMMISSIONERS:

HENRY L. DAWES,
TAMS BIXBY,
THOMAS B. NEEDLES,
C. R. BRECKINRIDGE.

ALLISON L. AYLESWORTH,
SECRETARY.

ADDRESS ONLY THE
COMMISSION TO THE FIVE CIVILIZED TRIBES.

DEPARTMENT OF THE INTERIOR,
COMMISSION TO THE FIVE CIVILIZED TRIBES.

REFER IN REPLY TO THE FOLLOWING
Cherokee D 74.

Muskogee, Indian Territory, August 13, 1902.

W. W. Hastings,

Attorney for the Cherokee Nation,

Muskogee, Indian Territory.

Sir:

There is herewith transmitted a copy of the decision of the Commission to the Five Civilized Tribes, rendered August 11, 1902, granting the application of James A. White for the enrollment of himself and his child, Willie G. White, as citizens by blood of the Cherokee Nation.

You are hereby advised that you will be allowed fifteen days from date hereof in which to file with the Commission such protest as you may desire to make against its decision, in granting the application of the above named persons. If you fail to file a protest within the time allowed, this decision will be considered final.

Very respectfully,

Tams Bixby

Acting Chairman.

Enc. C. No. 3.

CHEROKEE

D-74

James A. White et al.

Transferred to Cherokee 9499.

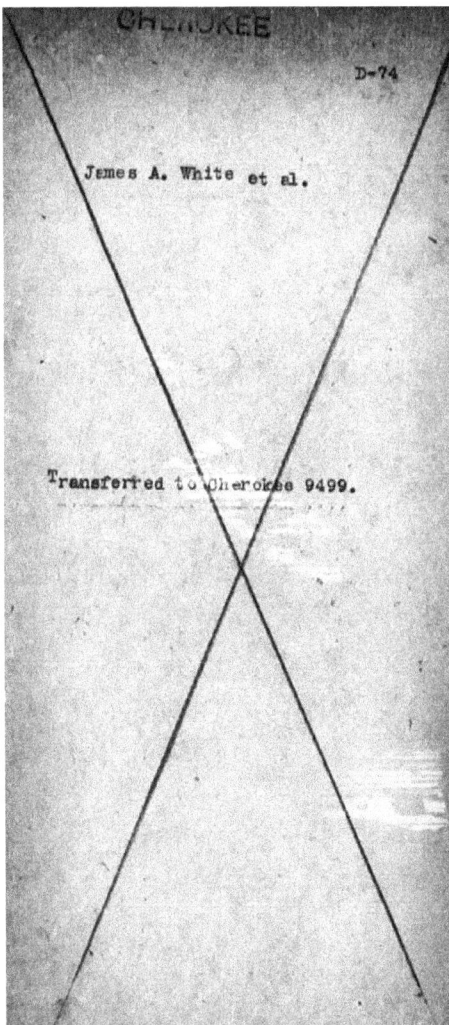

RESIDENCE: Flint DISTRICT.
POST OFFICE: Stilwell, I.T.

Cherokee Nation. Cherokee Roll.
(Not including Delawares, Intermarried, or Freedmen.)

CARD NO.
FIELD NO. 9189

Dawes' Roll No.		NAME.	Relationship to Person first Named.	AGE.	SEX.	BLOOD.	Tribal Enrollment Year.	Tribal Enrollment District.	Tribal Enrollment No.	Name of Father.	Year.	District.	Name of Mother.	Year.	District.
21572	1	White, James A.		26	M	1/8	1896	Going Snake	7620	Harrison White		non citz	Mary White		Flint
21573	2	" Willie G.	Son	3	"	1/16				No 1			Mary K White		non citz
	3														
	4	GRANTED													
	5	AUG 11 1902													
	6														
	7														
	8	CITIZENSHIP CERTIFICATE													
	9	ISSUED FOR NO. SEP 1904													
	10														
	11														
	12														
	13														
	14														
	15														
	16														
	17														
	18	See Cherokee R 570 & 9906		See NBH 2172											

Date of Application for Enrollment.

Cherokee D75 - George W. White

Department of the Interior.
Commission to the Five Civilized Tribes.
Bunch, I. T., August 2nd, 1900.

In the matter of the application of George W. White for enrollment as a Cherokee citizen; being sworn and examined by Commissioner Breckinridge, testifies as follows:

Q What is your full name? A George W. White.
Q What is your age? A 22.
Q What is your post-office? A Stilwell.
Q District? A Flint.
Q How long have you lived in Flint Dist.? A Four years.
Q Where did you live before that time? A Goingsnake.
Q How long did you live in Goingsnake? A One year.
Q Where did you live before that time? A Tahlequah.
Q How long did you live in Tahlequah? A One year.
Q Have you lived any longer than that in the Nation? A No.
Q That's the whole of your life in the Nation? A I lived about a month in Cooweescoowee district.
Q Where did you live before that? A In Georgia.
Q Have you a certificate of your admission? A Yes sir.
Q For whom do you apply now for enrollment? A Myself.
Q Only yourself? A Yes sir.

Mr. White, you present a duly authenticated certificate of admission to citizenship in the Cherokee Nation, signed by J. B. Adair, Chairman of the Committee on Citizenship, attested by Connell Rogers, Clerk of the Committee, approved and endorsed by J. B. Mayes, Principal Chief of the Cherokee Nation, and under the great seal of the Nation. It is dated Sept. 22, 1888, and it contains among others the name of George W. White.
Q Is that your name? A Yes sir.
Q Do you present this as your certificate of admission? A Yes sir.

You are duly identified in this certificate of admission and it is recognized as a duly authenticated certificate of the fact of your admission at the time states. It appears from the testimony that you were admitted to citizenship in 1888, but that for only something like half the time between the date of your admission and the present date have you been residing in the Cherokee Nation.

Q Are you on the roll of 1894? A Yes sir.
Q And the roll of 1896? A Yes sir.
1894 roll; page 1182, #3675, Geo. W. White, Tahlequah Dist.
1896 roll; page 814, #2622, George W. White, Goingsnake Dist.
Q Did you come to the Cherokee Nation on or about the time of your admission in 1888? A I come with my father in '90.
Q Some two years after your admission? A Yes.

Q And how long did you stay here? A Three months.
Q Did you then go back to Georgia? A Yes sir.
Q And when did you return again to the Cherokee Nation? A November 1894.
Q You were under age at that time? A Yes sir.
Q Did your father bring any household effects when he came in 1890?
A He brought his clothes and bedding; that's all.
Q Did you and your father and the family come for the purpose of making your home in 1890? A Well, I don't know myself; I don't know what their intention was then. I was just going with them.
Q Did all the family go back to Georgia? A Yes sir.
Q Did they take back all the household effects they brought with them in 1890?
A Yes sir.
Q Did I understand you to say that you returned again in 1894? A Yes sir.
Q Have you lived continuously in the Cherokee Nation ever since you returned in 1894? A Yes sir.
Q Are you making you home in the Cherokee Nation at this time? A Yes sir.

Mr. Baugh:

Q When you and your folks returned in 1894, did you or either of them make application to the Cherokee Nation Council for readmission to citizenship?
A I did not myself, because I was under age.
Q You don't know whether your father did either? A No sir.

I protest in the name of the Cherokee Nation against the enrollment of George W. White to Cherokee citizenship for the simple fact that he with his family removed out of the limits of the Cherokee Nation and taking all their effects, thereby forfeiting their rights to citizenship, and that on returning in 1894, they failed to avail themselves of the privilege granted by section 2nd, article one, of the Cherokee Constitution.

Com'r. Breckinridge:

Without meaning to indicate what the decision is or should be, will say, that your admission in 1888 to Cherokee citizenship is duly authenticated as shown in the testimony. You are duly identified upon the roll of 1894 and also upon the roll of 1896. It appears, however, that you and the other members of your family did not come to the territory for something like two years after your admission and that after a brief stay, you returned with the family to Georgia and did not again visit the Territory for something like four years. You appear to have resided consistently in the territory since the date of your last coming to the territory, a period of some six years; but, the question is raised of your citizenship having been forfeited and not renewed and that the Commission will take under advisement. For the present, therefore, your application will be placed upon a doubtful card. When the decision of the Commission is finaly[sic] made, you will be informed of it at your present post-office address, and whether that decision be favorable or unfavorable it, with the testimony, will be forwarded to the Honorable Secretary of the Interior for his approval.

Edward G. Rothenberger, being duly sworn by Commissioner Breckinridge as Stenographer to the Commission to the Five Civilized Tribes, he reported in full the testimony of the above named witness, George W. White, and that the foregoing is a full, true and correct transcript of his notes.

Edward G. Rothenberger

Sworn to and subscribed before me this 7th day of August, 1900.

Commissioner.

"R"

File with Cherokee D-75, George W. White.

Department of the Interior,
Commission to the Five Civilized Tribes,
Muskogee, I. T., February 17, 1902.

SUPPLEMENTAL TESTIMONY AND PROCEEDINGS in the matter of the application of Mary White for enrollment as a Cherokee citizen.

WILLIAM H. WHITE being sworn and examined testified as follows:

Appearances:
William H. White, for applicant;
W. W. Hastings, attorney for the Cherokee Nation.

BY COMMISSION:
Q What is your name? A William H. White.
Q How old are you? A I am 53 years old.
Q What is your post-office? A Stilwell.

BY COMMISSION: There is offered in evidence a certificate from the Cherokee Commission on citizenship, bearing date of September 22, 1888, admitting one Mary White and her children, Lewis R. White and Mary P. White to citizenship in the Cherokee Nation. The document is signed by J. T. Adair, Chairman of the Commission on citizenship, attested by Connell Rogers, Clerk of the Commission on citizenship, approved and indorsed by J. B. Mayes, Principal Chief of the Cherokee Nation, and bears the seal thereof. It is filed herewith.

It further appears that William J. White, whose name appears on doubtful card No. 69, is found in said certificate.

Q Is there any other statement you desire to make relative to the enrollment of these parties? A No sir not that I know of; I want to say something in regard to our youngest child; it was rejected; it is out youngest child; I would like to make some explanation if it is necessary. When that application was made for citizenship she was not born.

BY COMMISSION: That child will come in all right.

It further appears that the name of Thomas J. White is found in the certificate of admission admitting Mary White and others to citizenship in the Cherokee Nation on the 22nd day of September, 1888.

The name of James A. White appears in the certificate issued by the Cherokee Commission on citizenship admitting Mary White, and others to citizenship in the Cherokee Nation, on the 22nd day of September, 1888.

Q Any other statement you desire to make relative to the enrollment of your wife and children? A As to James A. White he was requested to bring a marriage certificate and it was left here with the other papers and never received it back. It was left with the Commission at the time he was placed on a doubtful list. Marriage certificate and also the certificate of the birth of his child.

BY COMMISSION: The name of George W. White appears in the certificate admitting Mary White and others to citizenship in the Cherokee Nation on the 22nd day of September 1888.

Q Do you submit this case to the Commission for final consideration? A Yes sir.

BY MR. HASTINGS: Cherokee Nation submits it.

M.D. Green, being first duly sworn, states that as stenographer to the Commission to the Five Civilized Tribes he correctly recorded the testimony and proceedings in this case and that the foregoing is a true and complete transcript of his stenographic notes thereof.

M.D. Green

Subscribed and sworn to before me this February 21, 1902.

T B Needles

Commissioner.

DEPARTMENT OF THE INTERIOR,
COMMISSION TO THE FIVE CIVILIZED TRIBES.

In the matter of the application of George W. White for enrollment as a citizen by blood of the Cherokee Nation.

DECISION.

The record in this case shows that on August 2, 1900, George W. White appeared before the Commission at Bunch, Indian Territory, and made application for his enrollment as a citizen by blood of the Cherokee Nation. A copy of the testimony in the matter of the application of Mary White for enrollment as a Cherokee citizen, taken at Muskogee, Indian Territory, on February 17, 1902, has been filed herewith and made a part of the record herein.

The evidence, and an examination of the records of the Cherokee Nation, in the possession of this Commission, show that George W. White was admitted to citizenship in the Cherokee Nation by the duly constituted authorities of said Nation on September 22, 1888. He is identified on the Strip payment roll of 1894, and the Cherokee Census roll of 1896.

The evidence further shows that said George W. White came with his parents to the Cherokee Nation in 1890, and a few months thereafter he returned with them to Georgia, and remained there until 1894, at which time he returned to the Cherokee Nation and has resided continuously therein ever since.

It is, therefore, the opinion of this Commission that George W. White should be enrolled as a citizen by blood of the Cherokee Nation in accordance with the provisions of Section twenty-one of the Act of Congress approved June 28, 1898 (30 Stats., 493), and it is so ordered.

COMMISSION TO THE FIVE CIVILIZED TRIBES.

Tams Bixby
Acting Chairman.

T.B. Needles
Commissioner.

C. R. Breckinridge
Commissioner.

Dated Muskogee, I. T.
this AUG 11 1902

COMMISSIONERS:

HENRY L. DAWES,
TAMS BIXBY,
THOMAS B. NEEDLES,
C. R. BRECKINRIDGE.

—

ALLISON L. AYLESWORTH,
SECRETARY.

ADDRESS ONLY THE
COMMISSION TO THE FIVE CIVILIZED TRIBES.

DEPARTMENT OF THE INTERIOR,
COMMISSION TO THE FIVE CIVILIZED TRIBES.

REFER IN REPLY TO THE FOLLOWING

Cherokee D 75.

Muskogee, Indian Territory, August 13, 1902.

W. W. Hastings,

Attorney for the Cherokee Nation,

Muskogee, Indian Territory.

Sir:

There is herewith transmitted a copy of the decision of the Commission to the Five Civilized Tribes, rendered August 11, 1902, granting the application of George W. White for enrollment as a citizen by blood of the Cherokee Nation.

You are hereby advised that you will be allowed fifteen days from date hereof in which to file with the Commission such protest as you desire to make against its decision, granting the application of George W. White. If you fail to file a protest within the time allowed, this decision will be considered final.

Very respectfully,

Tams Bixby

Acting Chairman.

Enc. C. No. 8.

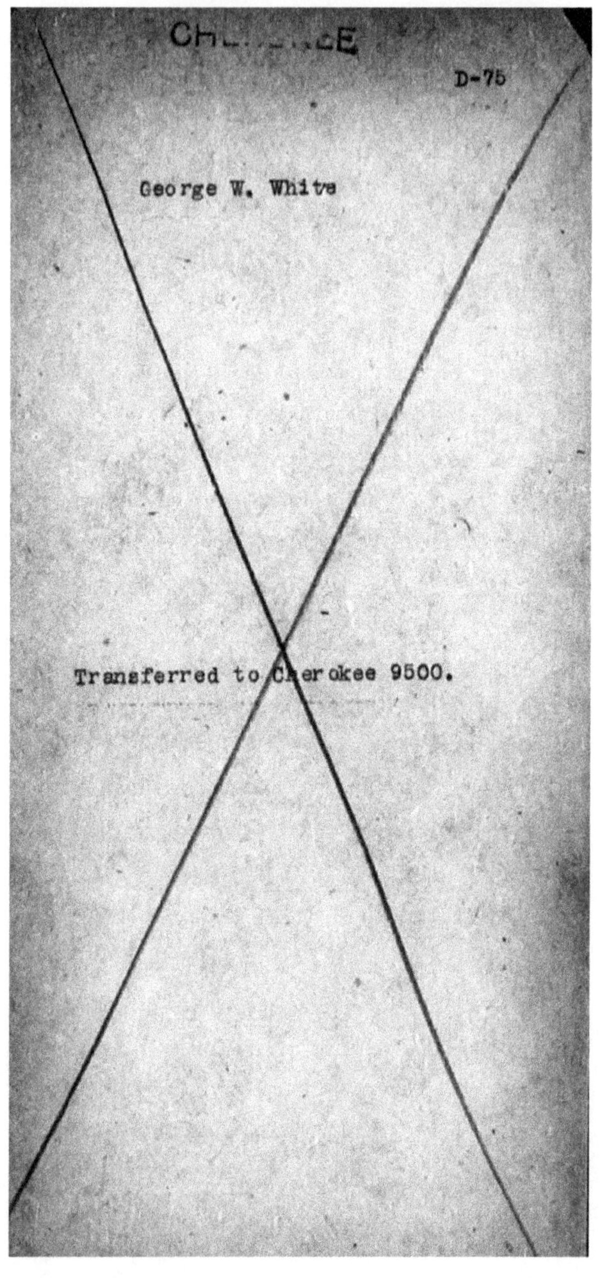
CH... ..E

D-75

George W. White

Transferred to Cherokee 9500.

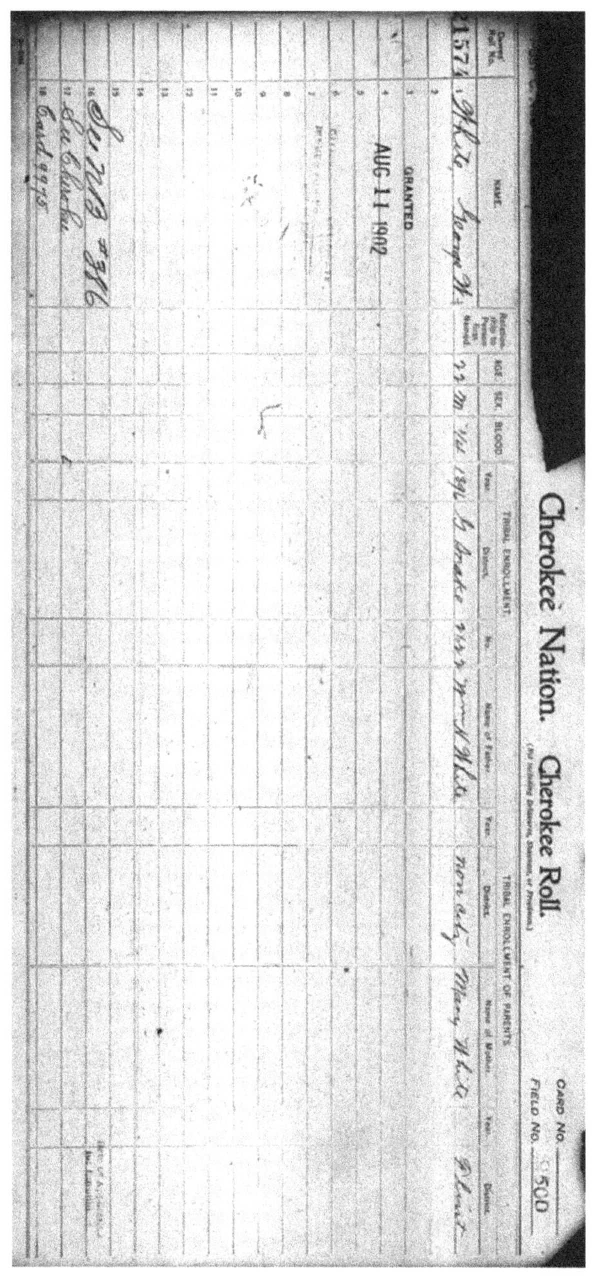

Cherokee Nation. Cherokee Roll.
(Not including Delawares, Shawnees, or Freedmen.)

CARD No.
FIELD No. 9500

Dawes' Roll No.	NAME.	Relationship to Person first Named.	AGE.	SEX.	BLOOD.	TRIBAL ENROLLMENT Year.	District.	No.	Name of Father.	Year.	District.	Name of Mother.	Year.	District.
2157[illegible]	1 White, George W.		22	M	1/4	1896	G Snake	[illegible]	Wm N White		non citz	Mary White		Flint

GRANTED
AUG 11 1902

See NB #386
See Cherokee
Card 9975

Cherokee D76 - Naomi A. Sitten by Solomon S. Sitten

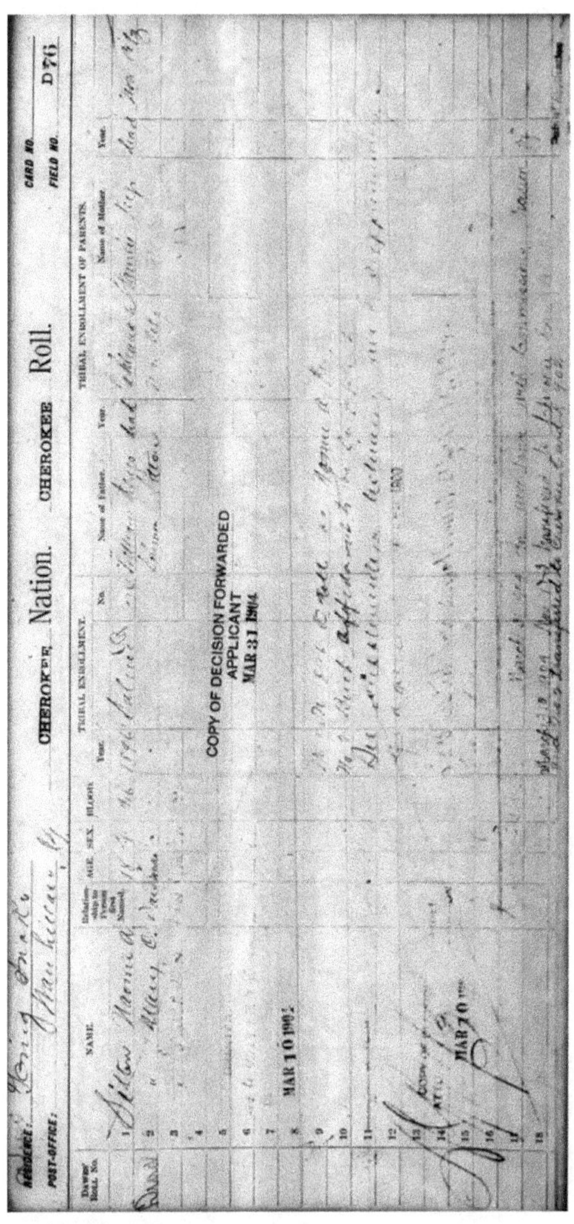

Department of the Interior,
Commission to the Five Civilized Tribes,
Bunch, I. T., August 3rd, 1900.

In the matter of the application of Solomon S. Sitton[sic] for the enrollment of his wife and child as Cherokees; being sworn and examined by Commissioner Needles he testifies as follows:

Q What is your name? a Solomon S. Sitton.
Q What is your age? A Twenty-one.
Q What is your post-office address? A Wauhillau.
Q Have you ever been recognized by the Tribal authorities of the Cherokee Nation as a citizen? A No sir.
Q Have you ever been enrolled by the Tribal authorities of the Cherokee Nation as a citizen? A No sir.
Q Your name does not appear upon any of the rolls? A No sir.
Q Who do you apply for? A For my wife and child.
Q What is your wife's name? A Naomi~~a~~ A Sitton.
Q How old is she? A Eighteen.
Q What is her post-office address? A Wauhillau.
Q In what district does she live? A Goingsnake.
Q How long has she lived there? A She aint been living in Goingsnake but about a year.
Q Where did she live before that? A She lived most of the time at the Orphan Asylum.
Q Is she a Cherokee by blood? A Yes sir.
Q What was her name before you married her? A Annie Keys.
Q What is the name of her father? A William C. Keys.
Q Is he living? A No sir.
Q Was he a Cherokee citizen? A Yes sir.
Q What is the name of her mother? A Fannie. She was a white woman.
Q Is her name upon any of the rolls of the Cherokee Nation? A Not as I know of.
Q How long has her father been dead? A Been dead about ten years.
1880 roll for wife's father: page 375, #750 as Wm. C. Keys, Flint District.
Q Have you got any proof of the marriage of William Keys to your wife's mother?
A No sir.
Q Your wife's father and mother both living? A No sir, both dead.
Q When were you married? A 3rd day of last September.
Q You don't know whether your wife was ever on any of the rolls or not? A Yes sir. She is on some of the rolls, she drawed[sic] her Strip money last summer after she was married.
1896 roll, page 1044 #74 Naomi A. Keys, Orphan Roll, Saline Dist.
1894 roll page 3 #42 Naomi Annie Keys, Orphan Roll Tahlequah Dist.
Q You know whether her father was admitted to citizenship or not? A Yes sir.
Q When was he admitted? A I couldn't tell you.
It has been several years ago, when he was just a boy.

-- -- --

Letha Bruner being sworn and examined by Com'r Needles testifies as follows:

Q What is your name? A Letha Bruner.
Q You know Naomi A. Sitton? A Yes sir.
Q You know what her name was before she was married? A Yes sir, Naomi Annie Keys.
Q Did you know her father? A Yes sir he was my first cousin, William Campbell Keys.
Q When did he come to the Territory? A In 1871.
Q Was he admitted? A Yes sir.
Q Under what name? A William Campbell Keys.
Q Did you know this girl's mother? A No sir, I didn't; I never seen her mother.
Q You don't know whether William Campbell was married to her or not then?
A No sir, I don't; I wasn't here when he married.
Q So you don't know anything about her? A No sir.
Examined by Cherokee Representative Baugh:
Q Did this man's wife's father come from North Carolina here? A No sir, he come from Alabama, Jackson County, right where I come from.
Q How was he admitted to citizenship? A I don't know.
Q He was admitted in 1870 you say? A Yes sir, he come here in 1871.

Com'r Needles:
He is dead is he? A Yes sir.
Q How long ago did he die? A Ten years. -Applicant recalled.
Q Have you got any children? A Yes sir, I have got a baby.
Q What is its name? A Mary C. Sitton[sic].
Q Have you got any certificate or license? A No sir, I have not got any.
Q When were you married? A The third day of Last September.
Q Who married you? A Jim Orr.
Q Is he a Minister? A Yes sir.
Q Didn't he give you a certificate? A No sir.
Q You didn't have any license? A Yes sir I had a license but it was returned to Muskogee and that have never been returned back to me yet.
Q Returned to Muskogee when? A 4th day of last September.
Q What did you send them to Muskogee for? A They went there to be recorded.
Q At the Clerk's office? A Yes sir.
Q There is a certificate on the license I suppose? A Yes sir.

Com'r Needles: Solomon S. Sitton[sic] applies for the enrollment of his wife, Naomi A., and his child, Mary C. The name of his wife is found upon the census roll of 1896 and upon the pay roll of 1894, and the name of his wife's father, William C. Keys is also found upon the authenticated roll of 1880. Satisfactory evidence is not presented as to the citizenship of Naomi A.'s mother, nor her identification upon the rolls of 1880. Applicant avers that his wife's mother's name was Fannie, and that her name appears upon the authenticated roll of 1880 with that of her husband, William C. The applicant also fails to present marriage license and marriage certificate, consequently the judgment as to the enrollment of said Naomi A. and her child Mary C. is suspended and their names will be placed upon a doubtful card.

M.D. Green, being first duly sworn, states that as stenographer to the Commission to the Five Civilized Tribes he reported the foregoing case and that the above and foregoing is a full true and complete transcript of his stenographic notes in said case.

M D Green

Subscribed and sworn to before me this 3rd day of August 1900.

T B Needles
Commissioner.

D. Card #76.

DEPARTMENT OF THE INTERIOR.
COMMISSION TO THE FIVE CIVILIZED TRIBES.
TAHLEQUAH, I.T., DECEMBER 3rd, 1900.

IN THE MATTER OF THE APPLICATION OF Naoma Anna Sitten - supplemental - for enrollment as a citizen of the Cherokee Nation, and she being sworn and examined by Commissioner, T. B. Needles, testified as follows:

Q What is your name? A Naoma Annie Sitten.
Q How old are you? A Eighteen.
Q What is your Post office? A Wauhillau.
Q What district do you live in? A Tahlequah.
Q Are you a recognized citizen of the Cherokee Nation by blood? A Yes sir.
Q What is your father's name? A William Keys.
Q Is he living? A No sir.
Q What is your mother's name? A Fannie Keys.
Q Is she living? A No sir.
Q Whom do you want to enroll? A Just myself.
Q Are you married? A Yes sir.
Q What is your husband's name? A Cicero Sitten.
Q Have you any marriage certificate? A Yes sir.

By Commissioner T. B. Needles: The applicant presents a marriage certificate, certifying that she was married on the 3rd day of September, 1899, to one. S. S. Sitten.

(1880 Roll, Page 375, #750, Wm. C. Keys, Flint District)
(1880 Roll, Page 375, #751, Fannie Keys, Flint District)

By Commissioner T. B. Needles: It is found upon an investigation of the rolls that the name of William C. Keys, father of Naoma A. Sitten, and Fannie Keys. mother of Naoma A. Sitten are found upon the authenticated roll of 1880, as indicated in the testimony.

The said Naoma Annie Sitten is fully identified as the child of William C. and Fannie Keys: Consequently, she is entitled to enrollment as a Cherokee citizen by blood, and her name will be taken from Doubtful Card #76, and placed upon a straight card.

The undersigned, being sworn, states that as stenographer to the Commission to the Five Civilized Tribes, he correctly recorded the testimony and proceedings in this case, and that the foregoing is a true and complete transcript of his stenographic notes thereof.

R R Cravens

Subscribed and sworn to before me this 3rd day of December, 1900.

T B Needles
COMMISSIONER.

"R"
SUPPLEMENTAL: D 76.

Department of the Interior,
Commission to the Five Civilized Tribes,
Tahlequah, I.T., November 26, 1901.

In the matter of the application of Naomi A. Sitten for the enrollment of herself and children as Cherokee citizens.

Appearances:
Applicant, Naomi A. Sitten, and Solomon S. Sitten, her husband;

TESTIMONY ON BEHALF OF THE APPLICANTS.

SOLOMON S. SITTEN, being sworn and examined testified as follows:
BY COMMISSION:
Q What is your name? A Solomon S. Sitten.
Q Have you any evidence of your marriage to your wife, Naomi A. Sitten? A I have if I could get them here, but I couldn't get no witnesses here.
Q Have you got a marriage license? A No sir, they come back to this clerk's office, and he sent them to Muskogee, and I never could get no account of it.
Q Couldn't you get a certified copy of them? A No sir, they never were recorded.

Q Do these two witnesses that you have with you know anything about your marriage? A They are on my father-in-law's marriage.
Q They don't know anything about your marriage? A No sir. I haven't got no witnesses here; there is plenty of them know about my marriage living 12 miles from here, but I couldn't get them to come.

SARAH L. PRICE, being sworn and examined testified as follows:
BY COMMISSION:
Q What is your name? A Sarah L. Price.
Q How old are you? A 64.
Q Your post-office is what? A Evansville.
Q Are you acquainted with Naomi A. Sitten? A Yes sir, she is a niece of mine.
Q You knew her parents did you? A Yes sir.
Q Are you a sister of her father? A No sir.
Q Of her mother? A Sister of her mother.
Q What was her mother's name? A Not of her mother, but of her grandmother. Her mother was my sister's daughter.
Q She is your grand-niece, her mother was your niece? A Yes sir, her mother was my niece.
Q What was her mother's name? A Fannie Keys.
Q Was she ever recognized as a citizen of the Cherokee Nation? A Yes sir.
Q Was she born here in the Cherokee Nation? A No sir, she was white herself, but then her father was Cherokee; Bill Keys was her father's name.
Q You mean Naomi's mother was a white woman? A Yes sir, she was a white woman, but her father was a Cherokee.
Q Was Naomi's mother a Cherokee? A No sir, she was white, but her father was a Cherokee.
Q What was her father's name? A William Keys.
Q Was her ever recognized as a citizen? A Yes sir, been here in the nation a good many years.
Q Was he here when the 1880 roll was made? A I think so.
Q Was he enrolled at that time? A Yes sir, I reckon so. This Bill Keys was on the 1880 roll, him and his wife both; they were married in about '78 or '9.
Q His wife was Fannie? A Yes sir; they were about to knock her out of her rights, and I just come down, I come down her last winter to try to help her out and they never called up no witnesses.
Q Do you know whether William Keys, and Fannie Keys the mother of Naomi A. Sitten were married? A Yes, sir, they were.
Q Were you present at their marriage? A Yes sir.
Q Where were they living at that time? A They were living up in Flint, close to the line, at Elm School House, married by a Cherokee preacher.
Q They were carried by a Cherokee preacher? A Yes sir.
Q Did they live together all the time? A Yes sir, as long as they both lived; they died in a month of each other.
Q You know whether either of them had been previously married?

A No sir, they never had been married. This lady(s[sic] mother was my niece and also her father was my husband's own cousin; I have known them ever since they was little children, well, in fact all their lives.
Q Do you know that this Naomi A. Sitten is the child of William Keys and Fannie Keys? A Yes sir.
Q And was born while they were living together as man and wife? A Yes sir.

LUCINDA ROSS, being sworn and examined testified as follows:
BY COMMISSION:
Q What is your name? A Lucinda Ross.
Q How old are you? A 54 years old.
Q What is your post-office address? A Evansville.
Q Are you acquainted with Naomi A Sitten, who was Naomi A. Keys?
A I knowed her mother and father; I aint knowed her all the time; I knowed her father and mother was married; I was there when they were married, at the church;
Q They were married by a minister of the Gosepl[sic]? A Yes sir, Cherokee preacher.
Q About how long ago was that? A I don't remember about how long.
Q Was it before the roll of 1880 was made, that was 21 years ago?
A Well it was along about that time sometime, I don't know just when; I have just plumb forgot it; I haven't never thought about it.
Q Did they have any children older than Naomi? A Yes sir, they had one when they lived by me, and it died, and they didn't have no more when they moved from where I lived.
Q Do you know they were lawfully married? A They was lawfully married at the school house and church house, at Elm School house.
Q Do you know they lived together up until they died? A Yes sir, they didn’t live in my neighborhood, but they lived together, and I think his wife died first and then he died.
Q They were always recognized as man and wife? A Yes sir, up until their deaths; after they left my neighborhood I knew them all the time, but I wasn't there in their family you know. I knowed the girl before she was married and I knowed the man before he was married.
Q You know whether either one of them were ever married before?
A No sir, I don't think they was, if they was I don't know it. I don't know anything about that.

Applicant's husband, SOLOMON S. SITTEN, re-called and further examined, testified:
BY COMMISSION:
Q Your wife has been enrolled as Naomi A. Sitton, Sitton being spelled S-i-t-t-o-n; is that the way you spell your name?
A Some of them spells it that way and some of them spell it Sitten.
Q How do you spell it? A S-i-t-t-e-n.
Q Is that the was[sic] you want to be enrolled? A Yes sir, that is the way I want it spelled; my father has it o-n.

Commission: This testimony will be filed and made a part of the record in case of Naomi A. Sitten, Cherokee D76.

------******------

M.D. Green, being first duly sworn, states that as stenographer to the Commission to the Five Civilized Tribes he correctly recorded the testimony and proceedings in this case and that the foregoing is a true and complete transcript of his stenographic notes thereof.

M D Green

Subscribed and sworn to before me this November 26th, 1901.

T B Needles

Commissioner.

CHEROKEE D 76

DEPARTMENT OF THE INTERIOR,

COMMISSION TO THE FIVE CIVILIZED TRIBES.

Muskogee, Indian Territory, February 27, 1902.

In the matter of the application of Naomi A. Sitten, et.al. for enrollment as Cherokee citizens.

Supplemental Statement.

--oOo--

There was filed with this Commission on the 26th day of November, 1901, the affidavit of Solomon S. Sitten, duly executed on the 26th day of November, 1902, from which it appears that Mary C. Sitten, the daughter of Solomon S. and Naomi A. Sitten died on the second day of November, 1900.

It is directed that copies of this statement be filed with the testimony in the above case.

T B Needles
Commissioner.

BCJ

Cherokee D-76

Department of the Interior,
Commission to the Five Civilized Tribes,
Cherokee Land Office,
Tahlequah, I.T., August 27, 1903.

In the matter of the application of Naomi A. Sitten for the enrollment of herself and her children, Mary C. and Theodore L. Sitten, as citizens by blood of the Cherokee Nation.

SUPPLEMENTAL TESTIMONY.

Cherokee Nation not represented;
Principal applicant present in person.

NAOMI A. SITTEN, being duly sworn and examined by the Commission, testified as follows:

Q What is your name? A Naomi A. Sitten.
Q Hoe[sic] old are you? A 21.
Q What is your postoffice address? A Maple, I.T.
Q Did you have a child named Mary C. Sitten? A She died.
Q When did she die? A 2nd day of November, 1900.
Q You have a child named Theodore L., have you? A Yes sir.
Q When you can first remember, where were you living? A In Sequoyah District.
Q Have you lived all your life in the Cherokee Nation? A Yes sir.
Q Are you living in the Cherokee Nation now? A Yes sir.
Q Have you ever lived out of the Cherokee Nation for any length of time?
A No sir.
Q Never lived out of it at all? A No sir.
Q When were you married? A 3rd day of September, '99.
Q Your husband is named Solomon S. Sitten? A Yes sir.
Q Where was he living when you married him? A He was living in Flint District, I think it was.
Q In the Cherokee Nation? A Yes sir.
Q Has he lived out of the Cherokee Nation since you and he married? A No sir.
Q You have been living with your husband continuously then in the Cherokee Nation ever since you were married? A Yes sir.

++++++++++++++++++++

Mabel F. Maxwell, being duly sworn, states that, as stenographer to the Commission to the Five Civilized Tribes, she correctly recorded the supplemental testimony in this case, and the above and foregoing is a true and complete transcript of her stenographic notes thereof.

Mabel F. Maxwell

Subscribed and sworn to before me
this 2nd day of September, 1903.

Samuel Foreman
Notary Public.

MFM

Cherokee D-76

DEPARTMENT OF THE INTERIOR,
COMMISSION TO THE FIVE CIVILIZED TRIBES.

In the matter of the application for the enrollment of Naomi A., Mary C. and Theodore L. Sitten as citizens by blood of the Cherokee Nation.

D E C I S I O N.

The record in this case shows that on August 3, 1900, Solomon S. Sitten appeared before the Commission at Bunch, Indian Territory, and made application for the enrolment of his wife, Naomi A. Sitten, and their minor child, Mary C. Sitten as citizens by blood of the Cherokee Nation. Further proceedings in the matter of said application were had at Tahlequah, Indian Territory, on December 3, 1900, November 26, 1901 and August 27, 1903. On November 26, 1901, there was filed with this Commission an affidavit wherein it is shown that Mary C. Sitten died on November 2, 1900. Thereafter on April 17, 1902, there was filed with this Commission an affidavit wherein it is shown that Theodore L. Sitten, minor child of Naomi A. Sitten, was born on September 30, 1901.

The evidence shows that Naomi A. Sitten is a citizen by blood of the Cherokee Nation and was married on September 3, 1899, to Solomon S. Sitten, a white man. As a result of that marriage the minor applicants were born. The said Naomi A. Sitten is identified on the Cherokee strip payment roll of 1894 and the Cherokee census roll of 1896; Theodore L. Sitten is identified by a birth affidavit made a part of the record herein. Mary C. Sitten is shown to have died subsequent to the application for her enrollment, prior to September 1, 1902. An affidavit to that effect is made a part of the record herein. The evidence further shows that Naomi A. Sitten has lived in the Cherokee Nation all her life.

Section twenty-five of the act of Congress approved July 1, 1902 (32 Stats., 716), provided:

"The roll of citizens of the Cherokee Nation shall be made as of September first, nineteen hundred and two, and the names of all persons then living and entitled to enrollment on that date shall be placed on said roll by the Commission to the Five Civilized Tribes."

It is, therefore ordered by this Commission that the application for the enrollment of Mary C. Sitten as a citizen by blood of the Cherokee Nation be, and the same is hereby dismissed; it is further ordered that Naomi A. Sitten and Theodore L. Sitten be enrolled as citizens by blood of the Cherokee Nation, in accordance with the provisions of section twenty-one of the act of Congress approved June 28, 1898 (30 Stats., 495), and it is so ordered.

COMMISSION TO THE FIVE CIVILIZED TRIBES.

(SIGNED). *Tams Bixby.*

Chairman.

(SIGNED). *T. B. Needles.*

Commissioner.

(SIGNED). *C. R. Breckinridge.*

Commissioner.

(SIGNED). *W. E. Stanley.*

Commissioner.

Dated Muskogee, Indian Territory,

this MAR 10 1904

COMMISSIONERS:
TAMS BIXBY,
THOMAS B. NEEDLES,
C. R. BRECKINRIDGE,
W. E. STANLEY.

ALLISON L. AYLESWORTH,
SECRETARY.

DEPARTMENT OF THE INTERIOR,
COMMISSION TO THE FIVE CIVILIZED TRIBES.

REFER IN REPLY TO THE FOLLOWING
Cherokee D 76

ADDRESS ONLY THE
COMMISSION TO THE FIVE CIVILIZED TRIBES.

Muskogee, Indian Territory, March 10, 1904.

W. W. Hastings,

Attorney for the Cherokee Nation,

Tahlequah, Indian Territory.

Dear Sir:

There is herewith inclosed a copy of the decision of the Commission to the Five Civilized Tribes, dated March 10, 1904, granting the application of Solomon S. Sitten for the enrollment of his wife, Naomi A. Sitten, and their minor child, Theodore L. Sitten, as citizens by blood of the Cherokee Nation, and dismissing the application for the enrollment of Mary C. Sitten, she having died on November 2, 1900.

You are advised that you will be allowed fifteen days from the date hereof within which to file such protest as you may desire to make against the action of the Commission in this case. If you fail to file such protest within the time allowed this decision will be considered final.

Respectfully,

T B Needles

Encl. V-20 Commissioner in Charge.

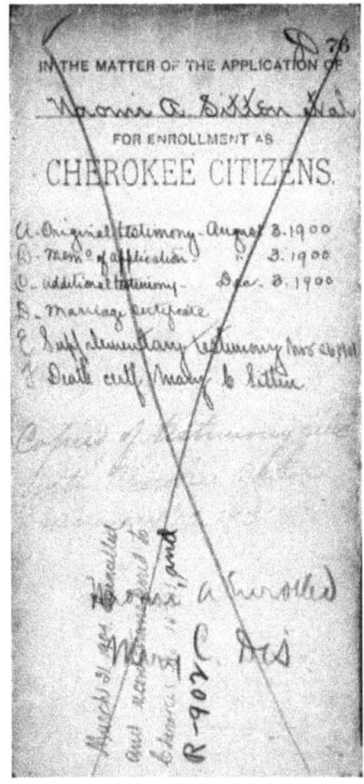

76

IN THE MATTER OF THE APPLICATION OF

Naomi A. Sitten et al

FOR ENROLLMENT AS

CHEROKEE CITIZENS.

A. Original testimony - August 3. 1900
B. Mem° of application " 3. 1900
C. additional testimony - Dec. 3. 1900
D. Marriage certificate
E. Supplementary testimony
F. Death cert Mary C Sitten

Naomi A Enrolled
Mary C. Dis
R-907

RESIDENCE: Going Snake DISTRICT.
POST OFFICE: Kansas (?) I.T.

Cherokee Nation. Cherokee Roll.

(Not including Delawares, Shawnees, or Freedmen.)

CARD NO.
FIELD NO. 10711

Dawes' Roll No.		NAME.	Relationship to Person first Named.	AGE.	SEX.	BLOOD.	TRIBAL ENROLLMENT Year.	District.	No.	TRIBAL ENROLLMENT OF PARENTS Name of Father.	Year.	District.	Name of Mother.	Year.	District.
31698	1	Sitter, Naomi A.		18	F	1/16	1896	Saline O.R.	74	William Key	dead	[illegible]	[illegible] Key	dead	[illegible]
31699	2	" Theodore L.	Son	7mo	M	1/32				Solomon S. Sitter		[illegible]	[illegible]		

GRANTED
MAR 10 1904

CITIZENSHIP CERTIFICATE
ISSUED FOR NO.
OCT 3 1904

No. 1 on 1896 C. Roll as Naomi [illegible]

See Supplementary testimony and Supplementary judgment Dec 3 1900

No. 2 listed for enrollment April 17, 1902.

See Cherokee Card No. E 902 See M.B. #2006

Date of Application for Enrollment. On Cherokee Card No. D 76 August 3, 1900; On this Card March 31, 1904

Cherokee D78 - Nellie Chuculate

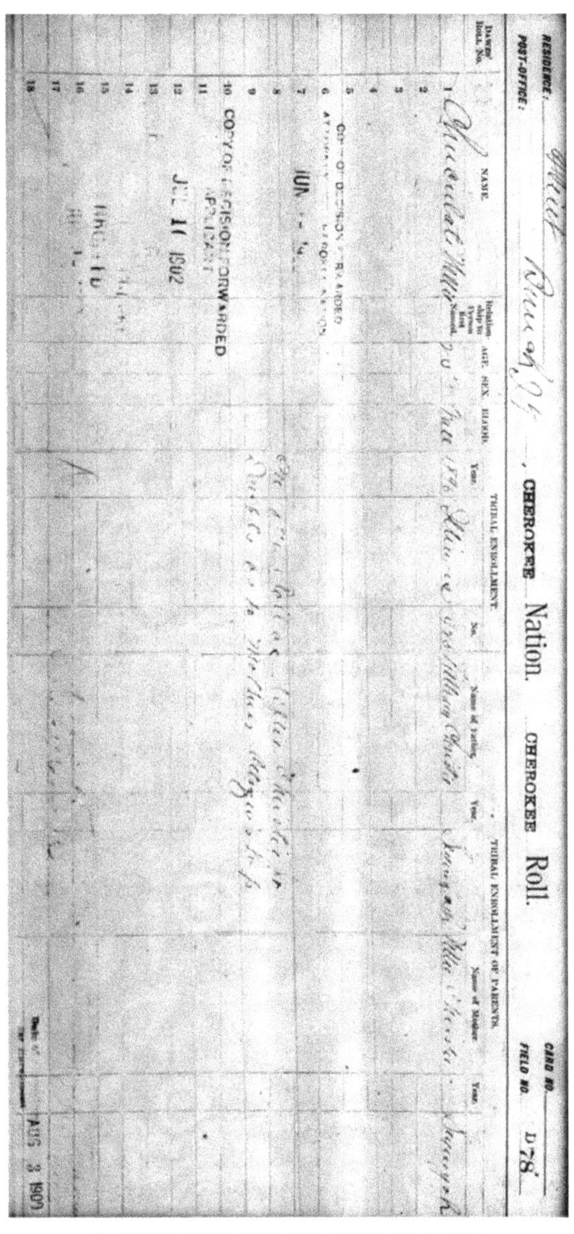
RESIDENCE: ... POST-OFFICE: ... CHEROKEE Nation. CHEROKEE Roll. CARD NO. ... FIELD NO. D78

COPY OF DECISION FORWARDED APPLICANT JUL 11 1902

AUG 3 1900

Department of the Interior,
Commission to the Five Civilized Tribes,
Bunch, I. T., August 3, 1900.

In the matter of the application of Isaac Chuculate et al for enrollment as Cherokee citizens; being sworn and examined by Commissioner Breckinridge he testifies as follows:

Walkingstick, Interpreter:

Q What is your full name? A Isaac Chuculate.
Q What is your age? A Twenty-three.
Q What is your post-office? A Bunch.
Q What is your district? A Flint District.
Q How long have you lived in Flint? A Lived in the District about ten years.
Q Where did you live before that? A I lived in Sequoyah District about ten years.
Q Have you lived in the Cherokee Nation all your life? A Yes sir.
Q Are you a full-blood Cherokee? A I think so, I don't know exactly.
Interpreter: Applicant says sometime they call him "Ice."
Note: 1896 roll page 656 #471 as Isaac Chucarlate[sic], Flint District, aged nineteen.
Q How did you get your money in 1894, did you get it when the other people got it, or did you get it by act of Council? [sic] I got my money at Council.
Q You belonged then to those they overlooked, and the Council just made it up to you? A I think so, that must be about the way, he says I never got my money at the time of the payment. They couldn't find my name at least on the rolls.
Q And the Cherokee authorities then saw that you got your money? A Yes sir, I think so. Because I got my money down there when Council convened that fall following the payment.
Q What was the name of your mother? A Culstiyah.
Q Do you know her name in 1880? A No, I couldn't say.
Q What was the name of your father? A Wesley Chuculate.
Q What was his name in 1880; was he living ther[sic] and carrying that name?
A Yes sir.
Note: 1880 roll page 357 #330 Wesley Chucalate[sic], Flint Dist.
A Do you remember your mother? A Very little.
Q Was she a full-blood Cherokee? A Yes sir, she was a full-blood.
Q You apply for your wife also do you? A Yes sir.
Q What is her name? A Nellie Chuculate.
Q Do you apply for any children? A No sir.
Q What was she before you married her? A Nellie Christie.
Q How old was she? A Twenty I think.
Q Is she on the roll of 1880 ad a Christie? A Yes sir.
Note; 1880 roll examined for applicant's wife, and name not found thereon.
Q When were you married? A In 1899.
1896 roll, page 849 #425 Nellie Christie, Jr., Illinois Dis't.
Q What is the name of your wife's mother? A Arneeley.

Note: 1880 roll examined for wife's mother; page 355 #256 Nelly Christie, Flint District.

Q Who here knows your wife as the daughter of Arnesley[sic] or Nelly Christie?
A No one here now.
Q Is your wife a full-blood? A Yes sir.
Q You don't know who drew your wife's money in 1894? A No sir I don't, her mother I guess.
Q Have you a certificate of marriage? A No sir.
Q Has your wife lived in the Cherokee Nation all of her life? A Yes sir.
Q You and she live together at this time? A Yes sir.

Com'r Breckinridge: This applicant is identified on the roll of 1894 and 1896; he appears to be among those Cherokees who were overlooked in making the regular roll payment of 1894, and he is not found on that roll; but he seems to have received his money at that time by the action of the Cherokee authorities. He cannot be identified on the roll of 1880 and has probably borne a number of names since that time. He is clearly a full-blood Cherokee, and he will be enrolled now as a Cherokee by blood.

In your application for your wife, there is a lack of satisfactory testimony; she is identified on the roll of 1896, but upon no other roll. You say you were married in 1899, and there should be some form of testimony sustaining that marriage, and in the lack of any further tribal testimony of record character, your wife should be identified by satisfactory personal testimony with her mother, who is found dult[sic] enrolled in 1880. Therefore, at present your wife's name will be placed upon a doubtful card, and you are [illegible] to come down to Sallisaw and produce additional testimony. You say that her father and some of her people are living down there; if you cannot produce any other testimony at least produce personal testimony as to your marriage, identifying her under her present name, and also personal testimony identifying her with her mother, who was enrolled in 1880.

M.D. Green, being first duly sworn, states that as stenographer to the Commission to the Five Civilized Tribes he reported the foregoing case and that the above and foregoing is a full true and complete transcript of his stenographic notes in said case.

M D Green

Subscribed and sworn to before me this 6th day of August 1900.

T B Needles
Commissioner.

Supl.C.D.#78.

Department of the Interior,
Commission to the Five Civilized Tribes,
Muskogee, I. T., February 17, 1902.

SUPPLEMENTAL in the matter of the enrollment of NELLIE CHUCHULATE[sic] as a citizen of the Cherokee Nation:

Applicant was notified by registered letter January 31, 1902, that this case would be taken up for final consideration by the Commission on the 17th day of February, 1902, and the she would on said date be given an opportunity to introduce any additional testimony affecting her case. She had acknowledged receipt of registered letter and has been called three times and fails to respond either in person or by attorney and the case is closed.

C. R. Breckinridge

J.C.R. Commissioner.

Cherokee D 78

DEPARTMENT OF THE INTERIOR,

COMMISSION TO THE FIVE CIVILIZED TRIBES.

Muskogee, Indian Territory, March 11, 1902.

In the matter of the application of Nellie Chuculate for enrollment as a Cherokee citizen.

Supplemental Statement.

---oOo---

Upon further examination of the authenticated tribal roll of 1880 Nellie Christie, the mother of Nellie Chuculate, is found to be identified thereon as a native Cherokee.

Nellie Chuculate is found under the name of Nellie Christie, Jr. upon the 1896 roll at the page as indicated in the testimony, and her age is there given as fifteen years.

It is directed that copies of this statement be filed with the testimony in the above case.

T B Needles
Commissioner.

Cherokee D 78

DEPARTMENT OF THE INTERIOR,
COMMISSION TO THE FIVE CIVILIZED TRIBES.

In the matter of the application for the enrollment of Nellie Chuculate as a citizen by blood of the Cherokee Nation.

D E C I S I O N.

The record in this case shows that on August 3, 1900, Isaac Chuculate appeared before the Commission at Bunch, Indian Territory, and made personal application for the enrollment of himself and his wife Nellie Chuculate as citizens by blood of the Cherokee Nation. Isaac Chuculate was listed on a regular care and is not therefore embraced in this decision.

The evidence shows that Nellie Chuculate is the child of Nellie Christie, who is identified upon the authenticated tribal roll of 1880 as a Native Cherokee. She is identified on the Cherokee Census roll of 1896, and appears to have been born subsequent to the preparation of the 1880 roll.

She has resided in the Cherokee Nation all her life and was a resident of said Nation at the time of the application herein.

It is, therefore, the opinion of this Commission that Nellie Chuculate should be enrolled as a citizen by blood of the Cherokee Nation in accordance with the provisions of Section twenty-one of the Act of Congress approved June 28, 1898 (30 Stats., 495), and it is so ordered.

COMMISSION TO THE FIVE CIVILIZED TRIBES.

Tams Bixby
Acting Chairman.

T.B. Needles
Commissioner.

Dated Muskogee, Indian Territory,

this JUN 9 - 1902

C. R. Breckinridge
Commissioner.

COMMISSIONERS:

HENRY L. DAWES,
TAMS BIXBY,
THOMAS B. NEEDLES,
C. R. BRECKINRIDGE.

ALLISON L. AYLESWORTH,
SECRETARY.

ADDRESS ONLY THE
COMMISSION TO THE FIVE CIVILIZED TRIBES.

DEPARTMENT OF THE INTERIOR,
COMMISSION TO THE FIVE CIVILIZED TRIBES.

REFER IN REPLY TO THE FOLLOWING
Cher. D-78.

Muskogee, Indian Territory, June 9, 1902.

W. W. Hastings, Esq.,

Attorney for the Cherokee Nation,

Muskogee, Indian Territory.

Sir:

Enclosed herewith please find copy of the decision of the Commission rendered June 9, 1902, in the matter of the application of Nellie Chuculate for enrollment as a citizen of the Cherokee Nation.

You are hereby advised that you will be allowed fifteen days from date hereof in which to file with the Commission such protest as you desire to make against the enrollment of the person above names as a citizen of the Cherokee Nation. If you fail to file protest within the time allowed this applicant will be regularly listed for enrollment.

Yours truly

Tams Bixby
Acting Chairman.

Encl. D-78.

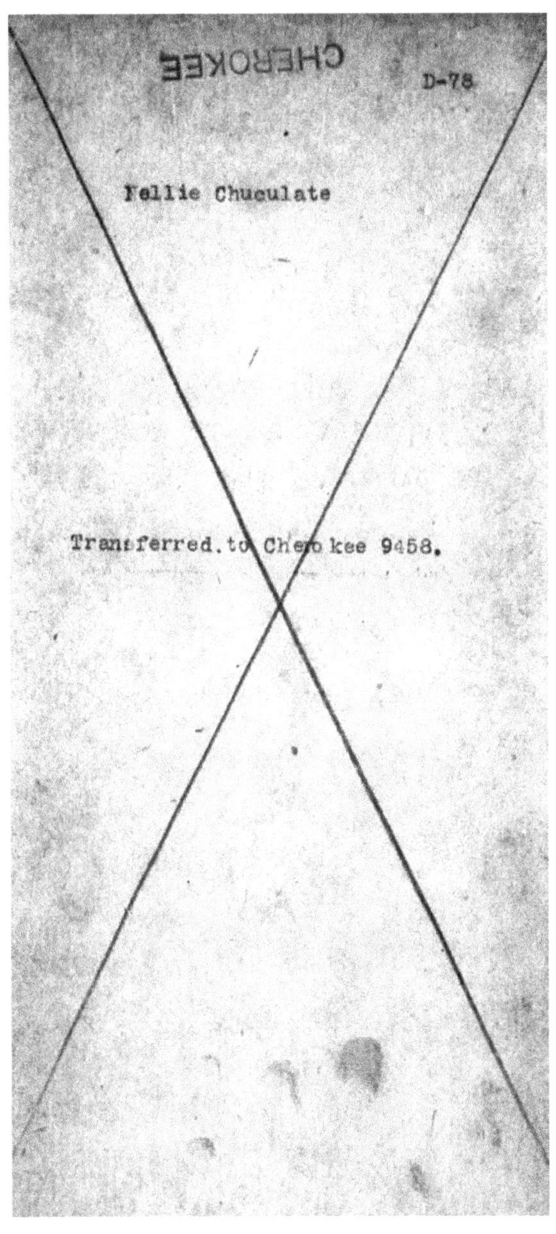
CHEROKEE D-78

Nellie Chuculate

Transferred to Cherokee 9458.

RESIDENCE: Flint DISTRICT.
POST OFFICE: Bunch, I.T.

Cherokee Nation. Cherokee Roll.
(Not including Delawares, Shawnees, or Freedmen.)

CARD NO. ______
FIELD NO. 9458

Dawes' Roll No.	NAME.	Relationship to Person first Named.	AGE.	SEX.	BLOOD.	Tribal Enrollment: Year.	Tribal Enrollment: District.	Tribal Enrollment: No.	Name of Father.	Year.	District.	Name of Mother.	Year.	District.
1518	1 Chuculate, Nellie		20	F	Full	1896	Illinois	405	William Christie		Sequoyah	Nellie Christie		Sequoyah
	2													
	3													
	4 GRANTED													
	5 JUN - 9 1902													
	6						On 1896 Roll as Nellie Christie Jr.							
	7													
	8													
	9													
	10													
	11													
	12													
	13													
	14													
	15													
	16													
	17													
	18													

Date of Application for Enrollment.

Cherokee D79 - Effie Denton

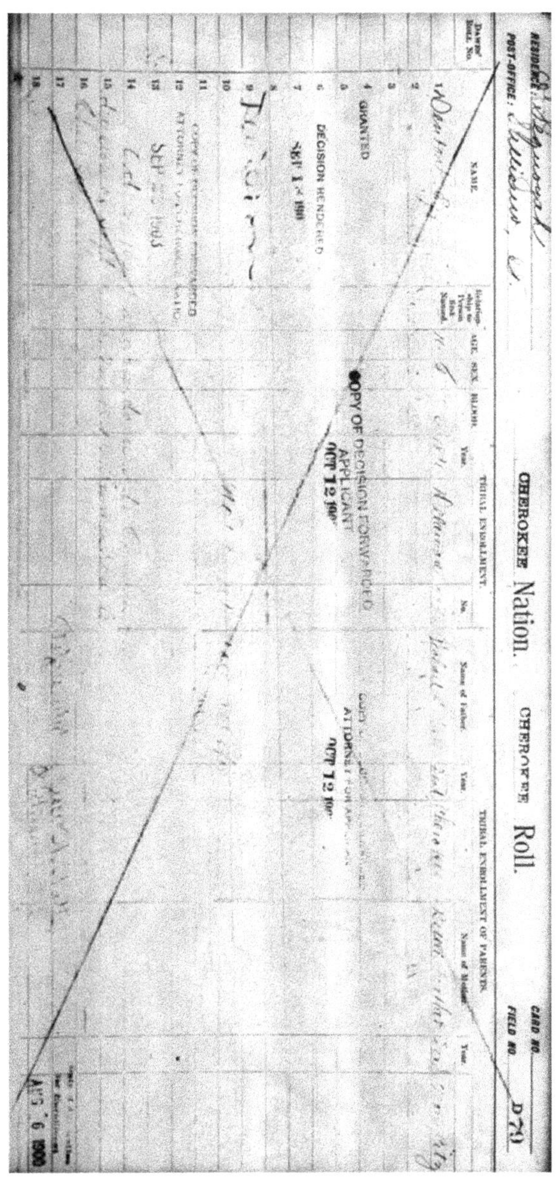
CHEROKEE Nation. CHEROKEE Roll.

CARD NO.

FIELD NO. D79

GRANTED

DECISION RENDERED

COPY OF DECISION FORWARDED
APPLICANT

Department of the Interior,
Commission to the Five Civilized Tribes,
Sallisaw, I.T., August 6, 1900.

In the matter of the application of Effie Denton for enrollment as a Cherokee by blood; being sworn and examined by Commissioner Breckenridge[sic], she testified as follows:

Q What is your full name? A Effie Denton.
Q What is your age? A 16.
Q Why doesn't your mother or father apply for you, are you an orphan?
A Yes, sir.
Q What is your post office? A Sallisaw.
Q What is your district? Sequoyah? A Yes, sir.
Q How long have you lived in Sequoyah district? A As long as I can remember.
Q All your life? A Yes, sir.
Q Do you claim as a Cherokee by blood? A Yes, sir.
Q Are you married or signal[sic]? A I am married.
Q Are you on any of the rolls of the Cherokee Nation? A Yes, sir.
Q Are you on the roll of 1894, when they drew the strip money? A Yes, sir.
Q What was your name in 1894? A Effie Prather.
Q When were you married? A The 14th of last March.
Q Have you a certificate of marriage? A Yes, sir, this is it.
Q How old did you say you were? A I am 16, but it is 18 down there.
Q This madam, is a duly authenticated certificate and license of your marriage, showing that you were married as stated on the 15th day of March in this year. I believe you stated that you were married on the 14th of March, but this is not a very great deal of difference. This identifies you under your new name. I return this to you. Is your mother living? A No, sir.
Q Is she on the roll of 1880? A No, sir, she is a white woman.
Q What was your mother's name? A Bettie Prather.
Q Were your father and mother married in 1880? A Why I don't know.
Q Are these other children in the family besides yourself? A Yes, sir.
Q Some older than you? A Yes, sir.
Q What is the age of the oldest of the children? A 20, I believe.
(On 1894 roll, page 445, No. 2208. Effie Prather, Delaware dist. On 1896 roll, page 514, No. 2352, Effie Prather, Delaware dist. 12 years old.)
Q Mrs. Denton, you present here a transcript from the Journam under date of 1870, showing the decision of what I understand to be the Supreme Court of the Cherokee Nation, on December 19, 1870, to the effect that one Caroline C. Prather is a Cherokee by blood and is entitled to the full rights and privileges of a Cherokee citizen. Was that Caroline C. Prather your grandmother? A Yes, sir.
Q Here is also a duly certified transcript from the record of citizenship in 1880, page 12, "A". This states a certain list therein stated contains the names, or at least is of the Prather family, and that it is copies from the official record made in the

Executive Department on June 21, 1871, by the Supreme Court acting as a Court of Commission, and it further says in the transcript to which allusion is made that the said report is of record in this case. Now that document is signed W. P. Doudinott[sic]. Executive Secretary, November 26, 1886.

In the list of names referred to occurs that of Caroline C. Prather. Is that your grandmother? A Yes, sir.

Q Do you claim that your grandfather's name is in that list or your father's?

A Why, I don't know whether it is or not.

Q Here is Richard L. Prather, is that the name of your father? A Yes, sir.

Q Now this record shows that these names were reported to this Department by the Court, but it does not clearly indicate what the decision of that Court was with respect to these names, whether it was favorable or unfavorable. It seems that the Cherokee law provided that the Court shall report to the Executive Department its decision upon all applicants for citizenship, whether favorable or unfavorable, and therefore the fact that these names have been reported to the Executive Department does not of itself carry a favorable conclusion. Now reference is made in this transcript to the report, as it is called, of the Court supplying these names to the Executive Office. Do I understand you as saying that the first transcript referred to, dated December 19, 1870, is all that is furnished relative to said report? A Yes, sir, that is all.

Q Now that report which you speak of contains only the name, as herein evidenced, of Caroline C. Prather; can you explain that discrepancy? A I don't know, sir, that is all that can be found.

Q Now Mrs. Denton, you hand me here another paper, a duly authenticated transcript from the records of the office of the Committee on Citizenship, Tahlequah, Cherokee Nation, June 27, 1887, page 243, showing proceedings dated June 27, 1887 and August 11, 1887, in regard to the Prather claim to citizenship. The case appears to have been continued until August 18, 1887, and appears to be a final hearing of the old and original case of December 19, 1870, to which reference is made in the first paper of these proceedings submitted. Now in this present decision of the Commission it is determined out of all that has preceded that R. A. Prather and Caroline Prather are duly entitled to citizenship. Now I observe in the evidence of December 19, 1870, that one Caroline C. Prather is spoken of as having been admitted at that time, and that of all the names gives[sic] in the list heretofore referred to from the record of citizenship, only the name of Caroline C. Prather is included at this time. This apears[sic] to be conclusive as regards Caroline C. Prather, and perhaps also as regards R. A. Prather, though it does not appear where or when his name entered into the proceedings. Now that R. A. Prather was the husband, was he, of Caroline C. Prather? A Yes, sir.

Q And therefore he was your grandfather? A Yes, sir.

Q Was your father living in August, 1886? A Why, I don't know, it has been about 6 years since he died.

(The Cherokee Nation introduced in evidence the Act of its Council approved December 3, 1869, and found on page 125 of the First Annual Report of the Dawes Commission; and also an amendatory act to the same, approved November 17, 1870, which will be hereafter furnished.)

Q I understand you to say, Mrs. Denton, that neither your father nor your mother are upon the roll of 1880? A I dont[sic] know whether they are or not.

(Roll of 1880 examined, and their names not found thereon.)

Q How old was your father when he died? A I don't know how old he was.

Q Your father was living before 1870, was he? A Yes, sir, I think so.

Q You have a brother, I think you said, 20 years old? A No, sir, I have a sister 20 years old.

Q So he was living in 1879 and had acquired considerable age at the time the action was first had on your grandmother's application? A Yes, sir.

Mrs. Denton, your application will be placed upon a doubtful card for further consideration by the Commission, and when a decision is finally arrived at, you will be informed at your present post office address of the result, and the decision, whether favorable or unfavorable, will finally be referred to the Honorable Secretary of the Interior for his approval.

--------o--------

Bruce C. Jones, being duly sworn, says that as stenographer to the Commission to the Five Civilized Tribes he reported the testimony of the above named witness and that the foregoing is a full, true and correct translation of his stenographic notes.

Bruce C Jones

Sworn to and subscribed before me this the 6th day of August, 1900.

Clifton R. Breckinridge
Commissioner.

"R"

Cherokee D 79

Department of the Interior,
Commission to the Five Civilized Tribes,
Muskogee, I T., February 17, 1902.

SUPPLEMENTAL PROCEEDINGS, in the matter of the application of Effie Denton et al., for enrollment as Cherokee citizens.

Appearances:
Jess W. Watts, Sallisaw, I.T., Attorney for applicants;
W.W. Hastings, attorney for Cherokee Nation.

BY MR. WATTS: Let the record show that the Cherokee Act approved December 3, 1869, and the amendatory act approved November 17, 1870, are to be filed, considered filed, and supplied hereafter.
BY COMMISSION: The attorney for the applicants will be given ten days in which to supply the acts referred to. Attorney for the applicants will also be given ten days in which to file brief, a copy with the Commission and a copy with the Representatives of the Cherokee Nation.

BY COMMISSION, of Mr. Watts:
Q Do you submit this case now to the Commission for final consideration? A Yes, sir.

M.D. Green, being first duly sworn, states that as stenographer to the Commission to the Five Civilized Tribes he correctly recorded the testimony and proceedings in this case and that the foregoing is a true and complete transcript of his stenographic notes thereof.

M D Green

Subscribed and sworn to before me this February 19, 1902.

T B Needles

Commissioner.

"R"

Cherokee D 79.

Department of the Interior,
Commission to the Five Civilized Tribes,
Muskogee, I, T., February 20, 1902.

SUPPLEMENTAL PROCEEDINGS in the matter of the application of Effie Denton for the enrollment of herself and child as Cherokee citizens.

APPEARANCES:
W. W. Hastings, attorney for the Cherokee Nation.

BY COMMISSION: W.W. Hastings, Representative of the Cherokee Nation, presents the following letter to the Commission, bearing date of February 19, 1902:

"Mr. W.W. Hastings,
Muskogee, Indian Territory.
Dear Sir:- After further considering the cases of Effie Denton and Artie Welch vs. Cherokee Nation, I shall not file briefs, but shall submit them as they now stand.
Very truly yours,
Jess W. Watts."

BY MR. HASTINGS: The Cherokee Nation desires to call attention of the Commission to the fact that Effie Denton claims that her father was Richard L. Prather, and the records show that Caroline Prather was admitted to citizenship in the Cherokee Nation in the year 1870, but that Richard L. Prather was not admitted at that time, and the certificate filed, signed by W.T. Boudinot, is an erroneous one, and does not properly represent the judgment of the court, because the judgment of the Court only states that Caroline Prather was admitted to citizenship in the Cherokee Nation.

The Cherokee Nation desires to further call the attention of the Commission to the fact that it is shown nowhere in the testimony that Richard L. Prather, the father of the applicant, was a minor at the time Caroline Prather was admitted in '70.

BY COMMISSION: The letter above quoted is filed in the application of Artie Welch, D 133.

M.D. Green, being first duly sworn, states that as stenographer to the Commission to the Five Civilized Tribes he correctly recorded the testimony and proceedings in this case and that the foregoing is a true and complete transcript of his stenographic notes thereof.

M D Green

Subscribed and sworn to before me this February 21, 1902.

T B Needles

Commissioner.

DEPARTMENT OF THE INTERIOR,

Commission to the Five Civilized Tribes,

Muskogee, I. T. August 26th 1902.

In the matter of the application of Effie Denton for enrollment as a citizen by blood of the Cherokee Nation. C. D. 79.

The testimony in this case shows that Effie Denton was sixteen years of age when she made her application for enrollment in this case, August 6th 1900; that she is a daughter of Richard L. Prather and a grand daughter of Caroline Prather; and the testimony shows that Caroline Prather was admitted to citizenship in the Cherokee Nation December 19, 1870, but the Cherokee Nation contends that it does not show that Richard L. Prather the father of the applicant was ever admitted to citizenship in the Cherokee Nation but it is contended by the Cherokee Nation that the certified copy of the report W. P. Boudinot filed in this case purporting to be a report of persons previously admitted to citizenship in the Cherokee Nation and made sixteen years after they were said to have been admitted was clearly erroneous and untrue because the record herein above referred to shows that one Caroline Prather was admitted to citizenship and none other and the decision of the Adair Court on June 27th 1887 was only as to R. A. Prather and Caroline Prather, husband and wife and did not include the said Richard L. Prather the father of the applicant hence there is no record whatever in this case that the said Richard L. Prather was ever admitted to citizenship in the Cherokee Nation or that he was a recognized citizen of the Cherokee Nation and there is no evidence tneding[sic] to show that the said Richard L. Prather was a minor at the time his alleged mother Caroline Prather was admitted to citizenship in the Cherokee Nation.

Again the testimony discloses that the applicants[sic] mothers[sic] name was Bettie and that she was a whitewoman[sic] and there is no testimony whatever tending to show that the father and mother were married or where they were married or where the applicant was born or is there sufficient testimony as to her residence.

In view of these facts we submit that they are insufficient to entitle the applicant to be listed for enrollment as a citizen of the Cherokee Nation by blood.

Respectfully submitted,

W W Hastings

J. C. S. Attorney for the Cherokee Nation.

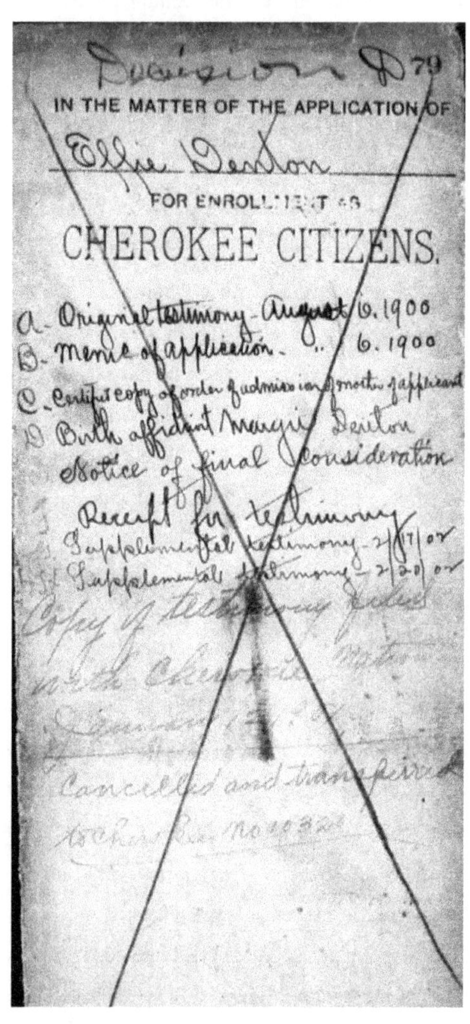

Decision D79

IN THE MATTER OF THE APPLICATION OF

Ellie Denton

FOR ENROLLMENT AS

CHEROKEE CITIZENS.

A- Original testimony- August 6. 1900

B- Memo of application. " 6. 1900

C- Certified copy of order of admission of mother of applicant

D Birth affidavit Maggie Denton

Notice of final Consideration

Receipt for testimony

Supplemental testimony- 2/17/02

Supplemental testimony- 2/20/02

Copy of testimony [illegible]

[illegible]

Cancelled and transferred

[illegible]

RESIDENCE: Sequoyah DISTRICT.
POST OFFICE: Sallisaw, I.T.

Cherokee Nation. Cherokee Roll.
(Not including Delawares, Shawnees, or Freedmen.)

CARD NO.
FIELD NO. [illegible]

Dawes' Roll No.		NAME	Relationship to Person first Named.	AGE.	SEX.	BLOOD.	Tribal Enrollment Year.	District.	No.	Name of Father.	Year.	District.	Name of Mother.	Year.	District.
29542	1	Denton, Effie		16	F	1/16	1896	Delaware	2952	Richard C. Prather	Dead	Cherokee	Nettie Prather	Dead	Non citz
29543	2	" Margie	Dau	6 mo	F	1/32				N. E. Denton		Non citz	Not		

CITIZENSHIP CERTIFICATE ISSUED FOR No. [illegible]

GRANTED
[illegible] 18 1903

No. 1 on 1896 Roll as Effie Prather
No. 2 Birth affidavit filed September 16, 1901

See N.B. #331

Represented by Jesse W. Watts, Sallisaw, I.T.

Date of Application for Enrollment. On Cherokee Card No. D-79, August 6, 1900; On this card October 12, 1903

Cherokee D80 - Augustus Brackett

RESIDENCE: Flint
POST-OFFICE: Stilwell, I.T.

CHEROKEE Nation. CHEROKEE Roll.

CARD NO.
FIELD NO. D80

Dawes' Roll No.	NAME.	Relationship to Person first Named.	AGE.	SEX.	BLOOD.	Tribal Enrollment: Year.	District	No.	Name of Father.	Year.	District	Name of Mother.	Year.	District
	1 Brackett, Augustus		21	M	[illegible]	[illegible]	[illegible]	10	[illegible]	[illegible]	[illegible]	[illegible]	[illegible]	[illegible]

DEPARTMENT OF THE INTERIOR,
COMMISSION TO THE FIVE CIVILIZED TRIBES
JUDGMENT RENDERED AND COPY
MAILED APPLICANT.
MAY 15 1902

COPY OF DECISION FORWARDED
ATTORNEY FOR CHEROKEE NATION
1902

Date of Application for Enrollment
AUG 6 1900

DEPARTMENT OF THE INTERIOR,
COMMISSION TO THE FIVE CIVILIZED TRIBES,
SALLISAW, I.T., AUGUST 6, 1900.

In the matter of the application of Augustus Brackett for enrollment as a citizen of the Cherokee Nation, said Brackett being duly sworn by Commissioner Needles, testified as follows:

Q What is your name? A Augustus Brackett.
Q Your age? A 21.
Q Your postoffice? A Stilwell.
Q Have you been recognized by the Cherokee tribal authorities as a citizen of the Cherokee Nation? A Yes.
Q Have you been enrolled by the Cherokee tribal authorities as a citizen of the Cherokee Nation? A Yes.
Q What district do you live in? A Flint.
Q How long have you lived there? A About 2 years.
Q Where did you live before that? A Tahlequah.
Q How long did you live there? A About 4 years.
Q Where did you live before that? A I stayed at the Orphan Asylum for about 4 years.
Q How long have you lived continuously in the Cherokee Nation? A For about 10 years.
Q Where were you born? A In Georgia.
Q Came from Georgia to the Cherokee Nation about 10 years ago? A Yes.
Q What is your father's name? A Bayless Brackett.
Q Is he living? A No sir.
Q Where did he die? A In Georgia.
Q What is the name of your mother? A Nancy.
Q Is she living? A No sir.
Q Where did she die? A In Georgia.
Q Are you married? A No sir.
Q What proof have you that you are a citizen of the Cherokee Nation? A I have a certificate.
Q Was your mother and father citizens of the Cherokee Nation? A My father was.
Q You present a certificate of admission as a Cherokee citizen issued by the Committee on Citizenship on the 16th day of August, 1889, admitting you to Cherokee citizenship, the said certificate is signed by Wm. P. Ross, Chairman of the Committee on Citizenship, approved and endorsed by J. B. Mayes, Principal Chief, under great seal of the Cherokee Nation, in which certificate appears the name of Augustus Brackett, aged 9 years, are you the identical Augustus Brackett named in this certificate? A Yes.
Q This certificate provides that it shall be the duty of the persons mentioned in this certificate to enroll their names and the names of their families from the date of their arrival in the Cherokee Nation, and that shall be within one year. Did you arrive in the Cherokee Nation within one year? A Yes.

Q On the back of this certificate is the following endorsement:
"Enrolled in the Executive Department, May 14, 1900."

Applicant on '96 roll, page 1041, number 10 as Guss Bracket.

On '94 roll, page 1, number 7, as Guss Brackett, Orphan roll, Tahlequah.

The name of Gus Brackett appearing upon the census roll of '96 and the pay-roll of '94, he also presenting certificate of admission to citizenship as described in the testimony, and makes satisfactory proof of his residence?[sic]

Now comes the representatives of the Cherokee Nation and for the present object to the enrollment of said Augustus Brackett, and ask that final judgment in his case be suspended until they can full investigate his rights to be enrolled as a Cherokee citizen. His name will therefore be placed upon what is known as a doubtful card.

Brown McDonald, being duly sworn, says as Stenographer to the Commission to the Five Civilized Tribes, he reported in full the testimony of the above named witness, and that the foregoing is a full, true and correct transcript of his notes.

Brown McDonald

Sworn to and subscribed before me this 17th day of August, 1900, at Muldrow, I.T.

T B Needles
Commissioner.

Cherokee D 80

DEPARTMENT OF THE INTERIOR,

COMMISSION TO THE FIVE CIVILIZED TRIBES.

In the matter of the application of Augustus Brackett for enrollment as a Cherokee citizen.

On the sixth day of August, 1900, Augustus Brackett appeared before the Commission to the Five Civilized Tribes and made application for his enrollment as a citizen by blood of the Cherokee Nation. The Cherokee Nation protested against his enrollment and at the conclusion of the evidence his name was placed upon a "Doubtful" card for further consideration.

No further evidence has been submitted by the Cherokee Nation and the case was ordered closed on the 17th day of February, 1902. The following decision is now rendered.

D E C I S I O N.

---oOo---

The evidence in this case shows that Augustus Brackett is a Cherokee by blood; that he was admitted to citizenship in the Cherokee Nation on the 16th day of August, 1889, by a decree of the Cherokee Commission on Citizenship. It appears that he removed to the Cherokee Nation and registered his name in the Executive Office of the Nation as required by the conditions of his admission on the fourteenth day of May, 1890. He has resided in the Cherokee Nation for ten years and he is identified on the Strip payment roll of 1894 and the Cherokee Census roll of 1896.

In making rolls of citizenship of the Cherokee Nation this Commission is governed by the following provisions of the Act of Congress approved June 28, 1898 (30 Stats., 495);

> "That in making rolls of citizenship of the several tribes, as required by law, the Commission to the Five Civilized Tribes is authorized and directed to take the roll of Cherokee citizens of eighteen hundred and eighty (not including freedmen) as the only roll intended to be confirmed by this and preceding Acts of Congress, and to enroll all persons now living whose names are found on said roll, and all descendants born since the date of said roll to persons whose names are found thereon; and all persons who have been enrolled by the tribal authorities who have heretofore made permanent settlement in the Cherokee Nation whose parents, by reason of their Cherokee blood, have been lawfully admitted to citizenship by the tribal authorities, and who were minors when their parents were so admitted; and they shall investigate the right of all other persons whose names are found on any other rolls and omit all such as may have been placed thereon by fraud or without authority of law, enrolling only such as may have lawful right thereto, and their descendants born since such rolls were made, with such intermarried white persons as may be entitled to citizenship under Cherokee laws."

In view of the facts and the law in this case it is considered that Augustus Brackett is entitled to be enrolled as a citizen by blood of the Cherokee Nation, and it is so ordered.

Tams Bixby

T B Needles

C. R. Breckinridge

Commissioners.

Dated at Muskogee, Indian Territory,

APR **23** 1902

Supl.-C.D.#80.

Department of the Interior,
Commission to the Five Civilized Tribes,
Muskogee, I. T., February 17, 1902.

SUPPLEMENTAL in the matter of the enrollment of Augustus Brackett as a citizen of the Cherokee Nation:

Applicant was notified by registered letter January 31, 1902, that on the 17th inst. this case would be taken up for final consideration by the Commission, and that he would be given an opportunity on said date to introduce any additional testimony affecting his case. He was also requested to supply the Commission with a certificate of his admission to citizenship in the Cherokee Nation. Applicant has acknowledged receipt of registered letter. He has been called three times and fails to respond, and the case is closed.

C. R. Breckinridge

Commissioner.

J.O.R.

COMMISSIONERS:

HENRY L. DAWES,
TAMS BIXBY,
THOMAS B. NEEDLES,
C. R. BRECKINRIDGE.

—

ALLISON L. AYLESWORTH,
SECRETARY.

ADDRESS ONLY THE
COMMISSION TO THE FIVE CIVILIZED TRIBES.

DEPARTMENT OF THE INTERIOR,
COMMISSION TO THE FIVE CIVILIZED TRIBES.

REFER IN REPLY TO THE FOLLOWING
Cherokee D-80

Muskogee, Indian Territory, April 23, 1902.

W. W. Hastings, Esq.,

Attorney for the Cherokee Nation,

Muskogee, Indian Territory.

Sir:

Enclosed herewith please find a copy of the decision of the Commission rendered April 23, 1902, in the matter of the application of Augustus Brackett, No. D-80, for enrollment as a citizen of the Cherokee Nation.

You are advised that you will be allowed fifteen days from date hereof in which to file such protest as you desire to make against the application of the said Augustus Bracket as a citizen of the Cherokee Nation. If you fail to file a protest within the time allowed, the applicant will be regularly listed for enrollment by this Commission.

Yours truly,

Tams Bixby

Acting Chairman.

Encl. D-80.

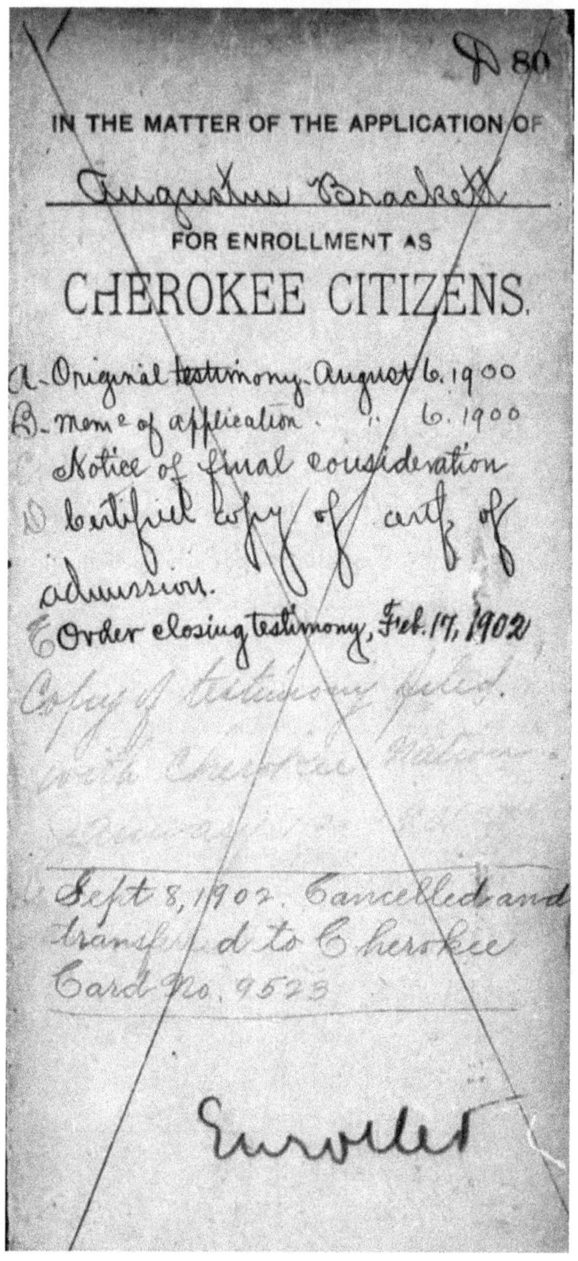

D 80

IN THE MATTER OF THE APPLICATION OF

Augustus Brackett

FOR ENROLLMENT AS

CHEROKEE CITIZENS.

A- Original testimony- August 6. 1900
B- Mem^e of application. " 6. 1900
C Notice of final consideration
D Certified copy of cert of admission.
E Order closing testimony, Feb. 17, 1902

Copy of testimony filed with Cherokee Nation [illegible]

Sept 8, 1907. Cancelled and transferred to Cherokee Card No. 9523

Enrolled

RESIDENCE: Flint DISTRICT.
POST OFFICE: Stilwell, I.T.

Cherokee Nation. Cherokee Roll.
(Not including Delawares, Shawnees, or Freedmen.)

CARD NO.
FIELD NO. 9523

Dawes' Roll No.		NAME.	Relationship to Person first Named.	AGE.	SEX.	BLOOD.	Tribal Enrollment Year.	Tribal Enrollment District.	Tribal Enrollment No.	Name of Father.	Year.	District.	Name of Mother.	Year.	District.
21595	1	Brackett, Augustus	Named	21	M	1/8	1896	Saline Og	10	Palmer Brackett	dead	Cherokee	Nancy Brackett	dead	Non-citz
	2														
	3														
	4														
	5	GRANTED													
	6	APR 23 1902													
	7														
	8							No 10 on 1896 roll as Guss Brackett							
	9														
	10														
	11														
	12														
	13														
	14														
	15												On Cherokee Card No		
	16												880 August 6, 1900.		
	17												On this card September		
	18	See Cherokee Card No 688											8, 1902 Date of Application for Enrollment.		

Cherokee D82 - Daniel Brackett

Department of the Interior,
Commission to the Five Civilized Tribes,
Sallisaw, I. T., August 6, 1900.

In the matter of the application of Daniel Brackett for enrollment as a Cherokee citizen; being sworn and examined by Commissioner Needles he testifies as follows:

Q What is your name? A Daniel Brackett.
Q What is your age? A About fifty-one.
Q What is your post-office address? A Sallisaw.
Q Have you ever been recognized by the Cherokee authorities as a Cherokee citizen? A Yes sir.
Q Your name appear[sic] upon the rolls of the Cherokee Nation? A Yes sir.
Q In what district do you live? A I live in this District, Sequoyah.
Q How long have you lived in Sequoyah District? A I have lived here five years.
Q Where did you live before that? A I lived in Flint District.
Q How long did you live in Flint District? A I lived in Flint about five years.
Q How long have you lived continuously in the Cherokee Nation? A Ten years.
Q What is your father's name? A Mige Brackett.
Q Is he living? A No sir.
Q Did he die before 1880? A No sir.
Q Was his name on the roll of 1880? A I don't know whether it was or not; he died in the old country.
Q What is the name of your mother? A Cynthia.
Q Is she living? A No sir, she died before I can recollect.
Q Are you married? A Yes sir.
Q What is the name of your wife? A Sarah C. Brackett.
Q Is she a citizen? A Yes sir I want to register her.
Q Mr. Brackett you present a certificate of admission to Cherokee citizenship issued by the Commission on Citizenship dated 16th day of August 1889, signed by William P. Ross, Chairman of the Committee, attested by D. S. Williams, Clerk of the Committee, approved and indorsed by J. B. Mayes, Principal Chief, under the Great Seal of the Cherokee Nation; in this certificate I find the name of Daniel Brackett, aged forty-four years; are you the identical Daniel Brackett mentioned in this certificate? A Yes sir.
Q This certificate requires that all persons who return to and permanently locate within the limits of the Cherokee Nation shall enroll their names with the names of their family upon the date of their arrival in a book to be kept in the office of the Principal Chief, and this shall be done within one year from the date of this certificate; have you done that? A I didn't enroll; they told me it wouldn't be necessary to enroll; they taken the census roll that same year we come here. I was here inside the limits.
Q Was you in the Cherokee Nation as a resident within one year from the date of this certificate? A Yes sir, I was at Sallisaw the 11th day of April.
Q When were you married? A I was married in 1867.

Q Does her name appear upon this certificate? A No sir, just me and my children.
Q Have you any children under twenty-one years of age? A No sir not now.
Q You are then applying simply for yourself? A Yes sir.
Q As I understand, you married your wife before you was admitted? A Yes sir.
Q And her name does not appear in here? A No sir.
1896 roll, page 1051 #65 Daniel Brackett, Sequoyah District, fifty years old.
1894 roll page 578 #264 Daniel Bracket[sic], Flint District.

Com'r Needles: The name of Daniel Brackett appears upon the census roll of 1896 and the pay roll of 1894; he also presents certificate of admission to Cherokee citizenship as described in the testimony now taken, and has made satisfactory proof as to his residence. And now come the representatives of the Cherokee Nation and object to the enrollment of said Daniel Brackett, consequently final judgment as to his enrollment will be suspended, and his name will be placed upon a doubtful card.

M.D. Green, being first duly sworn, states that as stenographer to the Commission to the Five Civilized Tribes he reported the foregoing case and that the above and foregoing is a full true and complete transcript of his stenographic notes in said case.

M D Green

Subscribed and sworn to before me this 7th day of August 1900.

T B Needles
Commissioner.

"R"

Cherokee

Department of the Interior,
Commission to the Five Civilized Tribes,
Tahlequah, I.T., November 16, 1901.

In the matter of the application of Sarah C. Brackett for the enrollment of herself as a Cherokee citizen by blood; being sworn and examined she testified as follows:

BY COMMISSION:
Q What is your name? A Sarah C. Brackett.
Q How old are you? A 50 years old.
Q What is your post-office address? A Sallisaw.
Q Haven't you been enrolled? A No sir, I aint never been before you before, this is the first time.

Q Do you apply for enrollment as a Cherokee by blood? A Yes sir, I am a Cherokee by blood.
Q What degree of Cherokee blood do you claim? A One-eighth or a quarter.
Q What district are you living in in the Cherokee Nation? A Sequoyah.
Q Do you apply for anyone besides yourself? A No sir, my husband there and children has all done enrolled.
Q Where were you born? A I was born in Georgia, Union County.
Q When did you come to the Cherokee Nation? A It will soon be 12 years since I come here.
Q Has you ever lived here before that time? A No sir.
Q Have you ever been recognized as a citizen of the Cherokee Nation by the tribal authorities? A Well I have since called over here and they said it was all right.
Q Did you apply for admission to citizenship when you came here? A Yes sir.
Q Have you any evidence of that admission? A I had one paper and I sent it to Washington; they said they would give me some more papers, but I never got them.
Q Were you admitted by an act of Council or by an act of the Commission on Citizenship? A I can't tell you.
Q Were you admitted at the same time that your husband was admitted?
A No sir, I was not admitted at the same time he was; I went ahead and made my proof since that and they said it was all sufficient, I had done all that was required of me.
Q How long ago was that? A About 10 years ago.
Q Did they give you a certificate of admission? A Well they gave me a copy of it, although I called for it.
Q Were you admitted or were you rejected? A I was not rejected, I sent it to Washington.
Q Have you ever drawn any money from the tribal authorities of the Cherokee Nation? A Yes sir, I drawed my Strip money.
Q Is your name on the Strip payment roll of 1894? A I reckon it is[sic]
Q Is your name on the roll of 1896? A I aint looked at the rolls, I don't know.
Q What is the name of your husband? A Daniel Brackett.
Q Daniel R. isn't it? A No sir, no R. to it.
Q How old is he? A He is about 54 years old, I reckon; he is older that I am
Q Is his post-office address at Sallisaw? A Yes sir.
Q When were you married to him? A 30 some odd years ago.
Q Have you and he been living together continuously since that time? A Yes sir, been living together all the while.
Q You are living together now? A Yes sir.
Q Is he a recognized citizen of the Cherokee Nation? A Yes sir.
Q Did he come to the Cherokee Nation when you came? A Yes sir, we all came at the same time.
Q Why didn't you apply for admission when your husband applied? A I was not here at this place at that time.
Q Then you didn't come when your husband came? A Yes sir, I came when he come[sic], but I wasn't here at that time.
Q When did you husband come? A He come at the same time I come; we have been here over 12 years.

Q What do you mean by saying you were not here? A I was not at this place.
Q Were you in the Cherokee Nation? A No sir, I was at my old home.
Q You came here with your husband 12 years ago? A Yes sir, not hardly 12 years it aint.
Q And you stated awhile ago that you were not here when he made his application?
A No sir, we was in the old country when our case were passed on and we were sent for and we come.
Q Then you were admitted to citizenship before you came to the Cherokee Nation?
A No sir, I was not.
Q Your husband was? A Yes sir.
Q How long after you came to the Cherokee Nation was it before you made application for admission? A Right the next fall.
Q Have you got any children? A Yes sir.
Q What are their names? A Emma Wilson, W.H. Brackett and Susan Adair.
Q They were admitted when your husband was? A Yes sir. Now the reason mine stayed the way it did was because there was no one to get for the witness.
Q You were never re-married to your husband after he was admitted to citizenship?
A No sir.

> 1896 census roll of citizens of the Cherokee Nation examined for applicant, and identified as follows:
> page 1051, No. 66, Sarah C. Brackett, Sequoyah District, native Cherokee, (with Daniel Brackett on this roll.)

Q What district were you living in when you drew your Strip money? A I was living in Flint District when we drew our Strip money.
Q Did you draw your money at the same time your husband drew his? A No sir.
Q You drew then by a special act of the Council did you? A Yes sir, I did.
BY MR. BAUGH:
Q That is the time then that you claim you were admitted to citizenship when they gave you your Strip money, is that it? A I reckon so, that's the time.

> 1894 payment roll of citizens of the Cherokee Nation examined for applicant and name not found thereon.

Q Did you ever have a child named Alice? A No sir.
Q Do you know any other Sarah Brackett living in the Cherokee Nation? A Yes sir, there is another Sarah Brackett besides me.
Q Do you know any of her children? A She has just got one child.
Q What is its name, do you know? A Minnie, Arminda I think she signs her name.
COMMISSION:

> Sarah C. Brackett applies for the enrollment of herself as a Cherokee by blood. She avers that she came to the Cherokee Nation some 12 years ago from the State of Georgia, and that after she came to the Cherokee Nation that she was admitted to citizenship by the tribal authorities. No evidence of said admission is introduces at the present time.

She is not identified upon the Strip payment roll of 1894. She is identified upon the census roll of 1896 as a native Cherokee and the wife of Daniel Brackett; said Daniel Brackett has been listed for enrollment as a Cherokee by blood on doubtful card No. 82; the applicant avers that she and her husband were married some thirty years ago, and that they have been living together continuously since that time, and are living together at present. By reason of the fact that the applicant does not produce any satisfactory proof as to her admission to citizenship she will be listed for enrollment as a citizen by blood, on a doubtful card, No. 82, that being the card of her husband. It will be necessary that the applicant furnish the Commission satisfactory proof as to her admission to citizenship in the Cherokee Nation by the tribal authorities of said Nation.

--**--

SUPPLEMENTAL:
To Judgment. (Of same date.)

DANIEL BRACKETT, being sworn and examined, testified as follows:

Present:

Applicant, Sarah C. Brackett, and husband, Daniel Brackett.
J. L. Baugh, for the Cherokee Nation.

BY COMMISSION:

Q What is your name? A Daniel Brackett.
Q How old are you? A I don't know my age exactly.
Q About how old? A Somewhere about 50 I reckon, 51 or 2, I don't know.
Q What is your post-office address? A Sallisaw.
Q Are you a citizen of the Cherokee Nation? A Yes sir.
Q By blood? A Yes sir.

BY MR. BAUGH:

Q Mr. Brackett, are you the same Daniel Brackett that applied at Sallisaw August 6, 1900 for enrollment? A Yes.
Q Is Sarah C. your wife? A Yes sir.
Q Why didn't you make application for her at the time you made application for yourself? A Why didn't I?
Q Yes sir? A I had some papers and introduced them and they shoved them back to me and never so much as looked at them I don't think.
Q Did you tell the Commission that you desired to enroll your wife as a citizen of the Cherokee Nation at that time? A No sir I didn't tell them that.
Q Why didn't you make application for your wife at that time? A I ought to have done it, but I didn't do it.
Q At that time were you cognizant of the fact that your wife had been admitted to citizenship, aw you claim now? A Why yes, that is what they claimed here you know, that she was admitted; that she had all the papers that was necessary.

Q Was there any citizenship papers ever placed in your possession? A Not in my hands, no sir.
Q Did you ever see any? A No sir, but she came here and got them and sent them to Washington City to the Secretary.
Q Got them from the Executive Department? A Yes sir.
Q I will ask you if you applied to the Executive Department for a copy of these papers since you have been here? A Yes sir.
Q What did you find there? A They said they had no record of it.
Q No record that she ever had been admitted? A No sir.
Q No record that she had ever applied? A Yes sir, I reckon there was a record that she applied. No I don't believe there was Mr. Baugh; that is, her individual self you know.
Q What was the nature of these papers you sent to Washington City? A She just sent for her removal money you know; you know those that paid their way to this country had a right to their removal money, 53 and 1/3 dollars per head.
Q Did she ever get her money? A No sir.
Q Do you know the reason why? A No sir, they wrote to her that the appropriation had give out; it was all right, but we would have to wait until more money was appropriated; that is what the Secretary said about it.

BY COMMISSION:

Q When was that Mr. Brackett, how long ago? A I don't know, I don't remember exactly, it has been about 4 or 5 years, I suppose; three or four; when they were paying out that removal money you know.
Q Did your wife actually draw the Strip money? A Yes sir.
Q What amount did she draw? [sic] Same amount the others drew.
Q What did they draw? A About 265 and something wasn't it?
Q Was that money paid to her by act of Council? A Yes sir.
Q Have you any evidence of your marriage to your wife? A Why I could produce plenty of evidence here in the country I suppose.
Q Well were you married in the State of Georgia? A Yes sir.
Q Then you procured a license and certificate did you not? A Yes sir, I could write back there I suppose to the Ordinary and get a marriage certificate if it is necessary.

BY MR. BAUGH:

Q How was this money paid to your wife, this money you claim she drew, did you get the money for it or was it paid in a warrant? A Got the money.
Q Direct? A Yes sir.
Q Who drew the money for your wife? A I drew the money myself.
Q Came here to Tahlequah and got it? A Yes sir.

BY COMMISSION:

Mr. Brackett, you had better get a certified copy of the marriage license and certificate and sent tit[sic] to the Commission, and you should also procure a certified copy of that act of the Council paying this 265 dollars to your wife, and mail it to the Commission.

--**--

M.D. Green, being first duly sworn, states that as stenographer to the Commission to the Five Civilized Tribes he correctly recorded the testimony and proceedings in this case and that the foregoing is a true and complete transcript of his stenographic notes thereof.

M D Green

Subscribed and sworn to before me this November 18, 1901.

J C Starr
Notary Public.

"R"

Cherokee D 82.

Department of the Interior,
Commission to the Five Civilized Tribes,
Muskogee, I. T., February 17, 1902.

SUPPLEMENTAL TESTIMONY AND PROCEEDINGS in the matter of the application of Daniel Brackett, et al., for enrollment as Cherokee citizens.

Appearances:
James H. Huckleberry, Sr., Sallisaw, I.T., Att'y for Appl'ts.
W. W. Hastings, attorney for the Cherokee Nation.

DANIEL BRACKETT, appearing before the Commission and being sworn and examined testified as follows:
BY COMMISSION:
Q What is your name? A Daniel Brackett.
Q How old are you? A I don't know my age, exactly, I am about 52 I suppose.
Q What is your post-office address? A Sallisaw.
BY MR. HUCKLEBERRY:
Q I wanted to ask him about the marriage of himself and wife: whereabouts were you married? A In the State of Georgia.
Q You remember what year? A I think it was '69, I aint certain about it; I aint positive of that fact, '68 or '9, I forget which it was.
Q What was her maiden name? A Sarah Mathews.
Q Was she a Cherokee by blood? A Yes sir.
Q On which side, on the father or mother's side? A On the mother's side.
Q What was the mother's name? A Jane McDaniel, Jane Mathews.
Q What was the father's name? A Allen Mathews.
Q When did you move to this country first? A Well I have been here 12 years, in April.

Q You came here in 1890 then? A Yes sir, 11th day of April we reached Sallisaw.
Q Did you ever come here before? A No sir, I never have been here before.
Q You notice that paper? A Yes sir.
Q Was that delivered to you at the time? A Yes sir.

BY COMMISSION: There is offered in evidence a certificate from the Cherokee Commission on citizenship bearing date of Agust[sic] 16, 1889, admitting Daniel C. Brackett and others to citizenship in the Cherokee Nation, and same is filed herewith.

Q Is there anything else you desire to offer in evidence in this case? A Yes sir. (Produces papers, copies of which are found to be on file.)

MR. HUCKLEBERRY: Here is also a certificate we want to introduce for Mrs. Brackett. (Hands to Commission.)

BY COMMISSION: There is offered in evidence a certificate from BW. Alberty, Assistant Executive Secretary of the Cherokee Nation, certifying that the name of Sarah C. Brackett appears as number 37 in the list of persons included in an act of the Cherokee National Council entitled "An act making appropriation for the benefit of persons residents of Tahlequah District omitted from the pay rolls and from participating in the distribution of the strip fund or the last per capita payment." Same is filed.

Q Is there any further testimony that you desire to introduce in this case? A No sir, we want at the same time to take up his children.
Q Do you submit this case to the Commission for final consideration?

MR. HUCKLEBERRY: Yes, sir.
APPLICANT: Yes, sir.

Q Do your submit, Mr. Hastings?

MR. HASTINGS: Yes, sir.

M.D. Green, being first duly sworn, states that as stenographer to the Commission to the Five Civilized Tribes he correctly recorded the testimony and proceedings in this case and that the foregoing is a true and complete transcript of his stenographic notes thereof.

M D Green

Subscribed and sworn to before me this February 19, 1902.

T B Needles

Commissioner.

Cher
Supp'l to D 82

Department of the Interior,
Commission to the Five Civilized Tribes,
Vinita, I.T., February 13, 1903.

In the matter of the application of DANIEL BRACKETT, for the enrollment of himself and his wife SARAH C. BRACKETT, as citizens by blood of the Cherokee Nation:

JOHN M. BRANNUM, being first duly sworn, and examined, testified as follows:

Examined by the Commission:

Q What is your name ? A John M. Brannum.
Q How old are you ? A I am sixty odd.
Q What is your post office ? A Sallisaw.
Q Are you a citizen of the Cherokee Nation ? A No sir.
Q How long have you been living in the Cherokee Nation ? A I have been here going on ten years.
Q Do you know Sarah C. Brackett ? A Yes sir.
Q Did you know her parents ? A Yes sir.
Q Her father's name was Allen Mathis ? A Yes sir.
Q He was a white man ? A Yes sir.
Q What was her mother's name ? A Jane.
Q Was she a Cherokee ? A Yes sir.
Q How long have you known her ? A Ever since I can recollect.
Q Where was she living ? A She was living then in Georgia, of course, where she was raised at, and where I was raised at; I first knew her when I was very small in Cherokee County, North Carolina.
Q And you knew here after that in Georgia ? A Yes sir. Knew her all my life up until after the war.
Q Was she a Cherokee Indian ? A Yes sir, that's been my understanding always.
Q Was there any doubt about it ? A No sir.
Q Did she look like an Indian ? A Looked like she might be a half breed. My understanding always has been that her father was about, or pretty near, a full blood.
Q When did she come to the Cherokee Nation ? A I can't tell you just when she came, but she was here when I first come here.
Q When did you come to the Nation ? A I come here, last August was nine years ago; but then I come from Texas here, I had left Georgia several years ago.
Q Was Sarah married over in Georgia ? A Yes sir.
Q You remember the occasion of her marriage, do you ? A No sir, I do not.
Q Where were they living in the Cherokee Nation when you come ?
A They was living up here on Coal Creek in Illinois or Flint district, close to the line.

Q Did Sarah's mother, Jane, come with her ? A I don't know.
Q When did Jane Mathis come to the Nation ? A Mr. Brackett can tell you, because she was here when I come here nine years ago.
Q Jane was ? A Yes sir.
Q What district were they living in ? A Flint District.
Q That was nine years ago ? A Last August yes sir.
Q Have they been living in Flint district ever since ? A No sir, they have been living the bigger portion of that time down in Sequoyah district near Sallisaw.
Q Is Jane Mathis living yet ? A No sir she's dead.
Q How long ago did she die ? A She died in October.
Q About four months you think ? A Yes sir.

DANIEL BRACKETT, being first duly sworn, and examined, testified as follows:

Examined by the Commission:

Q What is your name ? A Daniel Brackett.
Q How old are you ? A I am somewheres[sic] about fifty four or five I don't know exactly.
Q What is your post office ? A Sallisaw.
Q Are you a Cherokee by blood ? A Yes sir.
Q Were you admitted to citizenship in the Cherokee Nation ? A Yes sir, I was admitted here.
Q When ? A In August, 1889, I believe; my papers is here somewheres[sic].
Q Was your wife Sarah admitted with you ? A No sir.
Q How did that come ? A I don't know how that come.
Q Did you apply for admission to citizenship ? A Yes sir.
Q Yourself ? A Yes sir.
Q Who did you include in your application ? A I included her and the children, or had it done you know.
Q Who was your attorney ? A Gus Ivey.
Q Was that application made by you before you came here to the Cherokee Nation?
A Yes sir it was made before I came here.
Q Do you know who was admitted with you then ? A Well, my children was admitted with me.
Q But not your wife ? A No sir, she was not admitted at that time.
Q Was she admitted at any time ? A They claimed she were[sic], I don't know, I can't tell you about that.
Q You brought her with you from Georgia, didn't you ? A Yes sir.
Q She hadn't been admitted at that time ? A No sir.
Q Was she admitted afterwards ? A That's what they told me.
Q You would certainly know wouldn't you ? A I don't know about that, they claimed it was done in Council.

Q What year ? A That was about 1894, I reckon, somewhere along there. I don't know exactly the date.
Q Was her mother Jane Mathis admitted ? A No sir.
Q She never was admitted ? A No sir, not in this part of the country.
Q When did Jane Mathis come to the Cherokee Nation ? A It must have been ten or eleven years ago, I don't know exactly the date, she come after I come to the country,
Q You came shortly after your admission ? A Yes sir.
Q What year ? A In 1890.
Q Jane Mathis didn't come until after that ? A No sir, she come about the second year after I come.
Q You say she never was admitted ? A No sir, she never was admitted at all. My son wrote back but they never found her papers.
Q So she never claimed citizenship in this country did she ? A She claimed it but she never did get her papers like she ought to have had them.
Q Well, its[sic] probable then, that your wife was never admitted then, either ?
A It might be possible, I don't know. That's what they told us. She went to Tahlequah and got a certificate and sent it to the Secretary of the Interior.
Q Did Jane Mathis have any other children ? A Yes sir.
Q Did any of them come with her ? A No sir, one come with them, but they have gone out of the country.
Q Were they ever admitted to citizenship ? A No sir.
Q Did your wife ever make any effort to be admitted after she came here ?
A Yes sir.
Q Who was her attorney ? A Why Gus Ivey looking after the business.
Q But you don't know whether she was admitted or not ? A No sir, I can't be positive about that, they told her that she had done all that was necessary.
Q Who told her that ? A Parties told her that, up yonder at Tahlequah you know. She went back after that and got a certificate and send[sic] it to the Secretary of the Interior, about her removal.
Q You were lawfully married to her in Georgia ? A Yes sir.
Q Did you present your marriage certificate here ? A Yes sir my marriage certificate is here.
Q Your marriage certificate to this wife ? A Yes sir.
Q Is she your first wife ? A Yes sir.
Q And are you her first husband ? A Yes sir.
Q And have you been living together ever since you were married ? A Yes sir.
Q Never separated ? A No sir.
Q Have you been residing in the Cherokee Nation ever since you came here in 1890?
A Yes sir.
Q You and your wife ? A Yes sir.
Q Never lived outside the Cherokee Nation since that time ? A No sir.

E. C. Bagwell, on oath states that, as stenographer to the Commission to the Five Civilized Tribes, he correctly recorded that testimony and proceedings had in the above entitled cause, and that the foregoing is an accurate transcript of his stenographic notes thereof.

E.C. Bagwell

Subscribed and sworn to before me this March 7, 1903.

Samuel Foreman
Notary Public.

Cherokee D. 82.

DEPARTMENT OF THE INTERIOR
COMMISSION TO THE FIVE CIVILIZED TRIBES.

In the matter of the application for the enrollment of Daniel Brackett as a citizen by blood of the Cherokee Nation.

DECISION.

The record in this case shows that on August 6, 1900, Daniel Brackett appeared before the Commission at Sallisaw, Indian Territory, and made personal application for enrollment as a citizen by blood of the Cherokee Nation. Further proceedings in the matter of said application were had at Muskogee, Indian Territory, on February 15, 1902, and at Vinita, Indian Territory, on February 13, 1903. The application also included Sarah C. Brackett for enrollment as a citizen by intermarriage of the Cherokee Nation, but her status as such is not passed upon at this time and she is not embraced in this decision.

The evidence shows that the said Daniel Brackett was admitted to citizenship in the Cherokee Nation by the duly constituted authorities of said nation, on August 16, 1889, and is identified on the Cherokee census roll of 1896.

The evidence further shows that the said Daniel Brackett removed to the Cherokee Nation within the time limit specified in the certificate of admission, and has lived continuously for the past ten years in said nation, and that he was a resident therein at the time of this application.

It is, therefore, the opinion of this Commission that Daniel Brackett should be enrolled as a citizen by blood of the Cherokee Nation, in accordance with the provisions of section twenty-one of the act of Congress approved June 28, 1898 (30 Stats., 495), and it is so ordered.

COMMISSION TO THE FIVE CIVILIZED TRIBES.

(SIGNED). *Tams Bixby.*
Chairman.

(SIGNED). *T. B. Needles.*
Commissioner.

(SIGNED). *C. R. Breckinridge.*
Commissioner.

(SIGNED). *W. E. Stanley.*
Commissioner.

Dated Muskogee, Indian Territory,

this JUN 1 - 1903

C.P.R. Cherokee D 82

COPY

DEPARTMENT OF THE INTERIOR,

COMMISSIONER TO THE FIVE CIVILIZED TRIBES.

In the matter of the application for the enrollment of Sarah C. Brackett as a citizen of the Cherokee Nation.

D E C I S I O N

THE RECORDS OF THIS OFFICE SHOW: That at Sallisaw, Indian Territory, August 6. 1900, application was received by the Commission to the Five Civilized Tribes for the enrollment of Sarah C. Brackett as a citizen of the Cherokee Nation. Further proceedings in the matter of said application were had at Tahlequah, Indian Territory, November 16, 1901, at Muskogee, Indian Territory, February 17, 1902, and at Vinita, Indian Territory, November 13, 1903.

THE EVIDENCE IN THIS CASE SHOWS: That the applicant herein, Sarah C. Brackett, alleges that she is a Cherokee by blood, but a careful examination of the records of this office fails to show that she was ever admitted to citizenship in the Cherokee Nation by the duly constituted authorities of said Nation, or by the Commission to the Five Civilized Tribes acting under authority of the Act of Congress approved June 10, 1896 (29 Stat., 321), or by the United States Court in Indian Territory on appeal therefrom, or that she has ever been recognized in any manner as a citizen by blood of the Cherokee Nation. The evidence further shows that said applicant, on June 1, 1868, in the state of Georgia, was married to one Daniel Brackett, and it is considered, in view of the foregoing that she possesses no right as a citizen of the Cherokee Nation other than such right as she may have acquired by virtue of said marriage; that the Daniel Brackett was not, at the time of said marriage, a recognized citizen by blood of the Cherokee Nation, and did not become such until his admission to citizenship therein by the duly constituted authorities of said Nation, August 16, 1889, and the name of Sarah C. Brackett is not mentioned in the act admitting, among others, said Daniel Brackett to citizenship in the Cherokee Nation.

It is, therefore, considered that said applicant did not marry a citizen by blood of the Cherokee Nation prior to November 1, 1875.

Said Sarah C. Brackett is not identified on the Cherokee authenticated tribal roll of 1880.

IT IS, THEREFORE, ORDERED AND ADJUDGED: That in accordance with the decision of the Supreme Court of the United States, dated November 5, 1906, in the cases of Daniel Red Bird, et al., vs. the United States, Nos. 125, 126, 127 and 128, the said applicant, Sarah C. Brackett, is not entitled, under the provisions of Section twenty-one of the Act of Congress approved June 28, 1898, (30 Stat. 495), to enrollment as a citizen by intermarriage of the Cherokee Nation, and her application for enrollment as such is accordingly denied.

SIGNED Tams Bixby
Commissioner.

Dated Muskogee, Indian Territory,

this FEB 23 1907

COMMISSIONERS:
TAMS BIXBY,
THOMAS B. NEEDLES,
C. R. BRECKINRIDGE,
W. E. STANLEY.

ALLISON L. AYLESWORTH,
SECRETARY.

DEPARTMENT OF THE INTERIOR,
COMMISSION TO THE FIVE CIVILIZED TRIBES.

REFER IN REPLY TO THE FOLLOWING
Cherokee D-82.

ADDRESS ONLY THE
COMMISSION TO THE FIVE CIVILIZED TRIBES.

Muskogee, Indian Territory, July 9, 1903.

W. W. Hastings,

Attorney for Cherokee Nation,

Tahlequah, Indian Territory.

Dear Sir:

There is herewith inclosed a copy of the decision of the Commission to the Five Civilized Tribes, dated June 1, 1903, granting the application of Daniel Brackett for the enrollment of himself as a citizen by blood of the Cherokee Nation.

You are hereby advised that you will be allowed fifteen days from date hereof in which to file such protest as you may desire to make against the action of the Commission in this case, a copy of which protest you will be required to serve upon the applicant. If you fail to file protest within the time allowed, this decision will be considered final.

Respectfully,

T B Needles

Commissioner in Charge.

Enc. H-24.

REFER IN REPLY TO THE FOLLOWING
Cherokee D. 82

DEPARTMENT OF THE INTERIOR,
COMMISSION TO THE FIVE CIVILIZED TRIBES.

Muskogee, Indian Territory, February 23, 1907.

W. W. Hastings,
Attorney for Cherokee Nation,
Muskogee, Indian Territory.

Dear Sir:-

There is enclosed herewith a copy of the decision of the Commissioner to the Five Civilized Tribes, dated February 23, 1907, denying the application for the enrollment of Sarah C. Brackett as a citizen by intermarriage of the Cherokee Nation.

The decision, together with the record of proceedings had in the case, has this day been transmitted to the Secretary of the Interior for his review and decision. The action of the Secretary will be made known to you as soon as this office is informed of the same.

Respectfully,

Tams Bixby

Commissioner.

Encl. E-81
BLE

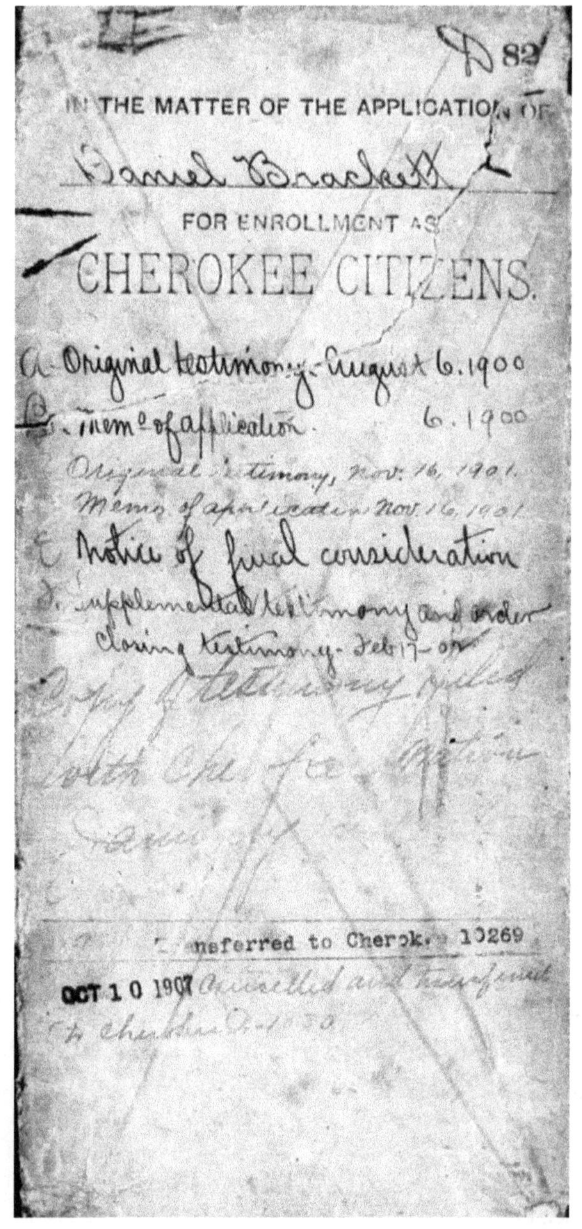

D 82

IN THE MATTER OF THE APPLICATION OF

Daniel Brackett

FOR ENROLLMENT AS

CHEROKEE CITIZENS.

A Original testimony - August 6. 1900
B Memo of application 6. 1900
Original testimony, Nov. 16, 1901.
Memo of application Nov. 16, 1901.
E Notice of final consideration
F Supplemental testimony and order closing testimony - Feb 17 - 04

Transferred to Cherokee 10269

OCT 10 1907 Cancelled and transferred to Cherokee D-1030

RESIDENCE: Sequoyah DISTRICT.
POST OFFICE: Sallisaw, I.T.

Cherokee Nation. Cherokee Roll.

(Not including Delawares, Shawnees, or Freedmen.)

CARD NO.
FIELD NO. 10259

Dawes' Roll No.	NAME.	Relationship to Person first Named.	AGE.	SEX.	BLOOD.	Tribal Enrollment Year.	Tribal Enrollment District.	Tribal Enrollment No.	Name of Father.	Year.	District.	Name of Mother.	Year.	District.
29817	1 Brackett, Daniel		51	M	1/16	1896	Sequoyah	65	Mige Brackett	Dead	Non-citz	Cyntha Brackett	Dead	Cherokee
	2													
	3 CITIZENSHIP CERTIFICATE ISSUED FOR NO. ______													
	4 MAR 4 1905													
	5													
	6													
	7 GRANTED													
	8 JUN 1 1905													
	9													
	10													
	11													
	12													
	13													
	14													
	15													
	16													
	17 See Cherokee													
	18 Card No D-82													

Represented by J H Huckleberry Sr, Sallisaw, I.T.

Date of Application for Enrollment: On Cherokee Card No D-82, August 6, 1900; On this card July 29, 1908.

Cherokee D83 - Andrusha Largent

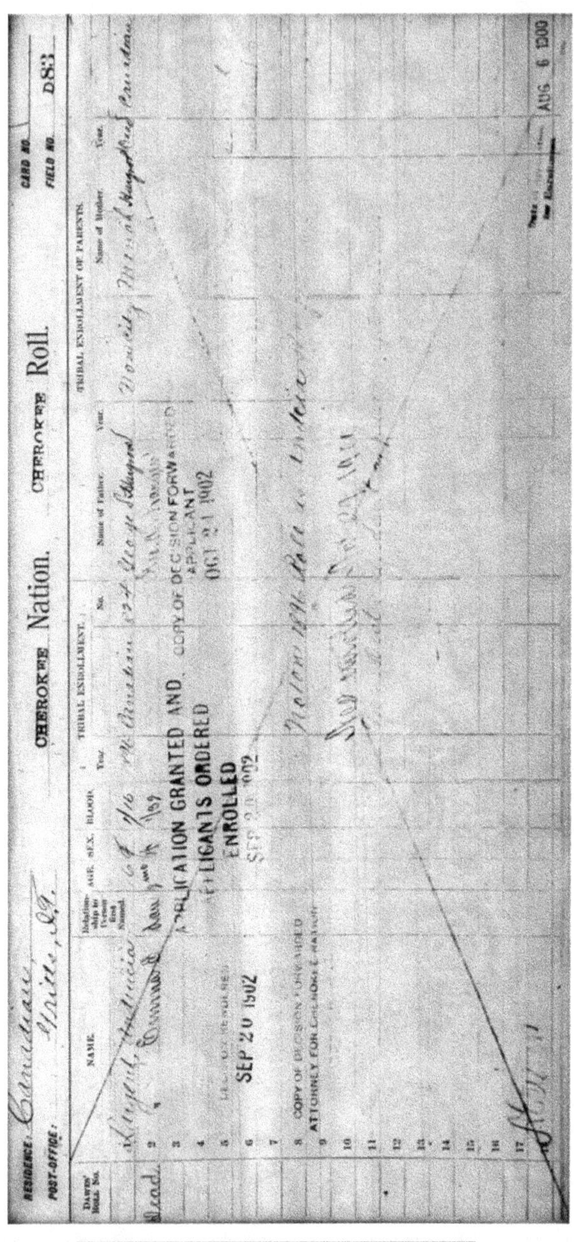

RESIDENCE: Canadian
POST-OFFICE:

CHEROKEE Nation. CHEROKEE Roll.

CARD NO.
FIELD NO. D83

Dawes' Roll No.	NAME	Relationship to Person first Named	AGE	SEX	BLOOD	TRIBAL ENROLLMENT Year	TRIBAL ENROLLMENT District	TRIBAL ENROLLMENT No.	Name of Father	Year	District	Name of Mother	Year	District

APPLICATION GRANTED AND APPLICANTS ORDERED ENROLLED SEP 20 1902

COPY OF DECISION FORWARDED APPLICANT OCT 21 1902

DECISION RENDERED SEP 20 1902

COPY OF DECISION FORWARDED ATTORNEY FOR CHEROKEE NATION

AUG 6 1900

Department of the Interior,
Commission to the Five Civilized Tribes,
Sallisaw, I.T., August 6, 1900.

In the matter of the application for the enrollment of Andrusha Largent for enrollment as a Cherokee by blood. George A. Largent, being duly sworn and examined by Commissioner Breckenridge[sic], testified as follows:

Q What is your full name? A George A. Largent.
Q What is your age? A 23.
Q What is your post office? A Gritts, I. T.
Q What is your district? A Canadian district.
Q How long have you lived in Canadian district? A About 3 years.
Q Where did you live before that? A I lived in the Choctaw country.
Q How long did you live there? A I lived there about 5 years.
Q Where did you live before that? A I lived in Arkansas.
Q For whom do you apply now for enrollment? A My wife, Andrusha Largent.
Q Before you and your wife were married her name was what?
A Hargrove.
Q How old is your wife? A She is 16.
Q Is she a Cherokee by blood? A Yes, sir.
Q What proportion of Cherokee blood do you claim for her? A 1/16, I suppose, as well as I know.
Q Do you apply for anybody but your wife? A No, sir, nobody but my wife.
Q What district does she live in, or did she live in when you married her?
A Canadian.
Q Did she always live in Canadian? A Yes, sir.
Q When were you married? A I was married in 1899.
Q Is your wife on the roll of 1896? A Yes, sir, I suppose she is.
Q And on the roll of 1894? A I suppose so.
Q What was her mother's name? A Her mothers[sic] name was Hargrove.
Q She had other children besides your wife? A Yes, sir.
Q What was her full name? A It was Maria Hargrove.
Q Do you think her mother is on the roll of 1880 as Hargrove? A I don't know whether her name is enrolled in 1880 or not.
Q Is her mother living now? A No, sir.
Q When did she die? A I can't tell you that, I have forgotten.
(Andrusha Largent on 1894 roll, page 82, No. 1716, Canadian dist. On 1896 roll, page 30, No. 824, Canadian district, Andcia[sic] Hargrove.)
Q Was her mother on the 1880 roll? A I don't know whether she was on the 1880 roll, she was admitted before 1880, that is my understanding.
Q Have you any written evidence of your wife's mother being admitted to citizenship? A No, sir.

Q Give your idea about your wife's mother being admitted, where she came from? A Andy Ross admitted her is the best of my knowledge, he was her father.

Q Where did she come from? A Arkansas.

Q Do you mean that she got admitted through him? A Yes, sir, through him, that is my understanding, I haven't got any written evidence of this at all.

Q Was your wife's mother a daughter of Andy Ross? A Yes, sir, that is my understanding, that she was a daughter of Andy Ross.

Q And then she married a man named Hargrove? A Yes, sir, George Hargrove.

Q Where was your wife born? A I suppose in Arkansas, William H. Ross is my wife's mother's brother.

Q Where was your wife born? A In Canadian district.

Q Have you any neighbors here who know about your being married to your wife? A I have Mr. Ross.

William H. Ross, being sworn and examined by Commissioner Breckenridge[sic], testified as follows:

Q What is your name? A William H. Ross.

Q And your post office address? A Webers[sic] Falls.

Q How long have you lived in this country? A I have lived here since about 1875 or 1876.

Q Mr. Ross, do you know the applicant here, George Largent? A Yes, sir.

Q Do you know his wife? A Yes, sir.

Q Is his wife kin to you? A Yes, sir.

Q What kin? A My niece.

Q Where were they married? A I cannot answer the question.

Q What is her name? A Andrusha Hargrove, it was before she married.

Q Have they been married 10 years? A No, sir.

Q Been married one year? A Yes, sir, been married about one year.

Q Have they lived together as husband and wife ever since they married?

A Yes, sir.

Q And are so living now? A Yes, sir.

A[sic] Now Mr. Ross, the age his wife is testified to as being is about 16, now who was her mother? A Her mother was Maria Hargrove.

Q She was your sister? A Yes, sir.

Q Isn't she on the roll of 1880? A No, sir.

Q Why not? A Her husband went to the states when they taken that roll.

Q You are on the roll of 1880 I believe? A Yes, sir.

Q And your sister was absent with her husband at that time? A Yes, sir.

Q Maria Hargrove is dead, isn't she? A Yes, sir.

Q When did she come back to the Cherokee Nation from that visit? A In 1881 or 1882, I would not be positive.

Q When did she die? A I can't answer the question.

Q How long was she visiting out of the Territory? A 12 months, to the best of my knowledge.

Q Where was your sister born? A She was born in the states.

Q When did she die? A I can't answer that question.

Q Been dead some year[sic], hasn't she? A Yes, sir, I can't exactly answer that question.

Q Has she been dead 10 years? A Yes, sir.

Q Has she been dead 15 years? A No, sir, she has not been dead 10 years, I was mistaken.

Q Did she live here in the Cherokee Nation from along about 1881 or 1882 until the time of her death? A Yes, sir.

Q And was this niece of yours, this man's wife, born here in the Cherokee Nation? A Yes, sir.

Q And lived here all her life? A Yes, sir.

Q Where was Maria Hargrove, the mother of this woman Andrusha Largent, married? A Married in the states.

Q What was her husband, was he a citizen of the Cherokee Nation? A No, sir, he was a citizen of the state of Arkansas.

Mr. W. T. Hutchings, attorney for Cherokee Nation: Were not you admitted to citizenship by some court of Commission? A Yes, sir.

Q When was that? A It was in 1885 or 1886, I will not be positive; in 1875 or 1876 I mean.

Q You were admitted by the Council then? A Yes, sir.

Commissioner Breckenridge[sic]: Was Maria Hargrove, your sister, admitted by any authority of the Cherokee Nation? A Yes, sir.

Q By the Council? A Yes, sir.

Q When? A When I was, in 1875 or 1876.

Q And then she left and went to Arkansas? A Yes, sir, they lived in the Nation quite a while and then went back and was out about 12 months.

Q And out there she married? A No, sir, she married before she came to the Territory.

Mr. Hutchings: Was she married here when she was admitted to citizenship? A Yes, sir.

Commissioner Breckenridge[sic]: She was admitted in 1875 or 1876 by the Cherokee authorities, and happened to miss the 1880 enrollment by being out of the Nation for a little while? A Yes, sir.

George A. Largent, recalled, testified:

Q Now Mr. Largent, your wife is duly identified on the roll of 1894 and also on the roll of 1896, but that simply gives us jurisdiction over her case, although it is true that it is to quite an extent persuasive, but it is not conclusive of her citizenship. The personal testimony establishes in a satisfactory manner the marriage of your wife to you, and her continued residence from her birth to this time in the Cherokee Nation, and in that was she is duly identified under her present name. It appears from personal testimony that your wife's mother, Maria Hargrove, was admitted to citizenship, or re-admitted, by the proper Cherokee authorities, under that name, along in 1875 or 1876, and that she failed to be enrolled on the roll of 1880 because of a temporary and brief absence from the Cherokee Nation, but that she came back to the Nation very soon after 1880, and lived here continuously until her death, and that her child, your wife, was born in the Nation. Now you are desired to procure and furnish to the Commission a certified copy of the proceedings of the Cherokee authorities supposed to be in 1875 or 1876, admitting your wife's mother to citizenship. Until that evidence is produced, your application for your wife will be placed upon a doubtful card, but when that evidence is produced, in the absence of any conflicting testimony, then your wife will be duly enrolled as a Cherokee by blood.

---------o---------

Bruce C. Jones, being duly sworn, says that as stenographer to the Commission to the Five Civilized Tribes he reportes[sic] the testimony of the above witnesses, and that the foregoing is a full, true and correct translation of his stenographic notes.

Bruce C Jones

Sworn to and subscribed before me this the 7th day of August, 1900.

Clifton R. Breckinridge
Commissioner.

Supl.-C.D.#83.

Department of the Interior,
Commission to the Five Civilized Tribes,
Muskogee, I. T., February 17, 1902.

SUPPLEMENTAL in the matter of the enrollment of ANDRUCIA[sic] LARGENT, ET AL., as citizens of the Cherokee Nation:

Applicant was notified by registered letter January 31, 1902, that her case would be taken up for final consideration on the 17th inst., and that she would on said date be given an opportunity to introduce any further testimony affecting her application. She has been called three times and fails to respond either in person or by attorney, and the case is closed.

C. R. Breckinridge

Commissioner.

Cherokee D 83

DEPARTMENT OF THE INTERIOR,
COMMISSION TO THE FIVE CIVILIZED TRIBES.

In the matter of the application for the enrollment of Andrusha Largent and Emma E. Largent as citizens by blood of the Cherokee Nation.

D E C I S I O N.

The record in this case shows that on August 6, 1900, George A. Largent appeared before the Commission at Sallisaw, Indian Territory, and made personal application for the enrollment of his wife Andrusha Largent, and his minor child Emma E. Largent, as citizens by blood of the Cherokee Nation.

The evidence shows that one Andrew Ross and children were admitted to citizenship in the Cherokee Nation by the duly constituted authorities of said Nation on December 8, 1877. It further appears that one of his children, namely; Maria, was married at the time of said admission to one Hargrove. As a result of that marriage the principal applicant in this case was born. It is further shown that Andrusha Hargrove married, in 1889, George A. Largent. As a result of that marriage Emma E. Largent was born. Andrusha Largent, nee Hargrove, is identified on the Cherokee Strip Payment Roll of 1894. She is further identified on the Cherokee Census Roll of 1896, as a native Cherokee.

It is further shown that subsequent to the admission of Maria Hargrove, and prior to 1880, she left the Cherokee Nation on a visit, and did not return in time to be enrolled. It is also shown that the principal applicant was born in the Cherokee Nation and has lived continuously therein, and was a resident thereof at the date of this application. Emma E. Largent is considered to have resided therein continuously since birth.

It is, therefore, the opinion of this Commission that Andrusha Largent and Emma E. Largent should be enrolled as citizens by blood of the Cherokee Nation in accordance with the provisions of Section twenty one of the Act of Congress approved June 28, 1898, (30 Stats., 495), and it is so ordered.

COMMISSION TO THE FIVE CIVILIZED TRIBES.

Tams Bixby
Acting Chairman.

T.B. Needles
Commissioner.

C. R. Breckinridge
Commissioner.

Dated Muskogee, Indian Territory,

this SEP 20 1902

COMMISSIONERS:

HENRY L. DAWES,
TAMS BIXBY,
THOMAS B. NEEDLES,
C. R. BRECKINRIDGE.

—

ALLISON L. AYLESWORTH,
SECRETARY.

ADDRESS ONLY THE
COMMISSION TO THE FIVE CIVILIZED TRIBES.

DEPARTMENT OF THE INTERIOR,
COMMISSION TO THE FIVE CIVILIZED TRIBES.

REFER IN REPLY TO THE FOLLOWING

Cherokee D 83.

Muskogee, Indian Territory, September 30, 1902.

W. W. Hastings,

Attorney for the Cherokee Nation,

Muskogee, Indian Territory.

Dear Sir:

Enclosed herewith please find a copy of the decision of the Commission to the Five Civilized Tribes, rendered September 20, 1902, granting the application of George A. Largent for the enrollment of his wife, Andrusha Largent, and his minor child, Emma E. Largent, as citizens by blood of the Cherokee Nation.

You are hereby advised that you will be allowed fifteen days from date hereof in which to file with the Commission such protest as you desire to make against the decision rendered in this case. If you fail to file protest within the time allowed, this decision will be considered final.

Respectfully,

Tams Bixby

Acting Chairman.

Enc. C. No. 123.

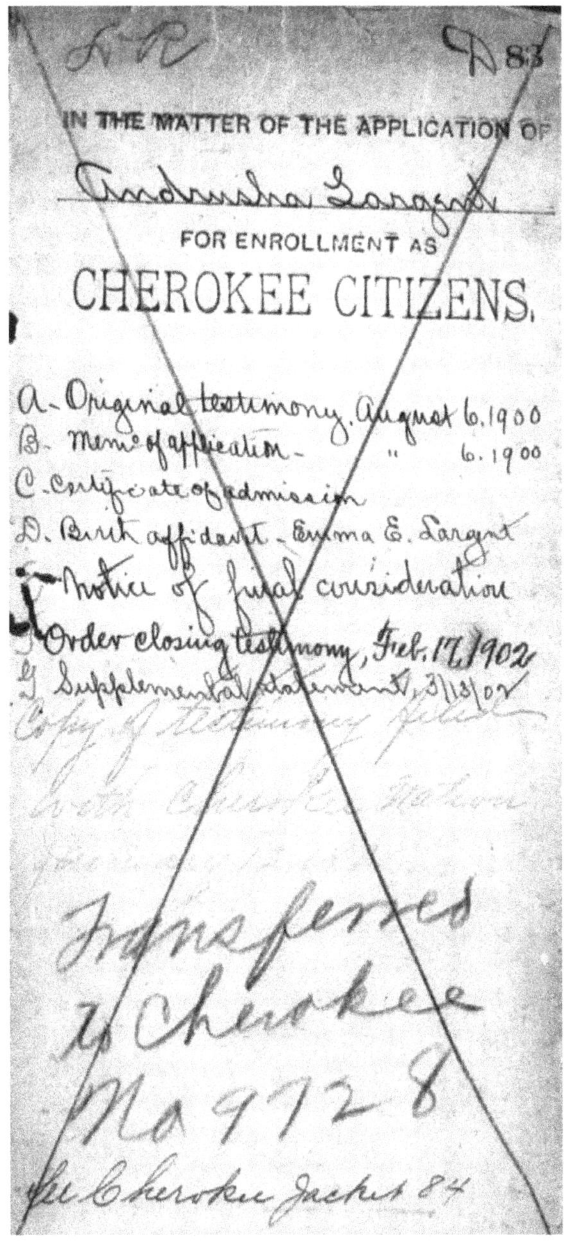

F R D 83

IN THE MATTER OF THE APPLICATION OF

Andrusha Largent

FOR ENROLLMENT AS

CHEROKEE CITIZENS.

A. Original testimony, August 6, 1900
B. Memo of application - " 6, 1900
C. Certificate of admission
D. Birth affidavit - Emma E. Largent
E. Notice of final consideration
F. Order closing testimony, Feb. 17, 1902
G. Supplemental statement, 3/13/02

Copy of testimony filed with Cherokee Nation

Transferred to Cherokee No 9728

See Cherokee Packet 84

RESIDENCE: Canadian DISTRICT.
POST OFFICE: Gritts, I.T.

Cherokee Nation. Cherokee Roll.
(Not Including Delawares, Shawnees, or Freedmen.)

CARD NO.
FIELD NO. 9728

Dawes' Roll No.		NAME.	Relationship to Person first Named.	AGE.	SEX.	BLOOD.	Tribal Enrollment Year.	Tribal Enrollment District.	Tribal Enrollment No.	Name of Father.	Year.	District.	Name of Mother.	Year.	District.
21864	1	Largent Andrucha		16	F	1/16	1896	Canadian	834	George S. Hargrove		Non citz	Mariah Hargrove	dead	Canadian
[illegible]	2	" Emma E.	dau	2mo	F	1/32				Geo. W. Largent			No. 1		
	3														
	4														
	5			APR		1905									
	6														
	7	GRANTED													
	8	SEP 20 1902													
	9						No 1 on 1896 roll as Andrua Hargrove								
	10							No 2 enrolled Nov. 27, 1902							
	11														
	12														
	13					DISMISSED									
	14														
	15														
	16														
	17														
	18	See N.B. #736											Date of Application for Enrollment.		

Cherokee D84 - Magnolia Wilson

Department of the Interior.
Commission to the Five Civilized Tribes.
Sallisaw, I. T., August 6th, 1900.

In the matter of the application of Joseph C. Wilson for his wife, Magnolia Wilson, and child, for enrollment as Cherokee citizens; he being sworn and examined by Commissioner Breckinridge, testifies as follows:

Q What is your full name? A Joseph C. Wilson.
Q What is your age? A Going on 24 years old.
Q What's your post-office? A Webbers Falls.
Q What district do you live in? A Canadian.
Q How long have you lived in Canadian district? A About 8 years.
Q Where did you live before that? A Salomo[sic] Springs, Ark.
Q For whom do you apply now for enrollment? A My wife and one child.
Q Do you apply for your wife as a Cherokee by blood? A Yes sir.
Q What is your wife's name? A Magnolia Wilson.
Q And when you married her her name was Hargrove? A Yes sir.
Q How old is she? A 19 years old.
Q When were you married? A Married in '97.
Q Have you a certificate of marriage? A Yes sir.

You present here a duly authenticated marriage license and certificate showing that on the 2nd of July, 1897, you were married to Magnolia Hargrove and this identifies your wife under her present name. This is returned to you.

Q Was your wife living in Canadian district in '94? A Yes sir, I guess so.
Q Also in '96? A Yes sir, I guess she was.
Q Is your wife's mother's name on the roll of 1880? A I could not tell you; don't think it is.
Q What was her name? A Maria Hargrove.
Q Is your wife a sister of George Largent's wife? A Yes sir.
Q Is that Maria Hargrove who was the mother of George Largent's wife, the mother of your wife? A Yes sir, guess she is.
Q Do you understand that your wife's mother was admitted to citizenship by the Cherokee authorities in '75 or 1874? A In 1875 or '76, I guess.
Q She was admitted at that time as Maria Hargrove was she not? A Yes sir, guess she was.
Q Along about 1880 did she move out of the Cherokee Nation on a visit for a little while? A Yes sir, think she did.
Q And in that way she failed to get on the roll of 1880? A Yes sir.
Q Do you understand that your wife's mother came back to the Cherokee Nation a little while after the roll of 1880 was taken? A Yes sir.
Q And did she live in the Cherokee Nation all the balance of her like until her death? A Yes sir, think she did.
Q Was your wife born here in the Cherokee Nation? A No sir, don't believe she was.

Q You think she was born while her mother was on that visit? A I can't say about that.

1896 roll; page 30, #823, Magnora[sic] Hargrove, Canadian Dist.
1894 roll; page 82, #1715, Magnora Hargrove, Canadian Dist.

Q Give me the name of your child? A Houston.
Q How old is he? A 2 years old.
Q You have got a certificate of his birth have you? A No sir.

Com'r. Breckinridge:

The woman, Magnolia Wilson, for whom application is made by her husband, Joseph C. Wilson, is duly identified as on the roll of 1896 and on the roll of 1894 under her maiden name of Hargrove. The license and certificate of marriage which have been cited in the testimony identifies her under her present name as Magnolia Wilson. There is personal testimony to the effect that this woman's mother Maria Hargrove, was admitted to citizenship by the Cherokee Council Commission on Citizenship in 1874 or 1875 or 1876, and that she omitted to be enrolled in 1880 by reason of a brief absence from the Cherokee Nation, but that she returned to the Nation very soon after 1880 and lived here continuously for the number of years until her death. Now it is desired that a certified copy be procured from the Cherokee authorities of their action in admitting Maria Hargrove, the mother of Magnolia Wilson, at the time indicated. When that copy is supplied to this commission, then Magnolia Wilson will be enrolled as a Cherokee by blood; and it is desired also that a certificate of the birth of the child, Houston Wilson, be properly made out and attested. When the mother's enrollment is justified by the production of the testimony stated and the certificate of the child's birth duly made out and authenticated and supplied to this Commission, then the child will also be enrolled as a Cherokee by blood. For the present, this application will be placed upon a doubtful card.

Edward G. Rothenberger, being duly sworn by Commissioner Breckinridge as Stenographer to the Commission to the Five Civilized Tribes, he reported in full the testimony of the above named witness, Joseph C. Wilson, and that the foregoing is a full, true and correct transcript of his notes.

Edward G. Rothenberger

Sworn to and subscribed before me this 7th day of August, 1900.

Commissioner.

Supl.-C.D.#84.

Department of the Interior,
Commission to the Five Civilized Tribes,
Muskogee, I. T., February 17, 1902.

SUPPLEMENTAL in the matter of the enrollment of MAGNOLIA WILSON as a citizen of the Cherokee Nation:

Applicant was notified by registered letter January 31, 1902, that her case would be taken up for final consideration by the Commission on the 17th day of February, 1902, and that she would on said date be given an opportunity to introduce any further testimony affecting her application. She was also requested to supply the Commission with a duly executed affidavit as to the birth of her son. She has been called three times and fails to respond and the case is closed.

C. R. Breckinridge

J.O.R. Commissioner.

D-84.

Department of the Interior,
Commission to the Five Civilized Tribes,
Muskogee, I. T., May 5, 1902.

In the matter of the application of Magnolia Wilson et al for enrollment as Cherokee citizens.

SUPPLEMENTAL TO D-84.

Applicant represented by her husband, Joseph Wilson.
Cherokee Nation represented by W. W. Hastings.

ROBERT F. ROSS, being duly sworn and examined by the Commission, testified as follows:

Q What is your name? A Robert F. Ross.
Q How old are you, Mr. Ross? A I am 49 years old, sir.
Q What is your present postoffice address? A Webbers Falls.
Q Are you a citizen of the Cherokee Nation? A Yes, sir.

Q By blood or adoption? A By blood.
Q Are you acquainted with Magnolia Wilson? A Yes, sir.
Q Are you related to her in any way? A She's my sister's child, I would be her uncle.
Q What's her mother's name? Or what was her mother's name? A Her mother's name was Mariah P. Ross was her maiden name; married a man by the name of Hargrove.
Q Her maiden name was Ross and she married a man by the name of Hargrove?
A Yes, sir.
Q So Magnolia Wilson's maiden name was Hargrove? A Yes, sir.
Q Who was the father of Mariah Hargrove? A Andrew Ross.
Q Is Mariah Hargrove living now? A No, sir.
Q Do you know the year she was born? A She was born, sir, in '55.
Q In 1855? A 1855, yes, sir.
Q Where was she born? A She was born four miles south of Alden, in Scott County, Arkansas.
Q When did she come to the Indian Territory? A In '76 I think, sir.
Q Had she ever been recognized as a citizen prior to her removal to the Cherokee Nation in '76? A No, sir, she hadn't been in the Nation; that was the first time she had been in the Nation; she was raised there.
Q Was she ever admitted as a citizen by the Cherokee tribal authorities? A She was admitted with Andrew Ross and family, Andrew Ross and children, came with him, living with him when she was admitted.
Q Do you know whether or not her name appears upon the 1880 roll? A No, sir, it does not, I think, of course I never-- I don't think it does.
Q Was she a member of Andrew Ross's family and living with him at the time Andrew Ross was admitted to citizenship by the Cherokee tribal authorities? A I think, sir, she was living in the house with him; I don't think they had ever-- she was married but I don't think they had ever moved to their house.
Q She was married prior to the time her father was readmitted? A Yes, sir, when he was readmitted, now my understanding that he was readmitted; he was born and raised in the Nation, my father.
Q He was born and raised here? A Yes, sir.
Q Where was Mrs. Hargrove during the year 1880 at the time the 1880 roll was made up? A Well, sir, she had been in Arkansas, this man Hargrove was a white man, and his mother was a widow woman, and she wrote to him to come down and help her straighten up her business, they had some real-estate there, and wrote to him, she wanted him to come down and help them tend to that business and get it straightened up, and he went down to help her, on visits rather and to straighten up that business, and about the time he was ready to come back, the time they was making the 1880 rolls, to the best of my recollection my father wrote to him that they was taking the census and he had better come on back and get on the rolls, and one of his children taken sick, had two children then, his oldest child taken sick and died, and by the time he died another one he[sic] taken sick and died the same time. On account of sickness why he didn't get back until the rolls was closed.
Q Do you know when Mrs. Hargrove was married, what year she was married to her husband? A No, sir, I couldn't swear to that, couldn't be positive, Q But she was

married at the time Andrew Ross and his family was admitted by the tribal authorities of the Cherokee Nation, was she? A Yes, sir.
Q Well now Mr. Ross, after Mrs. Hargrove returned to the Nation was she ever readmitted by the Cherokee authorities to citizenship? A I think not, sir, I don't think that she was; they didn't take all the stuff out of the Nation, just left--
Q Is she older or younger than you are? A Younger.
Q How much younger is she? A I was born in '53 and she was born in '55.
Q You remember when she and her husband returned to the Nation from Arkansas? A Yes, sir.
Q What year was that? A Well I say I remember when he come back, but I couldn't tell you about the time.
Q How long after the 1880 roll had been made up? A It was in the spring to the best of my knowledge, it must have been the spring of 1881, I couldn't tell you just exactly to the time.
Q You know by your father having written to Mr. Hargrove that they were preparing the 1880 roll that they were away at that time? A Yes, sir, and they were away from here when that 1880 roll was made.
Q And they didn't return until the following spring? A I think not to the best of my knowledge, somewhere along about the first of March when they got back.

JESSE T. ROSS, being first duly sworn and examined by the Commission, testified as follows:

Q What is your name? A Jesse T. Ross.
Q Do you know the applicant in this case, Magnolia Wilson? A Yes, sir.
Q Is she related to you in any way? A Yes, sir.
Q State how? A Sister's child.
Q What was her mother's name? A Mariah.
Q Mariah what? A Mariah Ross first; her maiden name was Ross; then she married a man by the name of Hargrove.
Q How old was Mrs. Hargrove? A I don't know exactly, of course I am older than she is, why I think she was born in '55.
Q How old are you? A I am 51 years old.
Q What is your postoffice address? A Gritts.
Q Where was Mrs. Hargrove in 1880, if you know? A She was in Arkansas on a visit.
Q Then her name wouldn't appear upon the 1880 roll? A No, sir.
Q Was she ever admitted to citizenship in the Cherokee Nation? A Well, that was my understanding, when brother was admitted why the children was all admitted and of course that's the way it come to me. I know I was at Tahlequah with him and the names was put down there, he give them all the names, but then my understanding was that they just admitted him and his family, now, he and his children; of course I don't know just exactly.
Q Well do you remember how old Mrs. Hargrove was at the time of that admission? A No, sir, she was married.

Q She was married at that time? A Yes, sir, she was married I reckon in must have been in '76, the spring of '76 if I ain't mistaken; that's as near as I think she was married.
Q Do you know how many children your father applied for at that time?
A Why no, I don't know.
Q You know whether Mrs. Hargrove here was included in the number?
A Yes, sir, of course they put down all the names.
Q Was your name included? A Yes, sir.
Q Your brother's name too? A Yes, sir.
Q You base your citizenship upon that act of admission of your father and his family, do you, Mr. Ross? A Yes, sir.
Q Well after Mrs. Hargrove returned from Arkansas was she ever readmitted to citizenship by the tribal authorities of the Cherokee Nation? A I think not, I don't reckon they was out long enough for that, you know.
Q About how long were they out of the Territory? A Well I could not tell you, but they just went on a visit is all I know; they went down there, you see he was a white man and his mother was in Arkansas, and wanted him to wind up her business, her husband died and left some land or something down there.
Q You mean Hargrove was a white man? A Yes, sir.
Q How long has Mrs. Hargrove been dead? A Well I think she died in '84 as well as I recollect, '84 or '85 somewhere along there.
MR. HASTINGS: Where was Mrs. Hargrove married? A Married in Arkansas.
Q They were married in Arkansas? A Yes, sir.
Q In '76? A Yes, sir, I reckon it was '76 I think it was.
Q Where was Mrs. Hargrove born? A She was born in Arkansas.
Q Lived there up till the time of her marriage? A Yes, sir.
Q And then she come over here? A Yes, sir.
Q And then went back to Arkansas? A Well she went on a visit, they didn't move back.
Q How long had they been over here when they went back on a visit? A Why they had been here, I don't know, two or three years, they went back.
Q Well about how long did they live in Arkansas after they were married before they came here? A About six months I reckon; they married in the spring; I wasn't there.
Q You wasn't there? A No, sir, I was here.
Q She lived up there in Arkansas from the time of her birth up till after she was married? A Yes, sir.
Q And according to your best recollection a short time, six or eight months, after her marriage she came here and stayed awhile? A Yes, sir.
Q And they went back to Arkansas? A Yes, sir, on a visit.
Q Now do you know when she come back the last time? A Why she come back just a little too late to get on the 1880 roll on account of sickness.
COMMISSION: I believe you said Mrs. Hargrove was the mother of this applicant? A Yes, sir.
Q Mother of this applicant, Magnolia Wilson? A Yes, sir.

Arthur G. Croninger, being first duly sworn, states that as stenographer to the Commission to the Five Civilized Tribes he reported in full the testimony and proceedings in the above case, and that the foregoing is a true and complete transcript of his stenographic notes thereof.

Arthur G Croninger

Subscribed and sworn to before me this 5th day of May, 1902.

PJ Reuter
Notary Public.

Cherokee D-84.

DEPARTMENT OF THE INTERIOR,
COMMISSION TO THE FIVE CIVILIZED TRIBES.
---o---
In the matter of the application for the enrollment of MAGNOLIA WILSON and her minor children, HOUSTON WILSON and VERNON WILSON, as citizens by blood of the Cherokee Nation.
-- -- -- -- -- -- -- --

D E C I S I O N.
--:o:--

The record in this case shows that on August 6, 1900, Joseph C. Wilson appeared before the Commission at Sallisaw, Indian Territory, and made application for the enrollment of his wife, Magnolia Wilson, and his minor child, Houston Wilson, as citizens by blood of the Cherokee Nation. Further proceedings were had in the matter of said application on May 5, 1902 at Muskogee, Indian Territory.

The evidence shows that Andrew Ross and children were admitted to citizenship in the Cherokee Nation by the duly constituted authorities of said Nation on December 8, 1877. It further appears that one of his children, namely Maria, was married at the time of said admission to one Hargrove. As a result of that marriage, the principal applicant in this case was born. It is further shown that Magnolia Wilson, nee Hargrove, was married on July 2, 1897, to one Joseph C. Wilson. As a result of that marriage, Houston Wilson was born. It further appears that, subsequent to the date of the application herein, there was born to said Joseph C. Wilson and his wife, Magnolia Wilson, a male child, one Vernon Wilson.

Magnolia Wilson is identified on the Cherokee Strip Payment Roll of 1894 and on the Cherokee Census Roll of 1896 as a native Cherokee. Vernon Wilson is identified by a birth certificate, filed herewith. The evidence further shows that Houston Wilson died on October 5, 1900.

It is further shown that, subsequent to the admission of Maria Hargrove, and before 1880, she left the Cherokee Nation for a visit. During her absence from said Nation, Magnolia Wilson, nee Hargrove, was born. Shortly after 1880, said Magnolia Wilson, nee Hargrove, returned with her mother to the Cherokee Nation, and has resided therein continuously up to and including the date of this application. The minor child, Vernon Wilson, is considered to have resided in said Nation since birth.

It is, therefore, the opinion of this Commission that Magnolia Wilson and Vernon Wilson should be enrolled as citizens by blood of the Cherokee Nation, in accordance with the provisions of Section twenty-one of the Act of Congress approved June 28, 1898, (30 Stats., 495), and it is so ordered.

It is further the opinion of this Commission that the application for the enrollment of Houston Wilson should be, and the same is hereby dismissed, and it is so ordered.

COMMISSION TO THE FIVE CIVILIZED TRIBES.

Tams Bixby
Acting Chairman.

T.B. Needles
Commissioner.

C. R. Breckinridge
Commissioner.

Muskogee, Indian Territory,
this JAN 12 1903

DEPARTMENT OF THE INTERIOR,
COMMISSION TO THE FIVE CIVILIZED TRIBES.

IN THE MATTER OF THE APPLICATION FOR ENROLLMENT OF MAGNOLIA WILSON, ET AL., AS CITIZENS OF THE CHEROKEE NATION.

D--84

PROTEST OF THE CHEROKEE NATION.

Comes now the Cherokee Nation and respectfully protests against the decision of the Commission rendered on January 12th., 1903, in the above case, and asks that the same be forwarded to the Secretary of the Interior for review.

The testimony in this case shows that the mother of the principal applicant was born in 1855 in the State of Arkansas, where she continued to live with her father until after her marriage in 1876, when she was twenty-one years of age, after which time she came to the Cherokee Nation, and with the exception of some two or three years subsequent to that time, when she went back to the State of Arkansas, she has lived in the Cherokee Nation.

The decision of the Commission states that:

"The evidence shows that Andrew Ross and children were admitted to citizenship in the Cherokee Nation by the duly constituted authorities of said Nation on December 8th., 1877. It further appears that one of his children, namely, Maria, was married at the time of said admission, to one Hargrove. As a result of this marriage, the principal applicant in this case was born".

Now how the Commission could construe that the admission of Andrew Ross on December 8th., 1877 could admit Maria Hargrove, the mother of the principal applicant, who was then twenty-two years of age, and who had previously married in the State of Arkansas, is not clear. We contend that she was not at that time a member of his family, and that this admission of her father did not carry with it the admission of his married daughter. It was incumbent upon her, as decided by the Supreme Court of the United States in the Eastern Band of Cherokees vs. United States, 117 U. S. 288, that it was necessary for her to have been re-admitted to citizenship when she came to the Cherokee Nation, because the court in that case decided if Indians in that State, or in any other State, wish to enjoy the benefits of the common property of the Cherokee Nation, in whatever form if may exist, they must, as held by the Court of Claims, comply with the Constitution and Laws of the Cherokee Nation, and be re-admitted to citizenship as there provided.

We desire to emphasize the point that the court in that case held that they must "be re-admitted to citizenship as there provided" sas[sic], and was therefore not a citizen of the Cherokee Nation. She married there where Magnolia Wilson was born. Clearly then it was incumbent upon her to be re-admitted upon her coming to the Cherokee Nation. The Cherokee Constitution, Article I, Section 2, provided a way in which a person may be re-admitted by memorializing the Cherokee National Council, and this does not seem to have been done in this case.

We submit that the name of the applicant was placed upon the 1894 and 1896 roll without authority of law, because she was born a citizen of the State of Arkansas, never admitted to citizenship in the Cherokee Nation, was never legally enrolled as such, and that she should not now be enrolled as a citizen of the Cherokee Nation by the Commission or by the Secretary of the Interior.

Respectfully submitted,

W. W. Hastings
Attorney for the Cherokee Nation.

COMMISSIONERS:

HENRY L. DAWES,
TAMS BIXBY,
THOMAS B. NEEDLES,
C. R. BRECKINRIDGE.

—

ALLISON L. AYLESWORTH,
SECRETARY.

ADDRESS ONLY THE
COMMISSION TO THE FIVE CIVILIZED TRIBES.

DEPARTMENT OF THE INTERIOR.
COMMISSION TO THE FIVE CIVILIZED TRIBES.

REFER IN REPLY TO THE FOLLOWING

Cherokee D-84

Muskogee, Indian Territory, January 12, 1903.

W. W. Hastings,

Attorney for the Cherokee Nation,

Vinita, Indian Territory.

Dear Sir:-

There is enclosed herewith a copy of the decision of the Commission to the Five Civilized Tribes, dated January 12, 1903, granting the application of Joseph C. Wilson for the enrollment of his minor child, Vernon Wilson, as a citizen by blood, and for the enrollment of his wife, Magnolia Wilson, as a citizen by intermarriage of the Cherokee Nation, and dismissing his application for the enrollment of his minor child, Houston Wilson, as a citizen by blood of the Cherokee Nation.

You are advised that you will be allowed fifteen days from date hereof, in which to file such protest as you desire to make against the action of the Commission in this case, a copy of which protest you will be required to serve upon the applicant. If you fail to file protest within the time allowed, this decision will be considered final.

Respectfully,

Tams Bixby
Acting Chairman.

Enc. M-17

ATTORNEYS
L. B. BELL
W. W. HASTINGS
J. S. DAVENPORT
J. C. STARR, SECRETARY

OFFICE OF
ATTORNEYS FOR THE CHEROKEE NATION
CHEROKEE FREEDMEN ENROLLMENT

No. F. D.

Vinita, Indian Territory, January 19th., 1903.

The Commission to the Five Civilized Tribes,
Muskogee, Indian Territory.

Gentlemen:-

Enclosed herewith find Protest of the Cherokee Nation against the Commission's decision in the matter of the application of Magnolia Wilson, et al, for enrollment as citizens of the Cherokee Nation, Cher. D--84.

Yours truly,

COMMISSIONERS:

HENRY L. DAWES,
TAMS BIXBY,
THOMAS B. NEEDLES,
C. R. BRECKINRIDGE.

ALLISON L. AYLESWORTH,
SECRETARY.

ADDRESS ONLY THE
COMMISSION TO THE FIVE CIVILIZED TRIBES.

DEPARTMENT OF THE INTERIOR,
COMMISSION TO THE FIVE CIVILIZED TRIBES.

REFER IN REPLY TO THE FOLLOWING
Cherokee D-84

Muskogee, Indian Territory, February 28, 1903.

W. W. Hastings,
Attorney for the Cherokee Nation,
Vinita, Indian Territory.

Dear Sir:

You are hereby advised that the Commission's decision, dated January 12, 1903, granting the application of Joseph C. Wilson for the enrollment of his wife, Magnolia, and his minor child, Vernon Wilson, as citizens by blood of the Cherokee Nation, and dismissing his application for the enrollment of his minor child, Houston Wilson, was affirmed by the Secretary of the Interior on February 18, 1903.

Respectfully,

Tams Bixby
Chairman.

COMMISSIONERS:

HENRY L. DAWES,
TAMS BIXBY,
THOMAS B. NEEDLES,
C. R. BRECKINRIDGE.

ALLISON L. AYLESWORTH,
SECRETARY.

ADDRESS ONLY THE
COMMISSION TO THE FIVE CIVILIZED TRIBES.

DEPARTMENT OF THE INTERIOR,
COMMISSION TO THE FIVE CIVILIZED TRIBES.

REFER IN REPLY TO THE FOLLOWING

Cherokee D-84.

Muskogee, Indian Territory, January 30, 1903.

W. W. Hastings,
Attorney for the Cherokee Nation,
Vinita, Indian Territory.

Dear Sir:

You are hereby advised that the Commission has this day transmitted to the Secretary of the Interior, for review, the record of proceedings had in the matter of the application of Joseph C. Wilson for the enrollment of his wife, Magnolia Wilson, and his two minor children, Houston and Vernon Wilson, as citizens by blood of the Cherokee Nation, together with the decision of the Commission, dated January 12, 1903, granting said application as to Magnolia and Vernon Wilson, and dismissing said application as to Houston Wilson, and the protest of the Cherokee Nation against said decision, dated January 19, 1903.

The action of the Secretary will be made known to you as soon as the Commission is informed of same.

Respectfully,

Tams Bixby
Acting Chairman.

Contest this case -
Woman born & married
in state of Arkansas
& never admitted
See Cross-Ex on
May 5" 1902 =

[Transcription of above note]

Contest this case -
Woman born & married in State of Arkansas
& never admitted
See Cross-Ex on May 5", 1902.

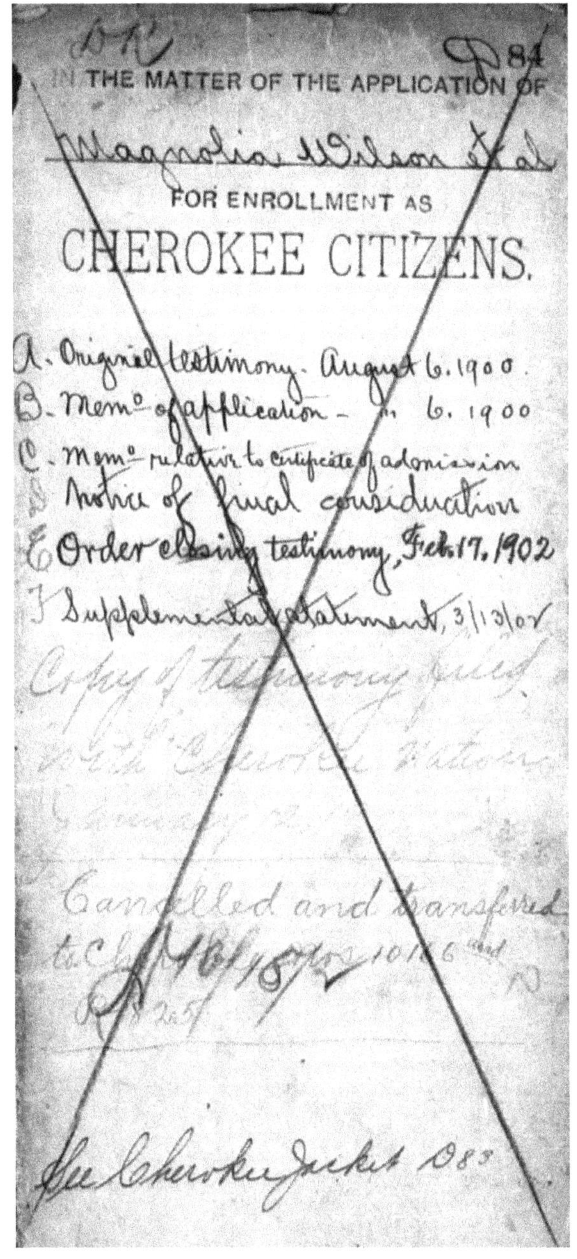

D R 84

IN THE MATTER OF THE APPLICATION OF

Magnolia Wilson et al

FOR ENROLLMENT AS

CHEROKEE CITIZENS.

A. Original testimony. August 6. 1900.
B. Memo of application – " 6. 1900
C. Memo relative to certificate of admission
D Notice of final consideration
E Order closing testimony, Feb. 17, 1902
F Supplemental statement, 3/13/0?

Copy of testimony filed with Cherokee Nation

Cancelled and transferred to Chy ... 10166 and

See Cherokee Jacket D85

RESIDENCE: Canadian DISTRICT.
POST OFFICE: Webbers Falls, I.T.

Cherokee Nation. Cherokee Roll.
(Not including Delawares, Shawnees, or Freedmen.)

CARD NO.
FIELD NO. 1[illegible]166

Dawes' Roll No.		NAME	Relationship to Person first Named	AGE	SEX	BLOOD	Tribal Enrollment: Year	Tribal Enrollment: District	Tribal Enrollment: No.	Name of Father	Year	District	Name of Mother	Year	District
26929	1	Wilson, Magnolia		29	F	1/16	1896	Canadian	823	George Hargrove		Non citz	Marah Hargrove	Dead	Canadian
26930	2	" Vernon	Son	2 mos	M	1/32				Joe Wilson		" "	No 1		
	3														
	4	CITIZENSHIP CERTIFICATE ISSUED FOR NO. OCT 6 1904													
	5														
	6	GRANTED													
	7	ACTION APPROVED BY						No 1 on 1896 Roll as Magnolia Hargrove							
	8	SECRETARY OF INTERIOR.						No 2, Birth affidavit approved Sept 6, 1902							
	9	FEB 18 1903													
	10														
	11														
	12														
	13														
	14														
	15												On Cherokee Card No		
	16					OK					Date of Application for Enrollment.		D-84, August 6, 1900.		
	17	See Cherokee											On this card, February		
	18	Card No R 825	See NB#			3019							28, 1903		

Cherokee D86 - Susan J. Adair by William D. Adair

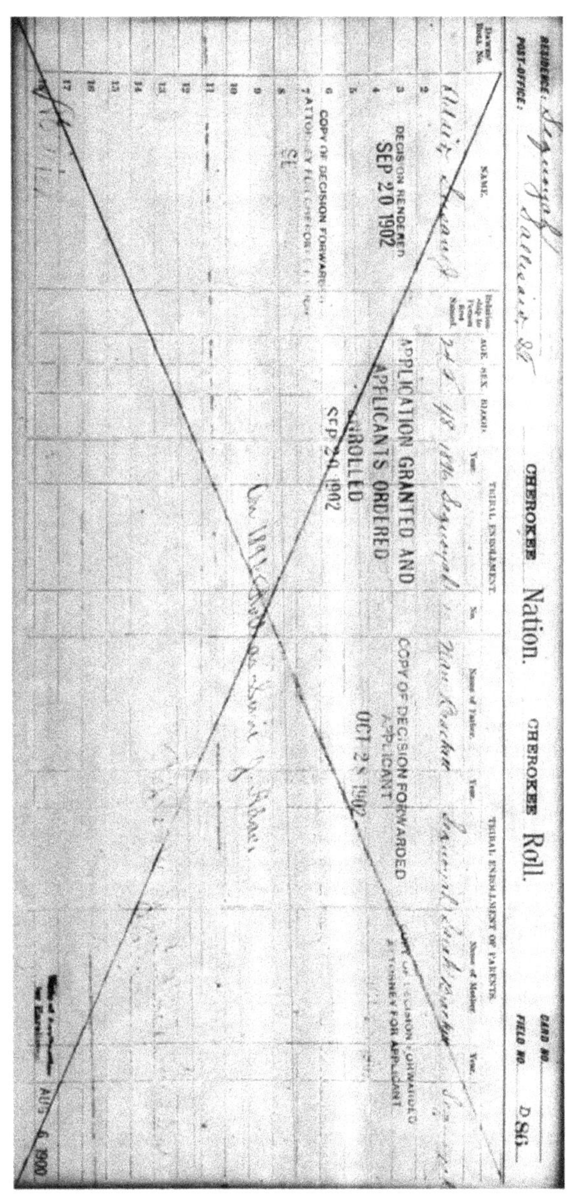
CHEROKEE Nation. CHEROKEE Roll.

FIELD NO. D86

DECISION RENDERED
SEP 20 1902

APPLICATION GRANTED AND
APPLICANTS ORDERED
ENROLLED
SEP 20 1902

COPY OF DECISION FORWARDED
APPLICANT
OCT 28 1902

AUG 6 1900

Department of the Interior,
Commission to the Five Civilized Tribes,
Sallisaw, I. T., August 6, 1900.

In the matter of the application of William D. Adair et al for enrollment as citizens of the Cherokee Nation; being sworn and examined by Commissioner Needles he testifies as follows:

Q What is your name? A William D. Adair.
Q What is your age? A Thirty-one.
Q What is your post-office? A Sallisaw.
Q Are you a Cherokee citizen by blood? A Yes sir.
Q What district do you live in? A Sequoyah.
Q How long have you lived there? A Six years.
Q How long have you lived in the Cherokee Nation? A All my life.
Q What is your father's name? A Chunoolosky Adair.
Q Is he living? A No sir. He died about two years ago.
Q What is your mother's name? A I think they put it down Maggie Adair. She has been dead about fifteen years.
Q Are you married? A Yes sir.
Q What is your wife's name? A Susan.
Q Is she a Cherokee citizen by blood? A Yes sir, she is Cherokee.
Q What was her name before you married her? A Susan J. Brackett.
Q Have you any children? A Yes sir.
Q What are their names? A Thomas, five years old; James C., three years old; Lujean, nearly two years old.
Q Have you got a marriage certificate? A No, I married according to Cherokee law.
Note: 1880 roll examined for applicant, page 348 #36 Wm. Adair Flint Dist.
1896 roll, page 1049 #18 Welliam[sic] Adair, Sequoyah District.
1894 roll, page 506 #11 William Adair, Flint District.
1896 roll, page 1049 #19 Susie J. Adair, Sequoyah District.
1894 roll, page 518 #267 Susan J. Bracket[sic], Flint District.
1896 roll, for children; page 1049 #20 Thomas Adair, Sequoyah Dist.
Q A certificate of citizenship is presented issued by the Commission to Citizenship at Tahlequah dated 16th day of August 1889 signed by William P. Ross, Chairman of the Committee on Citizenship attested by J. D. Williams, Clerk of the Committee, approved and indorsed by J. B. Mayes, Principal Chief of the Cherokee Nation under the great seal of the Cherokee Nation, certifying that Susan J. Brackett was admitted to citizenship on the 16th day of August 1889; is this Susan J. Brackett mentioned in this certificate your wife and the identical woman that you apply for here?
A Yes sir.
Q Was she a resident of the Nation on the 16th day of August 1889? A Yes sir.

Com'r Needles: The name of William D. Adair appearing upon the authenticated roll of 1880 as well as the census roll of 1896 and the pay roll of 1894, he being fully identified thereby, and having made proof of his residence, is listed for enrollment by this Commission as a Cherokee citizen by blood. His wife, Susan J. Adair, to whom he was married in the year 1894, her name appears upon the certificate of admission as described in the testimony, and her name also appears upon the census roll of 1896 and the pay roll of 1894, and proof has been made as to her residence but now come the representatives of the Cherokee Nation and object to the final enrollment of said Susan Brackett as a Cherokee citizen by blood, but not as a Cherokee citizen by intermarriage. And the name of his child Thomas being found upon the roll of 1896 and being duly identified thereby, will be listed for enrollment as a Cherokee citizen by blood, and also his two children, James and Lujean, who were born after the roll of 1896 was compiled, consequently their names are not upon said roll, they will be listed for enrollment as Cherokee citizens by blood when proper proof of birth is filed with the Commission.

M.D. Green, being first duly sworn, states that as stenographer to the Commission to the Five Civilized Tribes he reported the foregoing case and that the above and foregoing is a full true and complete transcript of his stenographic notes in said case.

MD Green

Subscribed and sworn to before me this 7th day of August 1900.

T B Needles
Commissioner.

"R"

Cherokee D 86.

Department of the Interior,
Commission to the Five Civilized Tribes,
Muskogee, I. T., February 17, 1902.

SUPPLEMENTAL PROCEEDINGS in the matter of the application of Susan J. Adair, for the enrollment of herself as a Cherokee citizen.

Appearances:
James H. Huckleberry, Sr., Sallisaw, I. T., attorney for applicant.
Daniel Brackett, relative.
W.W. Hastings, attorney for the Cherokee Nation.

BY COMMISSION: Attention is called to the certificate filed in the matter of the application of Daniel Brackett Cherokee Doubtful case No. 82, showing that Susan J. Brackett the applicant in this case, was admitted to citizenship on the 16th day of August, 1889, by the Cherokee Commission on citizenship. She was 14 years of age at that time. A copy of said certificate is filed with this case.

Q Do you submit this case to the Commission for final consideration? A
MR. HUCKLEBERRY; Yes sir yes sir.
Q Do you submit this case, Mr. Hastings:
MR. HASTINGS: Yes, sir.

M.D. Green, being first duly sworn, states that as stenographer to the Commission to the Five Civilized Tribes he correctly recorded the testimony and the proceedings in this case and that the foregoing is a true and complete transcript of his stenographic notes thereof.

MD Green

Subscribed and sworn to before me this February 19, 1902.

T B Needles

Commissioner.

Chero. 86.

Certificate of Admission to Cherokee Citizenship.

Office of Commission on Citizenship,
Tahlequah, Cherokee Nation.

To all whom it may Concern - Greeting:

This is to certify, That the following named, towit: Daniel Brackett aged Fourty-four[sic] years, Emily Brackett aged seventeen years, Willey H. Brackett age sixteen years, Susan J. Brackett aged fourteen years, Martha S. Brackett aged twelve years, did, pursuant to the provisions of an Act of the National Council of the Cherokee Nation, approved December 8th, 1886, entitled "An Act providing for the appointment of a Commission to try, and determine, applications for Cherokee Citizenship, "make such application to and before said "Commission" on the 3 day of Oct 1887; that the proof submitted by the above named applicants in support of the said application has been found, and is here by declared and certified to be sufficient and satisfactory to the said Commission according to the requirements of Section Seventh of said Act of the Nation Council and of the amendment thereto, dated February 7th, 1887, and that by virtue of such finding of fact by the Commission, and in conformity with the Fourteenth Section of said Act, the above named persons (

applicants for citizenship) are, from this the date of said finding and decision of the Commission as announced and recorded, re-admitted by the National Council, as provided in said Fourteenth Section, to the rights and privileges of Cherokee citizenship under Section 2, Article 1, of the Constitution of the Cherokee Nation upon the terms and conditions set forth in the Act of December 5th, 1888, entitled "An Act Creating a Commission on Citizenship," to-wit:

"That all persons to whom Certificate of Citizenship shall be issued by the decree of the Commission created by this Act, shall be required as a condition precedent to the delivery of said certificates to return to, and permanently locate within the limits of the Cherokee Nation, and it shall be further the duty of all such persons to enroll their names, with the names of their families (if any such), at the date of their arrival within the limits of the Nation, in a book to be kept for that purpose in the office of the Principal Chief, and no Certificate of Citizenship issued by said Commission shall entitle an applicant for admission into the Nation for (not) a longer period than one year from its date, who shall fail to become a bona fide citizen within that period."

And this certificate of the said decision of the Commission and of the re-admission by Council is made and furnished to the said persons accordingly.

In Witness Whereof, I hereunto sign my name, as Chairman of the of the Commission, on this the sixteenth day of August, 1889.

Will. P. Ross
Chairman Com. on Citizenship.

Attest: D. S. Williams
Asst. Clerk Com. on Citizenship.
(SEAL)

Approved and endorsed:

J.B. Mayes
Principal Chief C.N.

C. J. Harris
Asst Ex. Sec'y.

The undersigned, being duly sworn, states that as stenographer to the Commission to the Five Civilized Tribes, that he made the above copy and that the same is a true and complete copy of the original.

E. G. Rothenberger

Subscribed and sworn to before me this 14th day of April, 1902.

Philip G. Reuter
Notary Public.

C D 86

DEPARTMENT OF THE INTERIOR,
COMMISSION TO THE FIVE CIVILIZED TRIBES.

In the matter of the application for the enrollment of Susan J. Adair, as a citizen of the Cherokee Nation.

SUPPLEMENTAL STATEMENT
BY THE COMMISSION.

There is on file in the office of the Commission to the Five Civilized Tribes, a certificate of admission to Cherokee citizenship, issued from the Office of the Commission on Citizenship, Tahlequah, Cherokee Nation, bearing date 16th day of August, 1899, signed by Will P. Ross, Chairman Commission on Citizenship, and approved by J. B. Mays[sic], Principal Chief, Cherokee Nation, wherein, among others, there was admitted to citizenship Susan J. Bracket[sic], age at that time 14 years.

The original certificate, from which this information is derived, is filed in the case of Susan J. Adair, nee Brackett's father, Daniel Brackett, in case known as "C. D. No 82," and which is on file in the office of this Commission.

It is directed that copies of this statement be filed with the testimony in this case.

Dated at Muskogee, Indian Territory,
this 12th day of March, 1902.

Ella Mielenz, as stenographer to the Commission to the Five Civilized Tribes, states that the above is a true and complete transcript of her stenographic notes in this statement.

Ella Mielenz

Cherokee D 86

DEPARTMENT OF THE INTERIOR
COMMISSION TO THE FIVE CIVILIZED TRIBES.

In the matter of the application of William D. Adair for the enrollment of his wife Susan J. Adair, as a citizen by blood of the Cherokee Nation.

D E C I S I O N.

o-o-o-o

The record in this case shows that on August 6, 1900, William D. Adair appeared before the Commission at Sallisaw, Indian Territory, and then and there made personal application for the enrollment of his wife Susan J. Adair, as a citizen by blood of the Cherokee Nation. The application also included William D. Adair and his minor children Thomas, James C. and Lujean Adair, but as they are listed on Cherokee Roll Card Field No. 1005, their case is not passed upon at this time.

The evidence in this case shows that Susan J. Adair, nee Brackett, was admitted to citizenship in the Cherokee Nation on the 16th day of August, 1889. She was married to William D. Adair in the year 1894, and is identified on the Cherokee Census Roll of 1896 as "Susie J. Adair." The evidence is not clear as to the question of her residence between the 16th day of August, 1889 and her marriage in 1894, but it is considered that she has been a continuous resident of the Cherokee Nation from the date of said marriage up to and including the date of this application.

The authority of the Commission herein is defined in Par. 1, gee. 21, of the Act of Congress, June 28, 1898. (30 Stats., 495).

It is the opinion of this Commission that Susan J. Adair is lawfully entitled to be enrolled as a citizen by blood of the Cherokee Tribe of Indians in Indian Territory, and that the application for her enrollment as such should be granted, and it is therefore so ordered.

THE COMMISSION TO THE FIVE CIVILIZED TRIBES.

Tams Bixby
Acting Chairman.

T.B. Needles
Commissioner.

C. R. Breckinridge
Commissioner.

Muskogee, Indian Territory,
this SEP 20 1902

COMMISSIONERS:

HENRY L. DAWES,
TAMS BIXBY,
THOMAS B. NEEDLES,
C. R. BRECKINRIDGE.

ALLISON L. AYLESWORTH,
SECRETARY.

ADDRESS ONLY THE
COMMISSION TO THE FIVE CIVILIZED TRIBES.

DEPARTMENT OF THE INTERIOR.
COMMISSION TO THE FIVE CIVILIZED TRIBES.

REFER IN REPLY TO THE FOLLOWING
Cherokee D 86

Muskogee, Indian Territory, September 29, 1902.

W. W. Hastings,

Attorney for the Cherokee Nation,

Muskogee, Indian Territory.

Dear Sir:

Enclosed herewith please find a copy of the decision of the Commission to the Five Civilized Tribes, rendered September 20, 1902, granting the application of William D. Adair for the enrollment of his wife, Susan J. Adair, as a citizen by blood of the Cherokee Nation.

You are hereby advised that you will be allowed fifteen days from date hereof in which to file with the Commission such protest as you desire to make against the decision rendered in this case. If you fail to file protest within the time allowed, this decision will be considered final.

Respectfully,

Tams Bixby Acting Chairman.

Enc. C. No. 65.

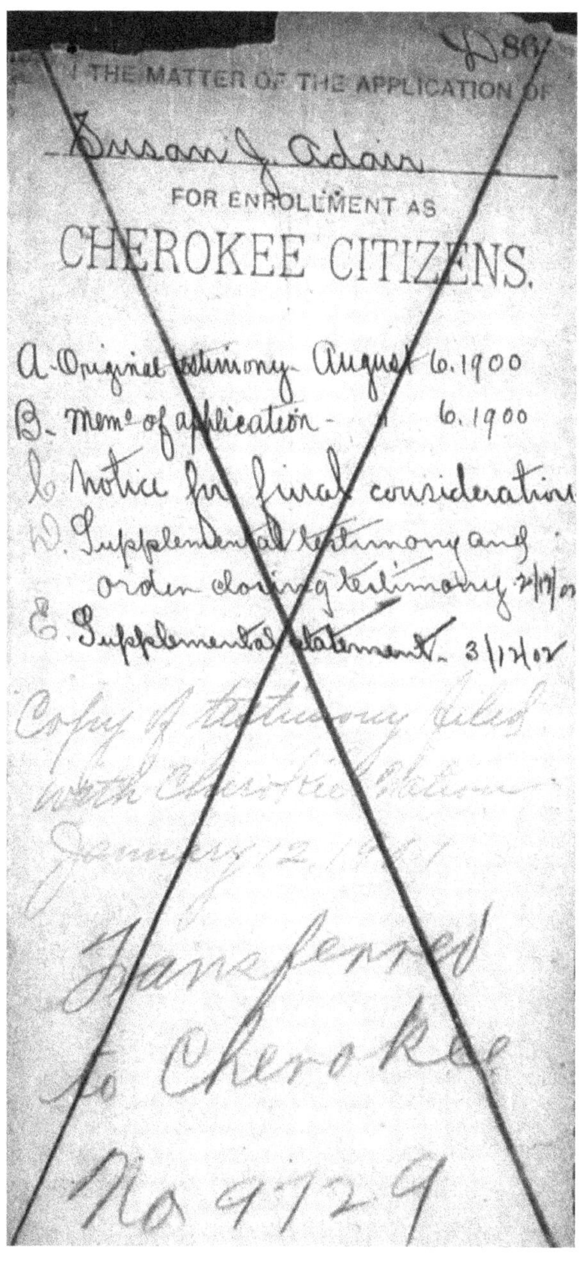

D 86

IN THE MATTER OF THE APPLICATION OF

Susan J. Adair

FOR ENROLLMENT AS

CHEROKEE CITIZENS.

A. Original testimony August 6.1900
B. Memo of application " 6.1900
C. Notice for final consideration
D. Supplemental testimony and order closing testimony 2/17/02
E. Supplemental statement 3/17/02

Copy of testimony filed with Cherokee Nation January 12 1901

Transferred to Cherokee No 9729

RESIDENCE: Sequoyah DISTRICT.
POST OFFICE: Sallisaw, I.T.

Cherokee Nation. Cherokee Roll.
(Not including Delawares, Shawnees, or Freedmen.)

CARD NO.
FIELD NO. 9729

Dawes' Roll No.		NAME	Relationship to Person first Named	AGE	SEX	BLOOD	Tribal Enrollment: Year	District	No.	Name of Father	Year	District	Name of Mother	Year	District
21865		Adair, Susan J.		W	F	48	1896	Sequoyah	19	Nann Brackett		Sequoyah D	Sarah Brackett		Sequoyah
	2	CITIZENSHIP CERTIFICATE ISSUED FOR NO.													
	3	MAY - 1905													
	4														
	5														
	6														
	7	GRANTED													
	8	SEP 20 1902					On 1896 roll as Susie J. Adair								
	9														
	10														
	11						Represented by J. W. Huckleberry Sr., Sallisaw								
	12						No 1 died July 1 1902; affidavit filed August 6, 1904								
	13														
	14														
	15														
	16														
	17														
	18														

Date of Application for Enrollment

Cherokee D87- William M. Wilson [William is white with a 1/8 blood wife and 4-1/16 blood children. Wife and children have a Dawes Roll Number.]

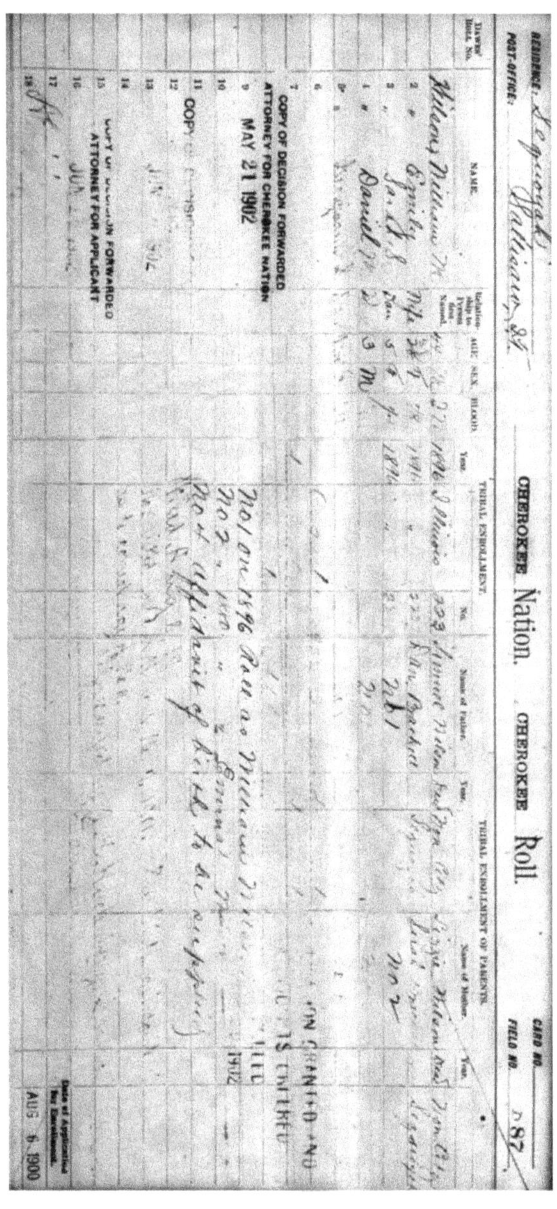
CHEROKEE Nation. CHEROKEE Roll.

COPY OF DECISION FORWARDED
ATTORNEY FOR CHEROKEE NATION
MAY 21 1902

Date of Application for Enrollment.
AUG 6 1900

Department of the Interior.
Commission to the Five Civilized Tribes.
Sallisaw, I. T., August 6th, 1900.

In the matter of the application of William M. Wilson et al for enrollment as Cherokee citizens; being sworn and examined by Commissioner Breckinridge, testifies as follows:

Q What is your full name? A William M. Wilson.
Q What is your age? A About 44.
Q What's your post-office? A Sallisaw.
Q What's your district? A Sequoyah.
Q How long have you lived in this district? A About 1 1/2 years.
Q Where did you live before that? A In Illinois district.
Q How long did you live there? A I lived there 3 years.
Q Where did you live before that? A Flint.
Q How long did you live in Flint? A 4 or 5 years.
Q Where did you live before that? A In Georgia.
Q Now for whom do you apply for enrollment at this time? A My wife and two children.
Q Do you apply for yourself? A I don't know about myself, I am adopted.
Q When were you married? A Was married in -(handing paper_
Q For whom then do you apply for enrollment? A Myself, wife and two children.
Q Do you apply as a Cherokee by blood? A No sir.
Q OR by intermarriage? A By intermarriage.
Q Is your wife on any of the rolls of the Cherokee Nation? A Yes sir.
Q What is her name? A Emma.
Q What was her name before you married her? A Brackett.
Q Was she admitted to citizenship by the action of the Cherokee authorities?
A Yes sir.

You present here, Mr. Wilson, a certificate of admission to Cherokee citizenship. It is signed by Will P. Ross, Chairman of the Committee, attested by D. S. Wilson, Assistant Clerk of the Committee and approved and endorsed by J. B. Mayes, Principal Chief of the Cherokee Nation and put under the great seal of the Nation, to the effect that on the 16th day of August, 1889, among others, Emily Brackett, aged 17 years, was admitted to citizenship.

Q Is that your wife? A Yes sir.
How old do you say that your wife is now? A About 28, I guess.

Your wife's name is duly identified on the certificate which you have presented and it is returned to you.

Q You say you apply for citizenship by intermarriage? A Yes sir.

You present here, Mr. Wilson, an official copy of a duly authenticated marriage license, issued Sept. 7th, 1894, by W. E. Whitnett, Clerk of Sequoyah District, authorizing the marriage between yourself and Miss Emma Brackett under Cherokee law. The certificate shows that this marriage was duly consummated on the 15th of Sept. 1894 and duly recorded in the Clerk's office. This will be filed with your application.

Q I suppose you are on the roll of 1896? A Yes sir, I suppose so.
Q Give the names of your children. A Sarah Savannah.
Q How old is that child? A 5 years old.
Q What's the next child? A Daniel M.
Q How old is he? A 3 years old.
Q Is her on the roll of 1896? A I don't know; seems like I had him put on. I forget.
Q Are these children both living at this time? A Yes sir.
Q Your wife is living at this time? A Yes sir.
Q You and she living together? A Yes sir.
Q Lived together ever since you were married? A Yes sir.

1896 roll; page 937, #223, William Wilson, Illinois Dist.
1896 roll; page 920, #2237, Emma Wilson, Illinois Dist.
1896 roll; page 920, #2238, Sarah S. Wilson, Illinois Dist.

This child, Daniel M., is too young to be on any of the rolls and you will have to identify that child by having properly filled out a certificate of birth. Form will be given you here.

Q Mr. Wilson, what do you know about where your wife lived after she was admitted as shown in the certificate in 1889? (No answer)
Q How long have you know her? A All my life almost.
Q Where did she live 5 years before you married her? A I think in Flint part of the time and in Illinois part of the time.
Q How long have you known her in the Nation? A Ever since she come here.
Q Your evidence shows that you haven't been here yourself but 8 1/2 years?
A I must have been mistaken; didn’t get at it right when you spoke of it.
Q Well how long do you mean to say you have been in the Cherokee Nation?
A About 16 years.
Q Where were you before that 4 years you spent in Flint? A I was in Flint most of the time until I moved to Illinois.
Q Have you lived continuously in the Cherokee Nation for the past 16 years?
A Yes sir, except 6 months in the Choctaw Nation.
Q Tell me as briefly as you can where you have lived in the Cherokee Nation during those 16 years? A I could not tell you exactly, I lived most of the time in Flint, 3 years in Illinois and the rest of the time down here in Sequoyah, about 1 1/2 years.
Q All the time of the time you lived in Flint except your little visit to the Choctaw Nation? A Yes sir.

That carries you back behind 1889 when the certificate shows your wife was admitted to citizenship here.

Q Did you know her here in the Nation in 1889? A I reckon I did, if she was here; and I guess she was here.
Q I want to find out whether or not it is a fact that when your wife was admitted in 1889, she went on and lived here in the Cherokee Nation or whether she lived some where else? A She lived here all the time.
Q Where did she live in 1889, 11 years ago? A I don't remember.
Q When did she come from Georgia? A I don't remember what year it was. I have a bad recollection.
Q You knew here back in Georgia? A Yes sir.
Q You came from Georgia about 16 years ago? A Yes sir.
Q Did she comer after you did? A Yes sir, good while after I came.
Q Do you remember when she first got here from Georgia? A No I don't remember what year or what date.
Q Do you remember that you knew it when she did come? A Yes sir, I come and helped them move.
Q Where did you meet them? A The other side of Sallisaw.
Q You know whether that was about the time she and the other members of her family were admitted to citizenship; before that move or after that? A I don't remember whether it was before or afterwards.
Q Has she live there ever since that time? A Yes sir ever since.
Q You and she have lived together ever since you were married? A Yes sir.
Q And lived in the Nation? A Yes sir.

Mr. Hutchings, representative of the Cherokee Nation, states that the Nation has received notice to-day of evidence that the admission by the Citizenship Commission of Emily Brackett was fraudulently obtained, and desire that judgment be suspended in this case until that evidence can be investigated and brought before the Commission.

Com'r. Breckinridge:

Mr. Wilson, the admission of your wife to citizenship is duly authenticated by the certificate of admission, dated Aug. 16th, 1889, as cited in the testimony. Your marriage to her in 1894 under Cherokee law is duly established by the marriage license and certificate of marriage filed with your application. Your child, Sarah S., is duly identified on the roll of 1896 and you and your wife are both identified on the roll of 1896. Your child, Daniel M. Wilson, is too young to be on any roll. It is testified that both of these children are living at this time and living with you and that you and your wife are living together, and have so lived ever since your marriage. Now you will be furnished with a blank form of a certificate of birth for your youngest child. It is desired that you have that certificate properly filled out and duly attested and that you supply this Commission with that certificate in that form. Now, as you are aware the representative present of the Cherokee Nation has requested that this case be held up for the present in order that inquiry may be made into the admission to citizenship of your wife on Aug. 16th, 1889. For the present, your application for yourself and all the members of your family, including your wife, will be placed upon a doubtful card, and the decision of the Commission will be held in suspense. If there is any evidence produced attacking the admission of your wife to citizenship that seems to need attention on your part or in her behalf, you will be given due notice so that both sides may be heard and the decision of the Commission when finally rendered will be made known to you at your present post-office address and then it will be forwarded to the Secretary of the Interior for his approval.

Edward G. Rothenberger, being duly sworn by Commissioner Breckinridge as Stenographer to the Commission to the Five Civilized Tribes, he reported in full the testimony of the above named witness, William M. Wilson, and that the foregoing is a full, true and correct transcript of his notes.

Edward G. Rothenberger

Sworn to and subscribed before me this 8th day of August, 1900.

Commissioner.

"R"

Cherokee D 87.

Department of the Interior,
Commission to the Five Civilized Tribes,
Muskogee, I. T., February 17, 1902.

SUPPLEMENTAL TESTIMONY AND PROCEDURES, in the matter of the application of William M. Wilson et al for enrollment as Cherokee citizens.

Appearances:

Mr. James H. Huckleberry, Sr., Sallisaw, I.T., Attorney for applicants;
W.W. Hastings, attorney for the Cherokee Nation.

MR. HUCKLEBERRY: All we want to do is to refer to that admission there.

BY COMMISSION: Attention is invited to the certificate from the Cherokee Commission on citizenship showinf[sic] that the applicants[sic] wife, Emily Wilson, was admitted to citizenship in the Cherokee Nation on the 16th day of August, 1889, by an act of the Cherokee Commission on citizenship; she is identified in said certificate as Emily Brackett, at that time 17 years old.

Q Do you submit this case to the Commission for final consideration?
A MR. HUCKLEBERRY: Yes sir.
Q Do you submit, Mr. Hastings? A Mr. Hastings: A Yes sir.

M.D. Green, being first duly sworn, states that as stenographer to the Commission to the Five Civilized Tribes he correctly recorded the testimony and proceedings in this case and that the foregoing is a true and complete transcript of his stenographic notes thereof.

M D Green

Subscribed and sworn to before me this February 19, 1902.

T B Needles

Commissioner.

Chero. D-87.

Certificate of Admission to Cherokee Citizenship.

Office of Commission on Citizenship,
Tahlequah, Cherokee Nation.

To all whom it may Concern - Greeting:

This is to certify, That the following named, towit: Daniel Brackett aged Fourty-four[sic] years, Emily Brackett aged seventeen years, Willey H. Brackett age sixteen years, Susan J. Brackett aged fourteen years, Martha S. Brackett aged twelve years, did, pursuant to the provisions of an Act of the National Council of the Cherokee Nation, approved December 8th, 1886, entitled "An Act providing for the appointment of a Commission to try, and determine, applications for Cherokee Citizenship, "make such application to and before said "Commission" on the 3 day of Oct 1887; that the proof submitted by the above named applicants in support of the said application has been found, and is here by declared and certified to be sufficient and satisfactory to the said Commission according to the requirements of Section Seventh of said Act of the Nation Council and of the amendment thereto, dated February 7th, 1887, and that by virtue of such finding of fact by the Commission, and in conformity with the Fourteenth Section of said Act, the above named persons (applicants for citizenship) are, from this the date of said finding and decision of the Commission as announced and recorded, re-admitted by the National Council, as provided in said Fourteenth Section, to the rights and privileges of Cherokee citizenship under Section 2, Article 1, of the Constitution of the Cherokee Nation upon the terms and conditions set forth in the Act of December 5th, 1888, entitled "An Act Creating a Commission on Citizenship," to-wit:

"That all persons to whom Certificate of Citizenship shall be issued by the decree of the Commission created by this Act, shall be required as a condition precedent to the delivery of said certificates to return to, and permanently locate within the limits of the Cherokee Nation, and it shall be further the duty of all such persons to enroll their names, with the names of their families (if any such), at the date of their arrival within the limits of the Nation, in a book to be kept for that purpose in the office of the Principal Chief, and no Certificate of Citizenship issued by said

Commission shall entitle an applicant for admission into the Nation for (not) a longer period than one year from its date, who shall fail to become a bona fide citizen within that period."

And this certificate of the said decision of the Commission and of the re-admission by Council is made and furnished to the said persons accordingly.

In Witness Whereof, I hereunto sign my name, as Chairman of the of the Commission, on this the sixteenth day of August, 1889.

Will. P. Ross
Chairman Com. on Citizenship.

Attest: D. S. Williams
Asst. Clerk Com. on Citizenship.
(SEAL)

Approved and endorsed:

J.B. Mayes
Principal Chief C.N.

C. J. Harris
Asst Ex. Sec'y.

The undersigned, being duly sworn, states that as stenographer to the Commission to the Five Civilized Tribes, that he made the above copy and that the same is a true and complete copy of the original.

E. G. Rothenberger

Subscribed and sworn to before me this 14th day of April, 1902.

Philip G. Reuter
Notary Public.

Cherokee D 87

DEPARTMENT OF THE INTERIOR

COMMISSION TO THE FIVE CIVILIZED TRIBES.

In the matter of the application of William M. Wilson for the enrollment of his wife Emily Wilson, and their minor children, Sarah Savannah, Daniel M. and Georgiaann S. Wilson, as citizens by blood, and for the enrollment of himself as a citizen by intermarriage of the Cherokee Nation.

DECISION.

o-o-o-o

The record in this case shows that on August 6, 1900, William M. Wilson appeared before the Commission at Sallisaw, Indian Territory, and then and there made personal application for the enrollment of his wife Emily Wilson, and their minor children, Sarah Savannah, Daniel M. and Georgiaann S. Wilson, as citizens by blood, and for the enrollment of himself as a citizen by intermarriage of the Cherokee Nation.

The evidence in this case shows that Emily Wilson, nee Brackett, was readmitted by Cherokee authorities to citizenship in the Cherokee Nation on the 16th day of August, 1889. William M. Wilson was married to the said Emily Brackett, in accordance with the laws of the Cherokee Nation, on the 15th day September, 1894. William M. Wilson, his wife Emily Wilson, and their daughter Sarah Savannah Wilson, are identified on the Cherokee Census Roll of 1896. Daniel M. and Georgiaann S. Wilson having been born subsequent to the making of the aforesaid roll, are identified by certificates of birth which are on file in the office of this Commission. William M. Wilson has resided in the Cherokee Nation for 16 years, with the exception of 6 months, wherein he resided in the Choctaw Nation. There is also filed an affidavit of the mother of Emily Wilson, for the purpose of identification.

The authority of the Commission herein is defined in Par. 1, Sec. 21, of the Act of Congress, June 28, 1898. (30 Stats., 495).

It is therefore the opinion of this Commission that Emily Wilson and her minor children Sarah Savannah, Daniel M. and Georgiaann S. Wilson, are lawfully entitled to be enrolled as citizens by blood, and William M. Wilson is lawfully entitled to be enrolled as a citizen by intermarriage of the Cherokee Tribe of Indians in Indian Territory, and that the application for their enrollment as such should be granted, and it is so ordered.

THE COMMISSION TO THE FIVE CIVILIZED TRIBES.

____
Acting Chairman.

T.B. Needles
Commissioner.

Muskogee, Indian Territory,
this MAY 20 1902

C. R. Breckinridge
Commissioner.

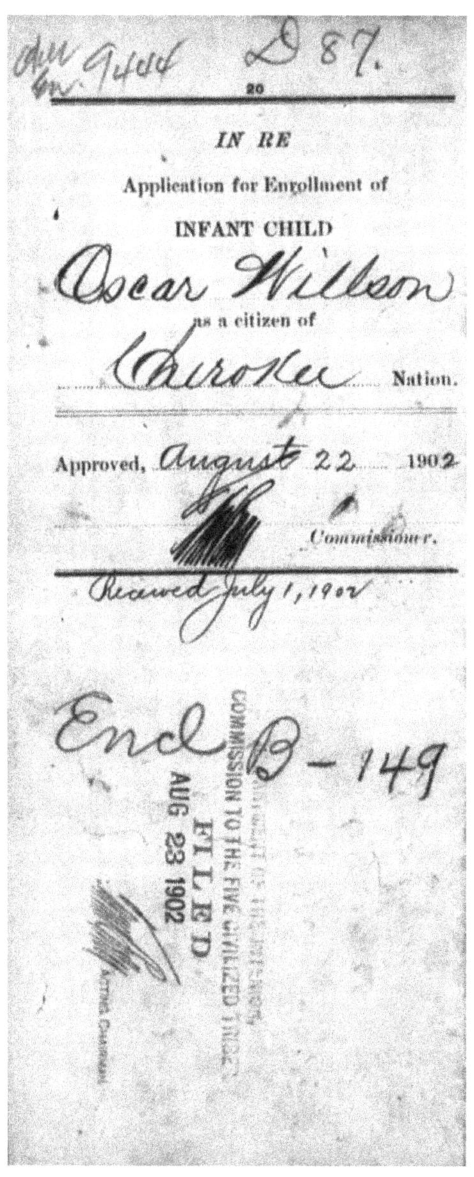

Aee 9404 D 87.

20

IN RE

Application for Enrollment of

INFANT CHILD

Oscar Willson

as a citizen of

Cherokee Nation.

Approved, August 22 1902

Commissioner.

Received July 1, 1902

End B-149

DEPARTMENT OF THE INTERIOR
COMMISSION TO THE FIVE CIVILIZED TRIBES
FILED
AUG 23 1902
ACTING CHAIRMAN

BIRTH AFFIDAVIT. 20

DEPARTMENT OF THE INTERIOR,
COMMISSION TO THE FIVE CIVILIZED TRIBES.

IN RE Application for Enrollment, as a citizen of the Cherokee Nation, of Oscar Wilson, born on the 24 day of June, 1902

Name of Father: Wm M Wilson a citizen of the Cherokee Nation.

Name of Mother: Emley Wilson (nee Brackett) a citizen of the Cherokee Nation.

Post-office, Sallisaw IT

AFFIDAVIT OF MOTHER.

UNITED STATES OF AMERICA, Indian Territory, Northern District.

I, Emley Wilson (nee Brackett), on oath state that I am 32 years of age and a citizen, by Blood, of the Cherokee Nation; that I am the lawful wife of Wm M Wilson, who is a citizen, by adoption, of the Cherokee Nation, that a Male child was born to me on the 24 day of June 1902 that said child has been named Oscar Wilson, and is now living.

WITNESSES TO MARK: Emily Wilson ~~Emley Willson~~

(Must be Two Witnesses)

Subscribed and sworn to before me this 28 day of June 1902

James G Denton NOTARY PUBLIC.

AFFIDAVIT OF ATTENDING PHYSICIAN, OR MIDWIFE.

UNITED STATES OF AMERICA, Indian Territory, Northern District.

I, Nancy J Howell, a Mid Wife, on oath state that I attended on Mrs. Emley Wilson (nee Brackett), wife of Wm M Wilson, on the 24 day of June, 1901; that there was born to her on said date a Male child; that said child is now living and is said to have been named Oscar Wilson

WITNESSES TO MARK: Nancy J Howell

(Must be Two Witnesses)

Subscribed and sworn to before me this 28 day of June 1902

James G Denton NOTARY PUBLIC.

COMMISSIONERS:

HENRY L. DAWES,
TAMS BIXBY,
THOMAS B. NEEDLES,
C. R. BRECKINRIDGE.

—

ALLISON L. AYLESWORTH,
SECRETARY.

ADDRESS ONLY THE
COMMISSION TO THE FIVE CIVILIZED TRIBES.

DEPARTMENT OF THE INTERIOR,
COMMISSION TO THE FIVE CIVILIZED TRIBES.

REFER IN REPLY TO THE FOLLOWING

D-87.

Muskogee, Indian Territory, May 21, 1902.

W. W. Hastings, Esq.,

Attorney for the Cherokee Nation,

Muskogee, Indian Territory.

Sir:

Enclosed herewith, please find a copy of the decision of the Commission rendered May 20, 1902, in the matter of the application of William M. Wilson et al. for enrollment as citizens of the Cherokee Nation.

You are hereby advised that you will be allowed fifteen days from date hereof in which to file with the Commission such protest as you desire to make against the enrollment of the above named persons as citizens of the Cherokee Nation. If you fail to file protest within the time allowed these applicants will be regularly listed for enrollment.

Very respectfully,

T B Needles

Commissioner in Charge.

Enc. D-87.

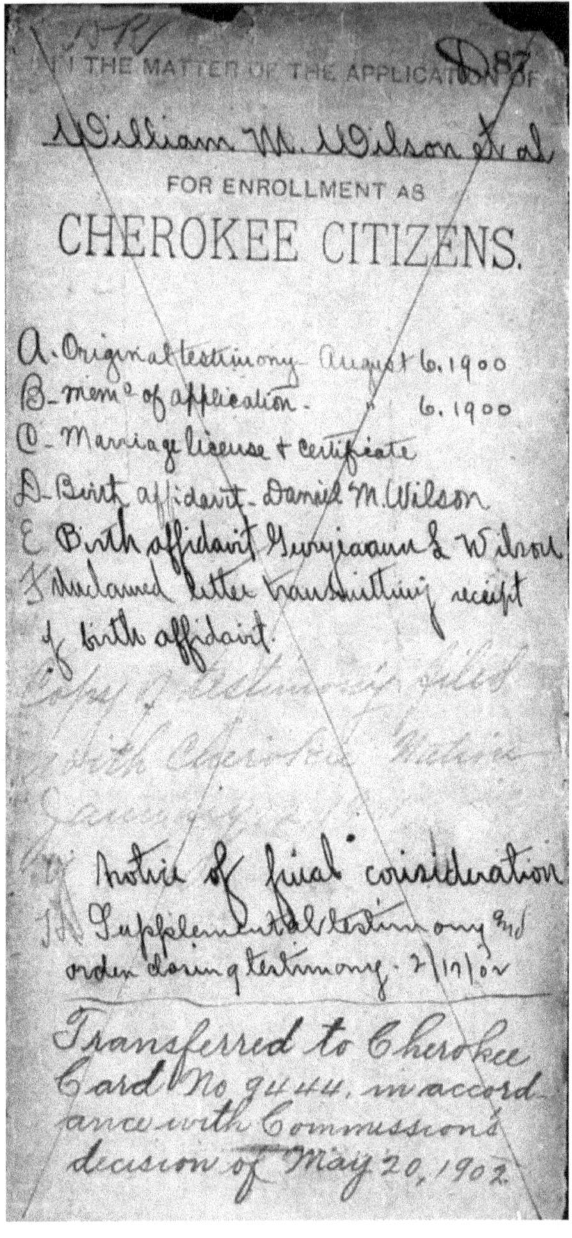

BRS D87

IN THE MATTER OF THE APPLICATION OF

William M. Wilson et al

FOR ENROLLMENT AS

CHEROKEE CITIZENS.

A. Original testimony August 6. 1900
B – mem^o of application " 6. 1900
C – Marriage license & certificate
D – Birth affidavit – Daniel M. Wilson
E Birth affidavit Georgiaann L. Wilson
F Inclosed letter transmitting receipt of birth affidavit.

Copy of testimony filed with Cherokee Nation January 1901

Notice of final consideration
Supplemental testimony and order closing testimony. 2/17/02

Transferred to Cherokee Card No 9444, in accordance with Commission's decision of May 20, 1902.

RESIDENCE: Sequoyah DISTRICT.
POST OFFICE: Sallisaw, I.T.

Cherokee Nation. Cherokee Roll.
(Not including Delawares, Shawnees, or Freedmen.)

CARD NO. ____
FIELD NO. 9414

Dawes' Roll No.		NAME	Relationship to Person first Named	AGE	SEX	BLOOD	Tribal Enrollment Year	Tribal Enrollment District	Tribal Enrollment No.	Name of Father	Year	District	Name of Mother	Year	District
		Wilson William M	X	44	M	I.W.	1896	Illinois	223	Samuel Wilson	dead	Non citz	Lizzie Wilson	dead	Non citz
21471	1	" Emily	Wife	31	F	1/8	1896	"	2237	Dan Brackett		Sequoyah	Sarah Brackett	"	Sequoyah
21472	2	" Sarah S	Dau	5	F	1/16	1896	"	2238	No 1			No 2		
21473	4	" Daniel M	Son	3	M	1/16		See note		No 1			No 2		
21474	5	" Georgiaann	Dau	2/mo	F	1/16		"		No 1			No 2		
21475	6	" Oscar	Son	2/mo	M	1/16		"		No 1			No 2		

CITIZENSHIP CERTIFICATE ISSUED FOR NO. 2
MAR 1 1905

GRANTED
MAY 20 1902

RESERVATION CERTIFICATE ISSUED FOR NO. 1
1905

No 2 died March 1 1906; Death affidavit filed June 14, 1906.
No 1 on 1896 Roll as William Wilson
No 2 " 1896 " " Emma Wilson
No 4; Birth affidavit to be supplied; filed August 8, 1900
No 5; " " " approved November 7, 1901
No 6; " " " approved August 22, 1902.

Date of Application for Enrollment: On Cherokee Card No D87 August 6, 1900
On this card, August 21, 1902.

Represented by J. H. Huckleberry, Sr. Sallisaw, I.T.

Cherokee D90 - John Overtaker for Fannie and Maggie Overtaker

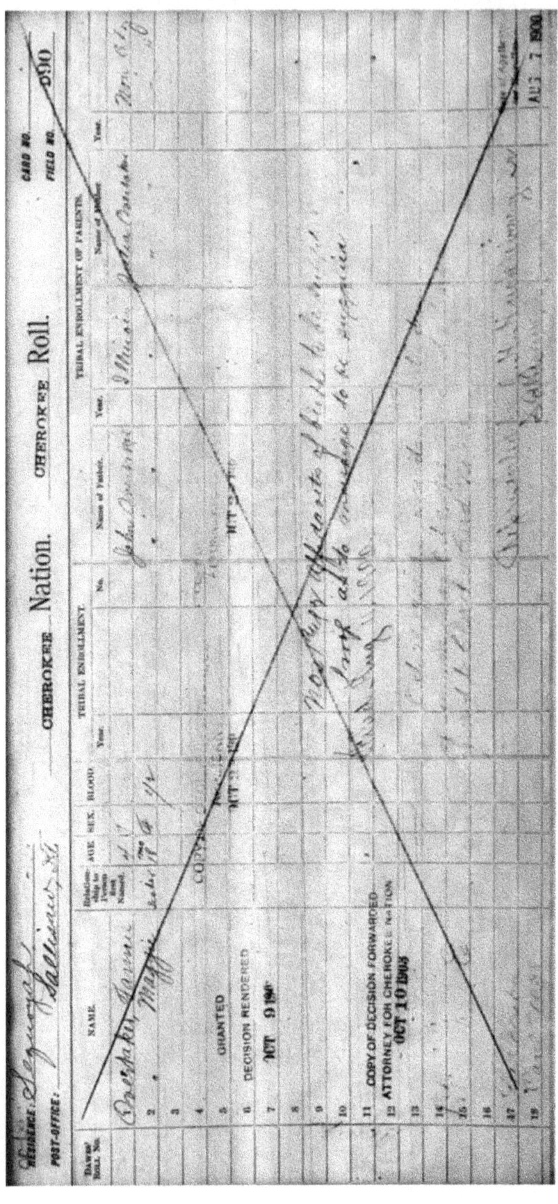

CHEROKEE Nation. CHEROKEE Roll.

RESIDENCE: Sequoyah
POST-OFFICE: Salina, I.T.

CARD NO.
FIELD NO. D90

Dawes' Roll No.	NAME	Relationship to Person first Named	AGE	SEX	BLOOD	Tribal Enrollment: Year	Tribal Enrollment: District	Tribal Enrollment: No.	Parents: Name of Father	Year	District	Name of Mother	Year	District
	Overtaker, Fannie								John Overtaker			Polly Overtaker		
	Maggie													

GRANTED

DECISION RENDERED
OCT 9 190[illegible]

COPY OF DECISION FORWARDED
ATTORNEY FOR CHEROKEE NATION
OCT 10 1903

AUG 7 1900

Department of the Interior,
Commission to the Five Civilized Tribes,
Sallisaw, I. T., August 7, 1900.

In the matter of the application of John Overtaker et al for enrollment as Cherokee citizens; being sworn and examined by Commissioner Needles he testifies as follows:

Q What is your name? A John Overtaker.
Q What is your age? A Forty.
Q What is your post-office address? A Vian.
Q Are you a Cherokee citizen by blood? A Yes sir.
Q What district do you live in? A I live in Illinois District.
Q How long have you lived there? A Not long. I have been living here in this district before I went to Illinois.
Q How long have you been living in the Cherokee Nation? A All my life.
Q Never lived out of it? A No sir.
Q What is the name of your father? A Charles.
Q Is he living? A No sir.
Q When did he die? A He died in time of the War.
Q What is the name of your mother? A Annie.
Q Is she living? A No sir, she has been dead about ten years.
Q What proportion of Cherokee blood do you claim? A I am about two-thirds I guess.
Q Are you married? A No sir.
Q Just applying for yourself? A No, I have got two children.
Q W~~h~~ere you ever married? A Yes sir.
Q What was your wife's name? A Julia Walker.
Q Was she a citizen or a white woman? A She was a white woman.
Q When did you marry her? A We wasn't legally married.
Q What are your children's names? A Fannie Overtaker, four years old; Maggie Overtaker, one and one-half years old.
Q Are these children alive and living with you? A Yes sir.
Q Did you ever live with this woman as your wife? A Yes sir, we lived together about five years.
Q What year did you commence living with her? A I don't know; it was about 1893 I reckon.
Q Did you live with her until she died? A She is not dead.
Q Why didn't you get married? A She is married.
Q Did you live with her all the time five years as man and wife? A Yes sir.
Q Have you any proof of that? A Yes sir.

Examined by Cherokee Representative Hastings:

Q Did this woman have any children before you married her? [sic] No sir.
Q You treated her as your wife? A Yes sir.
Q She lived in the house with you? A Yes sir.
Q Just you two? A Yes sir, and her mother.

Q When was the first child born? A Born February 24th 1896.
Q When did you commence living with that woman? A I think it was about 1893.
Q How long before this child was born? A About two years I guess.
Q She had lived with you continuously from the time you begun to live with her until the child was born, two years? A Yes sir.
Q You treated her as your wife? A Yessir[sic].
Q She treated you as a husband? A Yes sir.
Q No other man lived with her? A No sir.
Q When was the second child born? A She was born in 1898.
Q You were living with her at the time this second child was born or had you quit her? A I was still living with her.
Q How old was that child before you left her? A The child was about three or four months old.
Q What made you leave her? A I don't know.
Q Was it because of any jealousy of anybody else? A I didn't intend to leave her, she left me.
Q You were satisfied with her then, with the woman? A Yessir.
Q She became dissatisfied with you and left; is she living with somebody else now?
A Yes sir, she is married.
Q She was lawfully married to the next one? A Yes sir.
Com'r Needles:
Q Where are these children now? A There are here in town.
Q Who are they living with? A Their mother.
Cherokee Rep've Hastings:
Q Did she marry a citizen? A No sir.
Q Do they go by your name? A Yes sir.
Com'r Needles:
Q What is her present husband's name? A M. J. McClenathan.
Cherokee Rep've Hastings:
Q How long had she left you before she married this other man? A I reckon it was five or six months.
Q Did she live with any one in the meantime? A No sir.
Q Has she had any children since she quit you? A No sir.
Q You say that this child was born February 26th 1896? A 1896 I think.
Q Why didn't you enroll it in 1896? A I did enroll it, she is on the roll.
Q Did you enroll it under your name? A Yes sir.
1880 roll, page 712 #934 John Overtaker, Sequoyah District.
1896 roll page 1088 #1047 John Overtaker, Sequoyah District.
1896 roll, page 979 #992 John Overtaker, Sequoyah District.

Com'r Needles: The name of John Overtaker appearing upon the authenticated roll of 1880 as well as the census roll of 1896 and the pay roll of 1894, as indicated in the testimony, and he having made satisfactory proof as to his residence, he is ordered listed for enrollment as a Cherokee citizen by blood.

The names of his children, Fannie, four years of age, and Maggie, eighteen months old, their names not appearing on any of the rolls of the Cherokee Nation, they having been born since said roll of 1896 was compiled, satisfactory proof not being made as to his marriage with the woman whom he claims to be the mother of these children, named Julia Walker, judgment as to their enrollment is suspended, and they will be placed upon a doubtful card.

M.D. Green, being first duly sworn, states that as stenographer to the Commission to the Five Civilized Tribes he reported the foregoing case and that the above and foregoing is a full true and complete transcript of his stenographic notes in said case.

M D Green

Subscribed and sworn to before me this 8th day of August 1900.

T B Needles

Department of the Interior,
Commission to the Five Civilized Tribes,
Sallisaw, I. T., August 7, 1900.

In the matter of the application of John Overtaker for the enrollment of his two children, Fannie and Maggie, as Cherokee citizens; Joe Alfred, being sworn and examined by Commissioner Needles testifies as follows:

Q What is your name? A Joe Alfred.
Q What is your age? A Forty-seven.
Q What is your post-office? A Sallisaw.
Q You know John Overtaker? A Yes sir.
Q Did you know his wife, Julia? A Yes sir.
Q You know whether they were ever married or not? A I couldn't say, no sir.
Q You know whether they lived together as man and wife? A Yes sir.
Q How long did they live together as man and wife? A I knew them about three years.
Q They were keeping house as man and wife together? A Yessir[sic].
Q Did they have any children? A They had one that I know of when I got acquainted with them.
Q You know its name? A Fannie.
Q Did they have one afterwards? A Yes sir.
Q What is it name? A I don't know.
Examined by Cherokee Representative Hastings:

Q How far did you live from them? A I lived mile and a half.
Q How long? A I guess about four or five months; and difference places I saw them; I worked for the railroad company; I think they lived at McKey awhile, and here at Sallisaw awhile.
Q You know anything about their separation? A No sir.

Q You know anything about the cause of it? A No sir.
Q Did you know them prior to the birth of this first child, Fannie? A No sir.
Q You don't know whether they were living together when that child was born or not? A No sir.
Q You know whether they were living together when the second child was born?
A No sir; they moved away and I didn't see them.
Q You had no intimate acquaintance with them? A Yes sir, I have been about them right smart.

-- -- -- --

PICKENS BENGE, being sworn and examined by Commissioner Needles testifies as follows:

Q What is your name? A Pickens Benge.
Q What is your age? A Forty-two.
Q What is your post-office? A Marble.
Q Are you a Cherokee citizen? A Yes sir.

Examined by Cherokee Representative Hastings:

Q Do you know John Overtaker? A Yes sir.
Q You know the woman with whom he lived? A No sir. He worked for me about two years ago and lived with a woman they called Fannie, but I wasn't acquainted with them.
Q You know whether he had any children or not? A I seen a couple of children there, he said they was his children, but I don't know.
Q They were small children? A Yes sir.
Q You know when they separated? A No sir.
Q You don't know anything about the cause of the separation? A No sir, I just seen him with his family about two years ago; he worked for me about two months.
Q You know how long he lived with this woman? A No sir I do not.
Com'r Needles:
Q You don't know whether these children were that woman's or not do you?
A No sir.

M.D. Green, being first duly sworn, states that as stenographer to the Commission to the Five Civilized Tribes he reported the foregoing case and that the above and foregoing is a full true and complete transcript of his stenographic notes in said case.

M D Green

Subscribed and sworn to before me this 8th day of August 1900.

T B Needles
Commissioner.

"R"

Cherokee D 90.

Department of the Interior,
Commission to the Five Civilized Tribes,
Muskogee, I. T., February 17, 1902.

SUPPLEMENTAL PROCEEDINGS, in the matter of the application of Fannie Overtaker et al., for enrollment as Cherokee citizens.

Appearances:
James H. Huckleberry, Sr., Sallisaw, I. T., Attorney for the applicants;
W. W. Hastings, attorney for the Cherokee Nation.

BY MR. HUCKLEBERRY: I just want to submit that case. We have no additional proof.

BY MR. HASTINGS: Well, closed and submitted.

M.D. Green, being first duly sworn, states that as stenographer to the Commission to the Five Civilized Tribes he correctly recorded the testimony and proceedings in this case and that the foregoing is a true and complete transcript of his stenographic notes thereof.

M D Green

Subscribed and sworn to before me this February 19, 1902.

T B Needles

Commissioner.

Cherokee D 90.

DEPARTMENT OF THE INTERIOR,

COMMISSION TO THE FIVE CIVILIZED TRIBES.

In the matter of the application for the enrollment of Fannie and Maggie Overtaker as citizens by blood of the Cherokee Nation.

DECISION.

The record herein shows that on August 7, 1900, John Overtaker appeared before the Commission at Sallisaw, Indian Territory, and made application for the enrollment of himself and his two minor children, Fannie and Maggie Overtaker, as citizens by blood of the Cherokee Nation. John Overtaker is differently classified and is not embraced in this decision.

The evidence shows that the applicants are the minor children of John Overtaker, a Cherokee by blood, who is identified on the 1880 authenticated Cherokee roll, on the 1894 Cherokee strip payment roll and on the 1895 Cherokee census roll. The said minor children were born since 1880 and are identified by birth affidavits made a part of the record herein.

The evidence further shows that the said John Overtaker has resided in the Cherokee Nation all his life; and it is considered that the residence of said minor applicants has been with their father since their birth.

It is, therefore, the opinion of this Commission that Fannie Overtaker and Maggie Overtaker should be enrolled as citizens by blood of the Cherokee Nation, in accordance with the provisions of section twenty-one of the Act of Congress, approved June 28, 1898 (30 Stats., 495), and it is so ordered.

COMMISSION TO THE FIVE CIVILIZED TRIBES.

(SIGNED). *Tams Bixby.*
Chairman.

(SIGNED). *T. B. Needles.*
Commissioner.

(SIGNED). *C. R. Breckinridge.*
Commissioner.

(SIGNED). *W. E. Stanley.*
Commissioner.

Muskogee, Indian Territory,
this OCT 9 1903

COMMISSIONERS:
TAMS BIXBY,
THOMAS B. NEEDLES,
C. R. BRECKINRIDGE,
W. E. STANLEY.

ALLISON L. AYLESWORTH,
SECRETARY.

DEPARTMENT OF THE INTERIOR,
COMMISSION TO THE FIVE CIVILIZED TRIBES.

REFER IN REPLY TO THE FOLLOWING
Cherokee D-90.

ADDRESS ONLY THE
COMMISSION TO THE FIVE CIVILIZED TRIBES.

Muskogee, Indian Territory, October 10, 1903.

W. W. Hastings,

Attorney for Cherokee Nation,

Tahlequah, Indian Territory.

Dear Sir:

There is herewith enclosed a copy of the decision of the Commission to the Five Civilized Tribes, dated October 9, 1903, granting the application for the enrollment of Fannie and Maggie Overtaker, as citizens by blood of the Cherokee Nation.

You are hereby advised that you will be allowed fifteen days from date hereof in which to file such protest as you may desire to make against the action of the Commission in this case, a copy of which protest you will be required to furnish the applicants. If you fail to file protest within the time allowed this decision will be considered final.

Respectfully,

Tams Bixby

Chairman.

Enc. D-75

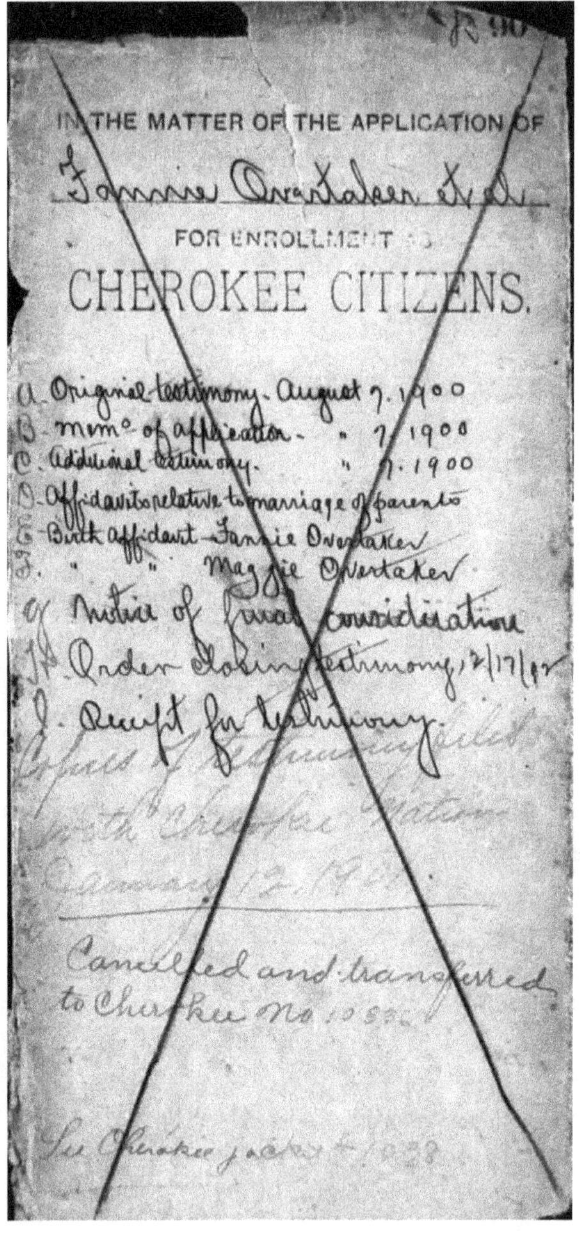

R 90

IN THE MATTER OF THE APPLICATION OF

Fannie Overtaker et al.

FOR ENROLLMENT AS

CHEROKEE CITIZENS.

A. Original testimony. August 7. 1900
B. Memo of application. " 7. 1900
C. Additional testimony. " 7. 1900
D. Affidavits relative to marriage of parents
E. Birth affidavit Fannie Overtaker
F. " " Maggie Overtaker
G. Notice of final consideration
H. Order closing testimony, 2/17/02
I. Receipt for testimony.

Copies of testimony filed with Cherokee Nation January 12, [illegible]

Cancelled and transferred to Cherokee No. [illegible]

See Cherokee packet [illegible]

RESIDENCE: Sequoyah DISTRICT.
POST OFFICE: Sallisaw, I.T.

Cherokee Nation. Cherokee Roll.
(Not including Delawares, Shawnees, or Freedmen.)

CARD NO. ______
FIELD NO. [illegible]

Dawes' Roll No.		NAME.	Relationship to Person first Named.	AGE.	SEX.	BLOOD.	Tribal Enrollment: Year.	Tribal Enrollment: District.	Tribal Enrollment: No.	Name of Father.	Year.	District.	Name of Mother.	Year.	District.
29607	1	Overtaker, Fannie		4	F	1/2				John Overtaker		Illinois	Julia Overtaker		Nowata
29608	2	" Maggie	Sister	[illegible]	F	1/2				"		"	"		"
	3														
	4														
	5														
	6														
	7	GRANTED						Nos 1 & 2, Birth affidavits required, filed August 9, 1900							
	8														
	9														
	10														
	11														
	12														
	13														
	14														
	15														
	16														
	17	See Cherokee													
	18	Card No 1051						Represented by J. H. Huckleberry, Sr, Sallisaw, I.T.							

CITIZENSHIP CERTIFICATE ISSUED FOR NO. 1 2
MAY 20 1905

On Cherokee Card No. D-90, August 7, 1900; On this card October 28, 1902

Date of Application for Enrollment.

Cherokee D92 - Sarah Brackett

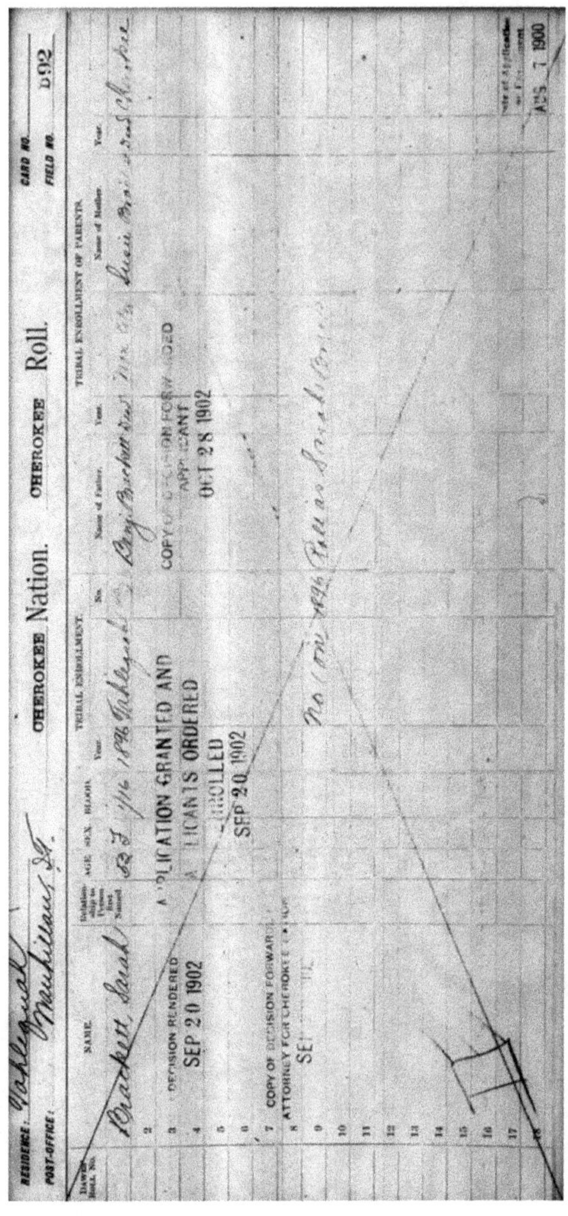
RESIDENCE: Tahlequah
POST-OFFICE: [illegible] I.T.

CHEROKEE Nation. CHEROKEE Roll.

CARD NO.
FIELD NO. D92

Dawes' Roll No.	NAME	Relationship to Person first Named	AGE	SEX	BLOOD	Tribal Enrollment: Year	Tribal Enrollment: District	Tribal Enrollment: No.	Name of Father	Year	District	Name of Mother	Year	District
1	Brackett, Sarah		52	F	1/16	1896	Tahlequah		Benj Brackett	Dead	Non Cit	[illegible]	Dead	Cherokee

DECISION RENDERED SEP 20 1902

APPLICATION GRANTED AND APPLICANTS ORDERED ENROLLED SEP 20 1902

COPY OF DECISION FORWARDED APPLICANT OCT 28 1902

COPY OF DECISION FORWARDED ATTORNEY FOR CHEROKEE NATION SE[illegible]

No 1 on 1896 Roll as Sarah [illegible]

Date of Application for Enrollment AUG 7 1900

DEPARTMENT OF THE INTERIOR,
COMMISSION TO THE FIVE CIVILIZED TRIBES,
SALLISAW, I.T., AUGUST 7, 1900.

In the matter of the application of Sarah Brackett for enrollment as citizens of the Cherokee Nation, said Brackett being sworn by Commissioner Needles, testified as follows:

Q What is your name? A Sarah Brackett.
Q Your age? A 53.
Q Your postoffice address? A Wauhillau.
Q Are you a recognized citizen of the Cherokee Nation? A Yes.
Q Name appear upon any of the rolls? A Yes.
Q What district do you live in? A Tahlequah.
Q How long have you lived there? A I lived in Tahlequah district 8 years and in Goingsnake district 2 years.
Q Lived in the Cherokee Nation 10 years? A Yes.
Q Where did you come from to the Cherokee Nation? A State of Georgia.
Q What evidence have you of your citizenship? A Certificate.

You present certificate of admission issued by the Commission on Citizenship of the Cherokee Nation, dated 16th day of August, '89, signed by William P. Ross, Chairman of the Commission, attested by D. S. Williams Clerk of the Commission, approved and endorsed by J. B. Mayes, Principal Chief. This certificate certifies that Sarah Brackett among other[sic] was admitted to citizenship on the 16th day of August, 1889. Are you the identical Sarah Brackett mentioned in this certificate? A Yes.
Q This certificate provides that it shall be the duty of the person named to enroll the names of their families when they arrive in the Nation, and they shall arrive in one year from the date of the certificate--- was your name enrolled? A It was on the pay-rolls.
Q Was it enrolled within one year when you came from Georgia? A No sir, it was not.
Q How long after this certificate was issued was it before you came from Georgia? On the 16th of August, '89, is the date this certificate was issued? A I came in March, '90.

Applicant's name on '96 roll, page 1134, number 83;
On '94 roll, page 1016, number 77.

Q Are you married? A No sir.
Q Have you any children under 21 years of age? A No sir.

The name of Sarah Brackett appears upon the census roll of '96 and the pay-roll of '94. She is duly identified thereby according to page and number of said rolls as indicated in the testimony. She also presents certificate of admission to citizenship in the Cherokee Nation issued on the 16th day of August, 1889, said certificate being described in the testimony. She has also made satisfactory proof as to her residence.

Now comes the representatives of the Cherokee Nation and onject[sic] to the enrollment of the said Sarah Brackett and ask that judgment as to her application be suspended until further evidence can be taken. Consequently judgment is suspended and her name will be placed upon a doubtful card.

Brown McDonald, being sworn, says a Stenographer to the Commission to the Five Civilized Tribes, he reported in full the testimony of the above named witness, and that the foregoing is a full, true and correct transcript of his notes.

Brown McDonald

Sworn to and subscribed before me this 23rd day of August, 1900, at Fort Gibson, I.T.

C R Breckinridge
Commissioner.

Supl.-C.D.#92.

Department of the Interior,
Commission to the Five Civilized Tribes,
Muskogee, I. T., February 17, 1902.

SUPPLEMENTAL in the matter of the enrollment of SARAH BRACKETT as a citizen of the Cherokee Nation;

Applicant was notified by registered letter January 31, 1902, that this case would be taken up for final consideration on the 17th inst., and that she would on said date be given an opportunity to introduce any further testimony affecting her application. Receipt has been acknowledged of the Registered letter and the applicant called three times and fails to respond either in person or by attorney and the case is closed.

C. R. Breckinridge

J.C.R. Commissioner.

Cherokee D 92

DEPARTMENT OF THE INTERIOR,
COMMISSION TO THE FIVE CIVILIZED TRIBES.

In the matter of the application for the enrollment of Sarah Brackett as a citizen by blood of the Cherokee Nation.

D E C I S I O N.

The record in this case shows that on August 7, 1900, Sarah Brackett appeared before the Commission at Sallisaw, Indian Territory, and made personal application for her enrollment as a citizen by blood of the Cherokee Nation.

The evidence shows that said Sarah Brackett was readmitted to citizenship in the Cherokee Nation by the duly constituted authorities of said Nation on August 16, 1889. Said Sarah Brackett is identified on the Cherokee Census Roll of 1896.

The evidence further shows that said Sarah Brackett removed to the Cherokee Nation in March, 1890, and has lived therein continuously up to and including the date of this application.

It is, therefore, the opinion of this Commission that Sarah Brackett should be enrolled as a citizen by blood of the Cherokee Nation in accordance with the provisions of Section twenty one of the Act of Congress approved June 28, 1898, (30 Stats., 495), and it is so ordered.

THE COMMISSION TO THE FIVE CIVILIZED TRIBES.

Tams Bixby
Acting Chairman.

T.B. Needles
Commissioner.

C. R. Breckinridge
Commissioner.

Dated Muskogee, Indian Territory,

this SEP 20 1902

COMMISSIONERS:

HENRY L. DAWES,
TAMS BIXBY,
THOMAS B. NEEDLES,
C. R. BRECKINRIDGE.

—

ALLISON L. AYLESWORTH,
SECRETARY.

ADDRESS ONLY THE
COMMISSION TO THE FIVE CIVILIZED TRIBES.

DEPARTMENT OF THE INTERIOR.
COMMISSION TO THE FIVE CIVILIZED TRIBES.

REFER IN REPLY TO THE FOLLOWING

Cherokee D 92.

Muskogee, Indian Territory, September 29, 1902.

W. W. Hastings,

Attorney for the Cherokee Nation,

Muskogee, Indian Territory.

Dear Sir:

Enclosed herewith please find a copy of the decision of the Commission to the Five Civilized Tribes, rendered September 20, 1902, granting the application of Sarah Brackett for the enrollment of herself as a citizen by blood of the Cherokee Nation.

You are hereby advised that you will be allowed fifteen days from date hereof in which to file with the Commission such protest as you desire to make against the decision rendered in this case. If you fail to file protest within the time allowed, this decision will be considered final.

Respectfully,

Tams Bixby Acting Chairman.

Enc. C. No. 66.

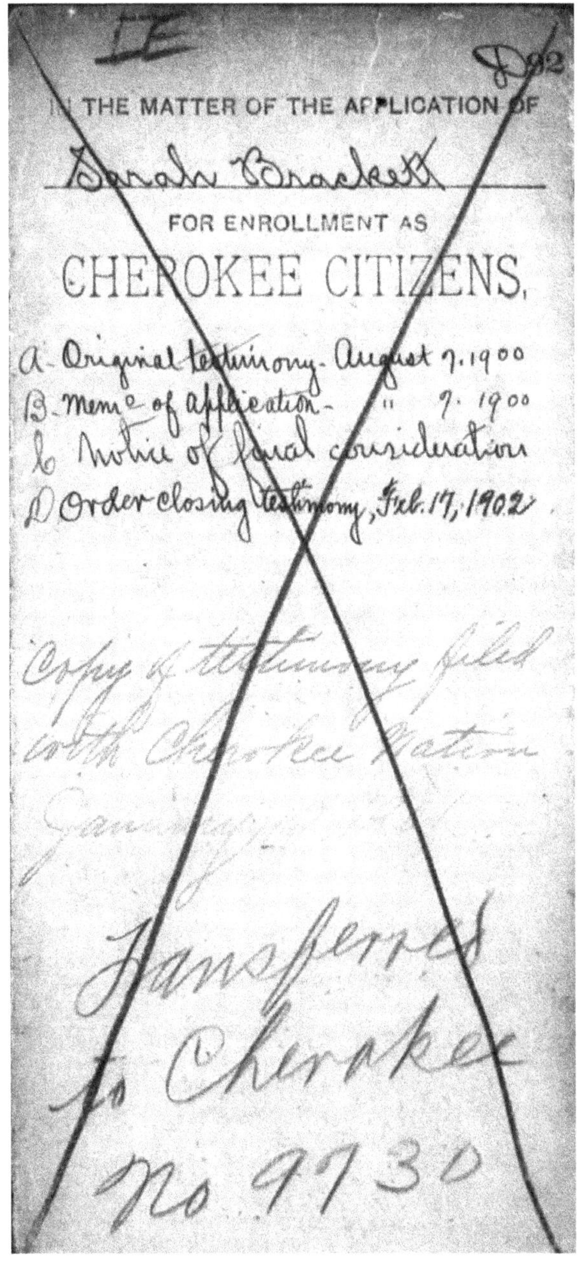

D 92

IN THE MATTER OF THE APPLICATION OF

Sarah Brackett

FOR ENROLLMENT AS

CHEROKEE CITIZENS,

A - Original testimony - August 7, 1900
B - Memo of application - " 7. 1900
C Notice of final consideration
D Order closing testimony, Feb. 17, 1902

Copy of testimony filed with Cherokee Nation

Transferred to Cherokee No 9730

RESIDENCE: Tahlequah DISTRICT.
POST OFFICE: Wauhillau, I.T.

Cherokee Nation. Cherokee Roll.
(Not including Delawares, Shawnees, or Freedmen.)

CARD NO.
FIELD NO. 9730

Dawes' Roll No.		NAME	Relationship to Person first Named	AGE	SEX	BLOOD	Tribal Enrollment: Year	Tribal Enrollment: District	Tribal Enrollment: No.	Name of Father	Year	District	Name of Mother	Year	District
21866	1	Brackett, Sarah		53	F	Full	1896	Tahlequah	83	Benj Brackett	dead	Non Cit	Susie Brackett	dead	Chicora[illegible]
	2														
	3														
	4														
	5														
	6														
	7	GRANTED					No 1 on 1896 roll as Sarah Brackett								
	8	SEP [illegible] 1902													
	9														
	10														
	11														
	12														
	13														
	14														
	15														
	16														
	17														
	18														

Date of Application for Enrollment.

Cherokee D93 - Adam Brackett

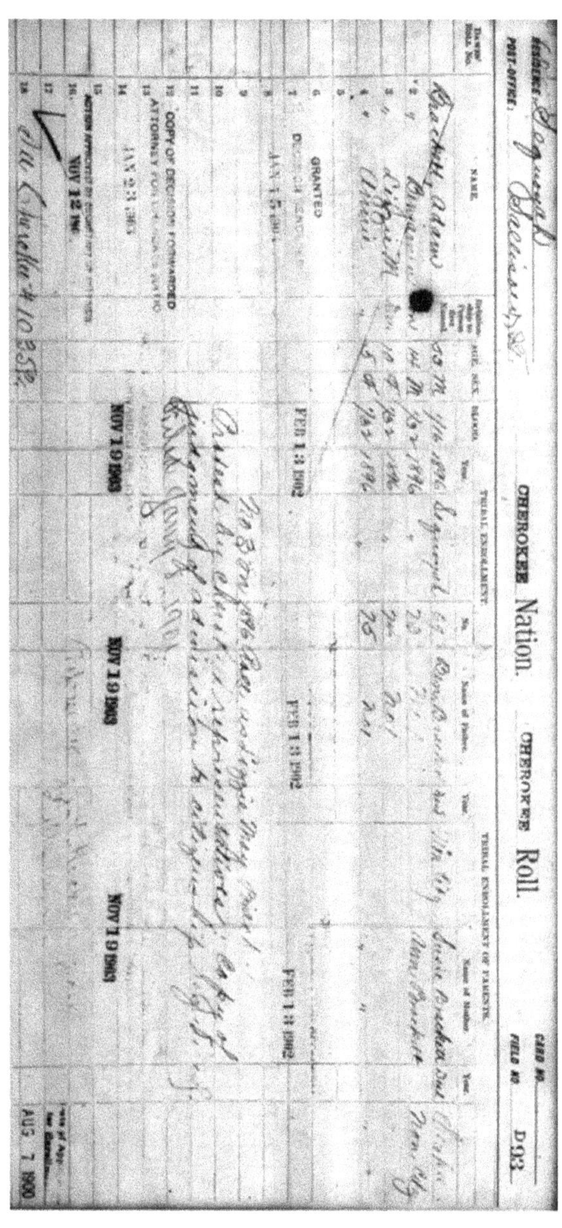

CHEROKEE Nation. CHEROKEE Roll.

CARD No. FIELD No. D93

GRANTED

FEB 13 1902

NOV 19 1903

NOV 12 1902

JAN 23 1903

AUG 7 1900

Department of the Interior.
Commission to the Five Civilized Tribes.
Sallisaw, I. T., August 7th, 1900.

In the matter of the application of Adam Brackett et al for enrollment as Cherokee citizens; being sworn and examined by Commissioner Breckinridge, testifies as follows:

Q What is your full name? A Adam Brackett.
Q What is your age? A 55.
Q What is your post-office? A Sallisaw.
Q What is your district? A Sequoyah.
Q For whom do you make application for enrollment? A Myself and children.
Q Do you apply for yourself as a Cherokee by blood? A Yes sir.
Q Are you on any of the rolls of the Cherokee Nation? A Yes sir.
Q Are you on the roll of 1880? A Think not.
Q Why are you not on the roll of 1880? A Wasn't here.
Q How did you acquire your citizenship; by the action of the Cherokee authorities? A Yes sir.
Q Where did you come from? A Georgia.
Q Have you your certificate of admission? A Yes sir.

Mr. Brackett, you present here a statement under seal by W.H. Mayes, Assistant Executive Secretary, Executive Department, Cherokee Nation, dated Tahlequah, Feb. 16th, 1892, stating that you among others were re-admitted to all the rights and privileges of Cherokees by blood by the Citizenship Commission of date 1889. It will be necessary, Mr. Brackett, for you to get from Tahlequah a certified copy of the judgment of the Commission rendering the decision, admitting you to citizenship.

Q Have you lived in the Cherokee Nation ever since the date you claim to have been admitted in 1889? A Yes sir.
Q Give me the names of your children? A Benjamin.
Q How old is he? A About 14.
Q What's your next child? A Lizzie Mayes.
Q How old is that child? A 10 years old.
Q What's your next child? A Annie.
Q How old is that child? A 5 years old.
Q Anymore? A That's all.
Q Now your child Benjamin was living at the time you claimed to be admitted to citizenship? A Yes sir.
Q Was he admitted the same time you were? A Yes.
Q His name is identified in the certificate that you have presented here from the Assistant Executive Secretary? A Yes sir.
Q Was Lizzie born since you were admitted to citizenship? A Yes sir.
Q And of course Annie was born since that time? A Yes sir.
Q Is the mother of these children dead? A No sir.

Q Was she admitted to citizenship the same time you were? A Yes sir.

Q What is her name? A She's not on the roll, she's adopted; she's a white woman.

Q Then she was not admitted to citizenship the same time you were? A No sir.

Q Who is Asalline Brackett mentioned in the certificate presented here? Was she your wife? A No.

Q What was she? A My oldest girl.

Q What is the name of the mother of these children for whom you apply?

A Annie Brackett.

Q She's not on any of the rolls of the Cherokee Nation? A No sir, I don't think she is.

Q What was her name when you married her? A Brewster.

Q How old is she? A I think she's about 45.

Q Were you ever married to her under Cherokee law? A Yes sir.

Q But you are not applying for her now? A We aint living together.

Q When did you marry her? A About ten years ago under Cherokee law.

Q When did you marry her under United States law? A About 25 years ago.

Q Have you a certificate or license proving your marriage to that woman?

A Yes sir.

Q Was Annie Brewster your wife and the mother of these children for whom you are applying for enrollment? A Yes sir.

Q And you say you married her under United States law some 25 years ago?

A Yes sir.

Com'r. A Marriage in '92 won't cover a marriage 25 years ago.

Q Have you any proof that you were married to Annie Brewster twenty five years ago.[sic] A Not in this country, I dont'[sic] think.

Q You and Annie Brewster were living together as husband and wife long before 1892 were you? A Yes sir.

Q Have you some one here that you can prove that by? A I reckon not.

Q Have you neighbors here that know you were living together as husband and wife? A I reckon not; were married back in the old country.

Q You claim to have come here in '89, you were living with her as her husband then were you not? A Yes sir.

Q And she came here with you? A Yes sir.

Q Well haven't you got some neighbors here who know that? A Yes there are people here who know it; I don't know whether there is anyone on the ground or not.

Witness, Norman S. Drake, being sworn and examined by Com'r Breckinridge, testifies as follows:

Q What is your age? A 55.

Q Your post-office? A McKee, I.T.

Q How long have you lived in this section of the country? A 20 years.

Q Do you know the applicant here, Adam Brackett? A Yes sir.

Q Do you know Annie Brewster that was, who is, or has been his wife?

A I know the woman who he lived with as his wife, but I don't know her name as Annie Brewster. She came here with him as his wife from Georgia. When I first knew them they were here as man and wife living together, about 12 years ago.

Q How long did the continue living as husband and wife? A Until about Strip Payment.

Q About '94? A About '93 or '94, along about that time.

Q Do you know whether she's considered to be the mother of his two children, Lizzie Mayes and Annie? A No sir. She's the mother of a young girl, a young woman now; I don't know.

Q Do you know anything about two children, one about 10 and one about 5?

A No sir, I don't know them.

Q Did I understand you to say you knew them to be living as husband and wife something like 12 years ago? A That's when I begun to know them, and occasionally met them until Strip Payment time.

Q Did they always appear [illegible] to along about the time of the Strip Payment as husband and wife before the community and did the people hold them out as such?

A I think so.

Q They were looked upon as husband and wife by the people? A I think so; I looked upon them as such and I guess the community did.

re-direct.

Q Did you draw money for your child Annie? A No sir.

Q Not for Annie but for Lizzie? A Yes sir.

Q Annie wasn't born at that time? A No I don't believe she was.

1894 roll; page 934, #81, Adam Bracket[sic], Sequoyah Dist.
1894 roll; page 934, #65, Benjamin Bracket, Sequoyah Dist.
1894 roll; page 934, #66, Lizzie M. Bracket, " "
1896 roll; page 1051, #69, Adam Brackett, " "
1896 roll; page 1051; #73, Benjaman[sic] Brackett, " "
1896 roll; page 1051, #74, Lizzie May Brackett, " "
1896 roll; page 1051, #75, Annie Brackett, " "

Q Mr. Brackett, are these three children living at this time? A Yes sir.

Q And are they living with you? A No, two little ones living with their mother.

Q But all alive at this time? A Yes sir.

Q Are you doing anything towards their support? A No sir; well I am buying them clothes.

Mr. Hutchings, representative of the Cherokee Nation:

Q Mr. Brackett, what is the date of the birth of that last child, Annie? A I can't tell you the day nor the month.

Q Hadn't you and she separated for good about the time that child was born or before? A No the child was done born. It was three or four weeks old when she left me.

Q Did she get a divorce from you? A No sir.

Q How did she marry Ecerett[sic]? A She aint married.

Q She's living with Everett? A She's living at his house.
Q There aint no other man living with her but Everett? A No sir.
Q Are you certain that you are the father of that last child, Annie? A Yes sir.
Q It was born when you were living together as man and wife? A Yes sir.

Mr. Hastings, representative of the Cherokee Nation:

Q You brough[sic] this woman with you from Georgia? A Yes sir.
Q Were you living with her when all these children were born? A Yes sir.

Mr. Hutchings, representative of the Cherokee Nation:

Q What was the longest time you and your wife were ever separated from one another by virtue of family quarrels, etc.? A She was gone one two monnths and a half I believe it was.
Q What county in Georgia did you come from to this country? A From Murray County.
Q What was your post-office? A Spring Place.
Q How long had you lived in that County previous to you coming to this Country? A About as well as I can recollect about 3 or 4 years.
Q From what county did you go to that County? A I went from Fannin County, Ga.
Q What was your post-office in that county? A Morgantown.
Q How long had you lived in Fannin County? A Two years I believe.
Q From what County did you go to Fannie County? A From Tennessee.
Q You mean the state of Tennessee? A Yes sir.
Q Give your county and post-office in Tennessee? A Severe[sic] County.
Q What was your post-office? A Severeville[sic].
Q Where were you born? A In Tennessee.
Q What County? A Hamilton County.
Q What Cherokee family do you possess to be a descendant from? From the Wilkinson; mother's side'; father was a white man.

Com'r. Breckinridge:

Mr. Brackett, the representative of the Cherokee Nation enters a protest against your enrollment in order that certain inquiries may be instituted in regard to your admission to citizenship by the Cherokee authorities in 1889, as I understand it.

You are duly identified on the roll of 1894, also on the roll of 1896. You present here an incomplete certificate or evidence of your admission to citizenship by the Cherokee authorities in 1889. Your son, Benjamin, for whom you make application, appears upon the same incomplete certificate of admission or evidence if admission. He is also identified on the rolls of 1894 and 1896. Your two younger children, Lizzie Mayes and Annie, born since you were said to have been admitted to citizenship, are identified on the roll of 1896, and the former, Lizzie Mayes, is identified on the roll of 1894. Your marriage to your wife is established in a satisfactory manner so far as the rights of these children are concerned, but the rights of all of you; that is, you and your children enumerated, for you make no application for your wife, flow from your purported admission to citizenship by the Cherokee authorities in 1889. Now, you are desired to get a duly certified copy of the judgment of the Cherokee Court or Commission by which you were admitted to citizenship in 1889, and by which as you claim your son Benjamin was also admitted in 1889, and you are desired to furnish this Commission with that duly certified copy. For the present the application for yourself and your children will be placed upon a doubtful card. If any allegations are brought forward in regard to your admission that seem to require attention on your part, you will be notified in order that you may take such steps as you think proper to protect your rights in the case, and the final decision of this Commission will be communicated to you at your post-office address.

Edward G. Rothenberger, being sworn and examined by Commissioner Breckinridge as Stenographer to the Commission to the Five Civilized Tribes, he reported in full the testimony of the above named witness, Adam Brackett, and that the foregoing is a full, true and correct transcript of his notes.

Edward G. Rothenberger

Sworn to and subscribed before me this 8th day of August, 1900.

Commissioner.

"R"

Cherokee D 93.

Department of the Interior,
Commission to the Five Civilized Tribes,
Muskogee, I. T., February 17, 1902.

SUPPLEMENTAL TESTIMONY AND PROCEEDINGS, in the matter of the application of Adam Brackett for enrollment as a Cherokee citizen.

Appearances:
James H. Huckleberry, Sr., Sallisaw, I. T., attorney for the applicant;
Daniel Brackett, relative of applicant;
W. W. Hastings, attorney for the Cherokee Nation.

DANIEL BRACKETT, being duly sworn and examined on behalf of the Cherokee Nation, testified as follows:
BY MR. HASTINGS:
Q What is your name? A Daniel Brackett.
Q What is your age? A I don't know, I declare I don't know, about 50, 52, or somewheres[sic] along there.
Q Do you know this Adam Brackett, the applicant? A Yes sir.

Q How long have you known him? A I have knowed him for years.
Q Well since you were a boy? A Yes sir.
Q Grew up together? A Yes sir.
Q You have known him ever since? A Yes sir, we have been together biggest part of the time.
Q You knew him in Alabama? A No sir, I lived in Georgia.
Q How far did you live from him there? A About 50 or 60 miles.
Q Did you know him when you lived in that country? A Yes, I saw him passing backwards and forwards.
Q I thought you said you knew him eber[sic] since you were a boy? A I know Adam, I say, he was passing back and forwards in the country where I lived.
Q Was he married out there? A Not that I know of.
Q Did you ever hear of him living with a woman and leaving her? A There that was in Georgia, yes sir.
Q He did live with a woman and leave her in there? A Yes sir.
Q Who did he come to this country with? A Why he came with Ann- I forget her name now, he married her since he come out here.
Q Married her after he come here didn't he? A Ann Brewster; yes sir
Q He never married her out there? A Not that I know of.
Q That is your family information aint it? A Yes sir.
Q He had been married out there in Georegia[sic] or Alabama before? A In Georgie[sic], yes sir.
Q Did he leave her out there? A Yes sir.
Q And married this woman? A Yes sir, the same he has got here, I don't think he married her out there; I think he just come off with her; I am called on for evidence and I will state the truth if I can.
Q You never heard of his being divorced from his first woman? A No sir.
Q You know in fact that he wasn't? A I don't suppose he was, now, to tell you the truth.
Q How long has he been in the country? A Oh he has been here, he was here before I came, I don't know how many years he has been here, Mr. Hastings; he has been here 15 or 20 years; he was here when I first came to the country.
Q You know Adam has got a young son named Been and a girl named Lizzie and one named Annie; they are children of this last woman, Ann? A Yes, I don't know much about them.
Q Do you know whether this Ann had any children when he took up with her or not? A I don't think she did.
Q You don't think she did? A No sir.
Q Do you know it? A No, I don't know it positive, I don't believe she did though.
Q Had she lived with anybody else out there as husband and wife? A Not that I know of; I wasn't right close to where she lived.
Q You never heard of it? A No sir.
Q You never heard of her having any children when she took up with him? A No sir.
Q About how long since they married in this country? A About ten or twelve years ago, it was since I come here at least.
Q They married since 1890? A Yes sir.

Q They married since you came to that country? A Yes sir. They married twice I think.

BY MR. HUCKLEBERRY:

Q Mr. Brackett, do you know of your own knowledge whether he was married to the first woman or not? A No sir, I never saw them married.

Q They lived together? A Yes sir, they was all just a little distance from me; 40 or 50 miles.

MR. HUCKLEBERRY: I want to call attention to what this gentleman says, that he appears on the roll of '51 or '2, known as the "Silar" roll. I don't know whether you have that or not.

BY COMMISSION: No, sir.

BY HUCKLEBERRY: He also appears on the blood roll. We then close this case.

BY MR. HASTINGS: Cherokee Nation submits it.

M.D. Green, being first duly sworn, states that as stenographer to the Commission to the Five Civilized Tribes he correctly recorded the testimony and proceedings in this case and that the foregoing is a true and complete transcript of his stenographic notes thereof.

MD Green

Subscribed and sworn to before me this February 19, 1902.

T B Needles

Commissioner.

DEPARTMENT OF THE INTERIOR,

COMMISSION TO THE FIVE CIVILIZED TRIBES.

In the matter of the application of Adam Brackett, et. al. for enrollment as Cherokee citizens, consolidating the applications of,

Adam Brackett, et. al. . . . .Cherokee D 93
Ann Brackett, ... " D 1465

DECISION,

--oOo--

The record herein shows that on August 7, 1900, Adam Brackett appeared before the Commission at Sallisaw, Indian Territory, and made application for the enrollment of himself and his three children, Benjamin, Lizzie M. and Annie Brackett as citizens by blood of the Cherokee Nation. Further proceedings were had in the matter of said application at Muskogee, Indian Territory, on February 17, 1902. On June 30, 1902, Emmet Starr appeared before the Commission at Muskogee, Indian Territory, and made application for the enrollment of Ann Brackett, the wife of said Adam Brackett as a citizen by intermarriage of the Cherokee Nation. Further proceedings were had in the matter of said application at Muskogee, Indian Territory, on July 16 and July 21, 1902.

An examination of the records of the Cherokee Nation, in the possession of this Commission show that Adam Brackett and his oldest son Benjamin Brackett were admitted to citizenship in the Cherokee Nation by the duly constituted authorities of said Nation on August 16, 1889. Lizzie M. and Annie Brackett have been born since the date of their father's admission to citizenship.

The evidence shows that Ann Brackett, the mother of the above named children, lived with the said Adam Brackett as his wife from about 1875 up to 1892, and that they were formally married on May 26, 1892, Adam Brackett testifies that he was previously married and that he separated from his form wife without a divorce about 1875.

Section 692 of the Compiled Laws of the Cherokee Nation (1892) provides:

> "All marriages which are herein prohibited on account of consanguinity between the parties, or on account of either of them having a former husband or wife then living, shall be absolutely void in this Nation, without any judgment of divorce or other legal proceeding, provided, that the issue from such unlawful marriage shall nevertheless be legitimate; provided, also that when a man having by a woman on or more children, shall afterwards intermarry with such woman, such child or children, if recognized by him, or proven to be his, shall thereby be legitimate"

All of the applicants herein are identified on the Cherokee census roll of 1896.

The evidence further shows that the said Ann Brackett lived with her said husband about four years following their marriage, and that she then left him and has not been living with him since that time.

Section 667 of the Compiled Laws of the Cherokee Nation (1892) provides:

> "Every person who shall lawfully marry under the provisions of this act, and afterwards abandon his wife, shall thereby forfeit every right and privilege of citizenship of this nation."

The evidence further shows that Adam Brackett has resided in the Cherokee Nation since 1889. The oldest child, Benjamin, is living with his father and the two younger children are living with their mother, who has resided in the Cherokee Nation since the date of her said marriage. The residence of said children has been continuous in the Cherokee Nation from birth up to and including the date of this application.

It is, therefore, the opinion of this Commission that Adam Brackett, Benjamin Brackett, Lizzie M. Brackett and Annie Brackett should be enrolled as citizens by blood of the Cherokee Nation, in accordance with the provisions of Section Twenty-one of the Act of Congress approved June 28, 1898 (30 Stats., 493), and it is so ordered.

It is further the opinion of this Commission that the application for the enrollment of Ann Brackett, as a citizen by intermarriage of the Cherokee Nation, should be denied under the provisions of the law above quoted, and it is, therefore, so ordered.

COMMISSION TO THE FIVE CIVILIZED TRIBES.

(SIGNED). *Tams Bixby.*
Chairman.

(SIGNED). *T. B. Needles.*
Commissioner.

(SIGNED). *C. R. Breckinridge.*
Commissioner.

Muskogee, Indian Territory,
this JAN 15 1903

[Transcription of Handwritten Letter on page 335-6]

Sallisaw I.T.

Oct 8, 1900

W.W. Hastings, Attorney for C.N.

Sir: Having met with Judge Littlejohn a fiew[sic] *days ago, and he informed me that the talk was going the rounds to the effect that one Mrs. Maggie or Margrette M^c^Kinnie was enrolled as a citizen by adobtion*[sic] *at Sallisaw by the Daws Com. Said Mrs M^c^Kinnie was ~~was~~ the widow of one John Overtaker Deciest*[sic] *and haveing*[sic] *married one Hiram M^c^Kinnie (who is a white man & a non citizen) since the death of said Overtaker would certainly fanfit*[sic] *her citizenship under Cherokee law. Also in the case of one Adam Bracket please watch carfully*[sic]. *It is said that said Bracket and his woman whos name is Ann never was lawfully married - that he Bracket left a wife in Allabama*[sic] *and sloped*[sic] *with said woman Ann and came to this country - Although the Brackets are put upon the doubtful list it will behoove you to watch this case in particular.*

Any information that I can give you or that I can find out in this case will let you know.- let me here from you.

Very truly yours

O.F. Adair

[Copy of Original Letter Transcribed on Previous Page]

(1)

Sallisaw I.T.
Oct 8. 1900

W.W. Hastings, Attorney for C.N.
Sir: Having met with Judge
Littlejohn a few days ago, and he
informed me that the talk was
going the rounds to the effect that
one Mrs. Maggie or Margaretta
McKinnie was enrolled as a citizen
by adoption at Sallisaw by the
Dawes com. Said Mrs. McKinnie
was ~~was~~ the widow of one John
Overtaker [illegible] and having
married one [illegible] McKinnie
(who is a white man & a non citizen)
since the death of said Overtaker
would certainly forfeit her citizenship
under Cherokee law. Also in the
case of one Adam Brassett

(2)

please watch carfully. It is said that said Bracket and his woman whos name is Ann, never was lawfuly married - that he Bracket left a wife in Allabama and eloped with said woman Ann and came to this country - Although the Brackets are put upon the doubtful list it will behoove you to watch this case in particular. Any information that I can give you or that I can find out in this case will let you know. - let me here from you.

Very truly Yours
O. F. Adair,

COMMISSIONERS:

HENRY L. DAWES,
TAMS BIXBY,
THOMAS B. NEEDLES,
C. R. BRECKINRIDGE.

—

ALLISON L. AYLESWORTH,
SECRETARY.

ADDRESS ONLY THE
COMMISSION TO THE FIVE CIVILIZED TRIBES.

DEPARTMENT OF THE INTERIOR,
COMMISSION TO THE FIVE CIVILIZED TRIBES.

REFER IN REPLY TO THE FOLLOWING
Cherokee
D-93 & D-1465

Muskogee, Indian Territory, January 23, 1903.

W. W. Hastings,

Attorney for the Cherokee Nation,

Vinita, Indian Territory.

Dear Sir:-

There is herewith enclosed a copy of the decision of the Commission to the Five Civilized Tribes, dated January 15, 1903, granting the application of Adam Brackett for the enrollment of himself and his three minor children, Benjamin, Lizzie M. and Annie Brackett, as citizens by blood, and rejecting his application for the enrollment of his wife, Ann Brackett, as a citizen by intermarriage of the Cherokee Nation.

You are hereby advised that you will be allowed fifteen days, from date hereof, in which to file such protest as you may desire to make against the action of the Commission in this case, a copy of which protest you will be required to serve upon the applicant.

If you fail to file protest within the time allowed, this decision will be considered final.

Respectfully,

Tams Bixby
Acting Chairman.

Enc. M-2104

COMMISSIONERS:

HENRY L. DAWES,
TAMS BIXBY,
THOMAS B. NEEDLES,
C. R. BRECKINRIDGE.

—

ALLISON L. AYLESWORTH,
SECRETARY.

ADDRESS ONLY THE
COMMISSION TO THE FIVE CIVILIZED TRIBES.

DEPARTMENT OF THE INTERIOR,
COMMISSION TO THE FIVE CIVILIZED TRIBES.

REFER IN REPLY TO THE FOLLOWING
Cherokee
D-1465 & D-93

Muskogee, Indian Territory, February 13, 1903.

W. W. Hastings,

Attorney for the Cherokee Nation,

Vinita, Indian Territory.

Dear Sir:

You are hereby advised that the Commission has this day transmitted to the Secretary of the Interior, for review, the record of proceedings had in the matter of the application for the enrollment of Adam Brackett et al., as citizens by blood, and for the enrollment of Ann Brackett as a citizen by intermarriage of the Cherokee Nation, together with the decision of the Commission, dated January 15, 1903, granting said application as to Adam, Benjamin, Lizzie M. and Annie Brackett, and rejecting said application as to Ann Brackett.

The action of the Secretary will be made known to you as soon as the Commission is informed of same.

Respectfully,

Tams Bixby
Acting Chairman.

COMMISSIONERS:

TAMS BIXBY,
THOMAS B. NEEDLES,
C. R. BRECKINRIDGE,
W. E. STANLEY.

ALLISON L. AYLESWORTH,
SECRETARY.

DEPARTMENT OF THE INTERIOR,
COMMISSION TO THE FIVE CIVILIZED TRIBES.

REFER IN REPLY TO THE FOLLOWING

Cherokee D-93.

ADDRESS ONLY THE
COMMISSION TO THE FIVE CIVILIZED TRIBES.

Muskogee, Indian Territory, November 19, 1903.

W. W. Hastings,

Attorney for Cherokee Nation,

Tahlequah, Indian Territory.

Dear Sir:

You are hereby advised that the Commission's decision dated January 15, 1903, granting the application for the enrollment of Adam Brackett and his three minor children, Benjamin, Lizzie M. and Annie Brackett, as citizens by blood of the Cherokee Nation, was affirmed by the Secretary of the Interior on November 12, 1903.

Respectfully,

Tams Bixby

Chairman.

W. W. Hastings, atty for C.N.
Tahlequah,
I. T.

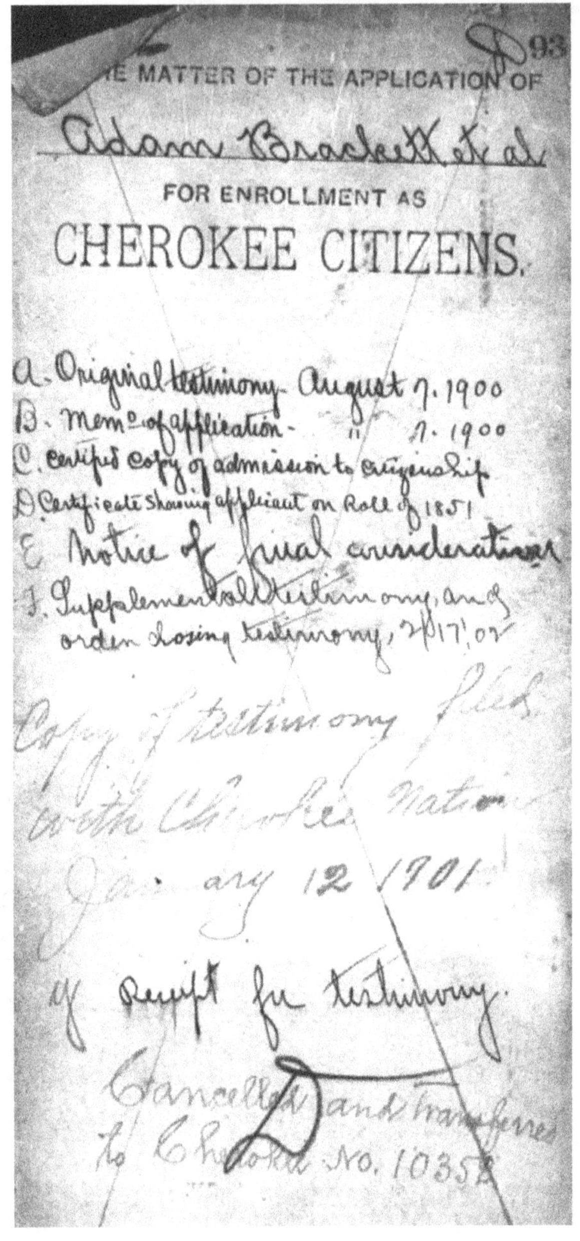

93

[IN TH]E MATTER OF THE APPLICATION OF

Adam Brackett et al

FOR ENROLLMENT AS

CHEROKEE CITIZENS.

A. Original testimony August 7. 1900
B. Memo of application " 7. 1900
C. Certified copy of admission to citizenship
D. Certificate showing applicant on Roll of 1851
E Notice of final consideration
F. Supplemental testimony, and order closing testimony, 2/17/07

Copy of testimony filed with Cherokee Nation January 12 1901

of Receipt for testimony.

Cancelled and transferred to Cherokee No. 10352

RESIDENCE: Sequoyah DISTRICT.
POST OFFICE: Sallisaw I.T.

Cherokee Nation. Cherokee Roll.

(Not Including Delawares, Shawnees, or Freedmen.)

CARD NO.
FIELD NO. 10352

Dawes' Roll No.		NAME.	Relationship to Person first Named.	AGE.	SEX.	BLOOD.	TRIBAL ENROLLMENT. Year.	District.	No.	TRIBAL ENROLLMENT OF PARENTS. Name of Father.	Year.	District.	Name of Mother.	Year.	District.
30776	1	Brackett, Adam		55	M	1/16	1896	Sequoyah	69	Ben Brackett	Dead	[illegible]	Susie Brackett	Dead	Cherokee
30777	2	" Benjamin	Son	14	M	1/32	1896	S.Q.	73	No 1			Ann Brackett		Non Citz
30778	3	" Lizzie M.	Dau	10	F	1/32	1896	"	74	No 1			" "		" "
30779	4	" Annie	"	5	F	1/32	1896		75	No 1			" "		" "
	5	CITIZENSHIP CERTIFICATE ISSUED FOR NO.													
	6		MAR 1 1905												
	7	GRANTED													
	8	ACTION APPROVED BY SECRETARY OF INTERIOR.						No 3 on 1896 Roll as Lizzie May Brackett							
	9	1905													
	10														
	11														
	12														
	13														
	14														
	15												On Cherokee Card No.		
	16											Date of Application for Enrollment.	D 93. August 7, 1900.		
	17												On this card November		
	18							Represented by J. M. Huckleberry, Sr. Sallisaw I.T.					19, 1903.		

www.ingramcontent.com/pod-product-compliance
Lightning Source LLC
Chambersburg PA
CBHW031136020426
42333CB00013B/408
* 9 7 8 1 6 4 9 6 8 1 7 3 7 *